A CONVENIENT VILLAIN

Charles A. Lindbergh's remarkable and
controversial legacy preparing the U.S. for war

JONATHAN D. REICH, MD, M SC ENGINEERING

authorHOUSE®

AuthorHouse™
1663 Liberty Drive
Bloomington, IN 47403
www.authorhouse.com
Phone: 833-262-8899

Published by AuthorHouse 11/15/2024

ISBN: 979-8-8230-0333-9 (sc)
ISBN: 979-8-8230-0331-5 (hc)
ISBN: 979-8-8230-0332-2 (e)

Library of Congress Control Number: 2023904682

Print information available on the last page.

Contents

Dedication

I'm told my great-grandfather listened to the radio every day to try to get news about what was happening to his family in Poland. He never found out. He died in 1943.

This book is dedicated to our grandparents.
May they rest in peace.
May our memories of them be a blessing.

Acknowledgements

During the pandemic I found I had time to do something I always wanted to do, write a book. I had the distinct advantage of having married a former journalist and copywriter for Jewish causes, who is also the daughter of a Holocaust survivor. She insisted I needed a hobby. Eternal thanks are due to my wife, Ellie, for lending me her writing experience. She read the book many times. She patiently put up with our lives suddenly being ensconced in the 1930s and my travels to Minnesota, New Haven, and endless museums and libraries. None of this would be possible without her perspective, support, and fortitude.

My children deserve recognition. Aaron, Zachary, Isaac, and Abraham, get thanks for their encouragement, positive attitude, and willingness to help whenever help was requested. The one who dedicated the most time was Isaac. He wrote part of the chapter on high altitude aviation. Aaron read some chapters and helped with computer issues. Zachary met me in New Haven and when I was done looking through Lindbergh's papers, he drove me home. And no one is a bigger fan than Avi.

I also must thank other members of my family. My brother Andy and my father read multiple chapters and my two other brothers (Gary and Jim) gave me valuable advice. Various cousins volunteered to read chapters and helped when they could, as did some of my in-laws.

My friends: Stuart continually gave me encouragement to write the book, Brian helped me with the legal issues, and Steve read every chapter. When others were too busy or had enough, Steve never hesitated to read another chapter. Wayne and Chris also read chapters and gave me particularly insightful advice. Roy and a different Steve also gave me advice and help.

I must thank two physicians for reviewing medical chapters and general help: an extremely helpful anesthesiologist and an outstanding cardiac surgeon. A retired chairman of an engineering department, who is also a Holocaust survivor, reviewed the engineering chapters and gave me good technical advice. Accommodations and help were provided by the Mayo Clinic Library especially Rosemary Perry, Yale University Library, the American Engine Historical Society, and the Minnesota and Missouri Historical Societies.

I had other special editors with whom it was my privilege to discuss this project. My uncles Mal and Danny turned 90 years old while I was writing this book. They both remember the 1930s and 1940s and the controversy surrounding Lindbergh. My Uncle Mal watched Silver Shirts, American Nazis, parade past his bedroom window in Queens, NY. I sent them many chapters to review. I did not send them the engineering chapters, which I felt were too technical. After all, they are 90 years old, and I couldn't take up all their free time. No matter what happens with this project, the opportunity to discuss my uncles' childhoods in pre-World War II America was a bonus I will always cherish.

1: Preface

Do remarkable acts of bravery and patriotism that saved the lives of thousands of Americans earn consideration of forgiveness for distasteful actions, which hurt no one?

In 1954, Charles Lindbergh chose the location of the United States Air Force Academy to be in Colorado Springs, Colorado. Nine years later I was born there. My father was a captain in the Air Force, and my mother was a graduate student in history. She was writing her thesis on the presidential election of 1948 and how Harry Truman was able to carry the state of Colorado.

I do not know if I was the first Jewish child born at the U.S. Air Force Academy Hospital, but I was one of the first. My *brit* is family lore. A *mohel* flew down from Denver and the Academy brass attended, having never seen a *brit*.

When I was 6 years old, I watched a man walk on the moon while sitting with my great-grandfather. As a young man living in New York City, he had a hobby. He would go to Roosevelt Field on Long Island (where Lindbergh took off for Paris) to fly on an invention — airplanes. When his son Joseph was old enough, he would go too. That boy, my great-uncle Joseph Kappel, was awarded the Distinguished Flying Cross and the Silver Star for bravery in combat in World War II. He was awarded these medals for his heroism during the bombing of oil fields in Romania. With the pilot wounded, the navigator dead, and the landing gear shot out, my uncle belly landed his B-24 bomber saving the lives of the rest of the crew.

My major qualification to write about Charles Lindbergh's legacy is my connection to aviation. I earned a degree in engineering and went to work for the Navy. I designed and tested airplanes that would see combat in the First Gulf War. I have personally known two men who flew combat missions in this war. One was my next-door neighbor and the other's son had his Bar Mitzvah with mine. I am immensely proud that those planes functioned as we designed them, and all the planes I worked on returned safely.

I left my employment with the Navy to move to Israel to work on the latest Israeli airplane, the *Lavi*. Unfortunately, the *Lavi* was cancelled the week before I was to leave the U.S.. I went to Israel anyway, lived there for a year, learned Hebrew, and started to earn a master's degree in engineering at Ben Gurion University in Beer Sheva, Israel. I finished my degree at the University of Miami while I was in medical school. I did my training at Emory University and began practicing medicine in 1998. Additionally, I intermittently taught engineering through the 2010s.

I am not German. Despite my last name I have no German ancestry. My last name is a contrived last name. The name from which it was derived came with my great-grandfather when he immigrated from Austria at the age of sixteen, by himself, prior to World War I. None of my other seven great-grandparents came from Germany nor any German-speaking country. I also have no allegiance to Charles Lindbergh nor his family.

While I'm sure I will be accused of "*shagetz*-appeal" or a "bromance" for admiring a blond, blue-eyed gentile, I have no personal stake in Lindbergh's legacy. I admire Lindbergh for what he accomplished, especially what he accomplished in medicine and his record in combat, but it is of minor importance to me and certainly his legacy is of no personal consequence. If you believe Lindbergh was an anti-Semite, I disagree — but changing your mind did not inspire me to write this book. What is personal to me is the story of my father-in-law.

My father-in-law was born Abraham Swiatzki in Lithuania in 1921. His mother and brother were murdered by the Nazis. My father-in-law escaped from a labor camp by hiding in a chimney and followed the Red Army through eastern Europe eventually making his way to Italy.

While in a Displaced Persons camp he learned his father had survived Dachau and he went to Germany to be reunited. The two of them made their way to the U.S., there he met my mother-in-law, and my *b'shert* was born in Chicago.

My wife was born the same year my mother was awarded her degree in history. It was also the same year my father left the Air Force.

If I thought Lindbergh had contributed to any of my in-law's tragic saga, the extermination of my great-grandfather's family, or the demise of any European Jew, I certainly would not have written this book. My wife doesn't remember her father ever mentioning him. But my mother and my grandparents hated Lindbergh as much as the reader presumably hates Lindbergh.

So why re-evaluate Charles Lindbergh's legacy?

Because no aerospace engineer has ever done so, certainly not a Jewish one.

Historians aren't engineers. They have never understood nor appreciated the intelligence Lindbergh provided. Historians often unquestionably accept Lindbergh's established reputation. For example, there is the ubiquitous allegation Lindbergh "exaggerated" the strength of the German air force in 1938. (Nasaw, 2012) Even the most casual student of World War II knows it was impossible to exaggerate the effectiveness of an air force which would lay waste to its enemies and force them to surrender faster than anyone expected. Anything anyone said about the German air force in 1938 can only be an understatement, because no one could have conceived of anything as terrible as what happened.

Constantly repeating allegations makes them the accepted truth. As a result, those writing about Lindbergh have become sloppy. In November 2022, the *New York Times* wrote Lindbergh was on American radio in the 1930s spreading anti-Semitism. Lindbergh didn't even return to the U.S.

until April 1939 and never gave any such radio address. He gave five U.S. radio addresses prior to the U.S. entering the war, but in none of his radio addresses did he mention Jews. His public statement about the Jews in the decade of the 1930s was a letter to his best friend, Harry Guggenheim, who was Jewish. He wrote, "Of course I don't need to tell you I am not in accord with the Jewish situation in Germany." (Berg, 1998, p.361)

In his book, *5 Days in Philadelphia*, historian Charles Peters wanted to emphasize Lindbergh was so unpopular even his family disagreed with him. While some of Lindbergh's family did disagree with him, Peters wrote Lindbergh's father-in-law, Dwight Morrow, spoke at the 1940 Democratic Convention in favor of intervening in World War II. It is unlikely Morrow attended the 1940 Democratic Convention because he died in 1931. (Peters, 2005, p.144)

In his book, *Rendezvous With Destiny*, Michael Fullilove quotes Lindbergh at the Senate Foreign Relations hearings in February 1941, saying he preferred "to see neither side win". (Fullilove, 2013, p.179). Actually, this is what he said: "I have never taken the stand that it makes no difference to us who wins this war in Europe. It does make a difference to us, a great difference." (VSOTD, 1941) He then said he wanted England to persevere but emphasized the U.S. can't fight European wars every two decades nor sacrifice our weapons and soldiers. "I never wanted Germany to win this war. But I know England is not in a position to win it, even with our help."[1] Quite different indeed.

In her book, *The Ambassador,* Susan Ronald wrote, with no reference, that in 1939 Lindbergh was convinced Hitler was a "man of peace". (Ronald, 2021, p.227) Some public figures were so desperate to avoid another war they convinced themselves Hitler's intentions were peaceful — but not Lindbergh. While Lindbergh found fault on both sides, he told the Germans as early as 1936 their behavior would result in another war. Journalists who later became his staunch enemies lauded him for saying it. (Berg, 1998, p.358) Had he ascribed peaceful intention to Hitler, he would not have urged the British Prime Minister to build more Spitfires for England's protection in 1937. (Ross, 1964, p.276) His predictions of how a war would start named Hitler or Mussolini as the instigator. In February 1939, Lindbergh wrote war would start only if Germany started it and then anticipating Hitler would start a war, brought his family back to the U.S. in April 1939. (Lindbergh, 1970, pp.158-160)

There's also a generational issue of Lindbergh's legacy that hasn't been addressed.

I have no memory of a world prior to Israel's Six Day War in 1967. My parents' generation tells me that this war completely changed Jewish identity. It made American Jews proud of their identity and assertive. Prior to that war, Jews tried to blend into American society, and certainly in Lindbergh's pre-Israel era they were insecure about their status as Americans. On July 5, 1976, I was 12 years old in Jewish summer camp. The adults celebrated the Entebbe raid and tried to explain to us how remarkable it was that a Jewish army rescued Jews in trouble. I couldn't appreciate it. To me it seemed completely expected. I thought there was always an army of Jews, flying in airplanes with Jewish stars on the wings, rescuing Jews.

Lindbergh's legacy specific to the Jews has only been evaluated by Jews through a pre-Six Day War lens. Lindbergh's speech in Des Moines, Iowa on September 11, 1941, threatened the Jews' identity as Americans. Lindbergh not only knew it would, but he also knew if he addressed Jewish interests, he'd be vilified as an anti-Semite. Faced with an impending war that would take the lives of hundreds of thousands of Americans, he didn't think Jewish feelings, nor his reputation were more important than an open debate of our national interest. Having never questioned my identity as an American, nor ever felt a reason to hide or deny my identity as a Jew, I can understand his motive without necessarily agreeing with him. I can ask these questions: What did he really say? Was it true?

Perhaps it's time to evaluate Lindbergh's legacy from the perspective of our generation, devoid of the insecurities and fears of my grandparents' pre-Israel generation?

The part of Lindbergh's legacy which applies to all Americans hasn't been appreciated either.

Every year of the Depression the U.S. decreased its military budget. The first increase of $525 million was approved by Congress in the spring of 1939 while Lindbergh was still in Europe. (Klein, 2013) At the hearings held by both Appropriations Committees, nearly every witness who was in favor of increasing military allocations used intelligence Lindbergh provided. (Nasaw, 2012, p.369) Indeed, we had little other intelligence because we didn't have a foreign intelligence agency prior to 1942. (Reel, 2018)

While Lindbergh was convincing the U.S. military to take Germany's rise seriously, a Harvard undergraduate and son of the U.S. Maritime Commissioner, John F. Kennedy, reflected the common thinking of the era. While touring Europe he wrote his father, "The general impression also seems to be that there will not be a war in the near future and that France is much too well prepared for Germany." (Dalleck R., 2003, p.52)

Because most people thought like our then-future president, we were completely unprepared to enter World War II. As an example of our lack of preparedness, in the summer of 1940 U.S. Army divisions in Louisiana and upstate New York held combat exercises. The soldiers had no rifles and carried broomsticks instead. Instead of tanks, buses with the word "TANK" written in red letters were used, and there were no combat aircraft with which to prepare for combat. (Dalleck, 2017) This was the status of the U.S. military and specifically our air power prior to the start of war. Nearly the only exception to national lethargy and incompetence when it came to our national defense was Lindbergh.

The intelligence reports of Lindbergh's assessment of German airpower resulted in two separate allocations of hundreds of millions of dollars (add a zero for today's dollars) to construct new combat aircraft in 1939, two years before we entered the war. (Nasaw, 2012, p.369) (Berg, 1998, p.389) Lindbergh discussed his intelligence findings with the military, the president, the Secretary of War, NACA (the precursor of NASA), and nearly every American manufacturer of airplanes and airplane engines.

Lindbergh's visits to Nazi Germany enabled the U.S. Embassy in Berlin to send a comprehensive list of the locations of German airfields, airplane factories, parts factories, and *Luftwaffe* units to the U.S. Army in November 1939. (Hessen, 1984, pp.164-5) Can an honest Lindbergh critic dismiss the importance of this intelligence? Should Lindbergh's remarkable actions in defense of his country entitle him to dispensation when evaluating his later behavior?

As a result of his advocacy, bravery, and patriotism, Lindbergh deserves more credit than nearly any other American for state-of-the-art combat airplanes being ready early enough after we entered the war in December 1941 to defeat both Germany and Japan. (Berg, 1998, p.389-90) His commanding officer said the engine setting recommendations Lindbergh made while in combat, also shortened the war in Asia by months and saved thousands of American lives. (Ross, 1964, p.332)

People like my father-in-law survived the war because millions of brave Americans like my uncle risked their own lives. Half a million Americans didn't return home from World War II. But had it not been for Lindbergh it is doubtful my uncle would have had a plane to fly. Even if he'd had a plane, without Lindbergh's input, it would undoubtably have been technologically inferior to our enemies' planes and unsafe with antiquated oxygen equipment.

1930s-era pilot oxygen equipment often resulted in deprivation of oxygen, which causes delayed reaction time, confusion, and disorientation. Lindbergh's improvements in military oxygen equipment included the oxygen supply in the cockpit where my uncle sat and the A-14 oxygen mask my uncle wore. (Dill, 1954) (Berg, 1998, p.447) It is doubtful my uncle could have landed the airplane, nor could his crewmates have fought off German fighter planes, had they been deprived of oxygen. (see Glossary)

Absent Lindbergh's remarkable intelligence, it is as unlikely my uncle would have returned home as it is unlikely my father-in-law would have survived the war. Although too old to be required to serve, Lindbergh also risked his life to fight in World War II and fly prototype jet airplanes. His contributions to high-altitude aviation saved the lives of pilots who flew combat missions through the Vietnam War.

Historians can put words in Lindbergh's mouth and resurrect his father-in-law to criticize him, because once someone has been vilified enough, people stop questioning the narrative. But without Lindbergh's contributions, we may have lost World War II and had we won, we certainly would have won much later. The Germans were developing *Wunderwaffe* (wonder weapons), ballistic missiles and jet airplanes, which would render every World War II era weapon obsolete and dominate future warfare. Had the war lasted longer, and these weapons been fully deployed, they could have prevented us from winning. The Holocaust would certainly have lasted longer and there would have been fewer survivors. Without his contribution to American jet engine technology, we may have lost the Korean War as well.

And no matter how wrong his predictions of the future and his worldview, everyone is entitled to be quoted correctly, not vilified, not condemned based on private thoughts, and have their position understood.

It is inconceivable that every aspect of Lindbergh's life has not been described in detail and considered as part of his legacy. And as an American who was responsible for aircraft flown by Americans in a different war, this is personal to me too.

Works Cited

[1] Speech given by Charles Lindbergh in Minneapolis, May 10, 1941.

(In future references, Lindbergh's speeches will be designated as: (city, date))

Berg, A. (1998). *Lindbergh.* New York: Berkley Biography.

Dalleck, R. (2003). *An Unfinished Life, John F. Kennedy.* New York: Little, Brown, and Company.

Dalleck, R. (2017). *Franklin Roosevelt.* New York: Viking.

Dill, D. (1954). *Walter Boothby: Pioneer in Aviation.* Science, 688.

Fullilove, M. (2013). *Rendezvous With Destiny.* New York: Penguin Press.

Hessen, R. (1984). *Berlin Alert: The Memoirs and Reports of Truman Smith.* Stanford: Hoover Institution.

Klein, M. (2013). New York: Bloomsbury.

Lindbergh, C. A. (1970). *The Wartime Journals of Charles A. Lindbergh.* New York: Harcourt, Brace, and Jovanovich.

Nasaw, D. (2012). *The Patriarch.* New York: Penguin.

Peters, C. (2005). *5 Days In Philadelphia.* New York: Public Affairs.

Reel, M. (2018). In *A Brotherhood of Spies.* New York: Doubleday.

Ronald, S. (2021). *The Ambassador.* New York: St. Martin's Press.

Ross, W, *The Last Hero: Charles A. Lindbergh*, Harper and Row, NY, 1964.

VSOTD. (1941, Feb VII, 266-7). Retrieved from Vital Speeches of the Day: http://www.ibiblio.org/pha/policy/1941/1941-02-06a.html

2: Charles Augustus Lindbergh: 1902-1974

A most remarkable life

Charles Lindbergh was a flawed man, but his flaws have been documented. Despite his flaws he made as great a contribution to American security, in particular our preparations for World War II, as any other American. This has not been documented. Without him it is unlikely the Allies would have defeated Germany and if so, certainly later than 1945. Absent him, the Holocaust may not have ended, certainly not when it did. He also made some remarkable and unappreciated contributions to American society, medicine, and science. This book documents what he did — both good and bad — and lets the reader decide what his legacy should be.

On May 21, 1927, Charles A. Lindbergh landed his single wing, single engine, single pilot airplane at Le Bourget airfield in Paris. He was an unknown mail pilot whose life previously had been one of mostly failures. He had dropped out of college after missing his senior year of high school due to World War I. He had enrolled in a private flight school, which was a scam. Although he had finished at the top of his military pilot training class, he failed the oral exam and had never retaken it.

During his famous flight, he was awake for 55 consecutive hours. He had nearly nothing to eat and only water to drink. Due to sleep deprivation, he was tormented by mirages and phantoms inhabiting his airplane. Several times he was turned around and flew in circles. He flew so close to the ocean that the spray woke him up. Despite being severely deprived of sleep, and the first time he navigated without landmarks, he was within a few miles of his intended course using a handheld compass.

When he left North America, he deviated his flight plan to fly directly over St. John's, Newfoundland, so if he were never seen again, it could be documented. When he reached Ireland, he flew only a few hundred feet above the ground so he could speak to the people on the ground. He wasn't sure where he was, and he wanted to make sure he wasn't dreaming. As he crossed the English Channel, he had two thoughts: he had no visa to enter France and he was a few hours early and thought there would be no one at the airfield when he landed. He had no idea what he was about to accomplish: 150,000 people were waiting at the airfield, and no one would ever ask him for a visa.

On June 13, 1927, Charles Lindbergh had a parade in New York City that was attended by 4 million people — in a city of 3 million people. (Maeder, 2017) Lindbergh then went on a tour of the 48 U.S. states. Estimates are that a quarter of the American population attended at least one parade honoring this previously unknown 25-year-old mail pilot. (Berg A. S., 2015)

Lindbergh had other remarkable achievements in his life. Each one by itself would make him one of the most influential men in American history, but in the collective memory, they are unknown.

Lindbergh is responsible for the modern system of airports as well as a system of trains to connect cities to the airports, a development known as the "Lindbergh Line". (Lankiewicz, 2007)

He established the first national meteorologic system. This allowed people to know the weather in different cities.

He discovered a then-unknown physics professor at a college in Worcester, Massachusetts, named Robert Goddard, and raised the money for his research facility in New Mexico to develop rockets. He is thus responsible for our rocket program, both explorative and militarily.

Lindbergh co-invented the first cardiac perfusion pump.

He co-authored the most influential medical textbook of his era, *The Culture of Organs,* which was published in 1937.

He won a Congressional Medal of Honor at 25 and a Pulitzer Prize in Literature at 52 years of age. (Berg A., 1998)

Charles Lindbergh must be the only man with no musical ability to have a dance craze named after him: the Lindy Hop. Ninety years after it was invented, people not only still do the Lindy Hop, but compete to be the best at it. On YouTube a Flash Mob in Birmingham, United Kingdom does the Hop in 2017. According to the Ken Burns' Jazz series (episode 3), the Hop was integrated at a time when nearly all social events were segregated. When the white-only dance halls in Times Square closed, white revelers would go uptown to dance the Hop on integrated dance floors in Harlem. Movies show black and white dancers swinging their arms in circles to represent a propeller in joy together. In his autobiography, Malcolm X fondly recalled dancing the Lindy Hop with white girls in Lansing, Michigan.

Yet, despite sweeping America, there is no record Charles Lindbergh ever danced it or even commented on it. Although it never caught on like the Lindy Hop, Lindbergh also had a 15-scene opera written about him by Bertolt Brecht. It was called *Der Lindberghflug.* Perhaps more understandably, Lindbergh never commented on it either. (Berg A., 1998)

Neither was Lindbergh a particularly funny man, but references to him appear in popular comedies. In *Back to School* (1986) the hardest dive, performed by Rodney Dangerfield at the end, is called the "Triple Lindy". There are references to Lindbergh in *Up in the Air* (2009) and *Home Alone 2* (1992): Loving someone a lot, means Lindbergh would cross two oceans for them. Lindbergh is in several *Sesame Street* episodes and in *The Muppets* a wedge of cheese flies a propellor-driven airplane. The pilot's name is Charles Limburger.

Today's popular mirth somehow erases popular memory of the abuse of his privacy by the press, especially after the murder of his son. The sensationalism of the trial of the man convicted and executed for the murder is taught in law school today as the textbook example of an unfair trial. (Berg A., 1998) The trial was so spectacular it inspired Agatha Christie to write, *Murder on the Orient Express.* Lindbergh's experiences inspired federal law to be written: the "Lindbergh Law", known as Federal Statute 48-781, made it a federal crime to kidnap a minor punishable by death. (Legal Dictionary, n.d.)

For the rest of his life, people would show up claiming to be his son or newspapers would write articles claiming to have found Charles, Jr.. (Berg A., 1998) While writing Lindbergh's biography two decades after the famous aviator had died, the author A. Scott Berg was contacted by 6 people claiming to be the murdered Lindbergh boy, including a black woman. (Berg A. S., 2015) Other celebrities experienced trauma but none had to live with such repetitive unending trauma their entire lives.

In collaboration with Dr. Alexis Carrel, Lindbergh invented the first working cardiac perfusion pump. The cardiac perfusion pump was presented in Copenhagen in 1937 at the Congress of Experimental Cytology where it demonstrated that a cat's thyroid, a fallopian tube, and a pancreas could be kept functioning attached to an extracorporeal pump. This was the first time an organ was kept functioning outside of a body, an accomplishment which foretold a future of organ transplantation. A physician who saw this feat said, "Lindbergh's work as a scientist would probably be remembered long after his flight to Paris is only a dimly recalled event in aviation history." (Berg A., 1998)

He also developed a technique for separating and purifying tissue cultures, by himself, that was used unsuccessfully in attempts to make a polio vaccine in the 1930s. (Lindbergh C., 1939) Not bad for a man with an 11th grade education!

What was Lindbergh's Legacy Preceding U.S. Involvement in World War II? There are few more influential figures in the prelude to World War II. Millions of Americans heard his speeches, read his articles, or followed the news reports of his testimony to Congress. He bravely fought for this country against the Japanese — all before his 43rd birthday.

Of all his accomplishments, perhaps the least recognized is the credit due him for Congress' decision to rearm after a decade of military neglect. In 1939, Franklin Roosevelt presided over the first two allocations for military preparations since the start of the Depression. The first, in the spring of 1939, was approved by Congress after every witness who testified for it used Lindbergh's intelligence assessments as justification. (Nasaw, 2012, p.369) The second, in the summer of 1939, occurred after Roosevelt's only meeting with Lindbergh. (Berg, 1998, p.387) Each allocation was in the hundreds of millions of dollars (add a zero for today's dollars). Prior to him isolationism was defined not only as opposing military preparedness, but accusing those who wanted to prepare for a future war of financial motives.

Lindbergh was providing valuable and comprehensive intelligence on our future enemy's military capabilities when nearly no one else was. Every component of airplanes had a myriad of options. Building the right airplanes required intelligence. Lindbergh, nearly alone, provided this intelligence and personally met with nearly every manufacturer of airplane components to discuss it, at his own expense. (Ross, 1964, pp.290-1) The Chief of the U.S. Army Air Corps, General Henry "Hap" Arnold, said the best intelligence he ever received came from Lindbergh. (Berg, 1998, p.387) Obtaining this intelligence was a remarkable act of espionage. His contributions to our military preparedness for World War II began 6 years before the U.S. established a foreign intelligence agency; the Office of Strategic Services (OSS) in 1942.

His impact on American politics was revolutionary. The outsider, who holds no political office, nor ever ran for an office, who grabs the spotlight by accusing politicians of lying to convince you to fight in foreign wars because they are beholden to special interests, is not unique. One thinks of Donald Trump, Patrick Buchanan, or Ross Perot; but Charles Lindbergh filled this role half a century earlier. The savvy media personality who has the ability to dominate the modern inventions of mass communication while viciously criticizing mass communication sounds like Trump, but was actually Lindbergh 75 years earlier.

In speeches heard by millions of Americans, Lindbergh advocated there were limits to American power in international affairs. He advocated the United States should not try to remake the world in its image. He warned Americans that the office of the president must have limits to its power and that secrecy and deception were threats to American democracy. Every one of these issues is as much of a burning issue today as when Lindbergh advocated them. President Roosevelt colluded with the press and used his power to destroy the reputations of those who sought to peacefully exercise their rights to oppose America's involvement in a war. No one was a bigger target than Lindbergh who was investigated and his phone was tapped without a warrant.[1] (Olson, 2013, pp.326-7) This issue would certainly repeat itself many times in our history.

In a speech at a sold-out Madison Square Garden he said, "Democracy can spring only from within a nation itself, only from the hearts and minds of the people." (NYC, 5/23/1941) Taking his advice would have prevented much suffering in Vietnam and Afghanistan.

His accomplishments were achieved without speaking to the press. While many political figures criticize the press, most give the press access when the conditions suit them. Lindbergh gave the press nearly no access. Photographers broke into the funeral home housing his dead 2-year-old son's remains, pried open the casket, photographed his remains, and published them. He never forgave them. In April 1939, he met President Roosevelt, and other officials and refused to allow the press to photograph him. The press promised they would thereafter respect his privacy. He wrote in his journal, "Imagine a press photographer talking about his word of honor! The type of men who broke through a window of the Trenton Morgue to open my baby's casket and photograph his body — they talk to me of honor!" (Lindbergh, 1970, p.187)

The photograph of his son's remains can still be found on the internet.

<u>Anne Morrow Lindbergh (1906-2001):</u> A remarkable historical figure in her own right.

Lindbergh's need for privacy led him and his mother to spend Christmas in 1927 in Mexico City at the home of one of his financial backers, Dwight Morrow, the U.S. Ambassador to Mexico. There he was introduced to and fell in love with Morrow's daughter, Anne. Anne was a surprising choice to marry the most eligible bachelor, as she was quiet and shy. So was he. He proposed on their third date, he had never been on a date with anyone else. (Berg, 1998)

Anne and Charles were married for 45 years and had 6 children, 5 of whom lived to adulthood. Anne was the best-selling female author of the era and an accomplished navigator, airplane radio operator, and pilot. Her books documenting her travels with her husband, many to places never seen previously by English-speaking people, are part of the anthropologic record of this planet. (Berg, 1998) She was one of the leading feminist activists of the 20th Century.

Anne was the first woman in America to earn a glider's pilot license and she won the National Geographic Hubbard Medal in 1934 for her documentation of their explorations. She set two aviation records: the first for maintaining radio communication for 3000 miles, for which she won the Veteran's Radio Operator Gold Medal. The second was the record for speed on a transcontinental flight when she and her husband flew across North America in 1930. She was 7 months pregnant at the time. She was inducted into the American Aviation Hall of Fame in 1977 and the International Women in Aviation Hall of Fame in 1999. (Arntzenius, 2016)

On September 20, 1938, Charles Lindbergh was urgently summoned to London to meet with the U.S. Ambassador, Joseph Kennedy, Sr., the father of our future president. Charles' journal paused its description of diplomacy and the impending world war to be a proud husband. He described how nicely Anne landed the airplane in London despite thick clouds. (Lindbergh, 1970, p.71)

She won two National Book Awards in the 1930s and was the best-selling author for non-fiction in 1937. A decade later, she published her diaries chronicling her husband's fight against U.S. involvement in World War II, titled "*War Within and Without*". It won the Christopher Award for 'affirming the highest values of the human spirit', and half a century later (2018), it was used as the title of a *Star Trek* episode. It was one of 15 books she published. A later book, *Gift From The Sea* (1955), sold 3 million copies and was translated into 45 languages. It was the top non-fiction bestseller in 1955. (GFTS, nd) It was published by a Jewish refugee whose own books were burned by the Nazis. (Berg, 1998)

She was a controversial figure who took abuse for her political views. She wrote in her diary in 1941 that the press considered her the "bubonic plague". (Arntzenius, 2016) But politically she was a complicated figure. She supported her husband but came from a family of interventionists and often criticized isolationism. (Olson, 2013) Her sister's husband, Aubrey Morgan, performed the exact role for the British government that Lindbergh was accused of performing for the German government — a propaganda agent for a foreign government. (Olson, 2013, p.48) Having visited Nazi Germany, she said the U.S. should enter the war rather than risk similar anti-Semitism in our society. (Berg, 1998, p.427)

Two decades after her death, a passage from her book *North to the Orient* (1935), greets visitors as they enter our national airport (today Reagan National Airport):

> "Travelers are always discoverers, especially those who travel by air. There are no signposts in the air to show a man has

> passed that way before. There are no channels marked. The flier breaks each second into new uncharted seas."

She wrote this while her son's murderer was on trial.

<u>What part of their legacies does this book cover?</u> This book concentrates on the era from 1935 to 1955.

Any of these topics would make a fine book and other than the flight to Paris, none of Charles' nor Anne's contributions are currently recognized for their significance. Charles Lindbergh's legacy is clouded by a designation that he was either a Nazi or Nazi Sympathizer. This is inaccurate, facile, and a shame. Both Charles and Anne were complicated people who lived complicated lives at an extremely complicated time. Their motivations and goals have been lost in the collective memory, but neither ever belonged to nor communicated with any organization with any affiliation to fascism, let alone a foreign government. In 1942, an FBI investigation proved it. In addition, Charles was deposed in a U.S. civilian court and under oath no evidence was produced supporting it. His nemesis, Roosevelt's Secretary of the Interior, Harold Ickes, admitted it in the *Chicago Daily News.* (Berg, 1998, pp. 409, 445) (Cole, 1974, p.133)

This book covers only a few aspects of their complicated lives: his contribution to the war effort and legacy regarding the war, especially the ensuing conflict with the Jews. It focuses on an arbitrarily defined era: 1935-1955. In U.S. domestic affairs, this constitutes the time between the first Roosevelt administration and the Brown v. Board of Education unanimous decision. Both events heralded new eras. Unlike previous presidents dealing with economic crises, and although constitutionally questionable at the time, Roosevelt unleashed the power of the federal government. (Dalleck, 2017) Brown v. Board began the end of racial segregation. The unanimous decision was engineered by Chief Justice Earl Warren, who like Charles Lindbergh was the son of Swedish immigrants. This decision began a new era in which the promise that every American's human potential could be reached was begun.

In Lindbergh's life this era begins with the verdict in his son's kidnapping case, the ramifications of which forced him to take his family to Europe. This series of events resulted in a legacy as a Nazi Sympathizer but demonstrated remarkable patriotism. The period ends with an honorary promotion to Brigadier General and the sale of his rights to the screenplay *The Spirit of St. Louis* to a Jewish movie producer. The movie starred Jimmy Stewart, who as a boy in Pennsylvania had followed Lindbergh's flight on a home-made wooden board. He became a star opposing Nazism in a movie called *The Mortal Storm.*

The Spirit of St. Louis was a commercial flop because most Americans didn't remember the flight and many of those who did despised Lindbergh. (Berg A., 1998) This era constitutes the transformation of his life from an international figure of consequence in a field other than aviation until he became honored, ignored, and despised simultaneously. Despite the disdain of millions of Americans, his expertise was avidly sought by our military, and he made major post-war contributions to American security which this book also documents.

For the Jews it marks the most transformative era not just in Jewish history, but perhaps in the history of any ethnic, religious, or minority group. It begins with Hitler's rise to power in Germany which began the worst period of victimization in history, includes the creation of the state of Israel, and roughly ends with the Sinai War (1956), a mostly forgotten war. Yet, the Sinai War may have been Israel's most important war. It established the permanence of the state of Israel. (Golani, n.d.)

Understanding the first third of Charles' life (1902-1935) is critical. It explains who he was and what motivated him. His father was a congressman persecuted for opposing U.S. involvement in World War I. Lindbergh spent a significant amount of his childhood on Capitol Hill. He was a loner and spent his early adulthood as a wanderer. But he had remarkable confidence in his own abilities, which resulted in success. He never lost focus no matter the danger — 3 crashes as an air mail pilot, crossing the Atlantic, experimenting with high altitude aviation, and combat against the Japanese. (Berg A., 1998)

The last third of his life (1956-1974) is of unclear importance. It will mostly not be discussed. There are specific events and quotes worth noting but in general he was self-destructive. His marriage failed, he had a strained relationship with his adult children, and although he considered himself an environmentalist, he refused public attention and mostly traveled around the world aimlessly. He certainly was not forgotten; he received hundreds of invitations for honorary degrees, speeches, and awards but he very politely turned nearly all of them down. In response to nearly every invitation, he wrote a hand-written letter thanking the organization but saying he wanted to spend time with his family, which he did not do. (Berg A., 1998) He did a photo opportunity for the benefit of the space program but declined Nixon's invitation to be present when the astronauts landed in the ocean. He died of lymphoma in 1974, few people attended his funeral, and he is buried, by himself, in Hawaii.

Anne spent the last two decades of her life enjoying the company of her children and 17 grandchildren. In the 1990s she, her children, and her surviving sister, collaborated with Berg in the writing of her husband's biography, *Lindbergh,* which was published in 1998 and won the Pulitzer Prize. She died in Vermont at the age of 94 in 2001. She was cremated and her ashes scattered over Hawaii. She bequeathed their papers to Yale University Library and all of Charles' awards and mementos were donated to the Missouri Historical Society in St. Louis, where they sit in storage as few people request to see them. (Personal communication, 2020)

This book is not an attempt to redo Mr. Berg's work. It seeks to explore Lindbergh's contribution to the U.S. war effort and address the question of whether Lindbergh was an anti-Semite or a Nazi Sympathizer from a different perspective — that of a Jewish aerospace engineer. Ultimately it proposes what his legacy should be in relation to the U.S. involvement in World War II and the Jews. The contributions he made to science are reviewed. Some are new to historical scholarship and derived from his original laboratory notes. These contributions have been forgotten.

Why is this book necessary? Because what historians find interesting is not necessarily what is historically important.

Historians are not engineers, neither are the people who write about anti-Semitism or define who was an anti-Semite. Perhaps they find engineering to be technical and of little interest. This may be true, but the world doesn't work without it and by not understanding it, Lindbergh's legacy has been distorted. By the same reasoning, a person who doesn't understand how a computer works can't define Bill Gates' legacy. Lindbergh's legacy and particularly his actions visiting Nazi Germany (1936-9), can't be judged without understanding its impact on aviation and U.S. preparation for war. Lindbergh's contributions to high altitude aviation, oxygen equipment, jet engine development, and air defense strategy have been completely ignored. As a result, his legacy has been distorted.

For example, historians have exhaustively examined social events such as the 1936 Berlin Olympics, whose Opening Ceremonies the Lindberghs attended. While the stories of Jesse Owens and Marty Glickman are compelling, the author considers them ceremonial with no effect on strategy, logistics, or weapons. On the other hand, historians have mostly ignored the disparate development of airplane technology in the 1930s and Lindbergh's role in U.S. engineers being able to eliminate this gap by 1943. His visits to German air facilities in the late 1930s are glossed over, inadequate detail paid to what he was shown, the intelligence reports he generated ignored, and the effect these reports had on allied aircraft development is not explained.[2] These visits enabled the Allies to achieve air superiority. Absent this development, and absent Lindbergh's role in it, the Holocaust could not have ended.

How is Anti-Semitism defined in this book? Often the difference between anti-Semitism and a disagreement is the invocation of a conspiracy.

Anti-Semitism is not a disagreement in which the alleged offender states Jews act transparently to pursue their own interests. The anti-Semite accuses the Jewish people and their supporters of a conspiracy to injure the non-Jewish world. (Rosenberg, 2022) A conspiracy is an allegation devoid of a factual basis. When contrary facts are presented, the conspiracy enlarges to include the contrary evidence as part of the conspiracy.

The most dangerous anti-Semitism meets three criteria: the anti-Semite identifies a problem, blames the Jews for that problem, and then invokes the conspiracy theory. Conspiracies serve to deny challenges to the accusation that the Jews are responsible for the problem. (Prager) Conspiracies make political action to rectify the problem impossible, i.e. elect different representatives. Thus, the anti-Semite can justifiably replace activism with resentment.

For example, when Ilhan Omar made her infamous "it's all about the Benjamins" comment, the offense was not repeating "tropes" as the media charged. She was advancing a conspiracy theory. First, she identified a problem — Congress is too pro-Israel. Second, she blamed it on the Jews and third espoused a conspiracy theory: Congress is only pro-Israel because it has sold America's national interest for money. (Gambino, 2019) Or as the *Wall Street Journal* wrote when defending the decision to remove her from the Foreign Relations Committee in 2023, "(she said) powerful Jews are...buying the nation's politicians to set U.S. foreign policy (in order to) advance their own Jewish interests." (Kaufman, 2023)

Anti-Semitic conspiracies are often a bitter excuse for failure. In 1970, future Chief Justice William Rehnquist allegedly wrote a Nixon Supreme Court nominee's rejection was so only "Brandeises, Cardozos, and Frankfurters" would be confirmed. The Senate rejected the judge because of his racist past, but a facile conspiracy replaces an honest assessment – the enemy is secretly orchestrating a completely Jewish Supreme Court. (Perlstein, 2008, p.466)

Disagreeing with a version of the national interest, using democratic processes, is not anti-Semitism. Lindbergh emphasized Jews were entitled to advocate, but he didn't believe war was in the national interest. This advocacy was devoid of conspiracies and thus not anti-Semitism. When Lindbergh lost this fight, democratically, he didn't allege conspiracies.

Which Jewish heroes engaged in Anti-Semitism in Lindbergh's era?

During the era reviewed, historians identify two types of anti-Semitism: casual anti-Semitism and malignant anti-Semitism. (Groom, 2013) For example, Neal Gabler, Walt Disney's biographer wrote, "I saw no evidence, other than the casual anti-Semitism that nearly all gentiles at that time would have, that Disney was an anti-Semite." (Gabler, 2020) Casual anti-Semitism would be defined as not renting a house to someone because they're Jewish, while malignant anti-Semitism commonly consisted of blaming the Jews for Nazi persecution, using derogatory names (e.g., kike), or claiming the reports of the Jews being mistreated in Germany were a media conspiracy. Lindbergh never engaged in the casual anti-Semitism in his personal life nor business affairs nor did he espouse malignant anti-Semitism.

A classic example of 1930s anti-Semitism was the 'Jews aren't American enough' argument, most famously stated by First Lady Eleanor Roosevelt. In response to Nazi persecution, Mrs. Roosevelt famously said the Jews must, "wipe out…any feeling of difference by joining all that is being done by Americans." (Cook, 1999, p. 557) This theory blamed the Jews' problems on being different. The most egregious form of "difference" was to complain. Millions of Americans, including Jews, thought the way to fight anti-Semitism was to blend in and thereby not fight anti-Semitism. The damage this sentiment did is incalculable. As common as this sentiment was, Lindbergh never espoused it, neither for the Jews nor any other group of Americans.

Other experts on anti-Semitism have excused 'cultural anti-Semitism' when espoused by American Jewish heroes such as President Harry Truman. The director of the U.S. Holocaust Museum, Sara Bloomfield, said about Truman's comments about Jews, "(it was)...typical of a sort of cultural anti-Semitism that was common at that time in all parts of American society. That was an acceptable way to talk." (Ginsberg, 2021) The author contends such statements are "acceptable" only because it was Truman who said them, and he made a critical contribution to Jewish history. Lindbergh made an equally important contribution, thus the question of him being excused should also be considered.

<u>The Ground Rules:</u> The author has developed 5 rules which he applies to all public figures in the book.

In 1970, Charles Lindbergh agreed to have his wartime journals published, and although some segments were removed, they have been documented regardless. (see Apocrypha) In 1978, the rest of his journals were published posthumously and all of Anne's journals have been published. The editorial position of the author is journals are invaluable for determining peoples' motivation and schedule. Details they impart can be considered true unless there is evidence otherwise, but private thoughts and one-sided conversations can't be used to establish someone's legacy. People are entitled to write down their private thoughts without judgement, and in this case no one knew these thoughts until long after the event in question. Stated succinctly — it is unfair to call someone an anti-Semite because they wrote something anti-Semitic in a journal that no one knew about. It is especially inappropriate to do so if no one knew about it until after the writer was dead.

For example, when returning from Europe to New York in 1939, Lindbergh observed that most of the other passengers were Jewish, as would be expected given the political situation. The weather was awful and most of the passengers got seasick. With hours stuck in his cabin, Lindbergh wrote about how the captain told him the Jewish passengers got seasick more often than the other passengers. Then he began wondering whether the Jews were going to New York or a different destination. He decided it would be better if the Jews went elsewhere because New York had a lot of Jews and it'd be better if they spread out. He wrote a few Jews adds "character" but too many produces "chaos". (Berg, 1998, p.386)

This journal entry is trotted out as 'proof' Lindbergh was an anti-Semite. Stated publicly it is casual anti-Semitism because although it includes a compliment and was made in what he thought was the Jews' best interest, it does blame the Jews for a problem: chaos, and then espouses a conspiracy theory — there are too many in New York. But it was a private thought, unknown until 1970, therefore it is a footnote.

Furthermore, Ken Burns' sinister simulated Lindbergh voice in the *U.S. and the Holocaust* (2022) obscures that this private thought, unknown for 31 years, is the entire body of evidence supporting the charge Lindbergh was an anti-Semite in the 1930s. For patriotic reasons, Lindbergh placed himself in the most anti-Semitic environment known, had many conversations, wrote reports and hundreds of pages of thoughts, and all his critics can find to define him as an anti-Semite in this decade is one milquetoast private thought: there are too many Jews in New York. Publicly, there are only positive references to Jews for the entire decade. His journal contains other passages sympathetic to Jewish suffering, advocating for the civil rights of Black Americans, and supporting the rights of Jews to advocate for themselves. (Lindbergh, 1970, 8/23/39)

If you can disqualify someone as an anti-Semite based on their private thoughts, nearly everyone, certainly everyone of that era who was not Jewish and kept a journal, would be disqualified, and the accusation would then lose all meaning. For example, Truman wrote in his journal in 1947:

> "(The Jews) I find are very very selfish. They care not how many Latvians, Finns, Poles, Estonians, or Greeks get murdered or mistreated as DPs (displaced persons) as long as Jews get special treatment. Yet when they have power, physical, financial, or political, neither Hitler nor Stalin has anything on them for cruelty or mistreatment for the underdog." (Cornwell, 2003)

This statement is certainly anti-Semitic. It identifies a problem: others suffer, it is blamed on the Jews, and then espouses a conspiracy theory: the Jews use power to mistreat the underdog. It is exponentially worse than anything Lindbergh ever said or wrote, even in private. Yet, we can't judge Truman on his private thoughts because if he is an anti-Semite, the term is meaningless. Based on his actions, Truman represented Jewish interests probably better than any other president. This statement demonstrates how depressed and frustrated Truman was at one of the low points of his Presidency.

There's another reason you can't use someone's thoughts taken out of chronologic context to condemn them: if everyone is an anti-Semite (or racist or bigot) than no one is. This is frequently the defense used by the real racist as justification for real hate. A truly vile figure of this era was the manager of the baseball team the Philadelphia Phillies, Ben Chapman. Chapman's racist taunting of Jackie Robinson was legendary and vicious. If the reader wants to see what real hate looked like in the 1940s, one should watch the movie '*42*' because the author won't repeat those insults. Chapman's defense was that everyone did this, for example "we called Joe DiMaggio a 'wop' and Stan Musial a 'polack'", and to have given Robinson a pass would have been "unfair". (Barra, 2013)

There's no doubt there were other players of the era who were called ethnic names and other ballplayers who did so. But there's a big difference between a slur designed to get a competitive edge and hate. For example, the famous pitcher Dizzy Dean called Hank Greenberg

"Mose" (short for Moses) before game 7 of the 1934 World Series to try to get a mental edge. (Greenberg, 1989) While this is anti-Semitism, it isn't the equivalent of the vicious baiting Robinson consistently and repeatedly endured from opposing dugouts designed solely to humiliate him. Likewise, there's a huge difference between Nazis and someone stuck on a ship noodling in private about where the Jews are going.

Another controversy in Lindbergh's legacy is one-sided reporting of private conversations. Anne gave interviews after Charles' death and discussed private conversations. For example, other than a reference in Anne's diary in 1941, there's no record of how he felt about the creation of the state of Israel. After Charles passed, Anne claimed that he was a supporter of Israel's creation, but this can't be verified at its time in history. (Mitgang, 1980) It is possible but hardly critical whether Lindbergh did espouse such a sentiment. Conversely, Henry Ford claimed he had conversations about the Jews with Lindbergh, but Lindbergh's journal documents 84 conversations or references to conversations with Ford without a single mention of the Jews. Every conversation is about the war effort and aviation. (Siegel, 2019) (Lindbergh, 1970) In neither case should credence be given.

First ground rule: Every major figure of the era is to be judged not on what they wrote in their journals privately or what someone said they said, but only for publicly confirmable actions or statements. Interviews conducted by historians are valid for consideration, if properly referenced.

Second ground rule: Americans' First Amendment rights protect unpopular speech, including opinions inimical to Jewish interests. Saying it does not make one an anti-Semite. Lindbergh's public statements will be evaluated for anti-Semitism, but context must be considered.

Third ground rule: something can't be anti-Semitic if it's true, regardless of the conventional rules of the era. Lindbergh said Jews wanted the U.S. to enter World War II and some Jewish leaders were advocating the U.S. enter the war. (Cole, 1974) (Des Moines Speech, 9/11/41) Both statements were true. That these statements weren't allowed to be said in public at the time is not anti-Semitism.

Fourth ground rule: people are not responsible for the political opinions of their friends, business associates, family members, or people with whom they interact. Lindbergh's critics have spent years finding faults with Lindbergh's associates. It is true he was friendly with anti-Semites such as Henry Ford, but he also was friendly with Jews like the Guggenheim family. People are only responsible for their own actions and their own statements.

President Roosevelt had a cousin named Laura Delano who infamously said about the U.S. giving refuge to Jewish children, "20,000 charming children will all too soon turn into 20,000 ugly adults." (Rosen, 2006, p.85) This statement can't be attributed to President Roosevelt. It does not provide his motivation for not providing visas to these children, because he too isn't responsible for the statements of people he was associated with.

Fifth ground rule: you can't ascribe motives to people without evidence. It is easy to win an argument if you disqualify the actions of those that disagree with you by ascribing motives. For example, in 1945 President Roosevelt pled with the future king of Saudi Arabia to allow Holocaust survivors into Palestine. The king refused. (Dalleck, 2017, p.614) Roosevelt's critics claim Roosevelt only did this so these Jews wouldn't come to the U.S.. However, lacking evidence this was his motive, his action must be recognized as in the Jewish interest. Judging legacies requires evidence to disqualify actions based on motives.

Assigning altruistic motives to people without documentation is termed hagiography. Assigning malicious motives to people without evidence is vilification.

Given evidence, a person's legacy does include the issue of motivation. A person who uses a generalization the listener finds offensive should not be condemned like a person who is trying to demean, dehumanize, or humiliate. There is no evidence Lindbergh sought to do the latter. What he was trying to do was address the war in Europe and address individual interest groups' arguments. His motivation was what he believed was in the best interest of his country and expected everyone to defend their interpretation of the national interest.

Because Lindbergh advocated for a negotiated settlement in western Europe, the charge of anti-Semitism is buttressed by an accusation, he "exaggerated" German airpower prior to World War II. (Nasaw, 2012, p.339) The people who charge this refuse to recognize the devastation inflicted by German airpower from 1939-1942 was unimaginable before it occurred and therefore could not have been "exaggerated". This book attempts to examine the accuracy of his predictions.

A person's legacy includes their life's work and whether in total it hurt or helped the country or the Jews. Lindbergh's legacy is complicated, especially regarding the Jews, but there is no question he did much more than is generally recognized. His actions were neither motivated by anti-Semitism nor consistent with anti-Semitism as defined in his era. He expressed admiration for Jews in an era which few did, prominently acknowledged and condemned German mistreatment of the Jews in an era in which it was minimized, used his contacts in Nazi Germany to advocate for the Jews which no other negotiator did, did business with Jews, after *Kristallnacht* refused to perform any public action which could be seen as supportive of Germany and incurred great expense to do so, visited a liberated Concentration Camp and spoke to survivors on his own time, was an advocate of the Nuremberg Trials, and regretted he'd been labeled an anti-Semite. (Berg A., 1998) (Mitgang, 1980)

In all his business and personal interactions with Jews (some of which went badly) there is no documentation he resorted to a slur. This is despite it being so common in his era that others, such as Truman, are excused for doing so. In his era, his respect for others was very unusual.

Lindbergh's Legacy: Lindbergh never blamed Jews for their mistreatment nor advocating for their interests. Although he opposed it, he said he understood why Jews wanted to enter World War II, and unlike others he never said Jewish advocacy caused anti-Semitism.

Lindbergh said it was justified Jews advocate the U.S. enter the war to stop Nazi persecution. (Des Moines speech, 9/11/1941) In his era, for anyone to say this, let alone an isolationist, was remarkable. In contrast, the First Lady, a U.S. Senator, and a congressman all stated publicly the Jews were unamerican or nefariously pushing the U.S. into World War II. A future U.S. President (John F. Kennedy) blamed criticism of his father on the nefarious influence of Jews in the press. (Nasaw, 2012) Lindbergh was more supportive of Jewish interests than most American public figures of his era; including on some issues, more than people now considered Jewish heroes.

He was ahead of his time advocating for Black Americans. He asked how can we fight for democracy in Europe given the treatment of Black Americans in the U.S.? He was addressing civil rights in March 1939 before he became an isolationist, "What of our 10 million Negroes?... One thing is certain: if democracy is to continue on this earth it will not be by the blood of its soldiers but only by great changes in its present practices." (3/20/39, Lindbergh, 1970)

The same week Lindbergh was preparing a public demand for a discussion of the role of Black Americans in our democracy (Lindbergh C.A., 1970) 12/12/41 (Cole, 1974), Hitler was calling the U.S. "decayed" because it was a "mongrel nation", "half Judaised and half Negrified." (Dalleck, 2017, p.343) When the U.S. was at war Lindbergh was no longer an isolationist, but he was still advocating for Black Americans. He deplored the lynching of Black servicemen and complained that the press didn't give these atrocities the attention they deserve.deserve. (Lindbergh, 1970, 10/6/42) He certainly made an odd "Nazi"!

He also advocated for the humanity of the Japanese. Dehumanization of Japanese rivaled Nazi dehumanization of Jews. They were compared to rats. Theodore Geisel (Dr. Seuss) drew racist cartoons and future Chief Justice Earl Warren, denied a hundred thousand Japanese Americans due process. (Fleming, 2003) Lindbergh criticized his fellow soldiers' dehumanization of the Japanese and although he fought the Japanese, he called the use of the atomic bomb a war crime. (Cole, 1974)

The position that the U.S. can't fight for democracy abroad until Black Americans have the benefits of democracy at home, and that an Asian enemy isn't subhuman was Muhammad Ali's argument in his fight against conscription in 1967. Ali's right to box was returned to him by Supreme Court justice Potter Stewart — a founder of the isolationist movement who invited Lindbergh to speak at Yale University.

<u>Why Should Jews Reconsider How They Remember Historical Figures?</u>
Because often it's wrong.

When it comes to American history, Jews have a faulty recollection of their past. Ulysses Grant is an example. As a general in 1862, Grant issued the infamous General Orders 11 which tried to expel the Jews from the Tennessee military district to stop smuggling across Union lines (President Lincoln canceled them). But he was perhaps the best president the Jews ever had and perhaps the most popular among American Jews. He was the first president to visit a Synagogue, appointed more Jews to public office than any previous president, and was a staunch defender of Russian Jews being mistreated by the Czar. Grant was responsible for perhaps the single most symbolic act supporting Jews by a President in the pre-Israel era. When confronting Romanian mistreatment of the Jews, he deliberately chose a Jewish ambassador to represent the U.S. in Bucharest. (Sarna, 2012)

Domestically he supported Jewish interests as well. Protestants tried to use federal money for parochial endeavors which excluded Jews and Catholics. Grant stood for secular use of government funds. He stood for free non-sectarian public schools and his State of the Union address in 1876 pronounced the government's responsibility was "...forbidding the teaching of any atheistic, pagan, or religious texts." He died two days before the Jewish day of mourning, *Tisha B'Av,* in 1885. The *Philadelphia Jewish Record* wrote, "None will mourn (Grant's) loss more sincerely than the Hebrew...and tomorrow in every Jewish synagogue and temple in the land the sad event will be solemnly commemorated with fitting eulogy and prayer." (Sarna, 2012)

Unfortunately, the only thing American Jews know about Grant is what he did as general and they know nothing about his presidency. When asked to rank the presidents in terms of how they treated the Jews, Grant is at the bottom. In 1948, he was 28th of 29 presidents. In 1996 he was 38th of 41 presidents. (Sarna, 2012) In Grant's defense, he claimed General Orders 11 was a draft that was issued before he had a chance to review it. He claimed if he had been given the chance to review it, he wouldn't have issued it. (Miller, 2019)

Jewish Misunderstanding of the pre-World War II era

This same misunderstanding of events and who acted in Jewish interests infects the Jewish collective memory of the years preceding World War II. American Jews cling to a positive assessment of President Franklin Roosevelt, even though it has been known for decades that he used every means at his disposal to deny Jewish refugees visas to which they were entitled to escape Germany and Austria. The record demonstrates no economic nor political reason which withstands scrutiny. (Morse, 1968) Historians persist in claiming without documentation that "Roosevelt worked behind the scenes" to help the Jews.

Those who claim Roosevelt "worked behind the scenes" to pass legislation to help Jewish refugees, such as Ken Burns in the documentary *The U.S. and the Holocaust,* or Richard Breitman in *FDR and the Jews,* can't cite a single piece of legislation which passed the U.S. Congress prior to 1943 that helped Jews. FDR did act behind the scenes to prevent Jews from escaping to the Dominican Republic (Breitman, 2013, pp.131-2) and to kill a Congressional resolution demanding England let Jews into Palestine. (Dalleck, 2017, p.596) Simply because historians want something to be true does not give them the right to invent it. This book endeavors to document everything it claims.

The Roosevelt administration's deliberate obstruction of Jews fleeing Nazi Germany was documented by his own Treasury Department in 1943. (Morse, 1968, p.89) It has not been taught to Jewish children. Instead, excuses have been made for his complicity in the annihilation of Europe's Jews. Recently the Israeli press published an article about the puzzling American Jewish attachment to President Roosevelt. There is a controversy among American Jews about whether the truth is taught about what happened to the Jews prior to World War II. (Norwood, 2020)

With 80 years hindsight, the public statements Lindbergh made, compared to others in an era during which anti-Semitism was rampant and vicious, are so mild and borderline in their alleged anti-Semitism they appear meaningless. The author questions what those who impugned him so vigorously did for the Jews? Why do Jews continue to accept the vilification of Lindbergh by Roosevelt who had his own motives for vilifying him? Roosevelt consistently acted contrary to Jewish interests and the author documents this enabled the murder of perhaps over a million Jews. Why isn't this generally recognized?

<u>So, Let's Do This!</u>

Charles Lindbergh had a legacy as an authority on aviation and a public political figure. His legacy as an American aviation authority comprised nearly half a century and is remarkable and exemplary. He made fundamental contributions to U.S. national security that not only enabled us to win World War II but helped in the Korean and Vietnamese conflicts as well.

He was a public political figure for two years and his legacy is not good. He was wrong about aid to England, wrong that oceans would protect us, used poor judgement, engaged in specious justifications, and shamelessly advocated moral equivalency. Indeed, he advocated false moral equivalency the rest of his life. But whether he was an anti-Semite and what he said about the Jews, as opposed to what his critics (many of whom were anti-Semites) said, is certainly worth examining from a new generational perspective.

Historians have examined his record as a public figure but ignored the contributions he made to U.S. security. But these legacies are intertwined. His expertise in aviation was a foundation of his opposition to U.S. involvement in World War II. (Oklahoma City speech, August 29, 1941) They somehow must be merged and both aspects acknowledged.

This book will attempt to evaluate Lindbergh's actions; in his personal life, in public life, in business, in scientific research, helping the U.S. military, and evaluate his life's accomplishments. His critics' arguments will be evaluated. There is much to criticize Lindbergh for. The author makes no excuses, and certainly makes no exonerating claims without documentation. But just as the author was surprised to find Lindbergh's behavior, motivation, advocacy, and accomplishments were so completely different than his critics have portrayed them, so may the reader?

Let's examine this legacy...

[1]Roosevelt also had the IRS investigate Lindbergh. Lindbergh always paid an extra 10% with his tax returns as a "patriotic surcharge." As a result, this "scandal" died quickly. When informed the IRS was going to review his tax returns, Lindbergh quipped sardonically that he wouldn't expect his refund. (Ross, 1964, p.294)

[2]The first post-mortem biography of Lindbergh was Leonard Mosley's. Lindbergh's intelligence work is dismissed as "already known" without a reference. The cardiac perfusion pump, his briefing of General Arnold

in May 1939, the meetings with airplane manufacturers, and the Kilner Report are not mentioned. (see Table 1, p. 94) (Mosley, 1976, pp.217, 249) When relevant, historians traditionally include the role of engineering. For example, historian David McCullough's book on the Johnstown Flood (published in 1968), contains an impeccable discussion of the engineering failures which caused the flood. In evaluating Lindbergh's legacy, either historians don't appreciate the relevance of Lindbergh's engineering contributions or have chosen not to consider them.

Works Cited

Arntzenius, L. (2016). Couple of an Age. *Princeton Magazine.*

Barra, A. (2013). What Really Happened to Ben Chapman. *The Atlantic.*

Berg, A. (1998). *Lindbergh.* New York: Penguin.

Berg, A. S. (2015, November 15). *Speech Princeton NJ.* Retrieved from https://www.youtube.com/watch?v=BnW1s0V6OoI

Breitman, R. (2013). *FDR and the Jews.* New York.

Burns (Director). (2022). *U.S. and the Holocaust* [Motion Picture].

Cole, W. S. (1974). *Charles Lindbergh and the Battle Against U.S. Involvement in World War II.* New York: Harcourt Brace Jovanovich.

Cook, B. (1999). *Eleanor Roosevelt.* New York: Viking.

Cornwell, R. (2003, July 12). *Truman Diary Reveals Anti-Semitism.* Retrieved from The Independent: https://www.independent.co.uk

Dalleck, R. (2017). *Franklin Roosevelt: A Political Life.* New York: Penguin Publishing.

Duffy, J. (2010). *Lindbergh v. Roosevelt.* New York.

Fleming, T. (2003). *The New Dealers War.* New York.

Gabler, N. (2020, Feb 25). *Jerusalem Post.*

Gambino, L. (2019, February 11). Ilhan Omar Apologizes. *The Guardian.*

GFTS, https://en....org/wiki/Gift from the Sea

Ginsberg, G. (2021). *First Friends.* New York: Hachette Book Group.

Golani, M (n.d.), The Sinai War and Suez Crisis, 1956-7. Jewish Virtual Library: https://www.jewishvirtuallibrary.org/ israel-studies-an-anthology-the-sinai-war

Greenberg, H. (1989). In *The Story of My Life.* Chicago: Triumph Books.

Groom, W. (2013). *The Aviators.* Washington, DC: National Geographic.

Kaufman, E. (2023, February 7). Republicans Do Ilhan Omar a Favor. *Wall Street Journal.*

Lankiewicz, D. (2007, July). The Lindbergh Line. *Aviation History.*

Legal Dictionary. (n.d.). Retrieved from Lindbergh Act: https://legal-dictionary.thefreedictionary.com/Lindbergh+Act

Lindbergh, C. (1939, May 26). A Culture Flask for the Circulation of a Large Quantity of Fluid Medium . *Journal of Experimental Medicine*, pp. 231-8.

Lindbergh, C. A. (1970). *The Wartime Journals of Charles Lindbergh.* New York: Jovanovich.

Maeder, J. (2017, August 14). The Day New York City Threw a Ticker Tape Parade for Charles Lindbergh. *NY Daily News.*

Miller, D. L. (2019). *Vicksburg.* New York: Simon and Shuster.

Mitgang, H. (1980, April 20). *Lindbergh said to regret misperceptions of the Jews*. Retrieved from Lindbergh: An American Aviator: http://www.charleslindbergh.com/ny/105.asp

Morse, A. (1968). *While Six Million Died.* New York: Random House.

Mosley, L, Lindbergh: *A Biography*, Doubleday, 1976.

Nasaw, D. (2012). *The Patriarch.* New York: Penguin.

Norwood, S. A. (2020, December 1). Stop Whitewashing FDRs Abandonment of the Jews. *Israel National News.*

Olson, L. (2013). *Those Angry Days.* New York: Random House.

Perlstein, R, *Nixonland,* Scribner and Sons, NY, 2008.

Prager, D. (1983). *Why the Jews*, Simon and Shuster, NY.

Reel, M. (2018). *A Brotherhood of Spies.* New York: Doubleday.

Rosen, R. (2006). *Saving the Jews.* New York: Thunder Mouth Press.

Rosenberg, Y. (2022). Why Some People Still Don't Understand Anti-Semitism. *The Atlantic.*

Ross, W, *The Last Hero: Charles A. Lindbergh*, Harper and Row, NY, 1964.

Sarna, J. (2012). *The Redemption of Grant.* Retrieved from Reform Judaism. Com: https://reformjudaism.org/redemption-ulysses-s-grant

Siegel, S. (2019). The Anti-Semitism of Charles Lindbergh. *The Jewish Press.*

Wallace, M. (2003). *The American Axis.* New York: St. Martin's Press.

3: Charles A. Lindbergh, Childhood and Wandering

1902-1926

Both Charles Lindbergh and his father shared the same first name and middle initial, although Charles was not a junior because they had different middle names. In this chapter, "Charles" refers to the famous aviator while his father is called, by his initials "C.A.", as he was in his life. The story of Charles' childhood can be found in Andrew Scott Berg's book, Lindbergh. Unless otherwise noted, that is the source of this chapter.

The famous aviator Charles Augustus Lindbergh was born in Detroit on February 4, 1902. He was born into an illustrious but very troubled family and had an unusual childhood. His paternal grandfather, Ola Mansson, was an elected representative in Sweden but fled Sweden in 1859, leaving his wife and family behind, rather than be prosecuted for financial crimes. He fled to Canada with his 19-year-old mistress and her infant son who would be the father of the world's most famous aviator. Upon entering Canada, Mansson changed his name to August Lindbergh and his son was named Charles August Lindbergh, called by his initials, C.A.. August Lindbergh crossed into the United States and made his way to the new state of Minnesota. There he and his family became American citizens. They settled in the town of Little Falls, Minnesota which had a few thousand people. C.A. named his only son, Charles Augustus Lindbergh.

Charles' mother, Evangeline Land Lindbergh, returned to her hometown of Detroit to give birth because she wanted her uncle, Dr. Edwin Land, to deliver the baby. She was a chemistry teacher at the local high school when she met C.A., who was a successful businessman and banker and several decades older. He was a widower with two daughters. Her father, Charles Henry Land, Sr. was a prominent dentist who pioneered the use of porcelain in dental implants and held several patents for high-temperature gas furnaces. (Lindbergh, 1970) Charles was Evangeline's only child. Her marriage quickly disintegrated. She was frequently unstable and prone to wild swings of her temper. Historians speculate she suffered from mental illness. Her stepdaughter who lived to adulthood, Eva Lindbergh, certainly believed she was ill.

Charles grew up initially in Little Falls, but his father was elected to the U.S. Congress in 1906 as a Republican. This begins a childhood consistent for dislocation and isolation. He was frequently traveling between Little Falls, Detroit, and Washington, DC. His schooling was haphazard, and his mother intermittently decided to home-school him. He recalled never having started a school year on time nor remaining in one place long enough to finish the year. His parents rarely lived with each other, but because a divorce would have destroyed C.A.'s political career, they remained married.

His two half-sisters despised his mother and spent most of their childhood in boarding schools. Once they were old enough to make decisions, they refused to have contact with her. He thus had no siblings, and he also had no friends. The closest figure to a brother and friend was his mother's brother, Charles Land, Jr., who was 23 years older than he was. Uncle Charles called himself an inventor, and had several patents, but rarely made a living and had unlimited time for his nephew. Despite lack of schooling — having a chemistry teacher for a mother, an inventor for "best friend", and a grandfather who was a scientist resulted in Charles spending his childhood tinkering with devices. He spent his time in his grandfather's science laboratory in Detroit. He was fascinated with science the rest of his life.

His father's status as a congressman gave Charles opportunities few children get. He attended school with President Theodore Roosevelt's sons, but they weren't friends. As a child, he met the most important politicians of the day. Some of the men in Congress with his father would be the most powerful congressmen in the country 30 years later when Lindbergh would lead the opposition to President Franklin Roosevelt.

The most prominent member of the class of 1906 was William Borah of Idaho who would become the most powerful Republican in the country during the Depression and a leading isolationist. He was introduced to the long serving Speaker of the House, "Uncle" Joe Cannon of Illinois, the socialist mainstay "Fighting Bob" LaFollette of Wisconsin, and President Wilson. The legend is 11-year-old Charles Lindbergh was not intimidated when speaking to the President.

He rolled Easter Eggs on the White House lawn with President Taft watching and saw the Suffragettes parade up Pennsylvania Avenue. He sat in the front row for inaugurations and saw the construction of the Panama Canal. In June 1912, C.A. arranged for his son to see the Aeronautical Trials in Ft. Myer, Virginia. Charles saw an airplane for the first time in his life and decided he wanted to fly.

His father made enemies as one of the most radical members of Congress. He took the on the "Money Trust" of Morgan, Carnegie, and Rockefeller and attacked his fellow congressmen who he believed were corrupt in what were called the Pujo Investigations. His enemies would get their chance to get even. The chance would come in 1914 when World War I began.

World War I was a complicated and forgotten war. There are many proposed reasons for it. German historians frequently claim the main reason was Germany wanting to be a superpower. For decades Germany had been a world power economically, scientifically, and militarily. On land, it had humiliated France in the Franco-Prussian War (1870-1). What it lacked was a coastline and a navy. England and France expanded their empires, not by the consent of the governed, but by force. Germany saw no reason it could not forcefully obtain its empire and saw its opportunity in World War I. (Lind, 2014) An obscure Austrian corporal named Hitler would speak for millions when he wrote, "...if this struggle should bring us victory our people will rank among the great nations. Only then could the German Empire assert itself as the mighty champion of peace." (Berg, 2013)

Britain used its navy to impose a brutal naval embargo on the short German coastline. As a result, the German civilian population was starving. (Lind, 2014) The U.S. continued to trade with England, C.A. contended this trade was for the purpose of making fortunes for the money trust, so it was inevitable the U.S. and Germany would be drawn into a conflict. Even "civilian" goods being shipped to England such as food, were legitimate military targets as England was starving Germany. Evidence was suppressed England was dishonest, for while the media reported sunk allied shipping was peaceful; it often was not. And while historians have proposed other justifications for the U.S. entering the war, such as the atrocities the Germans committed against civilian populations, particularly Belgium, these issues had little effect on President Wilson's decision to declare war on Germany. (Schaepjdriver, 2014)

On February 4, 1915, Germany declared the waters around the British Isles a war zone. Prior to purchasing passenger tickets, prominent warnings were posted that consumers were purchasing tickets to enter a war zone with all the dangers inherent therein. On May 7, 1915, a German submarine sank a passenger ship, the *Lusitania*. 1,198 people perished, including 128 Americans, but the ship was also carrying rifle cartridges, shrapnel, fuses, shell casings, and explosives. Secretary of State William Jennings Bryan said the U.S. should rebuke England for using our citizens to "protect her ammunition." (Berg, 2013)

Germany had no interest in fighting the U.S., but British ships fraudulently flew U.S. flags. Nor could Germany let the U.S. feed and arm England while its people were starving. In addition, some of the ships sunk, which produced loss of American lives and opprobrium in the U.S. were British-flagged ships. Nevertheless, Germany tried to prevent the U.S. from entering the war. The German government stated on May 9, 1916, that it was "prepared to do its utmost to confine the operations of war for the rest of its duration to the fighting forces of the belligerents".

In the presidential election of 1916, women had been given the vote in 11 states. Woodrow Wilson carried 10 of them, and overwhelming support from women made Wilson the first Democratic president to win re-election since Andrew Jackson. Despite Wilson's narrow electoral victory over Republican Charles Hughes being due to female voters' support for his pledge to keep us out of war, 3 months after his inauguration Wilson declared war on Germany. Congressman C.A. Lindbergh opposed entering the war and claimed the war was for financial gain. His radical stance turned off his Congressional allies and his constituents. In 1916, C.A. resigned his seat and ran for Senate. He lost badly, finishing fourth.

During his run for Senate, C.A., who had never driven a car, took 14-year-old Charles out of school to drive him around Minnesota campaigning. Charles had learned to drive when he was 11 and did the family driving. In an era when road signs were paint marks on trees and roads were made of clay and sometimes took a week to dry after it rained, Charles drove 3,000 miles on punishing rural Minnesota roads so his father could campaign.

When his father returned to Washington, DC to finish his term, Charles drove his mother from Minnesota to San Diego to visit his dying half-sister and attended no school during the 40 days it took to make the drive there and the 40 days to drive back. In an era before driver's licenses, weather reports, maps, signage, or mechanics, Charles demonstrated an innate ability to navigate as well as fix the car, as the roads and weather took their toll. He was pulled over in California when his headlights failed, and the officer realized he was too young to drive. He and his mother appeared in court, paid a fine, and then he drove his mother back to Minnesota.

Back at the Capitol, C.A. refused to leave without a fight. He made a speech from the floor of Congress accusing an obscure politician from Ohio named Warren Harding of corruption. Harding would be our next president and is often considered the most corrupt president in our history. C.A. was one of only 14 congressmen who voted against arming U.S. merchant ships, the identical fight that his son would fight in 1940-41. C.A.'s next campaign would be for governor, railing against the "money trust", in 1918.

Events would change quickly while C.A. was out of office. On April 2, 1917, President Wilson declared war on Germany. In 1917 Congress passed the Espionage Act, and in 1918 it passed the Sedition Act which made it a crime to oppose U.S. involvement in World War I. Gubernatorial candidate C.A. Lindbergh was arrested in Madison, Minnesota in 1918 for expressing his opinion that our involvement in a war was immoral and motivated by financial corruption.

When not being arrested, his unsuccessful campaign was marked by harassment and vilification. His son would be treated similarly, but on a national scale, for expressing the same opinion: U.S. involvement in a European war was wrong, and it was a violation of presidential power to arm merchant ships. In 1941, Charles' wife Anne would write, "how strange it is to see Charles fight the same fight as his father."

The allegation the U.S. entered World War I because of a financial conspiracy was common. In the 1981 movie *Reds*, about the Russian Revolution of 1917, Warren Beatty, portraying the American Communist John Reed, promotes this theory. But the evidence is overwhelming President Wilson entered the war for two reasons. First, the German sinking of allied shipping and second the Zimmerman telegram. In February 1917, the Germans abandoned their policy trying to avoid sinking neutral shipping. Expecting the U.S. would enter the war, German Foreign Minister Arthur Zimmerman sent an encrypted message to Mexico, saying if Germany and the U.S. fought a war and Mexico allied herself with Germany, Germany would return to Mexico the territory lost in the Mexican War of 1848. British intelligence intercepted and decoded the message. Four days after the telegram was published in U.S. newspapers, Wilson declared war on Germany. (Andrews, n.d.)

Despite the lack of basis for his conspiratorial accusations, C.A. had been right — it was a mistake for the U.S. to enter World War I. World War I was a disaster for the U.S. and the future of Europe. Approximately 116,000 American men were killed with twice that many wounded. Many Americans saw the legacy of World War I as a war that had been a stalemate and would have, presumably, ended with a truce based on exhaustion. Instead, because of our intervention, it became a "victory" for our "allies" England and France, but not for the U.S., without whom no one would have won the war. As a result of "their" victory, England and France imposed brutal peace terms on Germany that impoverished Germany to the point of starvation and political instability, and resulted in the rise of the Nazis to power. Despite President Wilson's promises, World War I did not make the world safe for democracy, nor end all wars.

U.S. debt from World War I was $10.4 billion in 1918, in today's dollars this exceeds $200 billion. (Phillips, 2012) In the run-up to World War II, Charles Lindbergh would charge that England and France, were as responsible for the conditions that led to World War II as Germany, because they deceived us into entering the war and we won the war for them. As a result, they received reparations (we did not because the U.S. Senate didn't ratify the Versailles Treaty), and rather than addressing the imperialism which had been the cause of the war; we sacrificed lives to expand their empires.

Lindbergh believed World War I expanded others' immoral and corrupt colonial empires which oppressed indigenous people at the cost of 116,000 American lives and a huge debt which was not paid back. Lindbergh argued colonialism was not only immoral and cruel to the occupied, but corrupted the occupier as well. He contended France and England's economic decline and political instability between 1935-1941 was due to maintenance of immoral empires. He continued this argument even after Hitler had violated the Munich Agreement in March 1939. (Lindbergh, 1970, p.173) This, not anti-Semitism, was the foundation of Lindbergh's opposition to the U.S. entering World War II.

Sixteen-year-old Charles spent World War I operating his father's farm in Little Falls. Due to the need for food with most men overseas, boys who worked on farms were given school credit. Charles never attended his senior year of high school, but he was awarded a high school diploma. Charles was preparing to join the war when on November 11, 1918, Germany surrendered.

After the war Lindbergh floundered. He briefly attended the University of Wisconsin, but with little formal education and a lack of interest he failed and was dismissed by the university. He attended a flight school in Nebraska, but after paying the tuition he arrived to find no other students. He learned to repair airplanes (in the 1920s pilots had to repair their own planes) and was a barnstorming prop. He walked wings and did other stunts while a pilot flew the plane. He had less than a dozen hours of flying time and was never allowed to fly alone because he couldn't post a bond to insure the value of the plane.

In May 1923, C.A. bought Charles a World War I surplus airplane, a Curtiss JN4-D better known as a "Jenny". Charles traveled to Americus, Georgia to pick it up. In his memoirs, he would recall that there were no pilot licenses then, the men just let him take the plane. He wasn't able to get it off the ground. With instructions and weeks of practice, Charles took his plane to Minnesota to help C.A. run for Senate again. He slept on the ground under the wing of his plane. C.A. would lose again.

Charles began a career as a barnstorming pilot. On one flight, he gave a flight to a man named Marvin Northrop, who would start the aerospace conglomerate, Northrop Corporation. In October 1923, Charles enrolled in Army flight school. For the first time, he would take classes for something he wanted to do. He would finish at the top of his class.

While Charles was in flight school, C.A. was diagnosed with brain cancer by Dr. Charles Mayo who, along with his brother, Dr. William

Mayo, started the Mayo Clinic. Charles briefly left flight school to say goodbye to his father who died on May 24, 1924. Charles graduated second in his class but did not take an active-duty commission with the Army for two reasons. First, he failed the oral exam. Second, pilots were not needed in the post-World War I army and the pay was low. Charles became a mail pilot.

Being a mail pilot in the 1920s was hazardous. The country lacked airports, navigation signals, airplane maintenance infrastructure, or any means of knowing the weather in advance. Pilots frequently landed in fields when they saw bad weather ahead. Lindbergh had three crashes. These crashes demonstrated one of the remarkable aspects of his personality, one which would lead him to fame and glory. He was able to think clearly when confronted with danger. Whether he was sleep deprived, deprived of oxygen, in combat, or faced airplane mechanical failure, throughout his life Lindbergh remained focused and made the right decision. In 3 crashes neither Lindbergh nor any one on the ground was hurt. All 3 planes were wrecked beyond repair.

In 1919, an immigrant named Raymond Orteig, who owned two of Manhattan's finest hotels, offered $25,000 to the first aviator "of any allied country crossing the Atlantic in one flight, from Paris to New York or New York to Paris." In June 1919, two English pilots, John Alcock and Arthur Brown, took off from Newfoundland and crashed into a bog in Ireland. Using this flight as a model, all efforts afterwards comprised at least two pilots. As the Orteig Prize became the talk of aviation, including in the cafeteria where Lindbergh ate lunch in St. Louis, famous aviators tried more elaborate planes with more engines and more personnel unsuccessfully to make the flight. Quite a few perished in the effort.

Flying mail across the country gave Lindbergh time to think. He was south of Peoria, Illinois in 1926 when he devised his strategy, "I'll fly alone. That will cut out the need for any selection of crew or quarreling.

If there's upholstery in the cabin, I'll tear it out for the flight. I'll take only the food I need to eat, and a few concentrated rations. I'll carry a rubber boat for emergency, and a little extra water." Notice no mention of a parachute. Although it would be dangerous, it would be less dangerous than "flying mail for a single winter." In six words, Lindbergh's strategy was, "one engine, one wing, one pilot". More engines meant a greater chance of engine failure and another man meant more weight and as he explained to the engineer who would design *The Spirit of St. Louis*, "I'd rather have the fuel."

So, this unknown 24-year-old mail pilot decided to speak to potential backers in St. Louis to finance the construction of an airplane with which to compete for a prize that had only been contested by the most famous aviators in the world. This would not only result in history but would result in what was likely Lindbergh's first significant exposure to Jews.

Works Cited

Andrews, E. (n.d.). *What Was the Zimmerman Telegram.* Retrieved from History.com: https://www.history.com/news/what-was-the-zimmermann-telegram

Berg, A. S. (2013). *Wilson.* New York: Berkley.

Cole, W. S. (1974). *Charles Lindbergh and the Battle Against American Intervention in World War II.* New York: Jovanovich.

Lind, M. (2014). Germany's Superpower Quest Caused World War I. *The National Interest*.

Lindbergh, C. A. (1970). *The Wartime Journals of Charles Lindbergh.* New York: Jovanovich.

Phillips, M, *The Long History of U.S. Debt*, Atlantic Magazine, November 2012.

Schaepjdriver, S. (2014). *The Long Shadow of German Atrocities in World War I.* Retrieved from The British Library: https://www.bl.uk/world-war-one/articles/historiography-atrocities-the-long-shadow#

4: Hour of Gold, Hour of Lead

1927-1935

The title of this chapter is taken from the title of Anne Morrow Lindbergh's published diary of this era. "Hour of lead" is her description of having your child kidnapped and murdered. In April 1972, upon re-reading her diary, she wrote, "I still go blind with tears." (Berg, 1998)

This chapter describes two of the most remarkable events in human history: the solo flight across the Atlantic Ocean by Charles Lindbergh between May 20-21, 1927, and the kidnap and murder of Charles A. Lindbergh, Jr. followed by the trial, and execution of Bruno Richard Hauptmann. Entire libraries have been written about these two events, and the purpose of this chapter is not to rewrite them. This chapter focuses on several aspects of the events: first interactions with Jews, second a window into the personalities of Charles and Anne Morrow Lindbergh, and finally the wonder of the accomplishment and the horror of the murder and how the press put its mark on both overwhelmingly for the worse.

In addition, the author wants to emphasize the evidence Hauptmann committed the murder is overwhelming and discuss the legacy of the Jewish lawyer who convicted Hauptmann.

If asked, "who were the first men to fly over the Pacific Ocean?" few could answer the question. Everyone knows about Charles Lindbergh's flight, but only aviation buffs know that Clyde Pangborn and Hugh Herndon, Jr. made the first non-stop Pacific flight from Japan to Washington State in 1931.

Why this is, is a subjective question, but several reasons are apparent. First, the Orteig Prize generated much enthusiasm before Lindbergh's flight, millions of people all over the world were following the competition. Second, 1927 was a great year—Babe Ruth hit 60 home runs and boxing's 'long count' in the match between Gene Tunney and Jack Dempsey enthralled the nation, but 1931 was the worst year of the Depression.

There were also several technologic reasons for Lindbergh's sudden rise to sensation. First, the technology to transmit motion pictures over telegraph had been accomplished. Audiences in movie theaters saw motion pictures of Lindbergh's flight within days of the accomplishment, and these movies for the first time had sound. The first Movietone News reel containing sound was of Lindbergh's take-off from New York on May 20, 1927. (Foxmovie Tone)

Also important was Lindbergh's prior obscurity, solo flight, self-effacing personality, and movie star good looks. Winston Churchill said, "...he represents all that a man should say, all that man should do, and all that a man should be." Will Rogers said, he was "a prince. We only get one in our lifetime." *The New Republic* wrote he is "...ours...He is the U.S. personified." (Groom, 2013)

But in 1926 Lindbergh was not a prince. He was unknown, had saved $2,000 from a life-threatening career of delivering mail, and needed to raise roughly $15,000 to purchase an airplane and supplies to attempt to cross the Atlantic. In his meager financial position, he traveled to New York and likely had his first significant adult encounter with a Jewish American.

In November 1926, he met with the Board Chairman of Columbia Aircraft, Charles Levine. Mr. Levine offered to sell a suitable airplane, a Wright-Bellanca, for $15,000. Charles returned to St. Louis and raised the money, but when he returned to NY with a cashier's check, Mr. Levine insisted Columbia Aircraft would choose the crew. Lindbergh refused. Two wasted trips to New York weren't enough for Mr. Levine. Levine asked him to stay so he could investigate selling the plane outright. After a wasted day and night spent in New York City, which

Lindbergh could not afford, Levine asked Lindbergh if he'd changed his mind. Lindbergh refused and left.

If the "Lone Eagle" had a partner it would have been Donald Hall, the engineer for the Ryan Aeronautical Company in San Diego. The Ryan Aeronautical Company built *The Spirit of St. Louis* for $10,580, while the famous explorer Richard Byrd attempted the same flight in a $100,000 airplane. Hall appreciated Lindbergh's very precise and determined personality. He built the plane the way Lindbergh wanted it and Lindbergh approved the design and function of every component. Not a single ounce was wasted. To calculate fuel needs, they used a globe from the public library and a piece of string. The plane was designed to carry 400 gallons of gasoline with a minimum cruising radius of 3,550 miles at 1,550 rpm, an oil gauge, a temperature gauge, and an altimeter. *The Spirit of St. Louis* had 5 gas tanks, one of which sat directly in front of the pilot blocking vision in front of the airplane. Lindbergh used a periscope to see and alternated from the gas tank supply every 15 minutes throughout the flight to keep the airplane balanced. (Berg, 1998)

In April 1927 alone, there were three horrendous crashes of airplanes competing for the Orteig Prize, killing two pilots and injuring others. That month, Lindbergh took his first test flight in *The Spirit of St. Louis,* flying for 21 minutes above San Diego. He then took 23 more test flights, each time making adjustments and observations to share with Hall. (Berg, 1998) On May 8, 1927, two French pilots, Charles Nungesser and Francois Coli left Paris for New York. They were never seen again. (History.com, n.d.)

On May 10, 1927, Lindbergh took *The Spirit of St. Louis* from San Diego to New York to be in position to depart, should the primitive weather reports of the era allow it. He landed in St. Louis 14 hours after taking off from San Diego, which was a record for time. After a brief stop, he flew to Mineola, NY in 7 hours, which was also record time. While waiting for suitable weather over the North Atlantic he flew test flights, went over his supply list, and had the plane checked. His mother came from Detroit to see him. She feared it would be the last time she would see her only child.

At 4 AM on May 20, 1927, it stopped raining after a sleepless night of "businessmen" banging on his door with deals. He received weather reports the North Atlantic was clear. The airplane was filled with fuel and at 7:54 AM the plane left the ground. He navigated with a compass rather than landmarks as he had never flown over open water. He was over Nova Scotia at noon. Using a road map as a reference he concluded he was 6 miles off course. He flew over St. John's, Newfoundland at 7:15 PM. He had no contact with a human, and no one knew where he was until he reached Europe. (Berg, 1998)

After a night of fighting sleep, hallucinations, and storm clouds, the sun rose over the featureless Atlantic Ocean and at 9:52 AM he saw fishing boats. He flew low enough to ask "which way to Ireland" but no fishermen appear on deck. An hour later he saw Dingle Bay, Ireland. The town rushed out to wave to him. Once he confirmed his location, he calculated he was three miles off course and two and a half hours ahead of schedule. He had become the first man to cross the Atlantic by air and should there be engine trouble or bad weather he knew he could land.

While flying over England he was fighting sleep deprivation and other problems. The engine sputtered over the English Channel because he had forgotten to rotate fuel tanks and over France he couldn't find the airport. He was ahead of schedule because he had increased his speed to 110 mph to maximize daylight and arrived over continental Europe while the sun was setting. In the 1920s, pilots found landing strips at night by following beacons to a black patch of land, but because thousands of cars were converging on Le Bourget airfield, all he could see was a miasma of lights. He circled the airport three times at less than 1000 feet unable to land. He landed at 10:24 PM local time. He flew for 33.5 hours and went 55 hours without sleep. He had water but had nearly no food. (CharlesLindbergh.com, n.d.)

Two French pilots rescued him from the mob and took him to a hangar. They asked if he needed medical care. They drove him to the *Arc de Triomphe* (Lindbergh had no idea what it was) and to the U.S. Ambassador's residence where he was fed. The Ambassador returned home to find a stranger wearing his pajamas, as Lindbergh had no clothes. He told Lindbergh he would send a telegram to his mother and arrange for a tailor. Then Lindbergh went to sleep for the first time in nearly three days. 42 years later in a letter to Neil Armstrong, Lindbergh wrote, "I wonder if you felt on the moon's surface as I did after landing in Paris in 1927 — I would have liked to have had more chance to look around." (Berg, 1998)

The outpouring of joy on behalf of the accomplishment of another human, and the mind-boggling sensationalism which accompanied Lindbergh's landing in Paris, is a truly remarkable chapter in human history. To describe it in a book dedicated to a different subject would be a disservice. Only a few historical footnotes will be described here to provide insight into Lindbergh's personality.

Lindbergh was not unique because he was a sensation, other sensations have died penniless and forgotten. Lindbergh died a wealthy man and remained in the spotlight when few people had a memory of his flight and millions of people despised him — many still do. He did not accomplish this by shilling for toothpaste or dating Hollywood stars although he had every opportunity to do so. He endorsed no products and proposed to a painfully shy 21-year-old college student on the third date of his life. He became an authority on multiple subjects of his choosing, he received uncountable honors, and until he died, received more requests to provide his opinion than he possibly could have. He was an authority on subjects of his choosing solely because he chose to provide his opinion. No longer needing to make a living, he dedicated his life to the advancement of humanity.

The people he met included the King of England, his infant granddaughter Elizabeth, and President Coolidge. Through it all, Lindbergh's selfless and modest personality persisted. The first question he asked when rescued from the mob at Le Bourget airfield was whether there was news of the missing French pilots. After spending the night in the home of the U.S. ambassador, the first person he asked to visit was the mother of missing French pilot Charles Nungesser. Given 150,000 Francs by the Aero-Club of Paris he donated it to families of aviators killed in exploration. Coolidge sent the U.S. warship *The Memphis* to bring Lindbergh and *The Spirit of St. Louis* home. His first words upon seeing a Naval escort were, "It is a great and wonderful sight and I wonder if I deserve all this". (Berg, 1998)

In his first month in the U.S., Lindbergh was offered 5 million dollars in endorsements, from Lindy shoes to Lucky Lindy Bread, and a movie studio offered him a million dollars to appear in a movie in which he'd get married. Lindbergh turned down every offer, saying he had no interest in appearing in motion pictures or promoting commercial products. He said his sole interest was the expansion of commercial aviation. But his motivation was more complicated.

While still in Paris he had his first exposure to the corruption and sensationalism of the media. Prior to his departure he'd given a brief interview to a *NY Times* reporter. While in Paris he was surprised the reporter had written Lindbergh's "first-hand account" of the flight. From then on, he would give the press nearly no access and this trepidation extended to Hollywood. In response, the press would stalk him and regularly lie about him. On his first date with his future wife, he told her, "I read I was engaged twice last week and never met either of the ladies." (Berg, 1998)

At the age of 25, Lindbergh turned down newspaper mogul William Randolph Hearst's $500,000 offer for the rights to his life story. Lindbergh turned him down saying he had no interest, but later revealed how much he despised Hearst's newspaper empire for its values:

> "They seemed overly sensational, inexcusably inaccurate, and excessively occupied with the troubles and vices of mankind. I disliked most of the men I had met who represented him, and I did not want to be associated with the organization he had built." (Berg, 1998)

Perhaps the only undeserved honor Lindbergh accepted was the appointment as a Colonel in the U.S. Army Reserves. Undeserved at this point, because he had not earned a promotion by being on active duty. In 1954, he would accept an honorary promotion to Brigadier General. During the controversial period prior to World War II, he was dubiously introduced at public events as "Colonel" Charles Lindbergh. (Cole, 1974)

Initially Lindbergh chose to promote aeronautics. He established a network of wealthy and powerful associates, several of whom were notable. The first was his best friend and also Jewish: Harry Guggenheim. Harry was an accomplished aviator and the grandson of Meyer Guggenheim, a Jewish peddler who came to the U.S. penniless and acquired an enormous fortune. His father Daniel Guggenheim, established the Guggenheim Foundation for the Promotion of Aerospace. Upon Lindbergh's return to the U.S., Daniel arranged a 48-state tour that visited 82 cities and provided the shy Lindbergh with a platform to give 147 speeches and participate in countless parades. (LWTICOA, 1927) Daniel Guggenheim died in 1930 and left Harry as the benefactor.

Second, was the U.S. Ambassador to Mexico, Dwight Morrow. Morrow was a backer of *The Spirit of St. Louis.* He invited Lindbergh and his mother to Mexico City for Christmas in 1927. There Charles met his wife, Morrow's daughter Anne. On their first date, Lindbergh took Anne to the home of his Jewish friend Harry Guggenheim. Harry and his wife entertained Anne, while Lindbergh got his plane ready to take her for a ride.

The other members of Lindbergh's business circle included the most important men in aviation. For example, the president of the Curtis Airplane Company, Clement Keys, also owned a company called Transcontinental Airplane Company (TAT), which later became Transworld Airlines or TWA. TAT gave Lindbergh a bonus of $250,000 in stock plus $10,000 a year in salary. Juan Trippe, the President of Pan American Airlines, put him on its board. Together these men, built airports, new airplanes, and the infrastructure to support them. These men, including Lindbergh, built the foundation of a domestic commercial air network that would forever change this country. (Lankiewicz, 2007)

Due to the intense media pressure, Charles and Anne kept their relationship secret. Anne's mother wrote "I believe a beautiful thrilling life is ahead of them if only the papers would let them alone." They were married in secret in the Morrow's home in New Jersey on May 27, 1929, and secretly slipped away to a boat moored on Long Island Sound. The press found out and searched the waters north of Long Island looking for them. They found them off the coast of Maine and harassed the couple for 6 hours to get them to come on deck for a picture. (Cole, 1974)

In February 1934, Lindbergh had his first conflict with the new President Roosevelt over airmail contracts. The depression had badly affected the revenue of the airlines and transporting mail was an essential and reliable source of revenue. Based on an accusation by a Senator from Alabama, who would become one of this country's most remarkable Supreme Court justices, Hugo Black, that the process of awarding air mail contracts was corrupt, Roosevelt canceled the contracts and handed them to the army. According to the curator of the Smithsonian, Robert van der Linden, the charges were unsupported; the contracts had gone through a legitimate bidding process and the Democrat Black's only motivation was an attempt to smear the previous Republican Hoover administration. (Duffy, 2010)

Lindbergh's personality consisted of stubbornness, confidence, and an abject refusal to compromise. Lindbergh had flown both the mail and airplanes for the Army. He knew Army airplanes lacked the equipment necessary to fly in bad weather and Army pilots were not trained to fly mail routes. (Olson, 2013) He sent a telegram to the White House and released it to the press saying the army was unprepared to deliver the mail and the President was destroying the commercial air industry.

The White House's response was to accuse Lindbergh of being a publicity seeker. A few weeks after Roosevelt transferred mail delivery to the army, 12 army pilots had died in crashes and others were seriously injured. Roosevelt wanted to return air mail service to the private sector, but in Congressional hearings Lindbergh wouldn't cooperate in a face-saving exit for the President. (Berg, 1998)

When Roosevelt finally returned mail delivery to the private sector, there had been 66 crashes, killing those 12 pilots, dozens of injuries, and significant delays in delivering the mail. Furthermore, the Hoover-era contracts did not demonstrate corruption. Because he was right, Lindbergh refused to acknowledge that either he or the commercial air industry had been at fault. Lindbergh's performance in hostile Congressional hearings would foreshadow the conflict between him and Roosevelt. (Duffy, 2010) Lindbergh's defiance, refusal to compromise, and complete refusal to be intimidated by any adversary, would define his life's struggles. It would lead to him being despised by millions, but he would remain unapologetic for the rest of his life.

The solution was mail delivery was returned to the private sector but not to the previous companies. (Duffy, 2010) Those companies simply changed their names; for example, American Airways became American Airlines, and Eastern Air Transport became Eastern Airlines. So clearly Lindbergh won this fight. (Berg, 1998) For the first time Roosevelt had a political opponent who could defeat him. Roosevelt did not like to lose, and he did not forgive. Politically, he was no longer invincible, and Lindbergh was as popular as he. Roosevelt saw Lindbergh was not only a political adversary but a figure who might very well be his political opponent in the future. The feud between Lindbergh and Roosevelt would resume 6 years later and Lindbergh would lose the next fight. (Olson, 2013)

Constant press harassment led Lindbergh to buy a home in secluded Hopewell, New Jersey. Despite its seclusion and fencing, Lindbergh hired guards to keep gawkers away. It was not sufficient. In 1930, Anne gave birth to their first child, Charles Jr.. On March 1, 1932, Junior was kidnapped from his bedroom, using a homemade ladder, and despite paying $50,000 in ransom money, on May 12, 1932, his decomposed body was found a few miles away. Independently both Charles and Anne blamed the press for Charles Jr.'s loss. Anne wrote in her diary, "If it were not for the publicity that surrounds us, we might still have him." and Charles described the press as the "…personification of malice, which deliberately urged on the crazy mob." (Olson, 2013)

In September 1934, a gas station manager in Manhattan named Walter Lyle received a $10 bill in payment for 98 cents in gasoline. The bill was a "gold note" and it was supposed to have already been exchanged for a conventional bill. When Lyle balked at taking the unusual bill, the motorist bragged in a thick German accent that he had more at home. Suspicious, Lyle wrote down the license plate number on the bill. The bill's serial number marked it as ransom payment. The car belonged to an unemployed carpenter named Bruno Richard Hauptmann, who was soon arrested. He was interrogated for 24 hours without a lawyer and without a break (criminal defendants weren't entitled to a lawyer in 1934). The investigation was led by a police officer named Herbert Schwarzkopf. His son Norman would lead the U.S. military to victory in the First Gulf War. The Assistant Attorney General who prosecuted the case, David Wilentz, was Jewish. (Berg, 1998)

Wilentz was born in Latvia, he immigrated to the U.S. as a child, fought in World War I, and graduated from New York University Law School in 1919. After the Lindbergh case he became the Attorney General of

New Jersey and an important figure in New Jersey politics. In the 1980s, Hauptmann's widow sued New Jersey three times for her husband's "wrongful death". Wilentz spent the last years of his life defending the veracity of the verdict in the Lindbergh kidnapping conviction, and Anna Hauptmann lost her lawsuits. Wilentz' son became Chief Justice of the New Jersey Supreme Court, and his granddaughter is a columnist for the *New York Times*. He died in 1988. (DW, nd)

Hauptmann's trial was called the trial of the century and the "biggest story since the resurrection." It pushed FDR's State of the Union address off the front page of the *NY Times*. It was marked by media sensationalism and violations of standards regarding the conduct of a trial and the rights of a defendant, even in an era with fewer regulations. The press regularly released inaccurate or secret information to the public and respected no norms in prejudicing the outcome of the trial.

Hauptmann had a qualified defense attorney, Edward Reilly. Reilly wisely declined to cross-examine Anne, knowing challenging her grief would be damaging, but he too was compromised by the media. He was being paid by the *NY Journal* in exchange for the exclusive rights to Hauptmann's wife's story. And while books extolling the innocence of Hauptmann have been published, it appears certain he was guilty. He may have had an accomplice, but none has ever been produced, nor has a credible one been suggested. The man Hauptmann fingered, Isidor Fisch, had passed away. However, he had been an old sick pauper, who had neither the physical, technical, nor financial qualifications for the police to take the accusation seriously. (Berg, 1998)

There were no fingerprints nor eyewitnesses, but the circumstantial evidence led to a conviction. Hauptmann had $14,000 of ransom money in his possession ($300,000 today), and as a carpenter he had a standard tool set that was missing one tool; it was found outside the Lindberghs' window. The wood used to make the ladder matched wood taken from Hauptmann's attic floor down to the location of the nail holes. Every important date which would have required Hauptmann's personal presence, for example the day he received the ransom money, he missed work. He quit his job the day the ransom money was paid and began spending large amounts of money without a source of income.

Hauptmann entered the U.S. illegally from Germany where he was convicted of robbery using a homemade ladder. The contact information for the go-between was found in his house in his handwriting. Five handwriting experts testified he wrote the ransom note. Under oath the go-between and Lindbergh identified his voice as the one that accepted the money. The ransom note contained mistakes specific to a native German speaker; such as "haus" instead of "house". The cab driver who had driven the man to the ransom money drop-off identified Hauptmann. The last surviving juror, Ethel Stockton, said 50 years later, "the evidence was overwhelming." (Berg, 1998)

The half-baked alternative explanations for the kidnapping and murder of Charles, Jr. invariably ignore Hauptmann hanged himself by taking the stand in his own defense. Wilentz' withering cross-examination hurt his case, but the most damaging testimony was during his own lawyer's questioning. Hauptmann contradicted himself multiple times, for example, saying he'd given a handwriting sample voluntarily and then under duress. His handwriting sample in court misspelled "signature" exactly as it was misspelled in the kidnapper notes. Most appalling was he spelled "boat" as "boad". Everyone knew the post-ransom note gave the fake location of the "alive" Charles, Jr. as the "Nelly Boad". (Berg, 1998, p.324)

For the Lindberghs the trauma was compounded by violations of their privacy and a press that would divulge wrong and dangerous information. Anne and Charles each had no doubt it was Charles Jr.'s remains. For example, he was wearing the clothes they had put him to sleep in and his first and second toes overlapped. Yet newspapers kept "finding" the Lindbergh baby alive and well in different places. Movie companies rigged clandestine microphones and cameras to illegally record the proceedings.

Charles refused to show emotion. Anne tried to do the same, although clearly this made her trauma worse. In her diary, Anne wrote in January 1935, "I must not talk, I must not cry, I must not dream." (Berg, 1998) To add to their grief, Anne's older sister, Elisabeth Morrow, died on December 3, 1934, at the age of 30. Charles considered showing emotion to be weakness. He refused to speak about what happened to his oldest son and namesake for the rest of his life. (Olson, 2013)

On February 13, 1935, the verdict of "murder in the first degree" was delivered. Hauptmann was sentenced to death on March 18, 1935, all his appeals were exhausted by December 1935, and he was put to death on April 3, 1936. The hysteria and sensationalism only got worse as the execution date drew closer and the Lindberghs moved to Europe to avoid the unending press harassment and threats to their lives. Hauptmann proclaimed his innocence until the end; he turned down offers of life imprisonment and $100,000 to be given to his wife if he would admit his guilt. (Berg, 1998)

Before they left Lindbergh made a major advancement to the field of science.

Works Cited

(n.d.). Retrieved from CharlesLindbergh.com: http://charleslindbergh.com/history/timeline.asp

Berg, A. S. (1998). *Lindbergh.* New York: Berkley Biography.

Cole, W. (1974). *Charles A. Lindbergh.* New York: Jovanovich.

Duffy, J. (2010). *Lindbergh v. Roosevelt.* New York.

DW, nd, en....org/wiki/David T. Wilentz

Foxmovie Tone. (n.d.). Retrieved from Foxmovie Tone Newsreel Collection: https://www.foxmovietonenews.com/#:~:text=The%20Introduction%20of%20Sound&text=That%20all%20changed%20on%20the,piloting%20the%20'Spirit%20of%20St.

Groom, W. (2013). *The Aviators.* New York: National Geographic.

Lankiewicz, D. (2007, July). The Lindbergh Line. *Aviation History.* Retrieved from History.com.

LWTICOA, Lindbergh Will Tour in Cause of Aviation. (1927, June 29). *NY Times,* p. A1.

Olson, L. (2013). *Those Angry Days.* New York: Random House.

5: The Pump

A remarkable achievement, either forgotten or dismissed

In the 1930s, Lindbergh and his partner, Dr. Alexis Carrel of the Rockefeller Institute, invented the first working cardiac perfusion pump. (see diagram/photo 3) As remarkable as this achievement was, it has been forgotten as its design and function were eclipsed by better technology. Critics of both Lindbergh and Carrel tried to diminish the accomplishment because of the controversies that would later engulf both of their lives.

Later chapters that deal with technical aspects of Lindbergh's developments contain a paragraph in which the author says that if you have no interest in engineering or medicine, just absorb a couple of points and then feel free to skip the rest of the chapter. This chapter is different. The technical components of the pump are not discussed in detail because this particular pump design is not used in modern medicine. Its design and function are important only to those who are interested. Such readers are referred to Dr. Robert Sade's excellent review in the *Annals of Thoracic Surgery* in 2017.

A remarkable achievement needs to be understood in the context of its era. It demonstrates the personality, talent, and persistence of Lindbergh. But as important, understanding how the accomplishment has been diminished by Lindbergh's critics demonstrates how Lindbergh's legacy has been distorted. Lindbergh's critics could grudgingly acknowledge that Lindbergh, for all his faults, accomplished a great thing for the benefit of mankind. However, his critics (with questionable knowledge of medicine and engineering) have sought to invalidate a remarkable event because acknowledging Lindbergh's altruism would somehow invalidate unrelated charges against him.

This strategy is not unique to this achievement. Lindbergh's accomplishments have been distorted or diminished by people who lack the technical capacity to understand, let alone judge, his achievements and actions. It is important to read the chapter even if you have no interest in medicine.

First some background:

1. Dr. Alexis Carrel was the first surgeon to win the Nobel Prize in Medicine (1912). At 39 years old he was the youngest recipient to ever win the award and the first physician practicing in America to win the award.
2. Dr. Carrel met Lindbergh in 1930 when he was faculty at the prestigious Rockefeller Institute in New York City. He had pioneered surgical advancements mostly in the field of vascular surgery but also in wound care, cardiac surgery, and intubation.
3. Lindbergh and Carrel did not invent a cardiac bypass pump that was used in the treatment of a patient. They invented a pump that successfully demonstrated such a device could potentially be used. For example, their most famous demonstration in Copenhagen in 1937, demonstrated a cat's thyroid could be kept "alive" outside of a cat using their pump. (Friedman, 2007)
4. Modern bypass devices include a cardiac pump and a pulmonary component. The circuit must both circulate and oxygenate blood while removing carbon dioxide. The Lindbergh-Carrel pump included only the cardiac component. It would more accurately be termed an extracorporeal cardiac circuit. While the organ was bathed in a high oxygen content fluid there was no "respiratory component", i.e. oxygen was consumed passively and carbon dioxide was not removed.

Lindbergh and Carrel were so far ahead of their time that they could never have developed a working cardiac bypass device that could have been used in a patient. Because:

1. The understanding of antibiotics was too primitive. Alexander Fleming discovered penicillin in 1928, but maintaining a human on a bypass pump requires broad spectrum antibiotics which would not exist for decades after their achievement.
2. The understanding of anti-coagulation was too primitive. The anti-coagulant heparin was discovered in 1916, but the maintenance of a human on extra-corporeal circulation requires a range of anti-coagulants, reversal agents, and laboratory tests which had not been discovered. Indeed, heparin was not even studied clinically until 1935 nor available commercially until 1936. (Mandal, 2019) As expected, many of their experiments ended with clots or infections, but even when this was overcome with sterility and heparin, there were other impediment to use in humans.
3. The ability to transfuse autologous (from a human donor) blood didn't exist in 1930. The technology to type and match donors and recipients had existed since the early 1900s, but there were no blood banks and the use of stored and preserved blood to be used for routine human transfusions wouldn't start until the 1940s. (History of Blood Transfusions, n.d.) In nearly all cases, certainly in the 20th century, cardiopulmonary bypass requires the availability of autologous blood.
4. The materials Lindbergh had to work with, mostly glass, were heavy, fragile and couldn't withstand the extreme cold temperatures needed to store blood safely. (Morris, 2019) Glass is thrombophilic (prone to blood clots) and promotes hemolysis (destruction of red blood cells). Glass doesn't let carbon dioxide escape the way certain plastics can. This prevents buffering of metabolic acids. (Blood Bag, 2021) In the 1960s, Lindbergh revisited cardiac bypass and was intrigued to discuss the newest generation of machines with the doctors. They used specially designed plastics to overcome the issues noted above. (Berg, 1998)

In 1930, Lindbergh was a big celebrity. He was wealthy, had a new son, and a wife who would set aviation records with him such as crossing

North America in 7 hours. He would travel to places no English-speaking person had been, most famously regions of Canada and Scandinavia north of the Arctic Circle. (Berg, 1998) He chose to spend much of his time in a laboratory, mostly by himself, tinkering with devices to create something for which he had no education and no training. What was his motivation?

Since spending his childhood in his grandfather's laboratory, Lindbergh had been fascinated by science. Soon after becoming famous, he bought biology textbooks and a microscope. Upon getting married in 1929, he became interested in his sister-in-law's plight. Elisabeth Morrow had rheumatic heart disease. Her mitral valve regurgitation and the subsequent congestive heart failure had been diagnosed, and Lindbergh inquired why it could not be fixed. When it was explained the heart could not be stopped for surgery to be done, Lindbergh was determined to find a solution.

On November 28, 1930, he was introduced to Dr. Alexis Carrel at the Rockefeller Institute in New York and together they set forth to find a way to operate on Elisabeth's heart. Elisabeth died in 1934 never having received an operation. (Berg, 1998) Due to the urgency of Elisabeth's condition and the hysteria that surrounded him, Lindbergh published his first prototype urgently but anonymously. (Science, 1931)

Lindbergh then devised improved devices, which Carrel tested. Dr. Carrel was an advocate of strict aseptic technique which had not yet been completely accepted. He was also an early advocate of sterilizing surgical tools using an invention, the autoclave, which he and Lindbergh adopted for their new pump prototypes. (Malinin, 1996)

Between 1931 and 1935, Lindbergh and Carrel performed 898 individual perfusion experiments using various iterations of their pump. Only a handful of the experiments had to be aborted due to the malfunctioning of the pump or the apparatus, nearly all the issues involved infections and clotting, two problems which could not be overcome in the era of the experiments. (Redman, 2015) (Malinin, 1996)

The device demonstrated in Copenhagen at the Congress on Experimental Cytology in 1937 used a perfusion fluid rich in oxygen filtered by two platinum screens, which were designed to prevent infection and all components were autoclaved attempting to achieve sterility. (Malinin, 1996) Both the blood that entered the organ and the blood removed from the organ were passed through a silica and sand filter. Cotton was used to plug holes to try to prevent infection. A glass rotating pump, powered by compressed air, pumped the blood through the organ. (Sade, 2017)

Using this design, Lindbergh and Carrel demonstrated a cat's thyroid could function for 18 days, its heart could beat for about 12 hours, a fallopian tube would continue peristalsis (rhythmic contractions to move the fertilized ovum (egg) into the uterus), and a pancreas would secrete insulin. (see diagram, (Sade, 2017)) At the end of 12 hours the cat's heart was notably edematous and although still contracting, the contractions became sluggish. Lindbergh and Carrel ended the experiment. (Malinin, 1996)

Partially due to the gap caused by World War II, the Lindbergh-Carrel design was not continued in the next generation of experimentation by others seeking to develop a cardiac perfusion pump. The design was abandoned in the 1940s after Carrel's death. Later, others had difficulty duplicating their experimental results. In the 1960s, with Lindbergh's consultation, researchers at the U.S. Naval Research Institute reproduced a replica of the pump and reproduced their experimental results. (Malinin, 1996)

The next generation of cardiac pumps used a different design, a rotating steel cylinder and a screen oxygenator. (Morris, 2019) In 1953, Dr. John Gibbon performed the first successful open-heart surgery using cardiopulmonary bypass. When Dr. Gibbon published the case report, he gave credit to Lindbergh and Carrel for their work. (Sade, 2017)

Lindbergh's scientific curiosity didn't end with this endeavor. Lindbergh would be involved in scientific experiments for the rest of his life and scientific inquisitiveness was inherited by his children. (Berg, 1998) In 1944, while visiting his mother in his grandfather's house, he found his son Jon in the basement bending glass tubes using his great-grandfather's Bunsen burner. (Lindbergh, 1970) Jon Lindbergh (1932-2021) would have an admirable career in marine biology.

Critics argue this was a publicity stunt. They contend that while Lindbergh lent his name to Carrel's endeavor, he really didn't do anything. (Wallace, 2003, pp.99-103) Records exist to document this isn't true. (Malinin, 1996) Lindbergh commuted to New York City (2 hours each way) and spent hours in the laboratory. Records exist of many of Lindbergh's drawings and the subsequent prototypes he either built or had built. The experimental logs document experiments and trials he performed as well as important meetings he attended, conversations with laboratory personnel, technicians, other key personnel, and his personal involvement in nearly every design change in the development of these devices. (Sade, 2017) (Berg, 1998) (Redman, 2015) (Malinin, 1996) He also assisted in a reproduction of the Carrel-Lindbergh pump in the 1960s, which proves he was directly involved in its development. (Malinin, 1996)

In addition, Lindbergh performed unrelated experiments with different doctors and on his own. In 1939, the *Journal of Experimental Medicine* published a description of a device Lindbergh developed by himself to separate and purify cell cultures. (Lindbergh C., 1939) His description is remarkable for his efforts to maintain sterility. Two doctors at the Rockefeller Institute, Raymond Parker and Ralph Wykoff, used this device to develop a polio vaccine. (Friedman, 2007, pp.167-8) (Lindbergh, 1970, p.229) They were unsuccessful and eventually the war ended this endeavor.

Carrel is also criticized for later charges against him. Carrel died in a French prison in 1944 accused of collaborating with the Nazis. He never received a trial, but in the aftermath of liberation, "French justice" resembled vigilante hysteria — so even had there been a trial, it would have been unlikely to have adjudicated his culpability. He continued his career under Nazi occupation which implies Nazi consent. (Friedman, 2007) (Berg, 1998, p.462) However, the accusation is inconsistent with his established political position. In 1939, he gave a national French radio address exhorting his countrymen to fight the Nazis. In 1940, he wrote, "National Socialism (Nazism)...is radically opposed to the principles of Western Civilization." (Ross, 1964, p.239)

As for Lindbergh, he accomplished all this while dealing with the kidnapping and murder of his son. Although Lindbergh did more biomedical work in support of the war effort, world events ended his career in cardiac pump development.

To Lindbergh's critics, this invention provides an opportunity to diminish his accomplishments.

Another criticism argues because the pump that Lindbergh and Carrel demonstrated was not used when the first successful cardiac bypass surgery was performed, it was a whimsical non-serious development. (Wallace, 2003, pp. 101-2) This argument is made by people who ignore the history of medicine, technology, and progress. Often research does not become the standard of care. The theory that an organ could live outside of the body had been postulated in 1812, but until Lindbergh and Carrel demonstrated it, it had never been demonstrated. (Berg, 1998) (Friedman, 2007, pp.60-61)

Lindbergh and Carrel's experiments were revolutionary and their advancements in the medical sciences are nearly unparalleled. They demonstrated not only that organs could be kept alive unattached to an organism, but would continue to function without neural input from a central nervous system. For example, they demonstrated a pancreas continues to secrete insulin without central nervous system neural input (i.e. a brain instructing the organ). The higher the blood sugar, the more insulin the pancreas needs to secrete.

Once Lindbergh and Carrel demonstrated the pancreas functions independently, the impending follow-up question could be investigated: How does the pancreas know the proper amount of insulin to secrete? If you want to transplant a pancreas you need to answer this question. Lindbergh and Carrel's proof an organ can function separated from an organism opened entire new fields of research eventually leading to the ability to transplant organs.

Furthermore, Lindbergh (mostly alone) gets credit for introducing mechanical engineering to the field of medical research — a discipline today called biomedical engineering. A modern visitor to Carrel's laboratory would be surprised to find almost no machinery. Carrel had refrigerators, microscopes, and an autoclave but none of the machinery seen in a modern lab. (Friedman, 2007) On Lindbergh's first workday in December 1930, he came to work with supplies possibly taken from his garage in Little Falls: screwdrivers, pumps, and tubes. In early 1931, his first prototype used a rotating air pump. (Friedman, 2007) This may have been the first time these disparate technologies were incorporated.

Lindbergh's critics attribute Carrel's beliefs to Lindbergh. Carrel had bizarre and distasteful beliefs, including promoting eugenics – while disavowing violence or coercion.[1] (Berg, 1998, p.349) Carrel's beliefs also included profound admiration for Jews, especially his close Jewish friends. When asked to speak at a banquet in honor of his friend, the famous Jewish cardiologist Emanuel Libman (the co-describer of Libman-Sacks Endocarditis), Carrel obliged, "(Jews) lead the human soul to the heights of mysticism,…better philosophy, (and) more justice." In 1936, in response to a sermon about Nazi persecution he wrote a supportive letter to the Rabbi, "I am a Jew. I have been a Jew for 4000 years" and "We Christians will always respect the Jews." (Friedman, 2007, p. 143)

If Lindbergh's collaboration with Carrel made him a eugenicist, then it also made him a philo-Semite. Of course, it made him neither. People are only responsible for their own beliefs and actions.

Lindbergh's critics never discuss Carrel's advances in the field of medicine. He did more for humanity than any doctor in his era and was perhaps the greatest vascular surgeon ever. Carrel pioneered the use of small needles and non-absorbable sutures soaked in Vaseline for repairing blood vessels, which greatly reduced thrombosis. (Malinin, 1996) He developed a solution to cleanse wounds still used today. This solution prevented the writer, Ernest Hemingway, from having his leg amputated in World War I.

Carrel successfully transfused a newborn dying of hemolytic anemia by anastomosing her vessels to her father's blood vessels in 1908. There was no infection. 1908 was decades before blood transfusions became available and most physicians didn't wash their hands. (Friedman, 2007)

Historians of organ transplantation consider unsuccessful attempts at skin transplants in burn victims in World War II as the first attempt to understand organ rejection. (Stolp, 2019) In 1928, Carrel was unable to transplant a kidney from one dog to another despite absence of infection or clots. He described organ rejection decades before the principles of immunology were understood. (Friedman, 2007)

Smearing Lindbergh by condemning his associates for their private beliefs while ignoring their accomplishments, will be seen again. Major Truman Smith, a U.S. war hero in World War I, was the military attaché in Berlin from 1922-1939. He is often portrayed as a Nazi Sympathizer to minimize the value of Lindbergh's espionage between 1936-1938. As military attaché in Berlin, he fostered relations with German military personnel. Smith is accused of admiring Hitler, but this is based on his desire to meet Hitler for intelligence reasons. A Lindbergh critic, historian Leonard Mosley, disagreed with Smith's politics but admitted, "(Smith) always acted in the sincere belief he was helping…the best interests of his country." (Mosley, 1976, p.417) Also undermining the accusation is that, unlike others in the State Department, Smith recognized Hitler was a threat to democracy and did not discount his anti-Semitism in the years before he came to power. (Smith, 1936) (Hessen, 1984, p.69)

Smearing Smith requires making a hero out of his boss, William Dodd, the U.S. Ambassador to Germany from 1933 to 1937. (Mosley, 1976, pp.214-5) While Smith was also decorated for his service in World War II, Dodd's actions encouraged Nazi oppression. He told Jewish leaders when he was appointed that he would ignore the plight of Germany's Jews and refused to meet Jews to discuss their treatment. During his posting he refused to do anything about the treatment of the Jews, when asked his response was always that the situation of the Jews in Germany was "improving". (Medoff, 2019, p.21)

Lindbergh shouldn't be vilified through his associations, but reasonable people can choose to ignore the cardiac pump. It had nothing to do with the Jews or our preparation for entering World War II. Furthermore, without Lindbergh and Carrel we would still have organ transplantation and cardiopulmonary bypass today. While those arguments are probably true of every major medical advance (there would probably be penicillin regardless of Fleming's discovery), it doesn't diminish the accomplishment. It doesn't make the disingenuousness of its criticism irrelevant.

If people without any background in medicine are willing to deny Lindbergh credit for the first functioning cardiac pump, what other accomplishments in Lindbergh's life are they willing to misrepresent?

Charles Lindbergh was about to embark on one of the most controversial periods of his life. He would move his family to Europe in 1935 and make three public trips to Germany to evaluate the development of air power in Germany. He would write intelligence reports for U.S., English, and French intelligence. These reports would be presented to U.S. Congressional committees responsible for financial military allocations prior to his return. Upon his return to the U.S. he would personally discuss these reports with the President, the Chief of the U.S. Army Air Corps, the Secretary of War, nearly every manufacturer of airplanes and their components, discuss German experiments and research with NACA (the precursor to NASA), and sit on a board which would determine the future of the U.S. Air Force. (Lindbergh, 1970)

How has history judged these events? What background do Lindbergh's critics have to judge his medical advances? If they have none, then what background do they have to judge the intelligence reports regarding aviation? Why do critics feel qualified in making judgments on topics they do not understand? Do they have ulterior motives when judging these events?

Unfortunately, the nature of the criticism of the cardiac pump will be repeated when we examine the historical discussion of events about to happen. And there are few events more relevant both to the Jews and the U.S. as it prepares to enter World War II.

[1] Berg wrote that Carrel advocated voluntary eugenics to build a stronger human race, e.g. choosing whom to marry based on genetic considerations. (Berg, 1998, p.349) However, the adjective 'voluntary' does not confer absolution because it had a different meaning in the 1930s. As examples, the Supreme Court ruled that certain 'unfit' people could be sterilized (Buck v. Bell, 274 U.S. 200 (1927)), and the mentally ill were often incarcerated without obtaining their consent (e.g., Zelda Fitzgerald's death). In his book, *Man the Unknown* (1935), Carrel advocates controlling the reproduction of the 'inferior', which included humans he considered "weak minded" and mentally ill. (MTU, 1935, p. xix)

Others have accused Carrel of beliefs that bore an "uncanny resemblance to National Socialism", but these references referred to the treatment of the "criminally insane". (Mosley, 1976, pp.218-220) Advocating harsh treatment of violent criminals is hardly unique to Nazism. (See Additional Historical Notes for more discussion of Dr. Carrel's legacy.)

Works Cited

Berg, A. S. (1998). *Lindbergh.* New York: Berkley Biography.

Blood Bag. (2021). Retrieved from Science Direct: https://www.sciencedirect.com/topics/nursing-and-health-professions/blood-bag

Cole, T. (1974). *Charles Lindbergh and the fight against American Involvement in World War II.* New York: Jovanovich.

Friedman, D. (2007). *The Immortalists.* New York: Harper Collins.

Herman, A. (2000). *Joseph McCarthy.* New York: The Free Press.

Hessen, R. (1984). *Berlin Alert: The Memoirs and Papers of Truman Smith.* Stanford, CA: Hoover Press.

History of Blood Transfusions. (n.d.). Retrieved from The Red Cross: https://www.redcrossblood.org/donate-blood/blood-donation-process/what-happens-to-donated-blood/blood-transfusions/history-blood-transfusion.html

Lindbergh, C. (1939). A Culture Flask for the Circulation of a Large Quantity of Fluid Medium. *Journal of Experimental Medicine*, pp. 231-8.

Lindbergh, C. (1970). *The Wartime Journals of Charles Lindbergh.* New York: Jovanovich.

Malinin, T. (1996). Remembering Alexis Carrel and Charles A. Lindbergh. *Tex Heart Inst J*, pp. 23(1):28-35.

Mandal, A. (2019, February). *Heparin History.* Retrieved from News Medical Life Sciences: https://www.news-medical.net/health/Heparin-History.aspx.

Medoff, R. (2019). *The Jews Should Keep Quiet.* Philadelphia: Jewish Publication Society.

Morris, R. (2019). The History of Cardiopulmonary Bypass. *American College of Cardiology.*

Mosley, L, Lindbergh: *A Biography*, Doubleday, 1976.

MTU, Carrel, A, *Man the Unknown*, Harper and Brothers, NY, 1935.

Redman, E. (2015, September 9). To save his dying sister-in-law. *Smithsonian Magazine.*

Ross, W, *The Last Hero: Charles A. Lindbergh*, Harper and Row, NY, 1964.

Sade, R. (2017). A Surprising Alliance. *Annals of Thoracic Surgery*, pp. 2015-9.

Science, (1931), Apparatus to Circulate Liquid…, 1809:73, p. 566.

Smith, T. (1936). Letters from Smith to Lindbergh. *U.S. Embassy Berlin Germany.*

Stolp, J. (2019). Immune tolerance and rejection in organ transplantation. In A. Boyd, *Methods in Molecular Biology* (pp. 159-179). New York: Springer Nature.

Wallace, M. (2003). *The American Axis.* St. Martin's Press: New York.

6: Europe in the late 1930s

Lindbergh is asked to commit espionage

Charles Lindbergh took his wife and surviving son to Europe in December 1935 to escape the hysteria surrounding the impending execution of the convicted murderer of Charles Jr.. The Europe he found was in chaos. The worldview Lindbergh would bring to the debate over U.S. involvement in World War II was forged in this environment.

The original date for the execution of Bruno Richard Hauptmann for the kidnapping and murder of Charles Lindbergh, Jr. was January 17, 1936. The conviction and condemnation of Hauptmann let loose a series of threats against the Lindbergh family, but mostly against his surviving toddler son, Jon Lindbergh. In the fall of 1935, Jon was being driven home by his teacher when a truck forced the car off the road. The truck was full of "journalists" who photographed the terrified toddler and drove away. Lindbergh wrote in a letter to his mother, "Between the politicians, the tabloid press, and the criminals a condition exists which is intolerable for us." State Troopers were present but could do nothing, there were no laws to protect privacy. Charles decided to move his family to Europe. (Berg, 1998, p.339)

On December 21, 1935, the Lindberghs packed in less than 24 hours and left the U.S. at midnight on a ship to Liverpool. They arrived on New Year's Eve, 1935. They would live in Europe for roughly three and half years. Lindbergh was asked by the military attaché in Berlin, Major Truman Smith, to investigate German advances in aviation. Major Smith was a career military man who was familiar with tanks. He was concerned about the situation in Germany and major Nazi advances in aviation.

Lindbergh's legacy as a "Nazi sympathizer" is partly due to the public being unaware he was performing services for the U.S. government.

He was seen repeatedly visiting Germany and lending an aura of respect to the Nazis. Although Lindbergh's role was disclosed in several newspapers in January 1939 and in a *NY Times* article in April 1939, it was not publicized until Smith began publicly discussing it in the mid-1950s. (archives, 1984) (Berg, 1998, p.385)

Lindbergh's behavior, writings, and speeches of this era not only need to be evaluated with the understanding of his mission, but also with an understanding of Europe's governmental, economic, and societal instability.

A Distorted View of the Situation in Russia was Presented to Americans in the 1930s

Lindbergh's travels gave him a different perspective on Europe than most Americans. Lindbergh had been to the Soviet Union twice — in 1932 and 1934. He would go for the last time in 1938. He saw the deprivation and bleakness of Soviet life. He was in the Soviet Union for two of the worst genocides in history. In 1932, he was there for the murder of 7 million Ukrainians, the *Holodomor*, which was suppressed by Western press. (Library of Congress, n.d.) In 1938, he was given extensive tours of Russia while Stalin murdered 1.2 million fellow Russians for invented offenses of disloyalty in *The Great Terror.*

The press conspired to prevent Americans from knowing the truth. The *New York Times* reporter from Moscow, Walter Duranty, won a Pulitzer Prize for reporting for which he was being bribed. He filed fake news reports regarding life in Moscow and actively covered up the famine in Ukraine. (Applebaum, 2017) Gareth Jones of the *Evening Standard*, who reported honestly on the famine, was attacked by his colleagues. Indignant, Jones accused the West of being deceived by Russian censorship, "Censorship has turned them (other reporters) into masters of euphemism and understatement. Hence they give famine the polite name of 'food shortage' and 'starving to death' is softened down to 'widespread mortality from diseases related to malnutrition.'" (Applebaum, 2017)

Certain mantras became accepted and were uniformly used by the press to euphemize conditions in Russia. "Hungry but not starving" became the mantra of the western Soviet press corps to describe famine, yet 7 million people starved. (Applebaum, 2017) Slave labor was reported as "commitment to the success of the revolution", grinding poverty meant Russians were not interested in superficial affluence, and lack of dissent meant Russians had no reason to complain. The Stalin show trials of 1936-8 were reported as true jurisprudence. Uniform nationwide deprivation and penury due to mismanagement of the economy was reported as superior to the uneven distribution of wealth which defined Western economies. (Herman, 2000)

Lindbergh and much of the U.S. diplomatic corps saw Germany and Italy as a bulwark against Russia. Lindbergh's knowledge of Soviet crimes was a foundation of his isolationism. He would cite his travel experiences and personal knowledge of Russian crimes to justify opposition to an alliance with Russia. (San Francisco, July 1, 1941; Chicago, August 5, 1940)

Today these historical figures are suspected of fascist sympathies, but they were basing their diplomacy on a realistic understanding of Russia. After we allied ourselves with Russia in World War II, the American view of Russia was further distorted. Americans eventually learned the truth about Stalin's Russia, but damage had been done. Hundreds of Communist sympathizers or "fellow travelers" in our government, many Jewish, passed secrets to Russian agents. (Herman, 2000)

Lindbergh's View of England and France: Democracy, Paralysis, and Colonialism

The Lindberghs lived in England and France when their governments were paralyzed by political infighting and labor strife. They saw governments change, workers strike, national GDP shrink, and hunger. Between 1930-1940, France alone had 17 different governments due to labor disruptions. During the 1930s, French labor unions called roughly

12,000 strikes which idled 1.8 million workers. This made long-range planning impossible and left France unprepared for war. (Lyman, 2018)

Britain had some stability electing mostly Labour governments. Labour won elections through pacifism to avoid provoking Hitler. Labour ran for power with the slogan, "Armament Means War, Vote for Labour" and "Stop War. Vote Labour." (Lyman, 2018). Lindbergh was disgusted by England's lack of progress, writing that the country that started the Industrial Revolution had declined to producing mediocre goods. (Lindbergh, 1970, p.11)

Charles and Anne saw India in 1937. His plane needing repairs left them in Calcutta for two weeks. Lindbergh blamed imperialism for grinding poverty and English callousness. He already despised the empire for World War I. They also spent time flying over the ruins of ancient Greece. They concluded World War I only increased the size of empires, and all wars were wasteful. He and Anne decided because war was wasteful, they would dedicate their time to prevention of another war. (Berg, 1998, pp.363-5)

<u>Lindbergh's Exposure to Fascism:</u> The Lindberghs traveled extensively in Italy.

Both Hitler and Mussolini rose to power using the apparatus of dysfunctional weak parliamentary systems and then seized absolute power. They then used their power to murder or imprison their opposition and begin a national revival. They embarked on large infrastructure projects (as did the U.S.) and conscripted hundreds of thousands of people for their armed forces. This employed people and gave the appearance of an economic renaissance, but the money had to be borrowed, or in the case of Germany stolen from Jews. Eventually, arms production and borrowing resulted in war because assets needed to be acquired to pay back loans. Weapons are worthless if not used. (Groom, 2013)

The Lindberghs were not alone in questioning whether the economic growth and political stability of fascism was preferable to political turmoil of democracies. In Spain, democracy fell and resulted in armed conflict. Many observers were seduced by Germany's economic progress and political stability. In 1933, Anne McCormick, published the first interview with Hitler by the English-speaking press. Titled, "Hitler Seeks Jobs for all Germans" she is deceived by Hitler who she calls a "shy and simple man" and accepts his protestations that he is not anti-Semitic without question. (McCormick, 1933)

McCormick's interview, published July 10, 1933, is pro-Nazi propaganda. German laws had stripped Jews of citizenship, fired Jews from public jobs, schools had been limited to a Jewish enrollment of 1.5%, and professionals (doctors, lawyers, judges, dentists) were denied licenses. (Civil Service Law, passed April 1933) (Morse, 1968)p. 106) Yet, journalists, observers, and the Prime Minister of Canada publicly admired Hitler. (Pettinger, 2017) (WMK, 2021)

Both Hitler and Mussolini sought territorial expansion through war and in 1935, Italy attacked Abyssinia (today Ethiopia). Although England would don the mantle of victim, it was complicit in Ethiopia's victimhood and did nothing about Italian atrocities. Every Italian soldier and bullet had to pass through the Suez Canal, which Britain controlled. Like Germany, Mussolini used grievances stemming from the unfairness of the Versailles Treaty as his justification for a senseless attack on a peaceful independent country. (Archive, n.d.) Lindbergh noted England's duplicity.

A major difference between Italian and German Fascism was anti-Semitism. Mussolini's regime did not promote anti-Semitism, strip the Jews of their property, nor institute oppression against the Jews prior to Italy's first racial laws in 1938. The Italians mostly refused to deport Jews under their sovereignty or make them wear the yellow Jewish star. (History Channel, n.d.)

Lindbergh's travels in Italy made no mention of the atrocities committed by Italian soldiers in Africa nor the suppression of political opposition although he did mention the ubiquitous presence of soldiers. His writings demonstrate a man seduced by the building of edifices and pageantry, with no questioning the economics of what he's witnessing:

> "The twentieth-century dictator (Mussolini) prophesized that Italy would return for a third time to be the directing force of Western civilization. He would electrify the railways, drain the Pontine Marshes, increase the birth rate, and reclaim the Italian Empire. How imitative it was! A dictatorship, conquest, and power, armies marching off for Africa and Spain, great structures rising-one might be describing ancient Rome instead of Modern Italy." (Berg, 1998)

He may have been enchanted with the pageantry of fascism, but he didn't sympathize with anti-Semitism. Mussolini's Italy's lack of anti-Semitism led him to assume anti-Semitism was not integral to German fascism. Few contemporaries understood the difference. Lindbergh tried to explain to Germans their anti-Semitism was unnecessary and holding their country back from achieving the recognition it deserved. He writes with incredulity he was not able to find a single German who agreed with him although he said he sensed they were embarrassed by their anti-Semitism. (Lindbergh, 1970, p.129)

Lindbergh's Visits to Nazi Germany

With these influences defining his thinking — hatred of Communism, a commitment to pacifism, distaste of British imperialism, believing fascism and anti-Semitism were separable, and the stagnation and political stalemate of France and England — Lindbergh went to Germany three times to evaluate the status of German airpower. He did not hold a military rank although he had recently applied to be reinstated as a reserve officer. He had no control over his itinerary. He paid for all travel expenses himself and never requested reimbursement from the U.S..

During his visits he made a single public speech. At an Air Club Luncheon in his honor in 1936, he spoke about the future of aviation. He warned the Germans their pursuit and development of offensive air power capabilities would doom the world into a mutually destructive war. His explanation of the speech was, "I tried to issue a warning of the dangers involved in Nazi military development while keeping in mind that I was a guest of Nazi Germany on an invitation issued through the military branch of an American Embassy." He received uniformly positive feedback from the Western press regarding this speech. (Air Club Speech, 1936)

At this visit he received a telegram from Roger Straus, the co-chair of the National Council of Jews and Christians, which requested he do nothing which could be interpreted as recognizing the legitimacy of the Nazi regime. He received a note from Harry Guggenheim saying he had every confidence "you would so conduct yourself as to give no aid to anti-Semitism." (Berg, 1998, p.358) (Cole, 1974)

It is instructive his visit in 1936 garnered little press criticism and only a request about future behavior from prominent Jews, with which he complied. He never made such a statement. Later criticism was not due to a change in his behavior. He gave no speeches, and he never changed his behavior. He always presented himself as a guest of the Germans on an invitation of the American embassy. He didn't change — Germany changed. After the 1936 Olympics, German behavior towards the Jews got worse and the American public became more aware of the persecution. Americans began to demand he publicly denounce German behavior.

There are notable instances in which Lindbergh advocated for Jews prior to the winter of 1938-9. He obtained an exit visa for a Jewish physician named Richard Bing and he relayed messages of concern from Secretary of State Hull to the German government regarding the treatment of the Jews. But mostly he compartmentalized the treatment of the Jews as distinct from his mission to obtain information on German air power. (Berg, 1998)

In his private writings he described his revulsion over the mistreatment of the Jews in Germany, but at the same time felt these actions could be separated from what he describes as the "inevitable alternative to decline". (Lindbergh, 1970)

Both Lindberghs felt there was no alternative to some type of fascism to prevent what they lived through in England and France, but neither excused anti-Semitism. Initially he wrote mistreatment of the Jews "stupid", later he described it as "repulsive" and "counter-productive". (Berg, 1998)p.382) (Cole, 1974) As German behavior got worse, these journal entries increasingly seem to be rationalizations. Eventually Lindbergh stopped public visits to Germany. Whether it took Lindbergh too long is certainly a valid question.

Three Other Events Which Shaped Lindbergh's Legacy:

1) the visit to the Soviet Union in 1938
2) apartment hunting
3) the albatross

In August 1938, the U.S. government asked Lindbergh to evaluate Soviet air power. Lindbergh dutifully, at his own expense, flew to Russia and visited four Russian cities and Czechoslovakia. He saw some Russian airplanes, but the Russians did not reveal their air power and instead took him to an ice cream factory and the Moscow subway. His opinion of the Soviet Union did not get better. He found the people uninspired and frequently drunk. He suspected Soviet air power and its military were worse than U.S. intelligence indicated. His assessment would prove accurate in the Red Army's performance in the Winter War against Finland the following winter.

His visit to Czechoslovakia and his relationship with Czech president Edouard Benes was warm and welcoming, but this wouldn't change his position in a month when the Munich Conference took place. (Berg, 1998)

Some of Lindbergh's writings about the Soviet Union were made public. He was banned from the Soviet Union. (Berg, 1998, p.377) This embarrassed the U.S. government. (Wallace, 2003, p. 182)

Second, the time required for Lindbergh to make these trips to Germany were taxing on his personal and family life. Lindbergh could see war coming, he had already lost a son, and he desired to reduce his time away from his family. He and his wife considered buying property closer to Berlin to reduce the time away from their children. He wrote, continuing his naive misunderstanding of the nature of Nazi Germany, that such a domicile might reduce misunderstandings between Germans and Americans and help him learn more about Germany. (Cole, 1974) (Berg, 1998, p.379) Instead, they rented an apartment in Paris where they spent the winter of 1938 and spring of 1939. But consideration of buying property in Germany is cited to claim he was a Nazi Sympathizer. (Groom, 2013)

Third — the medal. At a banquet on October 18, 1938, the head of the *Luftwaffe,* Hermann Goering, awarded Lindbergh a civilian medal for aviation in recognition of crossing the Atlantic Ocean 11 years earlier. The American delegation was surprised by the award. Lindbergh did not speak German and did not know what was transpiring. He did what he always did, he accepted the medal and initially the press paid little attention. Anne and Major Smith's wife, however, both realized it was a public relations disaster. Anne labeled it "the albatross".

"The albatross" was a communication malfunction. The German government informed the American embassy the award would be given a few hours prior to the banquet, but the message wasn't delivered to the American delegation. (Berg, 1998, pp.377-8) Caught unaware, the American delegation didn't intervene because October 1938 was a sensitive time in American-German relations. The Munich agreement had just been signed, Hitler had not yet seized the rest of Czechoslovakia, and there was optimism war had been avoided. (Cole, 1974)

Lindbergh had another reason for not refusing the medal; he had a message to deliver from Secretary of State Hull to Goering after the banquet regarding Jewish refugees from Germany arriving penniless. (Berg, 1998) (archives, 1984) In his memoirs, Truman Smith stated the need to deliver this message was the reason Lindbergh did not refuse the medal. (Hessen, 1984, pp.127-8) One historian proposed Lindbergh's mission was to query Goering about whether his henchmen could be bribed to let more Jews out of Germany. (Ross, 1964, p.279) Coincidentally, Goering divulged critical military intelligence in the conversation that took place after the banquet. (Cole, 1974)

In 1944, the Chief of Staff of the U.S. Army, General George C. Marshall, was given a medal by the Soviet Union. Marshall was embarrassed, but he did exactly what Lindbergh did. He graciously accepted it. The alternative, offending an ally during the Normandy Invasion, would have been as foolish as offending Nazi Germany after the Munich Agreement. Despite being in the center of the conflicts with the Soviet Union, as the architect of post-war Europe and Secretary of Defense, there was no demand for him to return it. (Lelyveld, 2016, p.131)

Kristallnacht, November 9-10, 1938

Kristallnacht opened some eyes to the barbarity and ultimate intentions of Germany. Mobs of Germans destroyed Jewish businesses, beat up and murdered Jews, and hundreds were dragged away never to be seen while the police watched or participated. Lindbergh's position on Germany also changed. While his personal writings still contain an element of puzzlement as to why this would happen, he never again wrote anything positive about Germany or the German people. Instead, he wrote his faith in the German people had been "dashed against some rock" and in a letter explained that he would never do anything that would "seem to support German actions against the Jews." He had never publicly supported German actions, but now he refused to "seem to support" Germany. (Berg, 1998, p.380) (Cole, 1974) It will be noted later that Roosevelt and his administration, refused to name 'the Jews' as the victims of Nazi persecution; Lindbergh did.

A fourth visit to Germany was being planned prior to Kristallnacht, as part of a delegation including General Arnold. In the Munich negotiations, Lindbergh, Kennedy, and Smith were considering the capacity of newly built German airplane factories, and this visit was to assess it. Lindbergh wrote to General "Hap" Arnold, Chief of the U.S. Army Air Corps, on November 2, 1938 (7 days before *Kristallnacht*), proposing this trip and Arnold's return letter written 8 days after *Kristallnacht* said he was "100% in favor". But after *Kristallnacht*, Lindbergh chose not to go. In his return letter to General Arnold on November 29, 1938, he said "this is not an opportune time" because "conditions have changed rapidly" despite Lindbergh's belief "our own Air Corps would have profited greatly." (Hessen, 1984, pp.159-161).

Lindbergh's revulsion over *Kristallnacht* is not solely responsible for the visit's cancellation. General Arnold also mentioned the untenable political situation in Germany. Furthermore, Lindbergh was vague about his reasons, U.S.-German relations deteriorated in the year prior to the start of the war, and Smith mentioned the War Department discouraged interactions between German and U.S. personnel. (Hessen, 1984, pp.159-161) However, not crediting Lindbergh for a moral stand is a hard argument to make.

5. First, the break between western democracies and Germany can be relatively decisively dated to a date a few months later: March 15, 1939, the date Germany broke the Munich agreement. Second, Arnold's letter is dated 8 days after *Kristallnacht* and 4 days after Roosevelt's press conference regarding *Kristallnacht* and General Arnold is still considering this trip, albeit at a later

> date. Finally, regarding his interactions with Lindbergh in November 1938, Smith wrote, "Lindbergh distrusted the Nazi government of Germany and found its anti-Semitic policies abhorrent." (Hessen, 1984, p.163) Worth noting, General Arnold's embrace of a trip to Germany after *Kristallnacht*, demonstrates the U.S. government's policies towards Germany did not fundamentally change after *Kristallnacht*.

Many have tried to discredit Smith and Smith was aware of his critics. This is discussed in an earlier chapter. It can be reasonably suggested Smith had incentives to defend Lindbergh's reputation in the 1950s. But the memoir is inconsistent with this motive. Smith never defends anyone: not the actions of the Embassy, not even himself. As a military officer, Smith paid no attention to Jewish persecution. He mentions it only twice despite living in Germany for 17 years. His job was to obtain intelligence and he was an avid advocate for the fourth trip. Since Smith never expressed any concern for Jews nor how he would be remembered, it seems unlikely he emphasized Lindbergh's abhorrence of anti-Semitism for any other reason — it was his recollection of why Lindbergh canceled a proposed trip after *Kristallnacht*. (Hessen, 1984)

Lindbergh's decision to stop publicly visiting Germany after *Kristallnacht* was and still is nearly unknown. No mention of the fourth trip appears in Lindbergh's journal and there's only a brief mention in Berg's book. But Lindbergh's refusal to return the medal was widely publicized and as Anne predicted, an albatross. Immediately after *Kristallnacht*, he couldn't return it because he was making secret trips to Germany for the French government. (see pp. 178-188) When he returned to the U.S. in 1939, he claimed he didn't have the medal. It was at the Missouri Historical Society where it remains to this day with every other award he received. Later in life when asked if he should have returned it, he said he saw no reason to engage in a "spitting contest". (Berg, 1998, p.381)

On April 18, 1942, James Doolittle led a bombing raid on Japan in retaliation for Pearl Harbor. The 16 B-25 bombers had a souvenir for the Japanese. U.S. sailors who had visited Japan in 1908 had been given medals by the Japanese. They gave them to the Navy, which fastened them to the bombs dropped on Japan. (Groom, 2013) Lindbergh should have done something similar with his medal, the more flamboyant the better. The polite, deferential, and solicitous routine is appropriate when you're an obscure 25-year-old mail pilot being introduced to the King of England, but he'd been an international figure for 11 years and recognized as an authority. He acquired invaluable intelligence no one else could have acquired, but he was also used.

Two Questions Need to be Answered before Lindbergh is Demonized:

First, where was the anti-Semitism? Where is the speech, recorded conversation, or even a personal letter written by Lindbergh while in Europe from 1935-1939 which is anti-Semitic? Anti-Semitism was not only legal fact in Germany; but Romania, Lithuania, Italy, and Poland passed laws which stripped Jews of public employment or secondary education. (Medoff, 2019) How did the great American anti-Semite, Charles Lindbergh, whom authors state was an anti-Semite as accepted fact, say nothing anti-Semitic during four years of the worst, most widespread, most nefarious anti-Semitism in world history? (Peters, 2005) It is hard to name a non-Jew of this era who did not say something in public which was at best "socially acceptable" anti-Semitism, but Lindbergh did not.

Because there is no public anti-Semitism, Lindbergh's critics emphasize private thoughts in his journal. He wrote unpleasant entries admiring certain aspects of German society. Passages in his journal express admiration for German people, say Hitler is popular, and acknowledge Hitler has accomplishments — "good and bad" — but often the context is the future of democracy in an era of societal paralysis, poor leadership, and societal decline. These sentiments were repeated in two personal letters, but the letters don't condone the treatment of Jews. He wrote to his friend Harry Guggenheim, "Of course I don't need to tell you I am not in accord with the Jewish situation in Germany." (Berg, 1998)p.361)

Lindbergh's statements were common in an era when Germany and Hitler were complimented in pursuit of other motives such as peace. The Prime Minister of Canada, William MacKenzie King, said in 1938, "(Hitler) truly loves his fellow man." (WMK, 2021) Gandhi wrote to Hitler in 1940, "We have no doubt about your bravery or devotion to your fatherland, nor do we believe that you are the monster described by your opponents." As an old man Lindbergh was asked why he didn't object forcefully, he responded, "I was far from being in accord with the philosophy, policy, and actions of the Nazi government, but it seemed essential to France, and England, and even to America, that Germany be maintained as a bulwark against the Soviet Union." (Berg, 1998, p.376) (Suhrud, 2019)

Lindbergh's worldview notwithstanding, definitionally a statement can't be anti-Semitic if it isn't about the Jews. None of the offensive statements were about Jews. He never excused German behavior towards the Jews, used Jewish stereotypes, blamed the Jews for their treatment, nor expressed personal dislike for Jews. He should have publicly defended Jews, but unlike President Roosevelt, General Arnold, Prime Minister MacKenzie King, and Gandhi he changed his behavior after *Kristallnacht.*

Second, what did the State Department do to support Lindbergh? Lindbergh was an authority on aviation. He wanted to be re-commissioned in the Army Air Corps. A foreign affairs fiasco would put his commission at risk. The State Department is responsible for relationships with foreign countries. Why was Lindbergh put in the position of having to repudiate German behavior at his own risk? Isn't this the job of the ambassador or the Secretary of State?

The Germans shared military intelligence with Lindbergh because they saw him as one of their own. He could have criticized them and demanded justice for Jews, but only with back-up. On his own he'd be shunned, and nothing would change. He'd lose his commission and the opportunity to gain intelligence. Had he done so at the awarding of the medal he might have been blamed for the collapse of the Munich Accords and thus for World War II.

Lindbergh could only have repudiated Nazi Germany if the State Department backed him up.

Would they have? You'll have to keep reading.

Works Cited

Applebaum, A. (2017). How Stalin Hid Ukraine's Famine From the World. *The Atlantic.*

Archive, U. K. (n.d.). *Why did Mussolini Invade Abyssinia.* Retrieved from https://www.nationalarchives.gov.uk/ and https:// www.upi.com/Archives/1984/11/04/Lindberghs-spy-missions-inGermany

Berg, A. S. (1998). Lindbergh. New York: Berkley Books.

Castillo, D. (2003). *The German Economy in the 1920s.* Retrieved from http://marcuse.faculty.history.ucsb.edu/classes/33d/projects/1920s/Econ20s.htm#:~:text=As%20in%20most%20nations%2C%20the,to%20France%20and%20Great%20Britain.

Cole, W. (1974). Charles Lindbergh and the Battle Against American Intervention. New York: Harcourt, Brace, Jonvanovich.

Correll, J. T. (2014, August). The Cloud Over Lindbergh. *Air Force Magazine,* pp. 76-82.

Encyclopedia Britannica. (n.d.). Retrieved from https://www.britannica.com/place/Italy/Anti-Fascist-movements

Gilbert, M. (1993). *Churchill and the Holocaust.* Retrieved from Winston Churchill.org: https://winstonchurchill.org/the-life-of-churchill/war-leader/churchill-and-the-holocaust-the-possible-and-impossible/

Groom, W. (2013). The Aviators. Washington, DC: National Geographic.

Herman, A. (2000). Joseph McCarthy. New York: The Free Press.

Hessen, R. (1984). *Berlin Alert: The Memoirs and Reports of Truman Smith.* Stanford, CA: Hoover Institute.

History Channel. (n.d.). Retrieved from https://www.history.com/this-day-in-history/goebbels-complains-of-italians-treatment-of-jews

Home.UK, H. (n.d.). Retrieved from http://www.historyhome.co.uk/europe/weimar.htm

Lelyveld, J. (2016). *His Final Battle.* New York: Knopf.

Library of Congress. (n.d.). *Ukrainian Famine.* Retrieved from https://www.loc.gov/exhibits/archives/ukra.html

Lindbergh, C. (1970). *The War Time Journals of Charles Lindbergh.* New York: Harcourt Brace and Jovanovich.

Lyman, R. (2018). *Under a Darkening Sky.* New York: Pegasus Books.

McCormick, A. (1933). *Hitler Seeks Jobs for all German.* Retrieved from NY Times Archives: https://www.nytimes.com/1933/07/10/archives/hitler-seeks-jobs-for-all-germans-does-anything-else-matter-he-asks.html

Medoff, R. (2019). The Jews Should Keep Quiet. Philadelphia: The Jewish Publication Society.

Morse, A. (1968). *While Six Million Died.* NY: Random House.

Peters, C. (2005). *Five Days in Philadelphia.* New York: Publicaffairs.

Pettinger, T. (2017, November 13). *The UK Economy in the 1930s.* Retrieved from https://www.economicshelp.org/blog/7483/economics/the-uk-economy-in-the-1930s/#:~:text=The%201930s%20economy%20 was%20marked,higher%20unemployment%20and%20widespread%20poverty.

Ross, W, *The Last Hero: Charles A. Lindbergh*, Harper and Row, NY, 1964.

Suhrud, T. (2019, September 25). Read Gandhi's Letters to Hitler. *Time*, pp. https://time.com/5685122/gandhi-hitler-letter/.

WMK. (2021, February). Retrieved from The Canadian Encyclopedia: https://www.thecanadianencyclopedia.ca/en/article/william-lyon-mackenzie-king

7. Aviation and Intelligence

The specific impact Lindbergh had on our preparedness for war

This chapter details some of the unparalleled contributions Charles Lindbergh made to our preparation to enter World War II. It gives details of what he was shown on his much-criticized visits to Nazi Germany and how this information was provided to the U.S. military and airplane manufacturers.

Not reviewed here is the specific intelligence he provided regarding aircraft engine technology, manufacture, and performance. This intelligence was so critically important to U.S. preparation for World War II it requires its own chapter.

When the U.S. Air Force became strategically, numerically, and technically superior to Germany's, it was able to defeat Nazi Germany. Defeating Germany ended the Holocaust. The contributions Lindbergh made to U.S. airpower through the intelligence he obtained visiting Germany between 1936-1938, subsequent discussions with U.S. military authorities and aircraft manufacturers, and his contributions to the financial allocations made to U.S. airpower in 1939 enabled our victory. Arguably, Lindbergh did as much to end the Holocaust as any other American.

This chapter describes the state of airplane engineering, military intelligence, and strategy in the 1930s. It explains how Lindbergh enabled the U.S. Air Force to engage the *Luftwaffe* effectively. Lack of intelligence and guidance Lindbergh provided would have resulted in additional years of war and casualties. The 5th column in the table below provides the basis for this assertion.

Table 1: Charles Lindbergh's Contribution to Our Military Preparedness for World War II

Military Field/year	Status Pre-Lindbergh	Lindbergh's Contribution	Lindbergh's Effect	Source giving Lindbergh credit
Military Intelligence (MI)/1937	German buildup considered "hysteria"	Military Intelligence (MI) Report 155420	MI considers Germany to be a potential enemy	Major Truman Smith, Military Attaché, Berlin, 1936-1939[1]
Size of Air Force/1939	U.S.: 1700 combat planes, Germany builds 500 planes/ month	Meets President Roosevelt, White House, 4/20/1939	U.S. allocates money to triple the size of the Air Force	Arthur Krock, NYT DC Bureau Chief, 1939[2]
Air Force Strategy/1939	Lacking understanding of German strategy, pilot training	Briefing, General Arnold, West Point, NY, May 1939	Most accurate description of *Luftwaffe*, strengths, and weaknesses	General Henry H. "Hap" Arnold, Chief of the Air Corps, 1938-1941[3]
Combat effectiveness U.S. Airplanes/1939	Airplanes under development lack key technologic advances needed to fight German aircraft	Kilner Report, June 29, 1939	Improvements in speed, altitude, range, firepower, and payload while adding various safety devices	Official History of the U.S. Air Force, General Arnold[4]

NYT: *New York Times,* [1]Ricks, TF, *Foreign Policy,* 10/16/2013, [2]Krock, 1939, see works cited, [3]Berg, p. 387, [4]Craven; Ross, see works cited. The term "Air Force" is used interchangeably with "Air Corps" although the Air Force was not established as a separate equal branch of the military until June 20, 1941. Prior, our airborne military was the U.S. Army Air Corps (1926-1941).

Lindbergh's Responsibility for U.S. Allocations for Military Preparedness Prior to Entry into World War II

During the period between the World Wars, our military preparedness had waned. For example, in 1934 the U.S. had a total of 3,000 aircraft in our armed forces, out of which only 300 were operational at any time. (Groom, 2005) Between 1934-1939, the allocation for air power decreased every year. At the start of 1939 we had roughly 1,700 combat aircraft at the same time the Germans were building 600 airplanes a month. (USAPDWW2, n.d.) (Lindbergh, 1970, p.70)

On April 20, 1939, Lindbergh met President Roosevelt in the White House. It was their only meeting. Lindbergh and Roosevelt were wary of each other, having clashed in 1934 over the government canceling private contracts to deliver the mail by air, which led to the death of a dozen military pilots. (Berg, 1998, pp.291-2) Lindbergh, due to his hatred of the press, would not allow photographers to document meetings. The meeting was described by both as pleasant. They made small talk about Lindbergh's wife, Anne, having been a classmate of FDR's daughter. Lindbergh said speaking to Roosevelt was like speaking to a man "wearing a mask". (Berg, 1998, p.387) (see photo 9)

At the end of the meeting, Lindbergh was publicly credited by the *NY Times* with Roosevelt's appropriation of $300 million to upgrade our air forces. (Berg, 1998, p.389) This would calculate to 3,251 airplanes or roughly a tripling of our inventory of planes. This began wartime airplane production, which would build 300,000 aircraft. (USAPDWW2, n.d.) The Washington Bureau Chief of the *NY Times* wrote, "when the new flying fleet of the United States begins to take the air, among those who will have been responsible for its size, modernness, and its efficiency is Colonel Charles A. Lindbergh." (Krock, 1939)

This was the second pre-war allocation of resources for which Lindbergh gets credit. While Lindbergh was still in Europe in the Winter of 1938-39, President Roosevelt called for an unprecedented $2 billion peacetime allocation for military preparedness. The witnesses who testified before the House and Senate Committees on Military Affairs in support used intelligence provided by Lindbergh to support Roosevelt's request. The full $2 billion would be allocated. (Nasaw, 2012, p.369) The *NY Times* wrote, "Informed officials here, in touch with what Colonel Lindbergh has been doing for his country abroad are the authority for this statement, and for the further observation that criticism of any of his activities — in Germany or elsewhere — is as ignorant as it is unfair." (Krock, 1939)

What might have been — Our Lack of Intelligence Led to Catastrophe in Asia: Absent Lindbergh's intelligence, the U.S. performance in Europe might have been similar.

The most advanced military aircraft in 1941 was not an American or German airplane, but the Japanese Zero, Despite the Zero's action in China, the U.S. military underestimated its capabilities. The U.S. garrison in the Philippines fell in five months, losing 20,000 casualties and P.O.Ws. (Fleming, 2001, pp.45-6) Military historians uniformly attribute this disaster to a lack of intelligence. (see pp. 362-3)

Lindbergh's Trips to Germany 1936-1938

Table 2: Dates, events, and intelligence for each trip to Germany

Key Dates: 1) Munich Conference, September 29-30, 1938, 2) Battle of Britain, 7/10-10/30/1940

Trip	Dates	Social Events	Military Sites Visited/Planes Inspected	Planes (I) Inspected/ (F) Flown[5]	Intelligence Reports Generated
1	July 22-August 2, 1936	Air Club Speech, Olympic Games Opening Ceremony	Elite *Luftwaffe* Group, Air Research Institute, Heinkel/Junker Factories	I: JU 86,JU 52, Heinkel line: HE111, HE112, HE80, HE118, F: JU87	Communications, See below

2	October 11-25, 1937	Lilienthal Aviation Conference	ATS, Folke-Wulff/ Henschel Factories, Fw-109, Doering 17 TEB	F: DO 17, JU87, I: ME109, ME110.	Report 155420- General Estimate of German Air Strength as of 11/1/37
3	October 11-29, 1938	Medal Presented by Goering	Jumo engine factory, DO-17, JU-88, ME-110, ME-109	I: JU 90, JU-88, F: ME-109, ME-110	Kilner Board, Report issued, 6/29/39

Ref: Cole, W, pp.33-37, Hessen, R, pp. 94-137, see works cited. The ME109 was also called the Bf109.

Soon after arriving in England on December 31, 1935, Lindbergh was invited to visit European airplane factories and airfields. An article appearing in the *Paris Herald* in May 1936 regarding Lindbergh's visit to a French airplane factory, was brought to the attention of Major Truman Smith. Smith had been appointed Military Attaché to the American Embassy in Berlin. His responsibility was "…to report to Washington about the growth of the German army, including the development of new weapons and new battle tactics." Smith realized neither U.S. Ambassador William Dodd nor Washington appreciated the magnitude of Germany's buildup, especially its new air force, the *Luftwaffe.* (Berg, 1998, pp.355-7)

Major Truman Smith sent a letter to Lindbergh on May 25, 1936, on the letterhead of the American Embassy. It is a three-page letter which clearly specifies the main purpose of the visit is to provide information on German air power to America. Smith spells out his concerns, "I hardly need to tell you that the present German air development is imposing and on a scale unmatched in this world and until recently this development was highly secretive." He states if such visits improved relations with Germany that would be beneficial, but the primary reason is "high patriotic benefit." (Smith, 1936)

The third page of the letter contained a list of the details Smith wanted Lindbergh to obtain for each airplane. Smith requested for each German airplane Lindbergh provide U.S. intelligence with: airplane type, identification (model number on each plane), cost of the plane, weight, material, wingspan, wing area, number of engines, make of engine, the numbers stamped on the engines, horsepower of the engines, number of seats in the airplane, color of the airplane, and any information he could obtain on the equipment in each airplane; specifically information on the radio equipment. Smith's letter tells Lindbergh he would be allowed to fly certain airplanes (Smith, 1936) which wasn't his decision. Perhaps as a result, Lindbergh was eager to visit Germany. (Lindbergh C. A., 1970) (Berg, 1998, p.356) Smith encouraged Anne's attendance and made arrangements for her visit. (Smith, 1936)

Lindbergh's handwritten letter to Smith on June 5, 1936, makes it clear he is interested but wants no publicity or newspaper reporters present for the visits. He also strenuously discouraged social functions such as receptions. These requests were ignored. He listed German aviation advances he would be interested in: low-wing monoplanes, advances in high-altitude aviation, supercharging (a technology which can produce more engine power), and methods of landing in fog. He suggests the German Air Ministry make the itinerary. (Hessen, 1984, pp.91-2,99) Allied mastery of supercharging would be critical in World War II, although there is no mention of it nor techniques to land in fog in any of his visits to Germany nor subsequent intelligence reports.

1: <u>First visit to Germany, July-August 1936:</u> this visit established the German air force build-up couldn't be ignored. The U.S. Military starts to assess Germany's air power seriously. (Intelligence indented in italics) (Hessen, 1984, p.105)

> *-Lindbergh's visited two airplane factories, the Heinkel and the Junker Factories, where he inspected a variety of dive bombers, medium bombers, fighter planes, and observation planes.*

> *- Lindbergh inspected and flew the JU-87 Stuka (Stuka is an abbreviation of the German word for dive bomber). This plane incorporated the low-wing design Lindbergh requested to see. It was a critical advance in airplane technology.*

The *Stuka* is the airplane in documentary footage of Germany's invasion of Poland, terrifying civilians with its high-pitched whine as it dives to deliver its bombs and lay waste to the Polish army. (Cole, 1974) It would first see combat in Spain. While it was an effective airplane in the early campaigns, it was soon surpassed by better planes. Many were shot down over England due to their poor maneuverability and because diving exposed the planes to ground fire. (Junkers JU 87, n.d.)

> *-Lindbergh obtained the specifications and capabilities of the new Jumo (JU) 210 engine. This engine incorporated a critical design feature, a high-power liquid cooling system. The JU210 was designed for the JU86, a new bomber unknown to Western Intelligence.* (Hessen, 1984, p.97)

> *-The JU 210G model, developed in 1935, had a new feature unknown to Allied intelligence: a small pump which connected to each piston, injected fuel into the cylinder at a precise time in the intake cycle. Today we call this "fuel injection", it increases power while reducing fuel use.*

The importance of fuel injection and subsequent U.S. intelligence attempts to create engines capable of engaging in combat is critical to understanding WW II air combat. It is addressed in the next chapter.

In his writings, Lindbergh noted the German advances in technology and speculated contesting airplanes without such technology would be at a significant disadvantage. Lindbergh quickly realized German engineering was rapidly surpassing most other Western nations. (Berg, 1998) (Cole, 1974)

> *-Lindbergh visited the Richthofen Geschwader Group, an elite Luftwaffe Pilot Group where he learned how the Germans trained their pilots.*

Pilot training and pilot equipment were an interest of Lindbergh. Between 1942-1944, he would design the oxygen equipment in the B-24 bomber and design training programs for pilots. (Lindbergh C., circa 1943) (Berg, 1998, p.447) In 1936, the Germans were at least 5 years ahead of the Allies in pilot equipment and training. They pioneered heated gloves, pressurized pilot suits, and were addressing complicated physiologic questions of sudden depressurization, often unethically. (Kehrt, 2006)

Lindbergh was impressed with pilot morale and facilities but not with the quality of pilot training. (Hessen, 1984, p.96) Lindbergh gave a briefing on German pilot training to the Chief of the U.S. Army Air Corps, General Arnold, in 1939. (Berg, 1998, p.387) It is possible he based the pilot training program he developed at the Mayo Clinic on this experience. (Lindbergh C., circa 1943)

> *-He visited the Air Research Institute. He wanted to view German progress in the production and design of rockets. The German scientists would not discuss it with him.* (Hessen, 1984, p.96)

Lindbergh had a special interest in rockets because of his relationship with Robert Goddard. Lindbergh had discovered Goddard in 1929 and raised $100,000 from Daniel Guggenheim, enabling him to establish the first U.S. rocket research facility in New Mexico in 1930. Goddard invented the first liquid fueled rocket and had pioneered the use of duralumin for rocket construction which the Germans were now using in the construction of airplanes. (Berg, 1998, pp.348-9)

> *Intelligence was gathered through inadvertent divulging of information. Head of the Luftwaffe, Hermann Goering,*

> *made a comment during a social reception. Goering showed Lindbergh photographs of German airfields and mentioned "our first 70". Lindbergh concluded if the Germans had already built 70 airfields there must not only be planes in production to fill them up but a purpose for all this construction. He knew war was inevitable.* (Berg, 1998, pp.359-60)

Although rumored there was, no single intelligence report was generated by the U.S. military attaché from Lindbergh's first visit to Germany.[6] A series of communications between U.S. military personnel in Germany and their superiors at G2 military intelligence were performed for individual visits. For example, a report was prepared from the visit to the Heinkel factory on July 27, 1936. (Hessen, 1984, p.97) Some reported the superiority of German airplanes and their engines, but in others Lindbergh felt American airplanes were better. (Cole, 1974, p.34) (Harnett, 1984)

Lindbergh's assessment that Germany had the capacity to make airplanes faster than any European country was eye-opening to U.S. intelligence. In Smith's recollections, Lindbergh's intelligence led to efforts to acquire information on Germany's other military branches. (Hessen, 1984, pp.103-4)

<u>2: Second visit to Germany, October 1937:</u> this visit was notable for visits to facilities whose top-secret nature made them inaccessible to any other non-German. The subsequent intelligence report was widely viewed by U.S. officials as well as the English and French Air Forces.

Lindbergh returned to Germany in October 1937 under the guise of an aviation conference named for the German aviation pioneer Otto Lilienthal, who ironically is believed to have been Jewish. (Otto Lilienthal, n.d.) Lindbergh repeated much of the previous itinerary, visiting airplane factories, airstrips, and examining airplanes up close. This trip is notable for visits to facilities no American had ever visited.

In hearings before the Senate Foreign Relations Committee in February 1941, he testified he alone was allowed to see these facilities. No embassy staff was allowed to accompany him. (Committee, 1941)

> *-He visited the Focke-Wulf Airplane Factory in Bremen. He was the first American allowed to see the inside of this factory. (Berg, 1998)*
>
> *-Focke-Wulf made two critical aircraft which Lindbergh was the first to see.*
>
> *a) The FW-109, the Butcherbird. He observed a new type of engine, the radial engine, which allowed for more lift and larger payloads.* (FWC, n.d.)
>
> *b) A new contraption that could take off and land vertically. Today we call this a helicopter.*

The Focke-Wulf corporation was later one of the corporations which merged to form the modern corporation Airbus. (FWC, n.d.)

> *- Rechlin Air Testing station in Pomerania. No foreigner had seen this facility.* (Ricks, 2013)

It is known Lindbergh was exposed to the next German fighter airplane, the ME-110, which had a unique twin engine design. Whether he was exposed to German research on jet engines is unknown. References to jet technology appear in his journal (Lindbergh, 1970, p.959) however Smith wrote Lindbergh failed to gain intelligence on jet engine development. Smith considered this U.S. intelligence's greatest pre-war failure. (Hessen, 1984, p.165)

> *-Lindbergh inspected and sat in the cockpit of the newest German combat airplane, the Messerschmitt 109 (ME-109).*

The ME-109 had revolutionary design features which were relayed to U.S. intelligence: retractable landing gear, a revolutionary pilot canopy to allow egress, and a high power, liquid-cooled V12 700 Hp engine. He also provided its design criteria: top speed 400 km/hr (260 mph) but with a newly designed 1000 Hp engine the top speed could reach 520 km/hr (320 mph), it could ascend 6,000 meters (19,700 feet) in 20 minutes, and its top altitude was 10,000 meters (32,800 feet). Lindbergh documented the Germans planned on developing a 1500 Hp engine. It contained more and better machine guns than any previous combat aircraft. (Messerschmidt-Bf109, n.d.) (Hessen, 1984, p.111) (Hp=horsepower) Lindbergh would be allowed to pilot the ME-109 during his next visit.

> *-Lindbergh was provided the specifications and sat in the cockpit of the Dornier 17 (DO-17) Twin Engine Bomber* (Berg, 1998) (Hessen, 1984, p.111)

This DO-17 was one of the most effective enemy airplanes the Royal Air Force would fight during the Battle of Britain because it could fly at low altitudes, this meant it could avoid the primitive radar of the era. (FWC, n.d.) Despite the advances in aeronautics which would occur over the next 8 years, Allied pilots would fight these planes until the end of the war.

The DO-17 had a self-sealing gas tank which prevented fires and fuel loss if the plane was hit. Whether Lindbergh was made aware of this technologic development during this visit is unknown, but he would later be accused and cleared of providing this technologic secret to the Germans. (Messerschmidt-Bf109, n.d.) (Dornier DO 17, n.d.) (Wallace, 2003)

The information obtained by Lindbergh at these first two visits was detailed in Intelligence Report number 15540 which was titled "General Estimate of Germany's Air Power as of November 1, 1937."

3. <u>Details of *"General Estimate of Germany's Air Power as of November 1, 1937"*</u>

The General Estimate of Germany's Air Power as of November 1, 1937, was a report written by Lindbergh detailing new German airplanes and their engineering features. It reported Germany's air power had surpassed France's, achieved parity with England's, and would surpass America "by 1941 or 1942". This report was viewed by politicians and militaries in England, France, and the U.S.. Despite it, the U.S. Air Corps budget would be cut again in 1938. (Berg, 1998, p.368)

Briefly, this 4-page report reviews Germany's science laboratories and industry (46 factories, with details on production capacity, and a description of the airplane engines including their horsepower). For each airplane model, Lindbergh discloses their top speed and disposable pay load. He reports the number of first-line and reserve units, the size of German air military personnel including number of pilots, how many squadrons Germany has organized, and what percentage of each squadron has modern airplanes. A sample concerning pilot training:

> "While good potential pilots, the Germans must still be rated as unrefined. However, they have made great progress since 1933. The present units would be better if not for the air force expansion. Units have given up about half of their trained men every six months to form new units. There is a marked shortage of efficient squadron and group commanders." (Hessen, 1984, pp.113-8)

Lack of this type of information on the quality, training, and the subsequent disrespect for Japanese pilots was instrumental in the loss of the U.S. garrison in the Philippines in 1942. (see pp.362-3)

In the intelligence passage above, Lindbergh is noting German pilot training was deficient because experienced German instructors were removed from training units and weren't replaced by experienced instructors. American pilot training would be arranged differently. After a pilot flew a certain number of combat missions, he then worked as an instructor. It is possible, because of his previously mentioned briefing on German pilot training, Lindbergh influenced the decision to provide training American pilots with experienced instructors. (Berg, 1998, pp.387-8) In the Battle of Britain, German pilot training deficiencies were instrumental in the German defeat. (see pp.158-9)

Lindbergh's visits also enabled Smith to compile a list of the geographic location, production rate, and floor space of nearly every German aircraft factory and the location of every German airfield. There was also a list of the locations of many airplane parts factories and a list of the *Luftwaffe* units with the locations of their bases. The Embassy in Berlin provided these lists to the U.S. Army General Staff before U.S. staff left Germany in November 1939. (Hessen, 1984, pp.164-5)

4: <u>Third trip to Germany, October 1938.</u> This trip damaged Lindbergh's reputation. The intelligence collected was perhaps the most important intelligence collected in the pre-war era.

> *- Lindbergh piloted the ME-109*
>
> *-Lindbergh saw the specifications of the JU-88, an advanced plane, which prior to this visit had been unknown to Western intelligence.*
>
> *-He saw the production of a new engine, the Jumo-211. In his journal, Lindbergh related that the Germans told him not to tell anyone what he had seen.* (Lindbergh, 1970)
>
> *-He sat in the cockpit of the most advanced German fighter plane, the ME-110. He saw innovative advances in cockpit and engine design. He learned the details of piloting these planes and the unique control of the ailerons which adjusted these features automatically for the pilot based on manual pilot-controlled settings.* (Lindbergh, 1970)

This visit encapsulates why this book was written. Historians have treated this visit as unnecessary mostly because of "the albatross" (the medal Goering gave to Lindbergh). Historians have focused on the criticism Lindbergh received and assume enough intelligence was obtained on previous visits. (Berg, 1998, p.378) This criticism is made by historians because they have no background in engineering.

While "the albatross" did irreparable damage to Lindbergh's reputation, it had no effect on the war. Conversely, the intelligence Lindbergh collected on this trip was critical for the Allies to copy to obtain parity. Much of the airplane technology was completely unknown to Allied military intelligence. Obtaining this intelligence required a level of access to an enemy's technology which is unprecedented in the history of American espionage. Major Smith admitted even he didn't anticipate the wealth and quality of the intelligence Lindbergh collected on this visit. (Hessen, 1984, p.164) Unusual for Lindbergh, in a speech in 1941, he mentioned the trouble American engineers had trying to incorporate this intelligence into aircraft design. (St. Louis Speech, 5/3/1941)

Lindbergh piloted Germany's most advanced fighter airplane, the ME-109 and sat in the cockpit of the next generation German fighter plane, the ME-110. He had the features of the JU-88 explained to him. The JU-88 had never been seen by Allied intelligence. (Lindbergh, 1970, pp.107-8) (Berg, 1998) The JU-88 pioneered automatic flight settings. It was the most advanced and effective German combat airplane throughout World War II, and Lindbergh provided its specifications, capabilities, and weaknesses. The JU-88 could fly lower than a Spitfire at very high speeds and avoid the primitive radar of the era. It was the most effective German airplane in the Battle of Britain. (Junkers JU-88, n.d.) (see photo 7)

A sample of Lindbergh's intelligence from this visit, 10/21/38:

> "We were escorted to a line of four planes: the JU-88, the Me 110, and two Me 109s. It is probably the first time anyone but a German…has seen the 88. It was rather a strange-looking plane with its protrusions for machine

> guns, but it looked capable of high performance. It was mid-wing, all metal monoplane, with trailing edge flaps interconnected with the stabilizer-so that when flaps passed 30 degrees down they move the stabilizer automatically. Retracting landing gear, of course." (he then describes the exterior of the plane, the engines, and the hydraulic systems)
>
> "The interior arrangement of this bomber was also a departure from convention. It carries a crew of three. I was told the next 88's built would carry a crew of four. The crew positions were grouped so close together that each man could touch the other two without moving. The pilot and radio operator-gunner sit back to back. The bomber sits on a sliding seat beside the pilot. He also has a place where he can lie down to shoot below to the rear."

Note: First, Lindbergh's use of "of course" indicates the intelligence is intended for an audience versed in aviation. Second, the Germans provided him with intelligence of future developments. Third, there are combat implications of knowing which crew members had which responsibilities, for example the bomber couldn't shoot below and to the rear and drop bombs at the same time.

After examining the JU-88, Lindbergh piloted a version of the ME-109 which was one of the first fighter airplanes with a liquid-cooled engine and fuel injection. He marveled at the technology; especially its speed and agility while performing complicated maneuvers. He wrote it "handled beautifully". His experience flying this airplane would have a major influence on American military technology and strategy. (Lindbergh, 1970, p.108) (see pp. 127 and 132-3)

Table 3: Key intelligence Lindbergh (L) gathered on the third trip to Germany-October 1938:

	Intelligence Gathered	**Context**	**Comment**
Engines	Junkers Motors factory (Germany) produced 2 engines/ hour[7]	Allison Motors (U.S.) produced 8 engines/month[8]	L would brief Secretary of War, Army Air Corps immediately upon return of disparity
Airplane Performance	ME109 top speed=366 mph, target=450 mph[9]	In 1936, ME109 top speed=260 mph	Exceeding 450 mph became performance goal of U.S. engines
Airplane Design	Complete flight specifications of the JU-88 (see quote above)	Prior to L's visit, airplane unknown to Allied intelligence	Unique design features L described became standard in future fighter planes

Reference: [7]Lindbergh, 1970, p.101, [8]personal communication AEHS, 2021, [9]Lindbergh, 1970, pp. 103-4. AEHS: American Engine Historical Society

Military Strategic Implication of the Intelligence: Basic air strategy in World War II was to coordinate bombers and fighter planes as separate weapons. The bombers were slow, lumbering, and immobile. The fighter planes escorted bombers to their targets and the bombers unleashed their payload. But in future wars, airplanes with maneuverability and payloads found specific targets to destroy.

The JU-88 was maneuverable, fast (top speed = 390 mph), and carried a payload of about 2,000 pounds. It could be equipped for different situations and German strategy, particularly at Stalingrad, revolved around the flexibility of this particular airplane. Depending on the situation it was equipped to fight at night, for reconnaissance, drop torpedo bombs, lay mines, or had ordinance mounted specifically to destroy tanks and trains. (Shiner, 2021) (Dwyer, 2014)

Lindbergh's intelligence provided the Allies advanced knowledge of this advance in aviation. Six years later in combat against the Japanese, Lindbergh would demonstrate the Corsair F4U could carry sufficient payload to be used in a similar fashion. (Berg, 1998, p.455)

<u>Summary of the Political Implications of Lindbergh's Visits:</u> Lindbergh was used by the Germans for propaganda. Historians are remiss for not acknowledging successful espionage sometimes requires giving the enemy fodder for propaganda. He was also used by the U.S. Foreign Service.

Lindbergh tried to avoid being used for propaganda. His correspondence with Smith emphasizes he wanted no press coverage and no social functions. His requests were ignored. (Hessen, 1984, p.99) Regardless, when receiving intelligence in exchange for being used there comes a time when one must stop. Historians argue it should have come at the presentation of "the albatross", but this chapter and the next explain that the intelligence received after the banquet was critical, and the political situation, after the Munich Agreement but before *Kristallnacht*, was too fragile.

The event after which no moral person could continue to be used as propaganda was *Kristallnacht*, a two-day orgy of violence against German Jews. Coming after the Munich Agreement, it demonstrated German treatment of Jews would not improve nor would an agreement allowing them to leave be negotiated in good faith. (Nasaw D., 2012, p.360) Lindbergh too recognized this and in response pledged to not make any "...move which would seem to support German actions in regard to the Jews." (Berg, 1998, p.380) He did not, see the previous discussion of a planned fourth trip to Germany. (see p.86)

Major Smith admitted he used Lindbergh. (Ricks, 2013) Lindbergh paid with his reputation for the access to German military facilities Smith provided. Major Smith also unsuccessfully tried to use Lindbergh to obtain access to Hitler (Smith, July 1936), but the effect on Lindbergh's reputation was never considered. The culmination of being used by the Germans and the U.S. was the "the albatross" debacle. Lindbergh alone had his reputation destroyed — and it was destroyed by the U.S. government whose dysfunction led to his disgrace. He paid for these trips financially and with his reputation and his only reward was "high patriotic benefit." (Smith, May 1936)

Political background preceding Lindbergh's return to the U.S. in April 1939

Lindbergh's final public visit to Germany occurred between the Munich Agreement and Hitler breaking the Agreement and seizing the rest of Czechoslovakia. When Hitler broke the Munich Agreement, war was inevitable. Lindbergh brought his family back to the U.S. in April 1939, as Britain and France prepared for war. In August 1939, Hitler demanded land in Poland called the Danzig Corridor. He offered to resume negotiations, but this time England and France refused to negotiate with Germany. Hitler signed a non-aggression pact with Russia and on September 1, 1939, Germany invaded Poland.

Prior to Lindbergh's visits, many American public figures said news of Germany's intentions were hysterical exaggerations. Others believed, and newspapers reported, Hitler was a reasonable man who could be reasoned with. (Lyman, 2017) Major Smith said after the war, Lindbergh's reports forced the military to recognize Hitler was preparing for war. His intelligence was so thorough and so precise even doubters had to acknowledge a future war in Europe and prepare for it. (Harnett, 1984)

Politically however, both parties opposed entering another European war. The Republican party was dominated by three powerful isolationist politicians seeking the 1940 Presidential Nomination: Robert Taft of Ohio, Thomas Dewey of New York, and Arthur Vandenburg of Michigan. FDR also scrupulously avoided being portrayed as pro-war. Speaking during the 1940 campaign in Boston he said, "And while I am talking to you mothers and fathers, I give you one more assurance.

I have said this before and I shall say it again and again and again your boys are not going to be sent into any foreign wars." (Ambrose, 1983)

Lindbergh's Actions Upon Returning to the U.S. April 1939: Lindbergh met with President Roosevelt, NACA (precursor of NASA), the Secretary of War, and Chief of the U.S. Air Corps, General "Hap" Arnold. Lindbergh's contribution to the Kilner Board's report in June 1939 is the framework of the modern American Air Force.

Charles Lindbergh met "Hap" Arnold, the Chief of the U.S. Army Air Corps and they spent hours discussing Lindbergh's appraisal of German Air Power. Arnold said Lindbergh provided him with "the most accurate picture of the *Luftwaffe*, its equipment, leaders, apparent plans, training methods, and present defects" he ever received. (Cole, 1974) (Berg, 1998, p.387)

Lindbergh served on a committee chaired by Brigadier General Walter Kilner, known as the Kilner Board. The Board's report recommends airplanes have the supercharged high power inline liquid-cooled engines at Lindbergh's insistence. (Cole, 1974) (Culy, 2016) The specifications of the engines, including the recommended horsepower specifications, mimic the engines Lindbergh observed in his visits to Germany as detailed in his diary. (Lindbergh, 1970, p.107) The Kilner Board also recommended construction of the long-range bombers that destroyed our enemies' war capabilities. (LXB-30, nd)

The official Air Force history of the Kilner Board is while some airplanes and engines were already in production the changes recommended, "... greatly enhanced performance in such categories as speed, altitude, range, firepower, and payload while adding various safety devices." (Craven, 1958)

General Arnold said the recommendations of the Kilner Board were of "inestimable value" in getting the airplanes built that would win the war. (Ross, 1964, p.291)

Conclusion: Lindbergh made an Unparalleled Contribution to U.S. Military Preparation

According to Major Smith he convinced military intelligence and eventually the military itself to expect war. According to the *NY Times* he significantly increased the size of our Air Force. According to General Arnold he provided the U.S. Air Force "the most accurate picture of the *Luftwaffe*, its equipment leaders, apparent plans, training methods, and present defects" he had ever received. Arnold then asked Lindbergh to return to duty to "increase the efficiency of American (resources)." (Berg, 1998, p. 387) He provided the specifications and weaknesses of nearly every airplane and critical airplane components including the engines, how the Germans trained their pilots, and their research priorities. (Berg, 1998, pp.355-79) He was instrumental in providing the U.S. army the locations of all their critical infrastructure. (Hessen, 1984, pp.164-5)

According to the U.S. Air Force; the Kilner Board, of which he was one of five men, provided us with better range, speed, altitude, firepower, and payload as well as better safety features. This made our airplanes equal or superior to our enemies' airplanes. These contributions don't include Lindbergh started our rocket program, advised the largest assembly line of combat aircraft, test flew new airplanes, made recommendations derived from his test flights, designed much of the oxygen equipment used by our pilots, did life-threatening research in high-altitude aviation, obtained information about the German jet development program, and bravely served in combat.

We won World War II when we achieved air superiority. We destroyed our enemies' armies and raw materials. We bombed munitions factories and airfields. We earned air superiority because we eventually had better airplanes. Lindbergh's contribution is incalculable. The Holocaust ended because we won. Lindbergh's contribution deserves credit and gratitude — not vilification.

The historian Arthur Schlesinger, Jr. coined the term "Lindberghian future" to describe a dystopia in which the U.S. makes an alliance with an evil foreign power like Nazi Germany. (Peters, 2005) More appropriately, a "Lindberghian future" is one in which every American selflessly devotes themselves to preparing to fight and defeat just such an evil government at their own risk, expense, and loss of their personal reputation.

[5] "Flown" in some cases may include simulated flight, e.g. sitting in the cockpit and being allowed to adjust controls as though flying.

[6]The U.S. press reported Lindbergh authored a report called, "Report on German Aviation", but no quotes were provided, and the U.S. Embassy in Germany doubted this report existed. In 1953, Lindbergh was asked if such a report was prepared. Lindbergh said he believed the press was confusing a letter he sent to Ambassador Kennedy with a formal intelligence report. (Hessen, 1984, pp.153-4)

Works Cited

Allison1710. (n.d.). Retrieved from Allison 1710: https://airandspace.si.edu/collection-objects/allison-v-1710-33-v-1710-c15-v-12-engine/nasm_A19420027000

Ambrose, S. (1983). *Rise to Globalism.* New York: Penguin Publishers.

Berg, A. (1998). *Lindbergh.* New York: Berkley Biography.

BOB. (n.d.). Retrieved from Battle of Britain: https://en....org/wiki/Battle_of_Britain

Cole, W. (1974). Charles A. Lindbergh and the Battle Against American Intervention in World War II. New York: Harcourt Brace and Jovanovich.

Committee, S. F. (1941). *S. 275, "To Promote the Defense of the U.S.".*

Craven, W. (1958). *The Army Air Forces in World War II.* In Final Rpt. of Air Corps Board on Revision to the 5-Year Experimental Program, 28 June 1939 (Volume II). University of Chicago Press.

Culy, D. (2016, December). *Aircraft Engines of World War II.* Retrieved from Defense Media Network: https://www.defensemedianetwork.com/stories/aircraft-engines-world-war-ii/

Dalleck, R. (2017). *Franklin Roosevelt: A Political Life.* New York: Harcourt.

Dornier DO 17. (n.d.). Retrieved from https://en....org/wiki/Dornier_Do_17

Dwyer, L. (2014). *Junkers JU88.* Retrieved from Aviation Museum Online: http://aviation-history.com/junkers/ju88.html

Fleming, T. (2001). *The New Dealers War.* New York: Basic Books.

FWC. (n.d.). *Focke-Wulf Corporation.* Retrieved from Focke-Wulf 190: https://en....org/wiki/Focke-Wulf_Fw_190

Groom. (2005). *The Aviators.* New York.

Harnett, R. (1984). *Lindbergh's Spy Missions in Germany.* Retrieved from UPI Archives: https://www.upi.com/Archives/1984/11/04/Lindberghs-spy-missions-in-Germany/8186468392400/#:~:text=Lindbergh%20actually%20made%20four%20visits%20to%20Germany.

Hessen, R. (1984). *Berlin Alert: The memoirs and reports of Truman Smith.* Stanford, CA: Hoover Institute.

Junkers JU 87. (n.d.). Retrieved from https://en....org/wiki/Junkers_Ju_87

Junkers JU-88. (n.d.). Retrieved from Aviation History: http://aviation-history.com/junkers/ju88.html

Junkers Jumo 210. (n.d.). Retrieved from https://en....org/wiki/Junkers_Jumo_210

Kehrt, C. (2006). Higher, Always Higher' Technology, the Military, and the Science of Aviation Medicine During the Age of the Two World Wars . *Endeavor,* 30(4):138-43.

Klein, M. (2013). In *A Call To Arms.* New York: Bloomsbury.

Krock, A. (1939, February 1). In The Nation; The Invaluable Contribution of Colonel Lindbergh. *New York Times,* p. A1.

Lindbergh, C. A. (1970). *The Wartime Journals of Charles Lindbergh.* New York: Harcourt, Brace, and Jovanovich.

Lindbergh, C. (circa 1943). *Outline for 3-month indoctrination program.*

LXB-30, Lockheed XB-30, https://en....org/wiki/Lockheed_XB-30

Lyman, R. (2017). Under A Darkening Sky. New York: Pegasus.

Messerschmidt-Bf109. (n.d.). Retrieved from https://en....org/wiki/Messerschmitt_Bf_109

Nasaw, D. (2012). In *The Patriarch* (p. 369). New York: Penguin.

National Air and Space Museum. (2020). Retrieved from Allison V1710-33: https://airandspace.si.edu/collection-objects/allison-v-1710-33-v-1710-c15-v-12-engine/nasm_A19420027000

Otto Lilienthal. (n.d.). Retrieved from https://en....org/wiki/Otto_Lilienthal

Peters. (2005). *5 day in Philadelphia.* New York: Propublica.

Ricks, T. (2013, October 16). Six Facts About Truman Smith. *Foreign Policy,* https://foreignpolicy.com/2013/10/16/six-facts-about-col-truman-smith-that-should-interest-all-best-defense-readers/.

Rolls-Royce Merlin. (n.d.). Retrieved from https://en....org/wiki/Rolls-Royce_Merlin

Ross, WS, *The Last Hero: Charles A. Lindbergh,* Harper and Row, 1964.

Shiner, L. (2021). World War II in 65 Airplanes . *Air and Space Magazine,* 44-46.

Smith, T. (1936, May 25) Letter to Lindbergh from U.S. Embassy, Berlin, Germany.

Smith, T, (1936, July 15) Letter to Lindbergh from U.S. Embassy, Berlin, Germany

Wallace, M. (2003). *American Axis.* New York: St. Martins Press.

8: Engines

Perhaps Lindbergh's Most Important Specific Contribution to Allied War Preparedness

This chapter makes the argument Lindbergh deserves significant credit for America's ability to mass produce a liquid-cooled aircraft engine at the time of our entry into the war in December 1941. These engines enabled the U.S. to obtain air superiority over the Germans and thus win the war.

This argument is based on the following evidence:

1) *Lindbergh's intelligence included detailed information regarding German engine technology and in particular, liquid-cooled engines which were more advanced than ours. No other non-German had this level of exposure to German engine technology.*
2) *Lindbergh provided this intelligence to specific engine manufacturers of liquid-cooled engines and promoted liquid-cooled engines. After Lindbergh's visit, the manufacturer of the majority of liquid-cooled engines increased its capacity, years before it had a major government contract.*
3) *He made the use of liquid-cooled engines official policy of the U.S. military.*
4) *At the time (1939), the U.S. military had insufficient interest in liquid-cooled engines.*
5) *Liquid-cooled engines proved superior in both testing and combat to the competing engines the U.S. Army already had contracts to use in 1939.*
6) *The combat engines used by German and U.S. fighter planes were similar. This supports the argument Lindbergh's intelligence was critical to U.S. engine development.*
7) *When the U.S. obtained air superiority over the Germans in February 1944, the two planes given credit both used liquid-cooled engines (P-51 Mustang and the P-38 Lightning)**(see pp. 360-2)**.*

This chapter demonstrates the value of the intelligence Lindbergh gathered at the same visit he was awarded Goering's medal, indeed some of it was acquired the next day. The reader can decide whether a public display repudiating Germany at that moment would have served America's larger longer-term interests. (see timeline 1)

Every component of an airplane is critical. For example, the wing isn't more important than the instrumentation. If either is faulty the plane will crash. However, the airplane is designed around the engine. The wing provides lift, but lift depends on thrust and thrust depends on the engine. The engine determines the capabilities of the aircraft and in combat it is the most important determinant of strategy. In World War II nearly every improvement in aircraft technology was either an improvement in engine technology or was predicated on a previous improvement in engine technology. (Culy, 2016)

When people think of World War I aircraft, they think of biplanes (two wings), and when they think of World War II aircraft, they think of monoplanes (1 wing), but this isn't strictly accurate. Biplanes were used in World War II but mostly for transportation and non-combat roles. The U.S. Army Air Corps and the Navy were using biplanes in combat roles as late as 1938 and military planning included using them in a future war. (Grant, 2017) We were using antiquated technology because our engines were obsolete.

Because it has two wings a biplane can provide more lift for the same thrust. Therefore, using the same engine, a biplane can take off on a shorter runway, and a monoplane needs a longer wingspan to obtain the same lift. On an aircraft carrier, for example, runways are short and the capacity to store airplanes is critical and dependent on short wingspans. In this situation, biplanes could take off and more could be fit on a ship. Prior to Lindbergh's return to the U.S., our military strategy depended on antiquated engine technology. Absent dramatic improvements in engine technology this would have led to defeat.

Lindbergh had extensive exposure to German engine technology. Of these trips, the third is the most vilified trip because of the medal he was awarded by Goering. However, it was also the most important trip because he accessed the most advanced German engine technology. (Lindbergh, 1970) (Hessen, 1984, pp.128,135)

This chapter documents how Lindbergh used the information gathered on this trip to promote the liquid-cooled engine upon his return to the U.S. in April 1939. Prior to Lindbergh's visit, the U.S. Army Air Corps did not purchase liquid-cooled aircraft engines nor the planes that used them. (456th Fighter Squadron, n.d.) (Whitney, 1998, pp.31-41)(Dwyer, 2013) Lindbergh's advocacy helped this engine power the majority of our fighter aircraft. (Cole, 1974, p.68)

The German engine, the Jumo-211, and the American engine, the Allison V-1710, were similar engines. They were used for the same purpose, to power fighter planes, and were made in nearly identical numbers. The Germans developed their engines first, and at the time German engines were being developed (while Lindbergh observed), American liquid-cooled engine technology was far behind Germany's and not being promoted.

Engineers in both countries would eventually receive the enemy's engines to examinc from downed planes. (Whitney, 1998) But Lindbergh provided key intelligence to copy features of German liquid-cooled engines long before American engineers had access to German engines. Lindbergh neither designed the Allison V-1710 nor gets credit for its success. (see figure 1) However, without his advocacy and promotion it is doubtful U.S. combat engines would have been competitive and had they been, it would have been much later in the war.

<u>Principles Involved in the Design of Airplanes and Components</u>

State-of-the-art combat aircraft require years of design and manufacturing. During the design and manufacturing process changes and modifications are constantly being made. Many U.S. aircraft and their components were proposed or initially designed in the mid-1930s, before Lindbergh was involved. However, the lack of a national commitment to defense due to the monetary constraints and politics of the Depression made progress slow. (Klein, 2013)

As the war began and aircraft engaged in combat, the airplane companies were deluged with information and intelligence regarding the performance of their products, and changes in strategy, which required changes in the airplanes. Aircraft are made to be adjusted and modified, and the dies used to make the components are soft and changeable. During World War I the Packard Motor Company set out to make airplane engines, but they never made one. They received over 1,000 design changes and the war didn't last long enough for them to finish an engine. (Klein, 2013)

As intelligence became available, engineers modified the engines to provide better performance in combat conditions which differed depending on the location. No one person can be credited with any engine or even an engine feature. It is possible Lindbergh's intelligence resulted in small improvements in a wide range of engines rather than a single large improvement in one engine line. But judged chronologically and in terms of advocacy, Lindbergh had the most critical influence on the development of the Allison V-1710 engine lines.

Lindbergh's exposure to German engine technology

Lindbergh's visits to German military facilities are detailed in the previous chapter. Lindbergh was not an engineer and couldn't take photographs or notes during these visits. Everything he witnessed he had to remember. He would then explain what he had seen to Major Truman Smith, the U.S. Military Attaché in Berlin, who would then prepare intelligence reports. Major Smith had no background in aviation.

On his first visit to Germany, Lindbergh was given detailed exposure to an earlier line of Jumo engines, the Jumo 210 (July 30, 1936). Smith reported in his memoirs that Lindbergh was impressed with the quality and workmanship of the Jumo 210, and commented on the poor quality of equivalent American technology. (Hessen, 1984, p.97)

On October 18, 1938, Lindbergh visited the Junkers engine factory in Desau. He was given an in-depth briefing of Germany's transition from the Jumo 210 to the Jumo 211 engine. He learned how these engines were constructed, including their exact specifications. His briefing included not just engine details but how the technicians were trained and promoted. (Lindbergh, 1970, pp.100-2)

The next day, the day after the medal debacle, he saw the JU-88 combination fighter/bomber. Lindbergh documented the engines and engine bays of this airplane, noting that the location of the engine coils would lead one to assume these were air-cooled engines, but they were liquid-cooled engines. His description of the hydraulic system indicates he examined the engines in some depth. (Lindbergh, 1970, p.109) Lindbergh was told the ME-109 could fly at 600 km/hr (360 mi/hr) but the goal was to fly at 750 km/hr (450 mi/hr). In two years, German engineers had doubled the speed of the ME-109 and would seek to increase it by another 100 miles per hour. (Lindbergh, 1970, pp.100-9)

Lindbergh's interaction with U.S. Engine Manufacturers

Charles Lindbergh returned to the U.S. on April 14, 1939. While *en route*, appointments were made for him. Lindbergh met with Harry Woodring, the Secretary of War, General "Hap" Arnold the Chief of the U.S. Army Air Corps, President Roosevelt, and NACA (the National Advisory Committee for Aeronautics, the precursor of NASA). The meeting with Roosevelt is discussed in another chapter. The meeting with NACA presumably involved the status German research based on his testimony to Congress. The other meetings were debriefings on the status of German aviation. (Lindbergh C., May 1939)

He was then taken on a tour of Wright Air Base in Ohio. Wright Air Base was the location where the army would put aircraft engines through competitive testing to determine the best engines for combat. (Whitney, 1998, p.47)

The first appointment Lindbergh made was with a small manufacturer of aircraft engines, the Allison Motor Corporation, in Indianapolis, on April 27, 1939. In his journal, Lindbergh explains why he called Allison Motors to make an appointment with Ronald Hazen, the director of engineering: Allison Motors was the only manufacturer of airplane quality liquid-cooled engines in the U.S.. In engine testing in 1939, the Allison V-1710 did not perform well enough for the U.S. Army Air Corps to purchase it. (Whitney, 1998, p.45)

Lindbergh wrote that because it would take years for another manufacturer to make liquid-cooled engines, Allison needed more capacity. He noted that because Allison's factory was too small to manufacture sufficient liquid-cooled engines, they discussed how to expand capacity. They then discussed improving the engine's performance, including presumably competitive engine testing because Lindbergh had just reviewed its criteria. Advances in German liquid-cooled engine technology prompted Allison Motors to request and obtain a captured Jumo 211 engine to examine soon after we entered the war. (Lindbergh, 1970, pp.190-2)

In 1939, Allison Motors built an average of 8 engines a month. (AEHS, Personal Communication, 2021) After Lindbergh's visit in April 1939, Allison Motors began to double its workforce and triple the square footage of its factories, which was a significant financial risk.[4] (Pfeiffer, 2018) In June 1939, Lindbergh sat on the Kilner Board which determined the future of U.S. airpower. Lindbergh recommended, and the committee adopted his recommendation, that the future of U.S. airpower was high powered liquid-cooled engines and the airplanes that used them. (Cole, 1974, p.68) During the subsequent 3 and a half years of war, the Allison Motor corporation built nearly 70,000 high powered liquid-cooled combat engines which would power 60% of U.S. fighter combat aircraft. (Culy, 2016) (Allison V-1710-33, n.d.) Allison Motors was the only U.S. manufacturer of liquid-cooled engines for combat aircraft and their monthly output would increase 208 times their output prior to Lindbergh's visit.[1]

The Allison V-1710 provided power for the most effective fighter planes in World War II: the Mustang P51[2], the Bell P-39 and P-61, and the Curtiss P-40 series. (Whitney, 1998) Two Allison V-1710 engines would power one of the most effective fighter planes of the war, Lockheed's P38 Lightning. The engine was more effective in the Pacific than Europe because a shortage of tungsten affected its performance at high altitudes. But the P38 was used extensively throughout Europe and shot down so many German airplanes that the Germans nicknamed it "the fork-tongued devil". The Allison V-1710 would be modified for different fighting conditions in the European and Asian theaters and was used in the beginning of the Korean War. (National Air and Space Museum, 2020) (456th Fighter Squadron, n.d.)

Of course, every manufacturer of war equipment had an exponential growth in productivity during World War II. (Klein, 2013) But what appears to have been inevitable is often not. If one were to predict the engine company likely to be the main supplier of fighter plane engines in 1939, it would not have been Allison. Not only did Allison fail its first competitive engine test in 1939, but the U.S. army had little interest in liquid-cooled engines. (Whitney, 1998, p.45) Allison was able to develop them because the Navy needed them to power dirigibles. The first liquid-cooled engine the army bought, the Curtiss Conqueror, was a disappointment and abandoned by the army in 1936. (Dwyer, 2013) The Conqueror (officially designated the Curtiss V-1570) was unreliable, suffered significant coolant leaks, and was prone to overheating. (Curtiss V-1570, n.d.)

Lindbergh's intelligence revealed the target velocity German engineers were trying to achieve with the Jumo 211 engine in an ME-109 was 450 miles/hr. Upon his return, Lindbergh had conversations with airplane executives in which he discussed how American combat planes could surpass this velocity. They suggested the engine capable of powering fighter planes to achieve speeds of 500 mph in combat was a new engine, the "flat engine" made by Wright Aeronautical. (Lindbergh, 1970, p.190) This air-cooled engine, formally known as the Cyclone R-1820 series of engines, was the best-selling aircraft engine during peacetime and designed to achieve faster speeds in combat. The army had contracted with Wright Aeronautical in 1936 to produce these engines for high-speed combat aircraft. Wright was also a much larger company than Allison Motors. In the last 6 months of 1936 alone, Wright sold 700 Cyclone 1000 hp engines, or more than 100 per month. (Wright Aeronautical Engines, n.d.)

Although Wright made the engine on *The Spirit of St. Louis,* Lindbergh did not promote this engine, nor this company, and it did not power a significant number of U.S. fighter aircraft. These air-cooled engines would mostly power slower less-demanding bombers. Although a respectable number of Cyclone engines were made (roughly 25,000), this engine never matched the Allison V-1710 for production nor performance. (Wright Aeronautical Engines, n.d.) (Curtiss-Wright Aircraft Engine Shipments, 1920-1964, 1964).

The Wright Corporation would also be the subject of Congressional hearings into misuse of government funds during World War II. Infamously, the Wright Corporation used government funds to defame the government's main prosecutor as a defense tactic. This controversy made that prosecutor, an obscure Senator from Missouri named Harry Truman, a household name. (Levin Center, n.d.)

On August 4, 1940, Lindbergh met with Charles Sorensen, the chief engineer for the Ford Motor corporation to discuss aircraft engines. Ford Motor Company was making liquid-cooled engines for England to use in the Spitfire and Hurricane Hawker. (Klein, 2013) Lindbergh's journal reveals he and Sorensen discussed the Jumo 211 and Ford also requested the army provide them with a captured Jumo-211 engine so they could examine it. (Lindbergh, 1970, p.376)

Comparison of Air-Cooled and Liquid-Cooled Engines

In early 1940, British intelligence intercepted a message directly from Hitler, (translated) "I have decided to prepare a landing operation against England to eliminate England as a base of operation of the war against Germany. First the English air force must be reduced physically and morally so that it is unable to deliver any physical attack against the German crossing." (Peters, 2005) Thus, began the Battle of Britain which was the first battle fought entirely in the air and would be Germany's first loss in the war. The airplanes England used to fight the battle, the Spitfire and Hurricane Hawker, both used high-power liquid-cooled V12 engines. (Merlin Rolls-Royce, n.d.) Their performance demonstrated Lindbergh's recommendation in the Kilner Report was correct.

German engineers would meet their goal for peak velocity for the ME-109, powered by a Jumo 211 engine. It reached a velocity of 460 mph in 1942. (Junkers Jumo-211, n.d.) The maximum speed the Allison V-1710 achieved, in the Mustang P51A and the P38, was approximately 420 mph using model 81. However, peak obtainable velocity was not the most important determinant of combat effectiveness because the Spitfire's peak velocity never exceeded 400 mph and it effectively engaged in combat with the ME-109 during the Battle of Britain. (Allison V-1710-33, n.d.)

The two most important determinants of combat effectiveness were the length of time an engine could maintain high velocities and the power to accelerate to these velocities quickly. In these two parameters the liquid-cooled engine was superior to the air-cooled engine. This was because liquid cooling was a more reliable way to cool engines and the coolant could be directed to the parts of the engine which were most in need, enabling liquid-cooled engines to maintain top speeds longer. This resulted in better performance in combat.

U.S. Army Air Corps testing at Wright Field (today Wright-Patterson Air Base) and the record of these engines in combat would also confirm Lindbergh's contention that liquid-cooled engines were the superior technology. In addition to the advantages noted above, liquid-cooled engines had less aerodynamic drag and because they did not need to be placed behind the propeller, they were more versatile engines and allowed more creative and better-designed aircraft. (figures 2-3) The engine itself was lighter than air-cooled engines, but because it needed a separate cooling system the total weight was usually more. (Klein, 2013)

Lindbergh began advocating liquid-cooled engines and chose to contact and advise the only U.S. manufacturer of liquid-cooled engines more than a year before the combat performance of these engines would be known to the U.S. military. Had Lindbergh not made his recommendation and the outstanding performance of these engines been required to convince the Army Air Corps to purchase more liquid-cooled engines, U.S. technology development would have been delayed more than a year.

Similarities Between the Allison V-1710 and the Jumo 210/211

Figure 1 provides the important engine characteristics of the two engine lines Lindbergh had significant exposure to in Germany and the subsequent engine line developed by American engineers. Lindbergh does not get credit for specific details that were designed before he met with Allison in April 1939, nor the basic components which were similar in all engines of the era. The Allison V-1710 required thousands of man hours of engineering and technical labor independent of Lindbergh. However, the reader should notice:

1) The rapid development of German technology between 1935 and 1939. The Jumo 210 is a much smaller less powerful engine than the Jumo 211. It required significantly more fuel to achieve half the horsepower. Lindbergh commented on the rapid development of German technology in his intelligence reports and according to Major Smith made U.S. military planners aware. (Hessen, 1984, p.105)
2) Most of the characteristics of the Allison V1710 are either similar to the Jumo 211 or fall between the Jumo 210 and

the Jumo 211. Lindbergh saw a version of the Jumo 211 being developed and further modifications and improvements would be made which he would not see. The Allison V1710 resembles the Jumo 211 he would have seen in October 1938.

Differences Between the Allison V-1710 and the Jumo 210/211

There were differences between the two engines, for example German engines were designed with three valves per cylinder (2 intake, 1 exhaust) and American engines were designed with four valves per cylinder (2 intake, 2 exhaust). The larger the portion of the cylinder head composed of valves the more efficient the engine but in this case, there was not an appreciable difference. (AEHS, personal communication, 2021) The Germans attempted to place four valves on a cylinder head in one model of the Jumo 210 but didn't pursue this engineering feature. (Junkers Jumo-211, n.d.)

The most important difference was the incorporation of fuel injection. Although American engineers developed primitive fuel injection systems in the early 1930s, by the mid-1930s, American engineers were focused on supercharging. Lindbergh emphasized this in his communications with Smith in 1936.3

But Lindbergh was so impressed when he piloted combat airplanes with fuel injection, that he advocated for it rather than supercharging. (Hessen, 1984, pp.107-112) This intelligence was most likely provided directly to Allison Motors because they unsuccessfully tried to incorporate it into its engines, as did the U.S. military (Army Air Forces Engineering Division at Wright Field and U.S. Navy Aeronautical Engine Laboratory). German fuel injection technology was too advanced. When U.S. fuel injection became available, the systems were not copies of German technology. American engineers designed engines with original fuel injection designs. (AEHS, personal communication, 2021)

Engineering is complicated. A non-engineer unable to take notes or photographs will sometimes be unable to relay sufficient information for an engineer to copy the technologic advance.

<u>Parallel Development of Technology:</u> Determining the exact contribution of a single source of intelligence to a finished military product is impossible. The nature of military intelligence is that it is hard to trace.

Similarities may represent the state of the technology at the time and sometimes technologic advances occur in parallel without an intelligence contribution. A U.S. engineer invented self-sealing gas tanks in 1941 which reduced the incidence of fires and explosions in aircraft pierced with ordinance. (Self-sealing fuel tanks, n.d.) A similar, but not identical, technology was also found on downed German airplanes. The engineer accused Lindbergh of providing this technology to the Germans. Because the charge was chronologically impossible, the FBI cleared Lindbergh of this accusation. (Wallace, 2003) German and U.S. technology were not identical, and the JU-88 had a self-sealing gas tank before allied intelligence knew the plane existed and years before a U.S. patent was filed for the technology. (Self-sealing fuel tanks, n.d.) It appears both sides invented similar technology independent of each other.

<u>What might have been — The Italian Air Force (IAF)</u>

Although analogies are never completely appropriate, the record of the IAF demonstrates two important points. First, failure to adopt the use of liquid-cooled engines in combat aircraft resulted in inferior airplanes with inferior performance. Second, a time lag in producing combat-equivalent aircraft could have resulted in defeat. This demonstrates how critical Lindbergh's advocacy for liquid-cooled engines and his efforts to aid development of airplanes were in the U.S.'s efforts to fight World War II.

Until 1939 the Italian and American air forces were technologically similar, although Italy's Air Force was much larger. Italy had more fighter airplanes than England and France combined, but the airplanes were inferior. In its invasion of Abyssinia (1936) and its intervention in Spain (1937), the IAF relied on biplanes. It didn't start to introduce monoplanes until 1939. Around this time Lindbergh advocated liquid-cooled engines and their use became official policy. The U.S. began to build airplanes which adapted new technology as it was developed, the Italians did not.

Had Lindbergh not advocated liquid-cooled engines and taken a personal interest in Allison Motor Corporation, it can be assumed American fighter planes would have used the air-cooled Wright Flat Engine, because the Army had contracts to use this engine. Italian fighter airplanes used a similar Fiat line of air-cooled flat engines. As a result, Italy's fighter airplanes were inferior. Its premier fighter airplanes, the G50 Frecchia and the Macchi C-200, had top-speeds of only 300 mph, while American fighter airplanes' top speeds exceeded 400 mph.

Italian industry struggled to incorporate new technology and could not replace losses in Russia, Greece, and Africa with competitive airplanes. The Italians realized their planes were inferior and purchased liquid-cooled engines from Germany, but incorporating new technology is hard. Italy was too late to deploy these engines in significant numbers. Although the IAF remained loyal to its German ally, it had too few fighter planes left to be a factor in the Allied invasion of the Sicily (June 1943). By the time of the Allied invasion of mainland Italy in September 1943, Italy ceased to have an effective air force. (Italian Fighter Planes of World War II, n.d.)

<u>Lindbergh's Intricate Understanding of the Allison V-1710 engine</u>

While fighting in combat in the Pacific, Lindbergh advocated engine settings for the Allison V-1710 which reduced fuel consumption in the P-38 fighter airplane. This gave the plane more range. The history and strategy of this development is reviewed in a later chapter. The purpose of reviewing it here is to explain the change from an engineering standpoint and to demonstrate Lindbergh had an intricate understanding of engine technology. His advocacy for liquid-cooled engines was not based on something someone told him, but rather on experience gained from observing the intricacies of the engine and flying a series of airplanes with this type of engine, including flying them in combat.

In a 4-stroke diesel engine the piston compresses a fuel-air mixture in the cylinder which is then ignited by a sparkplug. The resulting combustion pushes the piston away from the sparkplug. This turns a crankshaft which pushes other pistons towards the sparkplugs in their cylinders in a cyclical fashion. The Allison V1710 had 12 cylinders, and in a 4-stroke engine the cycle is timed so when one piston is moving away from its sparkplug, the crankshaft compresses the fuel-air mixture in the other cylinders. (figure 4)

The number of times the crankshaft rotates is denoted revolutions per minute (RPM). The more air in the cylinder, the higher the pressure in the cylinder (the manifold pressure). A higher manifold pressure enables a lower RPM to achieve the same thrust and use less fuel. The pilot regulates the manifold pressure by opening and closing the throttle. An open throttle allows more air in the fuel/air mixture and raises the manifold pressure. Lindbergh demonstrated he could fly the same mission with less fuel by gradually opening the throttle while cruising. As he opened the throttle, he would carefully monitor the heat of the exhaust. This is called "engine-leaning".

Lindbergh extended the range of the P-38 through improved throttle settings, or engine-leaning techniques, which reduced engine speed to 1,600 rpm. He also set the carburetors for auto-lean and then flew at 185 mph (298 km/hr) indicated airspeed which reduced fuel consumption to 70 gallons/hour. This translates to roughly 2.6 additional miles per gallon. (Lockheed P38 Lightning, n.d.)

These settings appear in the engine's manual. (Whitney, 1998) But at the time, pilots believed at these settings the engines would explode. (Lockheed P38 Lightning, n.d.) Demonstrating courage, leadership, and an intricate knowledge of this engine, Lindbergh reassured his comrades both in combat and verbally, the engine would not malfunction, and the fuel savings would translate into potentially longer missions. Undoubtably, Lindbergh gave the U.S. a combat advantage which is discussed in a future chapter. (Berg A., 1998)

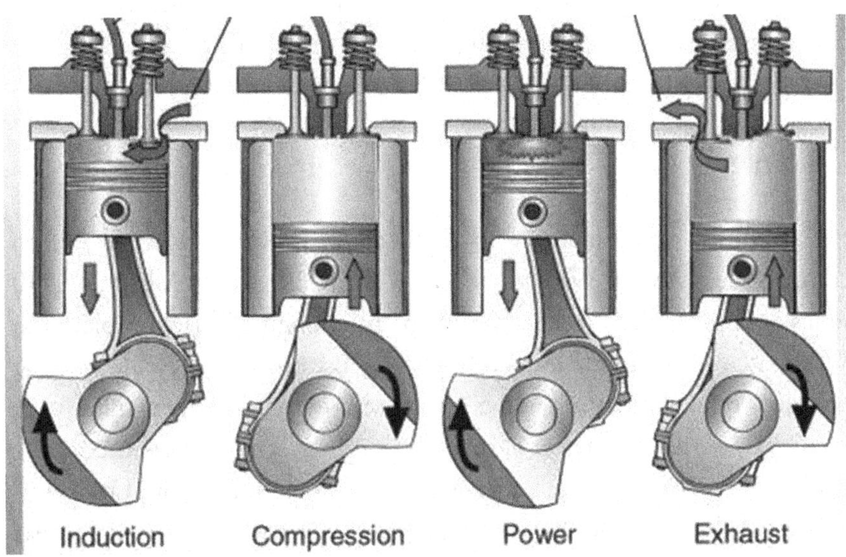

Figure 4: A 4-stroke internal combustion engine. During the induction phase, a fuel/air mixture enters the cylinder passively due to the vacuum created by the crankshaft withdrawing the piston (straight arrows). In fuel injection the fuel/air mixture is pumped into the cylinder rather than passively sucked into the cylinder. The composition of the fuel/air mixture is determined by the throttle. Lindbergh's use of a wide-open throttle provided the same power at a lower RPM and thereby reduced fuel consumption enough to improve airplane performance in combat.

According to the official history of the V-1710 engine:

> "When throttled back for cruise conditions the V-1710 was quite efficient. It was this feature, coupled with proper operating technique, which gave the P-38 its long-range capability. As detailed in the Allison engine Technical Orders, and later taught by Charles Lindbergh

> to airmen in the South Pacific, proper cruise control involved operating at reduced engine speed, but with the engine throttle "wide-open" (thereby minimizing pressure losses in the inductions system), and maintaining desired engine manifold pressure and power with the turbo. This shifted the burden of compressing the air to the turbo which had plenty of energy available." (AEHS, personal communication)

<u>Conclusion:</u>

Every engine manufactured by American industry was subject to competitive testing at Wright Air Base. (Klein, 2013) The Allison V-1710 series of engines did not become the premier engine in fighter planes in World War II because Lindbergh advocated for them; they became the premier engines because testing results and combat performances were eventually better than those of the other engines. The performance of the Royal Air Force during the Battle of Britain was also proof. But Lindbergh promoted these engines because he knew it was the better engine a year before the Battle of Britain. But why did Lindbergh need to promote this engine? After all, didn't U.S. airplane engineers know this too?

Some did, but engineers design engines to be sold. The largest consumer of airplane engines, the U.S. Army, had had limited interest in purchasing liquid-cooled engines in 1939. Previously the army had purchased liquid-cooled engines and they had been unreliable and abandoned. (Curtiss V-1570, n.d.) The army believed any additional system, such as a coolant circuit, meant more malfunctions. Engineers may have known the theoretical advantages of liquid-cooled engines, but they were also dealing with inferior technology. Without Lindbergh's advocacy, particularly on the Kilner Board, it is doubtful the engine technology would have improved, and it is doubtful the army would have been interested prior to late 1940.

Furthermore, no engineer had piloted an ME-109. Lindbergh knew the engineering advantages because his trips to Germany gave him access to more advanced liquid-cooled engine technology. But he also knew the tactical advantages because the Germans allowed him to fly both air-cooled and liquid-cooled fighter planes. Lindbergh was the only man who could testify to the Secretary of War, the Chief of the U.S. Army Air Corps, and the Kilner Board that the liquid-cooled engine was better both from an engineering and tactical standpoint. The Kilner Report gave a small airplane engine manufacturer the opportunity to produce fighter plane engines that outperformed, both in trials and in combat, the engines produced by a much larger company, which had a head start. Indeed, its competitor already had army fighter plane engine contracts.

If there was another pilot in the U.S. who had flown fighter planes with both liquid-cooled and air-cooled engines, he didn't have Lindbergh's resumé nor the knowledge of the intricate details of the engine. In any event, no one else's opinion was requested. Lindbergh, and Lindbergh alone, made this possible.

Although politically expedient, manufacturing thousands of airplanes which would later demonstrate inferiority in combat would have wasted millions of dollars and many lives. Despite the Curtiss Conqueror's failure in 1936, the Army showed some interest in liquid-cooled engines prior to 1939. However, partly due lack of funding, American liquid-cooled engines were unsuitable for combat. Engineering problems, e.g. poor fuel distribution, coolant leaks, and excessive vibrations, plagued their development. (Whitney, 1998, pp. 31-41) Mastering a learning curve takes time and money, and the impulse to not do so while preparing for a war is powerful. Yet, it had to be done. Lindbergh deserves significant credit that it was done.

For the Reader's Consideration:

In the author's experience when people are asked to describe Lindbergh's legacy, they say he was a Nazi. When asked why, if the person knows anything about Lindbergh, the response is he accepted a medal from Goering.

Due to President Roosevelt's use of this event to tarnish Lindbergh's reputation, people believe that when Hermann Goering unexpectedly presented Lindbergh with a medal, after a speech in a language Lindbergh did not understand, at a dinner in October 1938 that he should have refused it. Even if we ignore the State Department's responsibility for the diplomatic malfunction that preceded the awarding of the medal, the delicate situation caused by the recently signed Munich Agreement, and whether Lindbergh deserved blame for following U.S. Foreign Policy we are still left with the question: Was it was worth jeopardizing intelligence to make a symbolic statement?

Lindbergh's most valuable and most detailed experiences with liquid-cooled engines (as well as the flight specifications of advanced German airplanes never seen by Western Intelligence) were obtained during a visit to Germany, which the press at the time and historians today consider a disaster because of this medal. The medal was used to influence American domestic politics but had no effect on the war.

Lindbergh, using information he obtained on this visit to Nazi Germany, advocated for an engine technology and an engine company which was not favored at the time of his return to the U.S.. The technology Lindbergh advocated proved superior to the technology in use and preferred by the U.S. Army; both in combat and testing. His advocacy and intelligence shortened the gap between the development of German engine technology and Allied engine technology.

It is the reader's obligation to speculate how the war would have proceeded had we used inferior technology to power our combat aircraft. The reader should consider the record of the Italian Air Force because it exclusively used this inferior technology. It is the reader's obligation to speculate how many lives Lindbergh's actions saved and how much he shortened the war in Europe and Asia.

Most importantly, it is the reader's decision which was more important: obtaining information and advocacy, which led to the U.S. developing a competitive fighter aircraft engine or demonstrating disdain for Nazi Germany by refusing a medal in a symbolic act which would have had no effect on the war and would have ended Lindbergh's ability to acquire intelligence. It would have also ended Lindbergh's commission in the Army and possibly resulted in Lindbergh being blamed for the collapse of the Munich Agreement. While considering this question, the reader should remember that engine technology was only a small part of the intelligence Lindbergh provided.

If the lives of American Airmen and the soldiers on the ground they were supporting, and winning the war, were more important than a symbolic act of protest, then the reader agrees with the premise of this book: Lindbergh's legacy has been distorted by people who can't judge Lindbergh's legacy because they lack the qualifications to do so.

[1]The Ford Motor company was a U.S. manufacturer of liquid-cooled airplane engines during World War II. The engines it made were called the Rolls-Royce Merlin line of engines which is the name of an English manufacturer. Whether these are called "American" or "British" engines is of no importance. However, these engines did power some U.S. fighter planes, in particular the P-51.

[2]Initially the P-51 was powered by the Allison V-1710 but later versions used the Rolls-Royce Merlin engine.

[3]Supercharging is a similar technology to turbocharging. They both pump compressed air into the engine. Supercharging and fuel injection are not mutually exclusive. Some airplanes in World War II had both, including the P-51.

Figure 1: Characteristics of German airplane engines witnessed by Lindbergh and the subsequent American engine developed for the same purpose: (All measurements in metric units for consistency)

Ju 210 (Germany)	Ju 211 (Germany)	Characteristic	Allison (AM) V-1710 (U.S.)	Comment: Lindbergh (L)

1935	1938-39	Large Scale Production Year	1941	
Unknown	68,248	Number Made	69,233	
Inverted V12	Inverted V12	Engine Type	60 degree-V12	Predates L
Liquid	Pressurized liquid, Ethylene Glycol	Coolant	Pressurized liquid, Ethylene glycol	
690	1200*	Horsepower (Hp)	1250**	Range, depending on model
2700	2400	Revolutions Per Minute (RPMs)	2600^	Less RPMS=more power for equal fuel consumption
124 mm	150 mm	Bore	140 mm	
136 mm	165 mm	Stroke	152 mm	
19.7 Liters	35 Liters	Displacement	28 Liters	
442 kg	640 kg	Weight	633 kg	Dry weight, unequipped
3 Model 210H: 4	3	Valves/Cylinder	4	U.S. LCEs had 2 exhaust valves
6.5:1	6.5:1	Compression Ratio	6.65:1	
322-335 g/kW/hr	290 g/kW/hr	Fuel Consumption	298 g/kW/hr^^	
1.17 kW/kg	1.4 kW/kg	Power/Weight	1.76 kW/kg	
Only used for fighter aircraft	Superior record when used in fighters	Note-General	Only used in fighter aircraft	At L's visit (1938) 211 to be used only in fighters
Witnessed in depth-1936	Witnessed in depth-1938	Note-Lindbergh	Met with AM 1939, AM requests JU211	
1938	1945	End of Production	1951	

Engine characteristics vary by model and performance characteristics. Standard parameters source Jumo 210, Jumo 211, American Historical Engine Society (AEHS) and Allison V-1710 except as noted. LCE: Liquid-cooled engines, AM: Allison Motors, Ref: Whitney, 1998.

*The Jumo 211 would be developed with horsepower as high as 1500 hp, but at the time of Lindbergh's visit (1938) this was the specification of the engine. (Lindbergh, 1970)

**Horsepower is for the model G6

^RPMs for the Model C at cruising. During takeoff and diving all planes reach higher RPMs.

^^: For a Model E6 on a Bell airplane at 60% of full capacity. (Source, personal communication, AEHS, 5/2021)

[4] Exactly when Allison Motors received Army contracts to make the V-1710, and the relationship to Lindbergh's visit, is unclear. Whitney wrote the first contract was in the "spring of 1939", but he documents this contract was small (less than 1,000 engines), the terms were poorly written and confusing, and thus the large expansion of capacity involved a significant financial risk. (Whitney, 1998, pp.95-6, 108-9) Allison's major contract with the War Department, which would make it the premier fighter engine manufacturer, was in July 1941. (Pfeiffer, 2018) Absent Lindbergh's advocacy, insufficient capacity in 1941 would have caused delays fulfilling this contract.

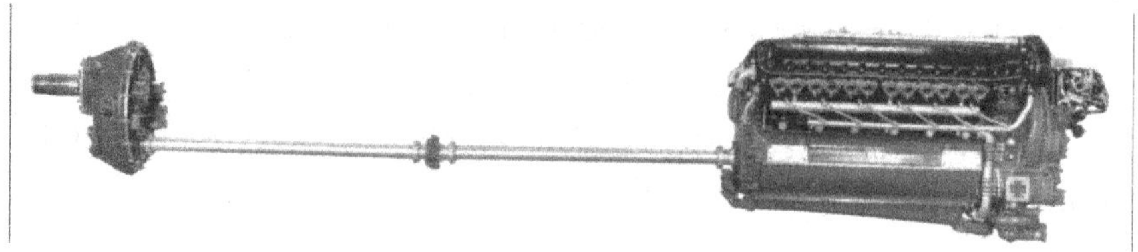

Figure 2: The Allison V-1710-E attached to the driveshaft (extension shaft) which attaches to the propellor mounting. Notice because the driveshaft could connect to the propellor, the engine did not need to be placed directly behind it.

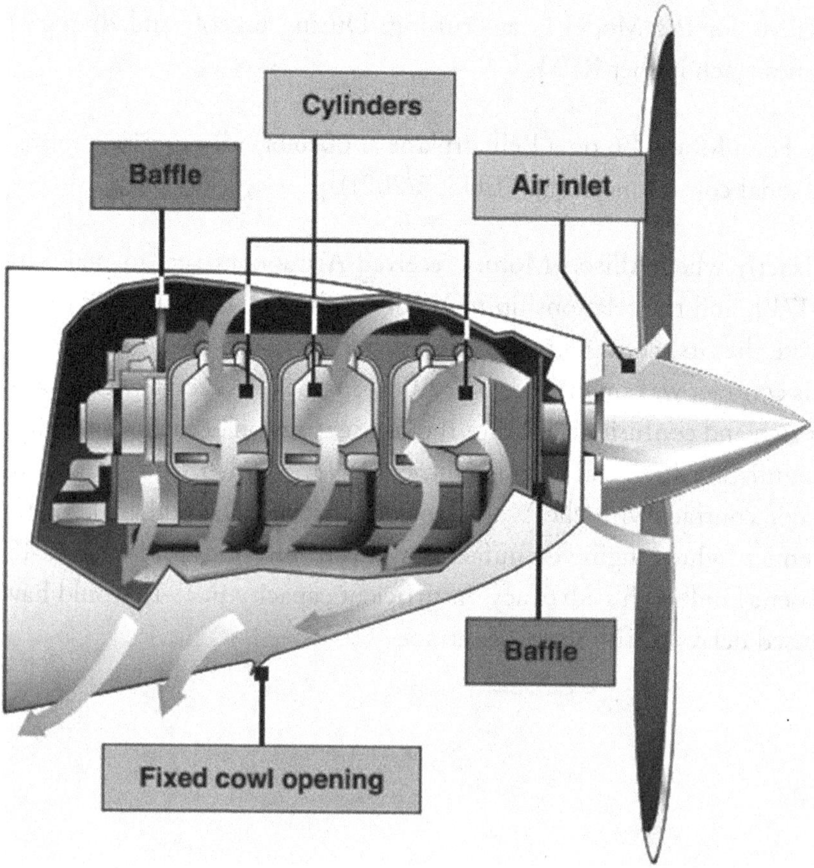

Figure 3: An air-cooled engine is placed behind the propeller in order for the air to have access to cool the engine.

Works Cited

456th Fighter Squadron. (n.d.). Retrieved from Allison V-1710: https://www.456fis.org/ALLISSON_V-1710.htm or http://www.aviation-history.com/engines/allison.htm

Allison V-1710-33. (n.d.). Retrieved from National Air and Space Museum: https://airandspace.si.edu/collection-objects/allison-v-1710-33-v-1710-c15-v-12-engine/nasm_A19420027000

Berg, A. S. (1998). *Lindbergh.* New York: Berkeley Biography.

Cole, W. (1974). *Charles Lindbergh and the Battle Against U.S. Intervention in World War II.* New York: Jovanovich.

Culy, D. (2016, September 28). The Aircraft Engines of World War II. *Defense Media Network.*

Curtiss V-1570. (n.d.). Retrieved from https://en....org/wiki/Curtiss_V-1570

(1964). *Curtiss-Wright Aircraft Engine Shipments, 1920-1964.*

Dwyer, L. (2013, October). *Allison V-1710.* Retrieved from Aviation History: http://www.aviation-history.com/engines/allison.htm

Grant, R. (2017). *Flight, The Complete History of Aviation.* New York: Penguin House.

Hessen, R. (1984). *Berlin Alert: The Memoirs and Reports of Truman Smith.* Stanford, CA: Hoover Institute Press.

Italian Fighter Planes of World War II. (n.d.). Retrieved from Military WWII: https://aerocorner.com/blog/italian-fighter-planes-of-ww2/

Junkers Jumo-211. (n.d.). Retrieved from https://en....org/wiki/Junkers_Jumo_211

Klein, M. (2013). *A Call to Arms.* New York: Bloomsbury Press.

Levin Center. (n.d.). Retrieved from Harry Truman and Invetigation of Waste, Fraud, and Abuse in World War II: https://www.levin-center.org/harry-truman-and-the-investigation-of-waste-fraud-abuse-in-world-war-ii/

Lindbergh, C. A. (1970). *The Wartime Journals of Charles A. Lindbergh.* New York: Harcourt, Brace, and Jovanovich.

Lindbergh, C. (May 1939). Military Aviation. *Congressional Hearings.* Washington DC.

Lockheed P38 Lightning. (n.d.). Retrieved from https://en....org/wiki/Lockheed_P-38_Lightning

Merlin Rolls-Royce. (n.d.). Retrieved from https://en....org/wiki/Rolls-Royce_Merlin

MNHS. (n.d.). Retrieved from https://www.mnhs.org/lindbergh/learn/other-occupations/scientist

Pfeiffer, C. (2018, May). *Liquid-Cooled Engines.* Retrieved from Indiana Historical Bureau: https://blog.history.in.gov/tag/liquid-cooled-engine/

Self-sealing fuel tanks. (n.d.). Retrieved from https://en....org/wiki/Self-sealing_fuel_tank

Whitney, D. (1998). *Vee's for Victory, the story of the Allison V-1710.* Pennsylvania: Schiffer Publishing.

Wright Aeronautical Engines. (n.d.). Retrieved from Aviation History: http://www.aviation-history.com/engines/wr-1937.htm

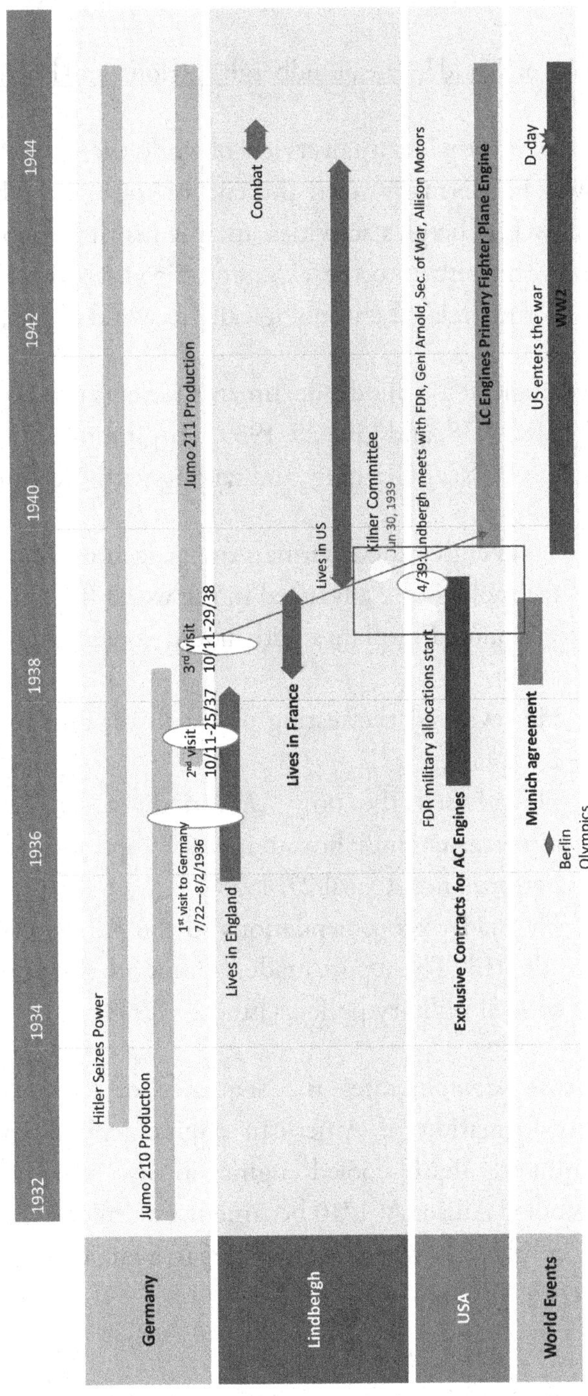
Timeline 1: Development of American Liquid Cooled Engines 1935 to 1945
Lindbergh's Interactions with German and American Engine Manufacturers and the Subsequent Predominance of LC Aircraft Engines vs. Air Cooled (AC) Engines
1932
1934
1936
1938
1940
1942
1944
Germany
Hitler Seizes Power
Jumo 210 Production
Jumo 211 Production
1st visit to Germany 7/22—8/2/1936
2nd visit 10/11-25/37
3rd visit 10/11-29/38
Lindbergh
Lives in England
Lives in France
Lives in US
Combat
Kilner Committee
Jun 30, 1939
USA
4/39: Lindbergh meets with FDR, Genl Arnold, Sec. of War, Allison Motors
FDR military allocations start
Exclusive Contracts for AC Engines
LC Engines Primary Fighter Plane Engine
World Events
Berlin Olympics
Munich agreement
US enters the war
WW2
D-day

AC: Air cooled engines, LC: Liquid-Cooled Engines

Timeline of World Events, Lindbergh's actions, and Engine Development:

The timeline provides an overview of world events from Hitler's seizure of power in Germany until the end of the war. The parallel lanes show how Lindbergh's activities; mainly his three public visits to Nazi Germany, his return to the U.S., and his visits with the U.S. military infrastructure, related chronologically to world events.

The rectangle in the middle documents 5 events that took place between October 18, 1938, and June 29, 1939 -- beginning with Lindbergh's last public visit to Nazi Germany and ending with the Kilner Report:

1) Lindbergh toured German engine factories which were the most technologically advanced in the world (October 18, 1938),
2) He piloted airplanes with liquid-cooled engines (October 19, 1939),
3) He reviewed the testing protocols for airplane engines (April 23, 1939),
4) He advised the only U.S. manufacturer of liquid-cooled airplanes engines: how to increase capacity and improve engine performance. (April 27, 1939),
5) He made recommendations to the Kilner Board which were adopted. The report made promotion of liquid-cooled engines official military policy. (June 29, 1939)

The arrow demonstrates the sequence of events concludes with the transformation of American engine technology to producing predominantly liquid-cooled engines for use in combat aircraft. The liquid-cooled Allison V-1710 became the premier U.S. fighter airplane engine in July 1941 when the War Department awarded a $240 million contract to Allison Motors.

9. Munich, 9/29-30/1938

Lindbergh's role in the Munich Agreement

For 80 years Lindbergh has been labeled a "Nazi-sympathizer". This chapter reviews a narrative which has been used to support this allegation: He spouted Nazi propaganda and was therefore instrumental in the decision of England and France not to come to Czechoslovakia's defense in September 1938. This allowed Germany to seize a part of Czechoslovakia called the Sudetenland in a negotiated settlement known as the Munich Agreement. The truth is complicated, but Lindbergh played a minor role in this historic event.

The reader should notice Lindbergh's assessment of German, British, and French air force capabilities; rather than being propaganda, mostly corresponded with estimates by German, French, and English Generals as well as U.S. intelligence estimates after the war.

On September 8, 1938, Hitler demanded Czechoslovakia cede the Sudetenland to Germany. Hitler threatened England and France with war if this territory was not ceded to Germany. The Sudetenland was a part of Czechoslovakia which had many German-speaking inhabitants. The German press had been manufacturing stories of atrocities committed against German-speaking Czech citizens by the authorities as a pretense for demanding the territory. The Munich Conference at the end of September 1938 was a negotiating session between France, England, and Germany to find a resolution to this crisis.

Czechoslovakia was not invited to the Munich Conference. England and France did not cede Czech territory to Germany without Czechoslovakia's consent. England and France made an agreement with Germany they would not come to Czechoslovakia's defense in exchange for a promise this would be Hitler's last territorial demand, i.e. there would be peace. Czechoslovakia was under no obligation not to defend herself; indeed, Czechoslovakia had been preparing for a decade for just such an attack. (Taylor, 2019) The Sudetenland was mountainous and defendable, once ceded the country was undefendable. Stalin promised to come to Czechoslovakia's aid if they chose to fight. Czechoslovakia's democratically elected government decided to cede territory to Germany. (Lyman, 2018)

-Lindbergh's advice to the English and French in 1938 (Cole, 1974, pp.52-56) (Lindbergh, 1970)

a) *England and France were unprepared for war. (Lindbergh privately noted France was hopelessly unprepared and doubted it would ever be in position to fight Germany)*
b) *If Germany's territorial ambitions were to the east, concessions should be made to Hitler to buy time, and hopefully any ensuing conflict would be isolated to a conflict between Russia and Germany.*
c) *In the interim, more and better planes should be built, and more pilots trained.*
d) *Neither England nor France had the ability to fight an air war over Eastern Europe. Both countries lacked planes, pilots, and bases. If a war needed to be fought, Lindbergh counseled England and France that they should fight to defend their homeland.*

Although modified, this position is very similar to his isolationist position in the U.S. two years later. This type of isolationism was unique for its emphasis on military preparation.

Much criticism has been leveled against Lindbergh, because in retrospect the agreement was a disaster. Germany seized the rest of Czechoslovakia in March 1939, and more territorial demands led to World War II starting on September 1, 1939.

History turned out as it did. But the criticism exaggerates Lindbergh's importance, ignores much of what he said was correct, and doesn't acknowledge the Germans conquered Europe faster and the war was worse than Lindbergh predicted, or anyone imagined.

First, Lindbergh's critics inflate his importance. It is true as wealthy famous people the Lindberghs socialized with important people with whom he had conversations about current events, but there's no evidence Lindbergh influenced England or France to accept a deal they would not have otherwise accepted. (Cole, 1974)

Between Hilter's demand and the Munich Agreement, Lindbergh met with only low-level English and French officials. He had dinner with the French Minister of the Air, Guy La Chambre, and spoke to intelligence officials at the Royal Air Ministry. (Lindbergh, 1970, p.70) Lindbergh is blamed for decisions made by leaders of democratic countries he didn't meet. Those decisions had been made before Hitler even made his demand, let alone Lindbergh became involved. (Bouverie, 2019)

Second, Lindbergh's assessment was mostly correct. The *Luftwaffe* was stronger than even Lindbergh estimated. In World War I, Germany's military spent 4 years and lost 2 million soldiers in grueling vicious seemingly endless combat and failed to capture Paris. In June 1940, Germany's air force captured Paris in 6 weeks. The French army had been so devastated by the *Luftwaffe,* it capitulated before the German army reached Paris. England tried to defend Western Europe and was humiliated. Defending territory much closer than Czechoslovakia, with bases and amenable infrastructure, England lost half its air force, half its pilots, and nearly all its tanks, personnel carriers, and heavy machine guns. (Klein, 2013) At the same time the *Luftwaffe* humiliated and destroyed the Royal Air Force (RAF), which Lindbergh's critics claim would have defeated Germany in a battle fought for Czechoslovakia, it also conquered 4 other countries.

England and France could not have defended Czechoslovakia in 1938. Given two years to prepare, England would defeat the *Luftwaffe* in the Battle of Britain *because it fought over its own territory.* (Dalleck, 2017)

Lindbergh recommended an agreement with Hitler for the same reason most Englishmen did, England was not prepared for war. (Cole, 1974) Lindbergh knew this better than anyone. (Berg, 1998) (Lindbergh, 1970) Furthermore, the 18-month gap between the Munich agreement and the Battle of Britain, enabled the English to build airplanes which (the Spitfire and the Hurricane Hawker) had high powered V12 liquid-cooled engines. (Lindbergh, 1970, p.23) (Rolls-Royce Merlin, n.d.)

The argument against Lindbergh

The charges against Lindbergh have been repeated every few decades, with many questions still unanswered. Lindbergh is accused of being either responsible for or instrumental in the Munich decision. His critics charge either he was a naïve fool or a willing tool of the German propaganda machine. The Germans fooled him into reporting what they wanted him to report, and this was that the German air force was formidable. Lindbergh then convinced the democratically elected prime ministers of England and France to concede to Hitler, which they would not have done otherwise. But in reality, Germany had a very weak air force. This narrative does not accuse Lindbergh of influencing the independent decision of the government of Czechoslovakia to surrender.

Chronology of Events: (**Bold** text indicates Lindbergh interaction, a section below reviews these events) Notice the important meetings and decisions took place nearly entirely before Lindbergh's involvement and Lindbergh's involvement was with officials with little political power.

a. August 30, 1938: Hitler had not made his demand and Lindbergh was in Russia. The British Foreign Minister, Lord Halifax, held a cabinet meeting in which he said, "Czechoslovakia cannot be defended." (Bouverie, 2019) This meeting was supposed to be secret.
b. September 1, 1938: The British newspapers published Halifax' comments. (Bouverie, 2019) Lindbergh was in Czechoslovakia

and he had not met any member of the English nor French government regarding a controversy which had not happened yet.

c. September 8, 1938: Hitler demands the Sudetenland.
d. **First Lindbergh interaction** — September 9, 1938: Lindbergh had an informal dinner conversation with a low-level official in the French Air Force, Guy La Chambre.
e. September 14, 1938: British Prime Minister Neville Chamberlain had a meeting with U.S. Ambassador to England, Joseph Kennedy. The next day, Chamberlain agreed in principle to cede the Sudetenland to Germany.
f. September 21-22, 1938: Hitler met Chamberlain and Deladier. The details of how Germany would annex the Sudetenland were discussed.
g. **Second Lindbergh interaction** — September 21, 1938: Lindbergh met with U.S. Ambassador Joseph Kennedy in London. Kennedy asked Lindbergh to prepare an intelligence assessment for the U.S. State Department.
h. September 21, 1938: The Czech government agreed to "make territorial concessions in return for an international guarantee against unprovoked aggression". (Nasaw, 2012, p.340)
i. **The Cable** — September 22, 1938: Lindbergh's intelligence assessment is sent to U.S. Secretary of State Cordell Hull.
j. **Third Lindbergh interaction** — September 22, 1938: Lindbergh had an informal dinner conversation with John Slessor, an official with the Royal Air Ministry. Over the next week he meets with various other low-level English officials.
k. September 29-30, 1938: Munich Agreement is signed.
l. October 1, 1938: German troops enter the Sudetenland.
m. March 15, 1939: German troops occupy the rest of Czechoslovakia.
n. April 7, 1939: **Lindbergh begins his voyage back to the U.S.**
o. September 1, 1939: Germany invades Poland, World War II starts.

p. March 7, 1940: Prime Minister of France, Edouard Deladier, tells U.S. envoy Sumner Welles that he is willing to continue negotiating with Hitler. (Fullilove, 2013, p.49)

Lindbergh's Interactions with France: 1) Lindbergh met with Guy La Chambre of the French Air Ministry on September 9, 1938, 2) The French assessment of its air power, 3) Events — September 10-20, 1938.

Lindbergh never believed others' estimates of French air power. Lindbergh was concerned about capacity to build new combat aircraft and postulated the French could build 50 airplanes a month or less than one-tenth of what he believed Germany could build. He sought to explain to the French they were in a desperate position. (Lindbergh, 1970, p.87) He contended the French officials agreed with him:

> "The condition of French aviation was even more deplorable (than the English). There was not a single squadron in France equipped with modern pursuit planes, and the French government was looking forward to the time when its aircraft production would reach a total of 200 fighting planes per month." (Germany was producing 436 planes/month-source below) ("pursuit plane" is a term for a fighter plane used in World War I)
>
> "I found that aviation circles in France, at that time, freely admitted that Germany would take supremacy of the air almost as soon as a war started." (Lindbergh C., 1941)

When Lindbergh met with Guy La Chambre of the French Air Ministry informally over dinner at the American Embassy on September 9, 1938, La Chambre said France was prepared to attack Germany despite its smaller air force. Lindbergh explained the French lacked both anti-aircraft guns, and gas masks, which they would need when Germany counter-attacked. (Lindbergh, 1970, p.70)

In the 10 days between this meeting and Kennedy's summons to London, both England and France negotiated with Hitler, but Lindbergh was not involved. He was discussing medical experiments with Dr. Carrel and sailing with his wife and son. (Lindbergh, 1970, pp.70-71) On September 14, 1938, Chamberlain met with Kennedy. Chamberlain told Kennedy, Britain's air power lagged far behind Germany's (Ronald, 2021, p.172) and he did not want to go to war over the Sudetenland. (Nasaw, 2012, p.338) On September 15, 1938, Chamberlain and Hitler negotiated the *Berchtesgaden Agreement* which in principle ceded the Sudetenland to Germany.

Other French officials heard about Lindbergh's conversation with La Chambre and a British embassy official complained Lindbergh was undermining the French will to fight. (Cole, 1974, p.53) But France's decision to not defend Czechoslovakia did not come from Lindbergh. Prime Minister Edouard Deladier lived to be an old man and gave many interviews. He admitted he knew Hitler wouldn't keep his promises and after Czechoslovakia it would be France's turn to be attacked, but France's military capabilities did not permit him to fight Germany in 1938. He said, "If I had 3 or 4 thousand aircraft, Munich never would have happened". He didn't mention Lindbergh. (Edouard Deladier, n.d.) Ironically, Lindbergh's critics claim France and England had 3-4,000 aircraft. (Mosley, 1976, p.414)

Because he needed airplanes, Deladier was trying to purchase aircraft from the U.S., (Edouard Deladier, n.d.) and Lindbergh's journal confirms this, which was not public knowledge. Lindbergh notes obstruction created by the Neutrality Acts and different English and metric measurements would create problems incorporating American fighter planes into the French air force. (Lindbergh, 1970, p.81) Lindbergh's attention to detail and knowledge of secret information belies the argument he was simply a German tool. (Cole, 1974, p.54) His critics don't address his objections nor address the details with which he supported them.

Lindbergh's meeting with Ambassador Joseph Kennedy

Lindbergh flew to England to meet Kennedy on September 20, 1938. Chamberlain was on his way to meet Hitler. Chamberlain had devised a strategy before Lindbergh met Kennedy and told Kennedy six days earlier. Chamberlain had already agreed, in principle, with Hitler five days earlier.

Lindbergh did not affect Kennedy's opinion. When Kennedy asked Lindbergh to draft an assessment of German air strength compared to her opponents, Kennedy had already given his opinion to Chamberlain. (Nasaw, 2012, p.338) Kennedy told Lindbergh although the English were ready to fight, the English weren't prepared, nor knew what they were facing. (Lindbergh, 1970, pp.72-3)

Kennedy told Lindbergh because Chamberlain did not want war, he would support him. Kennedy asked Lindbergh to compose a letter which would be dire, to support Chamberlain politically. Lindbergh's tone was what was asked of him. (Nasaw, 2012, p.339) (Ronald, 2021)

Lindbergh's assessment of the strength of Germany's air force compared to England and France's air force was cabled from Kennedy to Secretary of State Cordell Hull on September 22, 1938. (Lindbergh, 1970, p.73) (Berg, 1998, p.374) It is not clear who else saw it. U.S. Military Attaché Truman Smith said the cable was circulated only in the State Department: neither the War Department nor the White House received it. (Hessen, 1984, p.157) There is no evidence it affected anyone's opinion prior to the agreement. Lindbergh spoke to English government officials *after* Chamberlain and the Czechs agreed not to defend the Sudetenland. The historical record does not state the cable was presented to Chamberlain, Deladier, nor the Czech government. (Nasaw, 2012, p.340)

The Cable: Lindbergh's cable discussed England and France's capabilities in seven sentences. Kennedy then cabled it to his boss, Secretary of State Cordell Hull. Before Hull read the cable, the Prime Ministers of

England and France had already met with Hitler and Czechoslovakia had already agreed to cede its territory.

The letter starts out with three conflicting statements. First, Lindbergh says the Germans "now" have the capacity to build 20,000 airplanes a year. Second, he says the production can't be estimated. Third, he says the most reliable estimate is German airplane construction is between 500-800 airplanes per month (6,000-9,600/year). (Hessen, 1984) Based on this, Lindbergh is accused of overestimating German air strength. For example, the historian David Nasaw wrote Lindbergh composed "the most frightening scenario imaginable". (Nasaw, 2012, p.339)

The cable contains an initial assessment of total future capacity to build airplanes which appears to have been relayed from Major Smith. When asked, he referred interested Royal Air Force (RAF) officials to Major Smith. (Fredette, 1977) Major Smith obtained information the Germans were constructing new airplane factories and calculated when these factories were fully functional, the Germans would have the capacity to build 20,000 planes a year or 1,600 planes a month. (Hessen, 1984) "Now" may indicate Lindbergh "now" suspects the capacity of German air production will be 20,000 airplanes per year. Lindbergh's journal indicates the third estimate (500-800 planes/month) was <u>his</u> current estimate based on the factories he had seen during his visit in 1937. (Lindbergh, 1970, p.70)

But other than not attributing an estimate to its source and not clarifying whether it is a future estimate, the 7 sentences are correct:

1. France's air capabilities were "pitiful", and its leadership was poor — proven correct.
2. Lindbergh estimated German and English air power. Mostly correct, see below.
3. Lindbergh said Germany could destroy London from the air. He was temporarily wrong — Germany could not destroy London in 1938, but Germany <u>did</u> destroy London in 1940.

4. Lindbergh said Germany could destroy Prague or Paris if it wished — correct.
5. He said Russia's air capacity was overestimated — correct.
6. "(Germany) has the power to destroy the great cities of Europe" and
7. "I am afraid this is the beginning of the end of England as a great power." Both 6 and 7 were correct. (Ronald, 2021, p.174-5)

Lindbergh was human and in informal conversations he was occasionally wrong. Sometimes, he said he had insufficient information. In his meeting with John Slessor, Marshal of the RAF, he said he did not have enough time nor information to make such an assessment and referred him to the military attaché's estimate. (Fredette, 1977) But at the same dinner he stressed Germany could flatten most cities in Europe which at this point it could not. (Cole, 1974, p.55) In his informal dinner with La Chambre, he estimated Germany had 7,000 airplanes which is accused of being too high (Bouverie, 2019) but it was consistent with others' estimates. The Annual Air Report of the U.S. Embassy in Berlin in July 1938 estimated the Germans had 9,900 airplanes of all types. (Hessen, 1984, p.141)

But Lindbergh was remarkably correct in <u>his</u> estimate in the cable. His personal estimate of Germany's ability to build combat aircraft in the cable was 500-800 airplanes a month. (Lindbergh, 1970, p.70) (Hessen, 1984, p.154) After the war, the U.S. Strategic Bombing Service said the Germans produced 436 combat aircraft in October 1938 and in 1939 Germany built an average of 691 aircraft a month. (Fredette, 1977) Smith's much criticized prediction in Lindbergh's cable was also accurate. The Germans built more than 20,000 new aircraft in 1943 and more than 40,000 in 1944. (GAP, n.d.)

Some evidence supports all of Lindbergh's estimates being significant <u>underestimates</u>. After the war, the papers of the German Chief of the Air Ministry, General Hanesse, stated in October 1938 the Germans had 10,600 planes and produced more than 1,000 airplanes/month. (Hessen, 1984, p.142)

Furthermore, even Lindbergh's critics admit his previous intelligence estimates in the November 1937, *Report 155420-General Estimate of German Air Strength as of 11/1/37* which was circulated among British and French officials, were accurate. (Wallace, 2003, p.181) Lindbergh did not visit Germany between November 1937 and September 1938, so he based his opinion on correct information.

The cable had minimal immediate effect, but later it would. Americans didn't want to believe Germany represented a threat to peace. (Lyman, 2018) If Lindbergh exaggerated — it's a subjective charge — America needed to face reality and because of Lindbergh they would. During the Congressional hearings in the winter of 1938-9 Lindbergh's intelligence was reviewed. As a result, the *LA Times'* headline during Congressional Hearings in January 1939 was "Europe War Near". The U.S. began to allocate resources to rearm in the spring of 1939. (Nasaw, 2012, p. 369)

Seven sentences in a cable from a U.S. Ambassador to the U.S. State Department, did not result in democratically elected leaders' decisions. Indeed, Czechoslovakia had already conceded. The cable hadn't even been written when they met with Hitler. The future would prove the cable correct and perhaps an underestimate.

<u>Lindbergh's interactions with England:</u> 1) Britain's assessment of its air power, 2) Meeting with John Slessor, Royal Air Force, September 22, 1938, 3) Meetings with other English officials.

Lindbergh made the following assessment of England's air force capabilities:

> "At the moment of Munich, the Royal Air Force had only a few squadrons of modern fighters and bombers. The majority of their planes were obsolete. All of them together totaled a fraction of the German air force." (Lindbergh C., 1941)

Lindbergh met Slessor and Sir Cyril Newall, Britain's Chief of the Air Staff over dinner on September 22, 1938. Before dinner he heard press reports negotiations between Germany and England had broken down and his tone is one of disappointment. (Lindbergh, 1970, p.74) Slessor wrote he took Lindbergh's estimates with "a pinch of salt. But there was much truth in his story." (Cole, 1974, p.55) Slessor didn't need Lindbergh's warnings, because he had said "(no) British government could have brought itself to take the country into war in our then shocking state of unpreparedness in the air." (Fredette, 1977)

Lindbergh also met with others in the British Air Ministry and Air Intelligence prior to the signing of the Munich Agreement the next week. Lindbergh advised them, "to avoid war at any cost" (Cole, 1974, p.54) but it would appear they already chose this course of events. Lindbergh's contacts with the English government were low-level meetings which took place after Chamberlain had already conceded to Hitler (September 15th and 21st, 1938). (Lindbergh, 1970, pp.72-78)

Lindbergh's assessment was identical to recommendations of the British generals who were advising Chamberlain while Lindbergh was composing his cable. Lord William Douglas, the Marshall of the Royal Air Force, pled with Chamberlain at Munich to give the British another year to prepare for war. His letters and memoirs say England had only 100 fighter airplanes while Germany had 1,200 long range bombers. Lord Ironside, a senior general accompanying Chamberlain when he met Hitler (before Lindbergh met RAF officials) wrote in his journal, "We cannot expose ourselves now to a German attack. We simply commit suicide if we do...Chamberlain knows this. He dare not say it to the people." (Fredette, 1977)

British Prime Minister Neville Chamberlain died in August 1940. He left behind letters which have been published as "diaries", but they are incomplete and give conflicting accounts of his motivations. (Dutton, 2000) The generals who accompanied him on the trip are clearer. These records are consistent; they advised Chamberlain before Lindbergh met with RAF officials, they recognized England was unprepared for war, and they neither met nor mentioned Lindbergh.

A myth was created that the Germans moved airplanes around at night to fool Lindbergh into thinking they had more airplanes. It's apocryphal. (Berg, 1998, p.378) When asked for a source for this story, British historian Mosley said it's "very well known". (Fredette, 1977) Lindbergh himself mocked this accusation. (Radio Address, 8/8/40) In any event, it is irrelevant because Lindbergh's assessments of German, British, and French air power don't emphasize static number of airplanes. He based his assessments on the technologic capabilities of each aircraft model, air defenses, the number and quality of pilots, and most important, the capacity to build state-of-the-art airplanes. (Lindbergh C., 1941)

Future Events

Deladier's statement to Welles that he was still seeking an agreement with Germany in 1940, when Lindbergh had been in the U.S. for nearly a year, demonstrated the French desire for an agreement with Hitler was independent of Lindbergh's involvement.

The Accusation

> *Lindbergh gave a letter to Joseph Kennedy, the U.S. ambassador to England, on September 22, 1938. Kennedy, otherwise having no opinion, was scared by Lindbergh's letter and convinced Chamberlain. The German air force didn't exist in September 1938, but by acquiring factories and other assets in Czechoslovakia it became powerful in less than a year.* (Wallace, 2003)

The author agrees Lindbergh can be blamed in a general sense because he had influence on public and some government officials' opinions. But the stakeholders: Lindbergh, the U.S. (Joseph Kennedy), Britain (Chamberlain), the Czech government, and France (Deladier) came to similar conclusions independent of each other because it was the only realistic conclusion: They were incapable of fighting a war against Germany, especially in eastern Europe where they had no bases. The accusation isn't chronologically possible, nor does it address the details of each country's air power.

No one can be sure exactly how many airplanes Germany had, nor is it critical. Lindbergh's critics cite statistics claiming England and France had 4,000 airplanes and Germany only had 3,100. They ignore others' estimates as well as the quality of the airplanes, air defenses, logistics, and pilot training. For support, they recite diaries of German officers and Nuremberg testimony which claim Germany was in political turmoil in 1938 and had it not been able to seize Czechoslovakia, Hitler's government would have collapsed. (Mosley, 1976, p.414) This is valid but hardly definitive. People's recollections are not truth. Because no one was aware of it, they could not have negotiated based on it.

Questions posed by Lindbergh's defenders since the 1940s remain unanswered. For example, how did leaders who were responsible for the safety of their nation have a malleable opinion regarding the single greatest threat to their constituents, they let Lindbergh tell them what to do? How did a private citizen's opinion to whom the leaders did not speak, supersede the opinion of all the intelligence experts to whom these two Prime Ministers had access? And instead of people's recollections decades later, why not refer to what the experts who advised Chamberlain and Daladier said at the time? Was there any Allied general who said in 1938 that England and France could contend with the German air force?

This author believes the most important questions were: How were England and France going to defend Czechoslovakia? And if they really had 4,000 airplanes what were their capabilities? Lindbergh emphasized nearly all English and French planes were obsolete and explained in detail why he didn't believe England and France could defend themselves, let alone Czechoslovakia. He provided his understanding of the strength of the French and British air forces and even if there were airplanes of which he was unaware, the number of airplanes in British hangars doesn't translate into an effective defense of Czechoslovakia. They may have been obsolete and there were no bases from which to use them.

A base is not just a landing strip. It requires fuel, mechanics, and parts. Lindbergh had been to Czechoslovakia at the beginning of September 1938. He had seen their air force. Not only was it obsolete, but they were using old Russian airplanes. Their bases could not be used by western airplanes — parts wouldn't fit, and the mechanics couldn't repair the planes. (Lindbergh, 1970, pp.67-8)

Historians can challenge conventional wisdom, but the argument that Britain and France could defend Czechoslovakia in 1938 needs to be explained with specific explanations and descriptions of strategy. People's memories don't meet this standard. They also need to document which historic figures read Lindbergh's cable. If Smith was correct, and only officials at the U.S. State Department saw it, it had no effect on negotiations between English, French, and German officials.

If England and France were prepared to defeat Hitler in September 1938, it was not Lindbergh that convinced them otherwise. The opinions of British generals were consistent with Lindbergh's assessment, no one at the time believed England and France could fight a war against Germany.

Can Lindbergh be blamed for Munich? The historical record does not support blaming Lindbergh. Stakeholders came to the same conclusions simultaneously, independent of each other, before Lindbergh was consulted. The British military was unprepared and desperately needed time to build an air force. Lindbergh did not meet nor advise either prime minister. He did not convince them of something their own advisors weren't telling them.

Lindbergh's critics cite different statistics which uniformly report superficial numbers of airplanes without addressing technical issues nor Lindbergh's other concerns. These authors proceed with their arguments as though these are the right numbers, but no reason is given why these estimates are better than others' estimates.[1] (Mosely, 1976, pp.225-230,414) Furthermore, Lindbergh's intelligence report of November 1, 1937 reported the *Luftwaffe* had between 147 and 225 fully equipped squadrons, i.e. modern airplanes, pilots, support personnel, and airplanes in reserve. (Hessen, 1984, p.117) If Lindbergh's reports were "spoon-fed lies", then someone – Allied intelligence, U.S. Congress, or the War Department – would have questioned his report at the time. (Wallace, 2003) No one did.[2] Although Lindbergh had detractors in 1938, criticism he passed along German misinformation came later and was largely inspired by his politics and hindsight that the Munich Agreement was a disaster.

Munich had a benefit. As Lindbergh predicted, France could not improve her forces (Lindbergh, 1970, p.81) but the extra year Munich provided benefited England. All the combatants, including Hitler and Roosevelt, knew England needed time. In the fall of 1937, Hitler said he would discuss peace for a limited time because delay allowed England and France to reduce the armament gap Germany currently maintained. (Bouverie, 2019, p.143) President Roosevelt sent Welles on the peace initiative prior to the 1940 election with the expressed motivation that the longer the onset of a war was delayed in western Europe, the better prepared the Allies would be to defend themselves. (Dalleck, 2017, p.366)

In the Battle of Britain (summer and fall 1940), England would defeat Germany but would lose roughly 1,200 airplanes and 544 pilots. Germany lost roughly 1,600 airplanes, but most importantly over 4,000 trained Airmen (pilots, navigators) of which roughly 2,500 were killed. Unsustainable pilot attrition convinced Hitler to turn his aggression elsewhere. (BOB, n.d.) Germany could replace airplanes, but it couldn't train effective pilots quickly and the combat experience of the German Airmen shot down over England was irreplaceable.

This proves two of Lindbergh's arguments were correct. First, England's pilot attrition was much lower because it fought over its own territory.

English Airmen who safely ejected returned to the fight; equivalent German Airmen spent the war in P.O.W. camps. Second, as Lindbergh emphasized in his intelligence reports, German pilot training had serious deficiencies. (see pp.104-5) Lindbergh would brief General Arnold, Chief of the U.S. Army Air Corps, on pilot training and devise pilot training programs when he returned to the U.S. the following April. (Berg, 1998, pp.387-8) (see pp.315-6)

Conclusion: Munich was a disaster that continues to shape foreign affairs.

The legacy of Munich continues to guide world events. Three Israeli Prime Ministers — Ariel Sharon in 2001, Benjamin Natanyahu in 2015, and Naftali Bennett in 2021, all said Israel won't be Czechoslovakia. In 2022, Ukraine's Prime Minister accused former U.S. Secretary of State Henry Kissinger of living in 1938 when he suggested Ukraine cede land to Russia.

Two disastrous foreign policy decisions, the 1956 British intervention in the Sinai and U.S. escalation in Vietnam in 1965, were influenced by the legacy of what happened at Munich in 1938. Both U.K. Prime Minister Anthony Eden's decision to send his military to retake the Suez Canal (von Tunzelman, 2016) and President Lyndon Johnson's decision to send two additional Marine regiments to Vietnam were based on the stated fear of presiding over another Munich. (Darman, 2014, p.243)

Advocating for the Munich Agreement means being judged harshly by history. When Chamberlain returned from Munich on September 22, 1938, Winston Churchill told him, "You had a choice between dishonor and war, and you chose dishonor. And you will get war." Whether Lindbergh dishonored himself is the reader's judgment, but he deserved criticism. He influenced European opinion, and some estimates of German air capabilities were exaggerated. (Bouverie, 2019) (Cole, 1974, p.55) Lindbergh deserved to be criticized for his role in this disaster, but his role was minor, and he had little influence over events. Historian

Tim Bouverie wrote a 500-page book on the Munich negotiations, and it has only two references to Lindbergh. (Bouverie, 2019)

Because Munich was a disaster there is an impulse to say it was preventable, but this argument is selective and hindsight. Selective hindsight quotes from doubters in the German army make the reader ponder if Britain pledged to defend Czechoslovakia perhaps Hitler would have backed down. But, these officials had a reason to embellish Munich's legacy; it minimized their own complicity. Allied promises to aid Czechoslovakia would have been empty promises. This too would have had repercussions, because no country would have had any faith in future Allied promises of support.

England and France came to same conclusion as Lindbergh because air power is not the number of airplanes. Lindbergh's and Prime Minister Deladier's assessment of the French air force capabilities were the same and independent of each other. Lindbergh's assessment of English air power concurred with Lords Douglas and Ironside. (Fredette, 1977) Lindbergh stated France couldn't defend itself in the air regardless of how many airplanes it claimed it had. (10/1/38) (Lindbergh, 1970) Lindbergh was right. The Italian Air Force had more airplanes in 1938 than England and France combined, but Italy couldn't defend itself when the Allies invaded in 1943.

Lindbergh defined air power as the capacity to make state-of-the-art airplanes, each plane's tactical effectiveness, number and quality of pilots, and the status of air defenses. (Lindbergh, 1970, pp.70,80-81) When the accounts of Lindbergh's meetings with English and French officials are reviewed, the author is struck by the detail with which Lindbergh discussed air power and the lack of detail in his critics' arguments. Lindbergh's assessment of combatants' air power was accurate.

Furthermore, how was Germany able to vanquish her enemies in June 1940? Because it had established a military infrastructure that was unmatched in history. Lindbergh warned the Allies of this infrastructure, and he was entirely correct. His critics are obligated to acknowledge it.

Lindbergh's critics then argue that while it's true this capacity existed when Germany invaded Poland in September 1939 it did not exist in October 1938. (Wallace, 2003, p.180) This was the time to confront Germany, "when she was weak". Although Hitler occupied the Sudetenland in October 1938, he did not occupy the industrial part of Czechoslovakia until March 1939.

First, incompatible infrastructure can't be adapted and incorporated into an air force in 6 months. (Klein, 2013) Second, the *Luftwaffe* had demonstrated its prowess in Spain in 1937. Third, it's hindsight. Calling 1938 Germany "weak" is a comparison between her military in 1938 and 1940. The comparison the negotiators dealt with was between Germany and England in 1938, and every contemporary expert agreed: neither England nor France was prepared to fight a war in eastern Europe in October 1938, indeed they were unprepared to fight a war in western Europe in 1940. Credit that the U.S. had the capacity to arm England to wage war to *defend itself* in 1940-41 is partly due Lindbergh.

Lindbergh's assessment of German air power was the same as those people whose job it was to determine air power *at the time.* People agreed because they believed in the same definition of air power. It's the reader's decision whose opinion was proven correct by history.

Lindbergh's critics' arguments are summarized below. Compare them to the author's:

1) Germany was militarily weak even though it had laid waste to Spain. It then deluded Lindbergh, who had seen more of its military than any non-German, into thinking it was strong. Despite its underlying weakness it conquered Europe faster and more decisively than anyone imagined was possible.

2) England and France were militarily prepared to fight Germany despite having said publicly they weren't on August 31, 1938, when Lindbergh was in the Soviet Union. Then a few weeks later, once again

they were ready to fight Germany, but were convinced otherwise by a private American citizen with whom their leaders hadn't had any contact. It was Lindbergh alone who convinced them, even though all their generals and the Prime Minister of France said at the time they couldn't fight Germany. A year later, Lindbergh was in the U.S., but France was still trying to negotiate with Germany.

OR:

3) Germany started rebuilding its military in 1933 by devoting an enormous percentage of its GDP and brutally squashing dissent. Partly because England and France were democracies, they were paralyzed by pacifism, political gridlock, and an economic depression. As a result, in 1938, Germany was much stronger. When they demanded land, England and France conceded because they could not fight any war, certainly not a war in eastern Europe. A few years later, their armies were humiliated; but with an extra two years to prepare, U.S. help, and fighting over its own territory, England avoided being conquered. The combined might of the U.S., the entire British Empire, and the Soviet Union, combined with enormous resources, tens of millions of lives, and four years, finally defeated Germany. A few conversations Lindbergh had in 1938 with low-level officials, and a cable seen only by U.S. officials, had no bearing on these events.

Arguments 1 and 2 make no sense. Being human, Lindbergh was wrong on occasion but only in conversations. His formal intelligence assessments were neither excessively dire nor exaggerated, they were mostly correct. And as the war demonstrated underestimations.

Lindbergh's Munich legacy is muddled, and he deserves to be blamed for what he got wrong and any impact he had on public opinion. But he was a minor figure in this debacle. The responsibility for this blunder lies solely with the British, the French, the Czechs, and their democratically elected leaders.

[1]Mosley asserts the Luftwaffe had 3,300 airplanes in an unspecified month in 1938, and in May 1940, 4,665 airplanes, producing 150 airplanes a month. (Mosley, 1976, pp.225,414) Even if accurately cited, these statistics aren't credible, because Germany would have lost a third of its air force in the Battle of Britain (with nearly no ability to replace losses). It couldn't have controlled millions of square miles, from Scandinavia to North Africa, with an air force the size of America's in 1934. In 1941-2, Germany couldn't have forced the Red Army to retreat 300 miles in 10 days and then engaged them on a 1,800 mile front, repelled an invasion at Dieppe, and simultaneously conquered the Balkans and North Africa given Mosley's statistics. The Luftwaffe's performance was consistent with Lindbergh's estimates.

[2]One of the early biographies of Lindbergh reviewed the uniform acceptance of the *General Estimate* by military intelligence. There was only some political skepticism regarding Germany's imputed intentions. (Ross, 1964, p.276)

Works Cited

Berg, A. S. (1998). *Lindbergh.* New York: Berkley Biographer.

BOB. (n.d.). https://en....org/wiki/ Battle of Britain

Bouverie, T. (2019). Appeasement. New York: Random House.

Cole, W. (1974). *Charles Lindbergh and the Battle Against U.S. intervention in World War II.* New York .

Dalleck, R. (2017). *Franklin Roosevelt.* New York: Penguin.

Darman, J. (2014). *Landslide: LBJ and the Dawn of a New America.* New York: Random House.

Dutton, D. J. (2000). *The Neville Chamberlain Diary Letters.* Retrieved from https://reviews.history.ac.uk/review/256

Edouard Deladier. (n.d.). Retrieved from Jewish Virtual Library: https://www.jewishvirtuallibrary.org/edouard-daladier

Fredette, R. (April 1977). Lindbergh and Munich: A Myth Revived. *Journal of the Missouri Historical Society*, 197-202.

Fullilove, M. (2013). *Rendezvous With Destiny.* New York: Penguin Publishing.

GAP. (n.d.). *German Aircraft Production.* Retrieved from https://en....org/wiki/German_aircraft_production_during_World_War_II

Hessen, R. (1984). *Berlin Alert, The Memoirs of Truman Smith.* Stanford, CA: Hoover Institute Press.

Klein, M. (2013). *A Call to Arms.* New York: Bloomsbury Press.

Lindbergh, C. (1941, March 29). A Letter to Americans. *Colliers Magazine.*

Lindbergh, C. A. (1970). *The Wartime Diaries of Charles A. Lindbergh.* New York: Harcourt Brace Jovanovich.

Lyman, R. (2018). *Under A Darkening Sky.* New York: Penguin Books, Ltd.

Mosley, L, Lindbergh: *A Biography*, Doubleday, 1976.

Nasaw, D. (2012). In *The Patriarch* (pp. 338-339). New York: Penguin Press.

Ronald, S. (2021). *The Ambassador.* New York: St. Martin's Press.

Ross, W, *The Last Hero: Charles A. Lindbergh*, Harper and Row, NY, 1964.

Taylor, F. (2019). 1939. New York: MacMillan.

von Tunzelman, A. (2016). *Blood and Sand.* New York: Harper Collins.

Wallace, M. (2003). *The American Axis.* New York: St. Martin's Press.

Photographs

Photo 1: Charles and Anne Morrow Lindbergh, September 1929 a few months after their wedding. (public domain)

Photo 2: Charles Lindbergh at Wright Field (today Wright Patterson Air Base). The Air Corps Officer in the center is unidentified. The man in the straw hat is Orville Wright. (public domain)

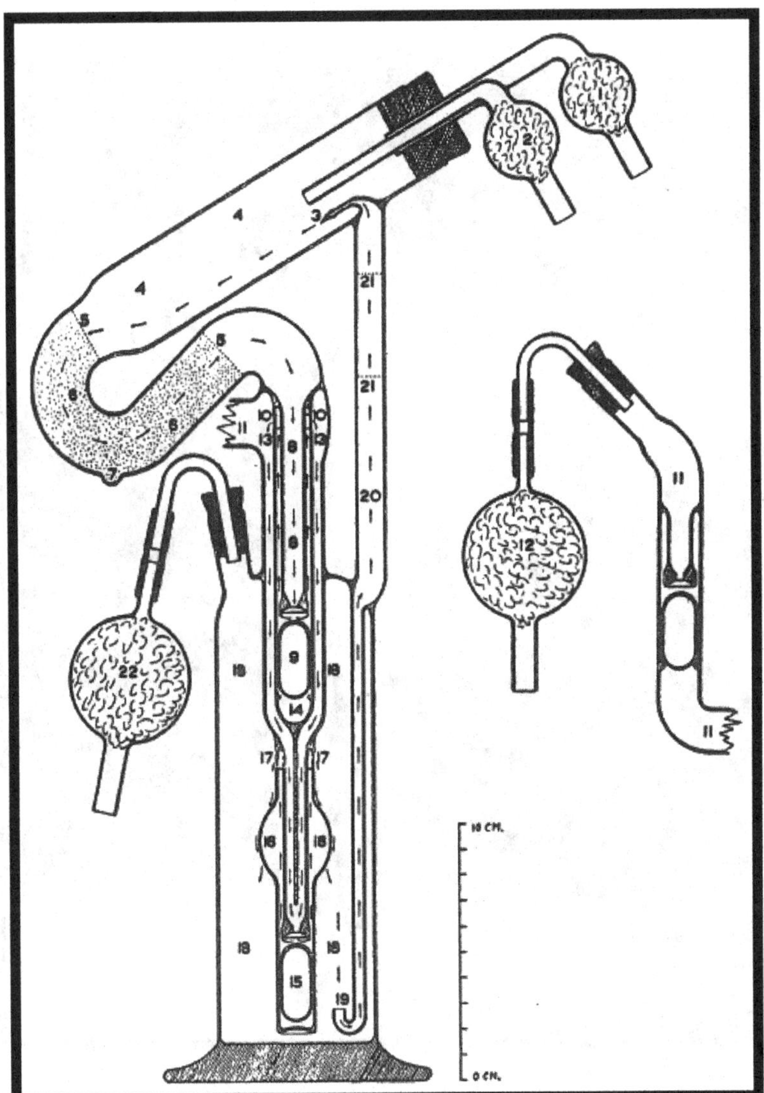

Photo 3: The first cardiac perfusion pump to ever successfully perfuse a human organ outside of a human body. Co-invented by Dr. Alexis Carrel and Charles Lindbergh in the 1930s. This pump kept a human heart beating, a pancreas secreting insulin, and a fallopian tube rhythmically contracting. This was publicly displayed at the Congress of Experimental Cytology in 1937. (permission to use diagram provided by C.C. Thomas Publishers)

Photo 4: Charles Lindbergh leaving a Bronx Courthouse in 1934 after testifying against Bruno Hauptmann in the kidnapping and murder of his son, Charles Lindbergh, Jr. in 1932. He is standing next to Herbert Schwarzkopf, the Superintendent of the New Jersey State Police (wearing the bowtie). That year Schwarzkopf would have a son, Norman; who would later command the U.S. forces in the First Gulf War. (public domain)

Photo 5: Charles Lindbergh standing next to Robert Goddard (middle), the father of American rocketry. Behind them is the base of a rocket. The man in the suit is Harry Guggenheim, Charles Lindbergh's best friend, who was Jewish. (public domain)

Photo 6: A Movietone News reel showing Charles Lindbergh carrying his son Jon off a ship in England on December 31, 1935. The Lindberghs moved to England in 1935 to avoid press hysteria surrounding the pending execution of their son's kidnapper and murderer in April 1936.

Photo 7: A Junkers-88 dropping bombs over England in 1940. Lindbergh was the first non-German to examine this airplane in 1938. He gave a detailed description of it to Allied intelligence, a sample of which is provided in Chapter 7. (public domain)

Photo 8: The Allison V-1710 aircraft engine. This liquid-cooled engine powered the majority of our fighter aircraft in World War II. Lindbergh took a personal interest in the Allison Engine Corporation and this particular engine when he returned to the U.S. in April 1939. He made the promotion of it the official policy of the U.S. Army Air Corps when he sat on the Kilner Board in June 1939. (Personal photograph)

Photo 9: Charles Lindbergh leaving the White House on April 20, 1939, after his only visit with President Roosevelt. About this visit Lindbergh wrote, "Roosevelt judges his man quickly and plays him cleverly." After this visit, Roosevelt allocated funds to significantly increase the number of airplanes in the U.S. arsenal. (Lindbergh, 1970, p.187) (public domain)

Photo 10: Charles Lindbergh testifying in front of Congress, circa 1940. (Public domain)

Photo 11: Charles Lindbergh speaking to advocate the U.S. not enter World War II. Ft. Wayne, Indiana, October 3, 1941 (Library of Congress)

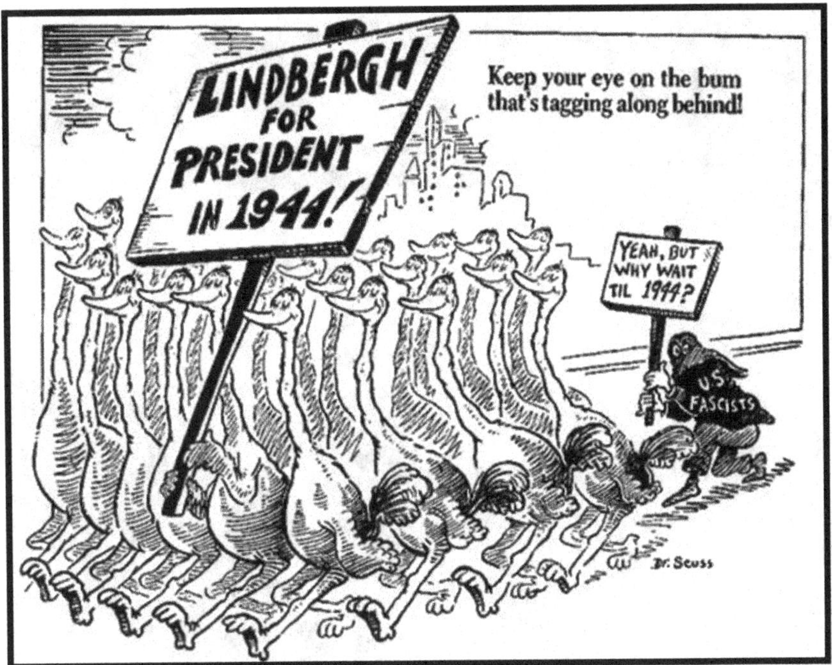

Photo 12: A political cartoon by Dr. Seuss (Theodore Geisel) criticizing Charles Lindbergh for his political stance against entering World War II. The birds are ostriches, known for sticking their heads in the sand when faced with danger. The accusation is Lindbergh is advocating for fascism as denoted by the black-caped character following the procession. (public domain)

Photo 13: Charles Lindbergh experimenting in high altitude aviation at the Mayo Clinic in 1942. (permission granted by the Mayo Clinic)

Photo 14: Charles Lindbergh second from right after a combat run in the South Pacific with three fellow Airmen, taken in 1944.

10. A Puzzle

Lindbergh's two secret visits to Germany in the Winter of 1938-39

Lindbergh's actions between October 1938 and April 1939 are controversial and not well understood. It is known he made two secret trips to Germany at the request of the French government, ostensibly to arrange a sale of German aircraft engines to the French government.

Author Introduction: In researching this book, the author has been dismayed to realize historians occasionally repeat each others' assertions and then use each others' books as references. This is true for this portion of Lindbergh's life: from the signing of the Munich Agreement until leaving Europe in April 1939. They pronounce Lindbergh was a fool. This chapter demonstrates a different verdict.

For example, in a book on Ambassador Joseph P. Kennedy, author Susan Ronald wrote Lindbergh's negotiations with Germany to arrange for the French to buy aircraft engines were "phony". Her source is a book on John F. Kennedy. (Ronald, 2021, p.227) Contrary to her assertion, the negotiations resulted in a German offer to sell aircraft engines to France. (Cole, 1974, p.60) Furthermore, Lindbergh also facilitated a series of meetings between German officials and a friend of his father-in-law, George Rublee, which unsuccessfully tried to arrange for Jews to leave Germany. (Lindbergh, 1970, pp. 139-141) Historians haven't recognized Lindbergh's successful actions nor the effort he made to help Jews.[1] (Breitman, 2013) (Rosen, 2006, pp.105-114)

Historical Introduction: On September 30, 1938, British Prime Minister Neville Chamberlain and French Prime Minister Edouard Deladier concluded the Munich Accords which allowed Hitler to seize the Sudetenland portion of Czechoslovakia without British or French intervention. Millions of people believed war had been avoided.

Lindbergh did not. Believing a European War had been avoided required either accepting, justifying, rationalizing, or ignoring German mistreatment of Jews. Lindbergh did not do this either. (Lindbergh, 1970)

On March 15, 1939, Hitler broke the agreement by seizing the rest of Czechoslovakia. As a result, England and France stopped negotiating with Hitler. Knowing war was inevitable, Lindbergh and his family moved back to the U.S. in April 1939. The war would start a few months later.

Lindbergh said in July 1936 war was inevitable. In his only public appearance in Germany, his speech at the Aeroclub Luncheon in July 1936, he stated that Germany's rearmament would result in a European War. (Aeroclub speech, 1936) He had been to Germany twice more and saw Germany rearming faster and with more technologically advanced weapons. Consequently, in his journal he states there will be a war and proposes three scenarios in which war was likely to start:

1. Mussolini would demand French territory such as Corsica. This would cause France and Italy to declare war. Germany would join the Italians and England would fight with the French.
2. Germany, similar to what it had done in World War I, would invade Belgium and Holland. Lindbergh felt this would accomplish too little for the response it would generate in world opinion and was thus unlikely.
3. Germany would attack a country to its east, most likely Poland.

Lindbergh felt the third option was the best of 3 bad options because German expansion to the east would inevitably lead to a conflict between it and Russia. The ensuing war would prevent Russia from dominating post-war Europe. Lindbergh was wrong about two future events. Like many military analysts of the time, he felt the *Maginot Line* would deter Germany from invading France and he failed to anticipate the non-aggression pact Hitler would sign with Stalin. (Lindbergh, 1970, pp.158-60)

Kristallnacht was a pogrom of terror, murder, and torture committed against Germany's Jews on November 9-10, 1938. Prior to *Kristallnacht* the position of the U.S. Foreign Service was the issue of Jewish mistreatment was best handled by constructive engagement with the Nazi regime. (Nasaw, 2013) While *Kristallnacht* invoked expressions of disapproval by the U.S. government, unlike the British government, the Roosevelt administration did not issue a protest nor formally rebuke Germany. Lindbergh however, publicly wrote because of *Kristallnacht* he would never again engage in any action which could be interpreted as showing support for Germany's mistreatment of the Jews. (Berg, 1998, p.380)

After *Kristallnacht*, Lindbergh kept his vow. He declined a fourth public trip to Germany, but he made two secret trips on behalf of the French government. To keep his visits to Germany a secret he arranged a cover story. At his own expense, he left his airplane at a Berlin airport so that if the press discovered he was in Germany, he could plausibly say he had only come to retrieve his airplane, which needed repairs. (Hessen, 1984, pp.139-141)

How these missions were arranged: Lindbergh's interactions with French Intelligence

As noted in the previous chapter, Lindbergh first met with French Air Ministry representative Guy La Chambre on September 9, 1938. Historians have dwelled on Lindbergh's estimate of German first-line strength at this meeting. The author instead finds importance in the discussion regarding French efforts to buy American fighter airplanes, because it is unusual for Lindbergh to divulge information in his journal that both sides wanted to keep secret. (Lindbergh, 1970, p.70)

Lindbergh was careful to only discuss intelligence matters with the State Department (Joseph Kennedy) and the military (Major Truman Smith). (Lindbergh, 1970) He saw no reason for the public to be aware of his actions. He wrote, "It (would) mislead the English and anger the Germans. There are few things which would cause more misunderstanding." (Lindbergh, 1970, p.140)

Because the restrictions of the Neutrality Acts limited his ability to send weapons to friendly nations, Roosevelt proposed to both the British and the French that the U.S. could sell airplanes by producing them in Canada. (Cole, 1974, p.58) This solution didn't solve the problem Lindbergh identified at the September meeting. American airplanes would be difficult to incorporate into the French air force. He identified another problem, American engines weren't powerful enough for France's needs. He proposed France buy engines from Germany. (Cole, 1974) (Lindbergh, 1970, p.70)

Lindbergh was in Germany until October 30, 1938. The next day Lindbergh met with La Chambre. He reviewed French military needs, and Lindbergh suggested exploring if Germany would sell France engines. But in the absence of stability in French politics, France still won't be able to defend itself. Lindbergh received the approval to go ahead with the mission on November 25, 1938. (Lindbergh, 1970, pp.112,120)

<u>The criticism of Lindbergh and the Historical Record:</u>

Lindbergh's critics' narrative: Lindbergh invented this "absurd" idea on his own and the French realizing the impossibility of the venture humored Lindbergh and told him to go to Germany. The Germans then had some fun "considering" this idea before turning it down. (Wallace, 2003) Lindbergh considered the Germans were not serious and suggested this to the Germans, but German insistence along with their tone and body language convinced Lindbergh they were serious.

(Lindbergh, 1970, 12/20/38) Besides, on November 25, 1938, Lindbergh wrote the French asked him to go. (Lindbergh, 1970, p.120)

As noted in the introduction, Lindbergh's critics fail to mention that Lindbergh was successful in arranging a deal for Germany to sell aircraft engines to France (Cole, 1974, p.60) and in addition at these meetings Lindbergh encouraged and facilitated meetings between German officials and George Rublee of the International Refugee Committee to help Jews leave Germany. (Lindbergh, 1970, pp.139-141) The engine deal ended when Germany seized Czechoslovakia in March 1939. (Hessen, 1984, p.141)

The narrative criticizing Lindbergh is hindsight. An agreement between France and Germany in 1939 was not only possible, it was suggested by figures at the time. France and Germany signed the Munich Accords in September 1938. From then until Hitler seized the rest of Czechoslovakia, separate deals between Germany and her adversaries were pursued, indeed one was signed between Russia and Germany later that year. In January 1939, the British Foreign Minister, Lord Halifax, warned the government that unless England rearmed, France might seek just such an agreement. (Bouverie, 2019)

French efforts to buy airplanes from foreign countries predated Lindbergh's first meeting with La Chambre. Lindbergh initially was hesitant to make suggestions. In fact, he wrote a letter to the famous French economist, Jean Monnet on October 9, 1938, in which he said he thought it was a bad idea for him to be involved in any effort on the part of the French to buy armaments. (Cole, 1974, pp.58-9)

Finally, Lindbergh's visit with La Chambre on October 31, 1938, is inconsistent with the French humoring him. (Lindbergh, 1970, p.112) La Chambre gave Lindbergh specific and technical instructions on what France needed and what France could incorporate into its air force. La Chambre explained to Lindbergh that France can produce airplanes faster than it can produce engines and specifically asked for the Junkers

211 engine. (Lindbergh, 1970, p.125) Suggesting a specific engine, particularly one Lindbergh was intimately familiar with, to purchase is inconsistent with mocking someone.

On October 1, 1938, Lindbergh flew the premier French fighter plane, the Moran 406. He thought it had potential but was too slow at a top speed of 300 mph. This was too slow because, for example, it was the same top speed as the lumbering B-24 bomber. He recommended France purchase surplus German engines because U.S. factories had neither the technology nor capacity to meet French military needs. (Lindbergh, 1970, pp.85,613) Lindbergh's premise was based on knowledge his critics lack.

Lindbergh's critics give him no credit for recognizing, nearly by himself, that U.S. engine technology was inferior, because they lack knowledge of aircraft engines. To those understanding French military needs and engine technology in October 1938, it seems logical he would suggest buying engines from Germany. Lindbergh consistently advocated for the same class of engines. Lindbergh's assessment of the lack of capacity of American engine factories he hadn't yet seen was particularly astute. (see p.122)

A curious claim is these negotiations were at the "behest of (convicted Nazi war criminal Hermann) Goering", which lacks a reference. (Ronald, 2021, p.229) The documentation demonstrates they were at the behest of the French who, because they had been unsuccessful at buying engines, asked Lindbergh to negotiate with the Germans. Goering was not part of these negotiations, although he signed off on the engine deal Lindbergh arranged with the other German officials. (Lindbergh, 1970, pp.120,125-142), (Ross, 1964, p.284)

Historians inventing convoluted interactions between Lindbergh and Goering will be seen again. When done, it's never mentioned Lindbergh's interactions with Goering were solely at the request of the U.S. government. (see p. 336)

Lindbergh's Secret Visits to Germany, December 16-20, 1938, and January 16-18, 1939

Lindbergh discussed the purchase of German engines with two high ranking members of the German military, State Secretary for Air, Erhard Milch, and German Air Minister, Ernst Udet. At the first meeting, they discussed which engines Germany could sell, how Germany would be paid, and who in the German government would have to approve the deal. At the second meeting they discussed which engines Germany could sell, how Germany would be paid, and again who in the German government would have to approve the deal. (Lindbergh, 1970, p.140)

In his journal, the engine deal is an afterthought. Lindbergh spends more time discussing the plight of the Jews. He points out the ubiquitous nature of anti-Semitism in Germany and the opinions of the Germans he met regarding the Jews. He expresses frustration that Germans believe anti-Semitic propaganda: Jews are responsible not just for Germany's economic collapse and Bolshevism but taking the best houses and consorting with the prettiest German women. (Lindbergh, 1970, p.139)

On January 16, 1939, Lindbergh's journal records his final pre-war conversation with German officials. Udet tells him the Germans have "made progress" on the Jewish issue. Lindbergh then discussed the engine transaction, saying if the Germans have no interest the issue need not be addressed, but Milch insisted the Germans are interested in selling airplane engines to France. They discussed details of which engines, how many Germany will sell, and how Germany is to be paid. Lindbergh again returns to the mistreatment of the Jews. Apparently Udet's assurances are inadequate. He finishes 3 years of discussions with Germans by recommending Milch and Udet speak to Rublee about ways to help the Jews. The first time he returned to Paris by train, thus leaving his airplane at Templehof Airport in Berlin. This time he took his airplane back to France. (Lindbergh, 1970, p.142)

The final meeting between Rublee and Hjalmar Schacht took place on January 20, 1939. Unfortunately, the Nazis were now asking not just for all the assets of those allowed to leave Germany, but also additional assets from foreign Jews. Jewish agencies refused to fund a future enemy's war preparations. Even if German extortion was paid, there was no country willing to take Jews. Rublee was unsuccessful in arranging refuge for Jews in countries like the Philippines. (Breitman, 2013, p.151)

Lindbergh did not return to Germany until after the war. His cover was blown on January 7, 1939, when the *New York Herald Tribune* published an article titled, "Lindbergh reported providing U.S. with data on Reich Air Force." Lindbergh felt much of the information was inaccurate, but because some of it was accurate and confidential, he suspected it had been leaked by the Roosevelt administration. (Lindbergh, 1970, p.135) The administration denied it and Lindbergh did not consider the likely source was the hearings underway in Congress by the armed forces appropriations committees that were reviewing his intelligence reports. (Nasaw, 2013, p.369) Although Major Smith received a communication the Germans did not believe the report, Lindbergh was distraught. (Lindbergh, 1970, pp.135-6)

<u>Follow-up discussions and negotiations</u>

Lindbergh returned to France on January 19, 1939, and met with La Chambre. The conversation mostly consisted of Lindbergh relaying the details of his meeting with Milch. One sentence referred to American Jews with whom he will soon battle. When they discuss the reaction in the U.S., Lindbergh said the agreement must be portrayed as contributing to peace to be accepted, because otherwise "Jewish influence" will oppose it. (Lindbergh, 1970, p.143)

There's no condemnation of Jews using their influence in an era in which Jews were routinely blamed for influencing news and public opinion. Lindbergh was vulnerable, he could be blamed for supporting Germany and an ensuing war. He did not lash out. Contrast Lindbergh's statement with Joseph Kennedy's on the Jews and their effect on his ability to prevent war. "If the Jews would pay less attention to advertising their racial problems and more attention to solving it, the whole thing would recede into its proper perspective. It's entirely out of focus now and it's chiefly their fault." (Perry, 2017)

University of Maryland historian Wayne Cole documented Germany agreed in March 1939 to sell the French 300 surplus aircraft engines. Hitler's occupation of the rest of Czechoslovakia on March 15, 1939, ended the deal. (Cole, 1974, p.60) The specific engine the Germans would sell to the French was designated to be the Daimler-Benz engine with 1250 horsepower. (Lindbergh, 1970, p.140) The most likely model was the DB600 which was developed in the late 1930s. This engine would have met Lindbergh's approval because it was a liquid-cooled engine capable of powering combat competitive airplanes. (see engines)

This deal supported Lindbergh's philosophy of "smart" rather than "hysterical rearmament". The wasteful acquisitions of weapons would also be opposed during U.S. rearmament. He wrote "hysterical rearmament" would leave the U.S. with a bloated obsolete air force. (Lindbergh, 1970, pp.135-6) This deal, had it been completed, would have met his approval; although he speculates either way he'd be criticized: either for enabling war or wasting money. (Cole, 1974)

France purchased a few airplanes from the United States, but it didn't matter. French fortunes were not determined by the number of airplanes nor the engines. As Lindbergh told La Chambre on October 31, 1938, in the absence of political stability France could not defend itself, and aircraft engines wouldn't matter. (Lindbergh, 1970, pp.112-3)

Conclusion:

The word "ostensible" in the introduction emphasizes Lindbergh may not have gone to Germany to arrange an airplane engine deal. His journal treats engine negotiations as an afterthought. It seems unlikely he would promote his reputation as a German sympathizer and be blamed for war, so France could purchase engines which would still not allow France to defend itself.

It is likely Lindbergh primarily went to Germany to assess whether a separate German-French peace deal was possible. In his journal he explains why a deal with France made sense for Germany's interests. (Lindbergh, 1970, pp.158-60) Before he left for Germany he wrote, "It seems to me that a closer German-French relationship is of utmost importance." (Lindbergh, 1970, p.120) Furthermore, Lindbergh believed that only he had the connections to arrange an agreement and only he understood Germany. (Lindbergh, 1970, p.173) He had said, "my greatest hope lay in the possibility that a war would be confined to fighting between Hitler and Stalin." (Berg, 1998)

Despite the mission being unsuccessful, Lindbergh deserves credit for persistently raising the issue of the Jews. He never accepted the U.S. position the Jews were an internal German matter. Unlike the U.S. Ambassador to Germany, William Dodd, when told the treatment of the Jews was getting better, he refused to accept it. (Medoff, 2019, p.21) (Lindbergh, 1970, p.139) He certainly deserved more credit than the repetition of a statement that Lindbergh's mission was "phony", cited as fact by historians writing books about peripheral subjects. (Ronald, 2021)

In 1935, two English Lords (Lord Allan and Lord Lothian) negotiated with Hitler and in 1937 another, Lord Halifax, traveled to Germany to negotiate peace terms with Hitler. None of them brought up Jewish persecution. In weeks of negotiations, there is no record of either Chamberlain nor Deladier representing Jewish interests in the Munich negotiations. (Bouverie, 2019)

In the spring of 1940, State Department official Sumner Welles was sent to Europe by Roosevelt to explore a peace agreement. In meetings with Hitler, Goering, Mussolini, Deladier, Chamberlain, and Churchill; Welles assembled the outline of a peace settlement but *never* mentioned the Jews. Regardless, Roosevelt rejected Welles' ideas when he returned to the U.S.. (Fullilove, 2013, pp.34-62)

Lindbergh alone negotiated with the Germans based on the premise that the persecution of Jews needed to be addressed. Ending the persecution of the Jews, not the future of aviation nor an engine sale, concluded four years of Lindbergh's interactions with the Germans.

Critics must give Lindbergh his due:

1. Lindbergh advocated for the Jews during these two visits. He encouraged high level meetings between German and refugee officials to reach an agreement to allow Jews to emigrate.[1] These negotiations failed because no nation would take the Jews and the Germans were demanding exorbitant payoffs which no one would pay.
2. Lindbergh's visits resulted in an offer from Germany to France to buy 300 premier aircraft engines. The deal was never completed because German aggression voided it. (Cole, 1974, p.60)

<u>Lindbergh's last 3 weeks in Europe:</u> March 15 – April 7, 1939

When Hitler seized the rest of Czechoslovakia and thereby broke the Munich Accords on March 15, 1939, war was inevitable because Britain and France refused to negotiate with Hitler. (Bouverie, 2019) At the time, Lindbergh did not say the Allies should continue to negotiate, but later in life he would contend he supported more negotiations with Hitler. His opinion regarding additional negotiations no longer mattered because when Hitler made his next demand, for part of Poland in August 1939, Lindbergh was in the U.S. and had no influence in European politics. (Cole, 1974) Lindbergh and his family had returned to the U.S. in April 1939. To spare his wife and children press harassment, their passage was booked separately.

Presumably, because his efforts to prevent war in Western Europe were a failure, the tone of Lindbergh's journal entries is bitter, and his thoughts are disturbing. His critics say they portray Lindbergh as a German sympathizer. Private thoughts which were not expressed in public, and wouldn't be read for 31 years, can't be part of someone's legacy. But they are valuable for providing insight into errors Lindbergh would make in the next two years fighting America's inevitable entry into World War II.

Some of Lindbergh's statements are qualified by his personal situation. For example, Lindbergh writes about greater "personal freedom" in Germany. This refers to freedom from press harassment which had defined his life for 12 years. Both he and his wife blamed the press for their son's murder, death threats against their second son, his son's remains being published on the front page of newspapers, being forced to leave the U.S., and now his blown cover. (Lindbergh, 1970, p.166) Similar but less excusable is Lindbergh's appreciation of German "order". He contrasted Germany with England and France where he saw instability, debauchery, and decline. (Lindbergh, 1970, p.163)

Lindbergh, however, never advocated totalitarianism. *All free societies wrestle with the same issues Lindbergh is discussing.* In his case, it was exacerbated by his personal loss, his desire for privacy, and the complete absence of rules prohibiting press harassment which exist today:

> "Newspapers cause all sorts of unnecessary troubles. I am inclined to think an irresponsible and completely unrestricted press is one of the greatest dangers of democracy, just as a completely controlled press is a danger in the other direction." (Lindbergh, 1970, pp.139-40)

Likewise, he never excused the mistreatment of Jews. But he justified and excused Germany's other actions and this was leading to war. When Germany violated the Munich Agreement and seized the rest of Czechoslovakia he wrote, "I cannot support her (Germany's) broken promises, but she has only moved a little faster than other nations have in breaking promises." (Lindbergh, 1970, p.173)

Berg wrote that at this stage, Lindbergh "stuck his head in the sand". (Berg, 1998) The author disagrees. His head was indeed stuck, not in the sand, but in World War I. He was still championing the issues his father championed. Still dwelling on Germany's grievances stemming from the Versailles Treaty Lindbergh wrote that war could be avoided if "Germany is given a reasonable opportunity for trade and influence" and that Britain, France, and the U.S. were as responsible as Germany for the current climate of impending war. (Lindbergh, 1970, p.158) Germany's trade was not being effectively limited in 1939 and its influence was unparalleled.[2] Britain and France had given Hitler everything he had demanded in exchange for an agreement he had broken. President Roosevelt made good relations with Germany paramount and abandoned the Jews of Germany.

Consideration of Hitler's call for further rectification World War I era grievances in March 1939 was motivated by desperation to avoid war. On April 1, 1939, Hitler gave a speech defending and celebrating the conquest of Czechoslovakia. In addition, to calling the Jews a fungus, he wallowed in grievances from the Versailles Treaty. He made the same tired old claims that he wanted peace but would use force to rectify these grievances. (Yale Law School Archives, n.d.) Few still gave credence to Hitler's victimhood grievances, but in response to Hitler's speech Lindbergh wrote, "The question of right and wrong is one thing by law and another by history." Lindbergh seems to be saying, "although Germany violated the Munich Agreement, historical wrongs still needed to be corrected". (Lindbergh, 1970, p.173)

This response may have made sense in 1933 but not in 1939. The wildest accusations of mistreatment due to the Versailles treaty had been rectified. In response, Hitler's behavior had only gotten worse and his demands more extreme. Hitler's response to concessions at Munich had been *Kristallnacht*. The Germans were not only mistreating

Jews, but also incarcerating and torturing homosexuals, gypsies, the handicapped, Communists, his political opponents, and even non-Jewish Czech civilians. (Taylor, 1992, p.314) The last group can't be explained by Lindbergh's logic because in Hitler's wildest conspiracies they had nothing to do with Germany's defeat in World War I and Hitler had demanded the Sudetenland specifically in the name of protecting Czech civilians. Events moved past the injustices of the Versailles Treaty, but Lindbergh didn't.

Also, although Lindbergh considered German expansion eastward being the best of three bad options, there must be consideration for the people who lived there. Lindbergh never considered the people of eastern Europe living in the path of Germany's expansion ambitions. They were humans too. What would happen to them if Lindbergh had succeeded in fulfilling his "greatest hope"? He never mentioned them.

Lindbergh believed he understood the Germans, but he badly misunderstood them and their goals. The logic of German expansion being exclusively eastward that Lindbergh felt made his proposals achievable, meant nothing to the Germans. (Lindbergh, 1970, p.159) Logic means nothing to the evil. The historical grievances Lindbergh endeavored to rectify were a ruse the Germans used to hide their objectives. Most Germans followed the Nazis blindly because they were seduced by power, and thus, accepted or participated in evil, and as a result became evil. Evil does not care if the persecution of Jews hinders economic agreements or international recognition.

Lindbergh's separation of the treatment of the Jews from Germany's other actions was not just a mistake, it was inexcusable. Lindbergh had been to Nazi Germany five times. The Germans never denied him access to anything he requested to see. If he misunderstood Germany, it's because he chose to. He had preconceived notions, perhaps based on his father's experience, and he blinded himself with the arrogance of believing only he understood Germany. Violence against the Jews would beget violence against others. By rationalizing German transgressions, he completely misjudged Germany's motivations and its objectives. Evil only wants more power.

Lindbergh boarded a ship to return to the United States on April 7, 1939, not understanding this.

Lindbergh would eventually understand the Nazis were evil. Unfortunately, he would have to see it with his own eyes to understand it.

[1]Hjalmar Schacht, head of the *Reichsbank*, met with George Rublee, head of the *Intergovernmental Refugee Committee*, to arrange refuge for German Jews between December 1938 and January 1939. (Rosen, 2006) When Lindbergh became aware, he met with Rublee to inquire how he could aid the negotiations. (Berg, 1998, p.381) Lindbergh's efforts included introducing a *Lufthansa* official named Otto Merkel and Major Smith to Rublee. At the meeting with Milch and Udet on January 16, 1939, Lindbergh encouraged these negotiations. He vouched for Rublee's character, honesty, and discretion. (Lindbergh, 1970, p.140)

[2]There were Jewish-led boycotts of German goods throughout the 1930s, but these boycotts were inconsistent, isolated, and had no effect on Germany's economy, including its ability to borrow large amounts of money to build weapons. Many of these loans were arranged by John Foster Dulles, who would become President Eisenhower's Secretary of State. President Roosevelt refused to support a boycott of German goods, although a poll in 1938 showed the majority of Americans supported a boycott. These boycotts were not adopted by any country. However, Lindbergh was not in the U.S. and was getting at least some (and while in Germany all) of his news from German propaganda. He may have believed Germany's claim that these boycotts were hurting its economy. (Medoff, 2019)

Works Cited

Berg, A. (1998). *Lindbergh.* New York: Berkley Biography.

Bouverie, T. (2019). *Appeasement.* New York: Random House.

Breitman, A. (2013). *FDR and the Jews.* London: Belknap.

Cole, W. (1974). *Charles A. Lindbergh and the Battle Against American Intervention in World War II.* New York: Harcourt.

Fullilove, M. (2013). *Rendezvous with Destiny.* New York: Penguin Press.

Hessen, R. (1984). *Berlin Alert: The Memoirs and Reports of Truman Smith.* Stanford, CA: Hoover Insitute Press.

Lindbergh, C. A. (1970). *The Wartime Journals of Charles A. Lindbergh.* New York: Harcourt, Brace, and Jovanovich.

Medoff, R. (2019). *The Jews Should Keep Quiet.* Lincoln: U. Nebraska Press.

Nasaw, D. (2013). *The Patriarch.* New York: Penguin.

Ronald, S. (2021). *The Ambassador.* New York: St. Martin's Press.

Roscn, R. (2006). *Saving the Jews.* New York: Thunder's Mouth Press.

Ross, W, *The Last Hero: Charles A. Lindbergh*, Harper and Row, NY, 1964.

Taylor, T. (1992). *The Anatomy of the Nuremberg Trials.* New York: Knopf.

Wallace, M. (2003). *The Ameican Axis.* New York: St. Martin's Press.

Yale Law School Archives. (n.d.). Retrieved from Avalon Project: https://avalon.law.yale.edu/wwii/blbk20.asp

11: Isolationism

The Great Debate, Sept. 1, 1939-Dec. 11, 1941

The "Great Debate" was America's public opinion and legislative conflict between the start of World War II, Germany's invasion of Poland, and Germany's declaration of war against the U.S. four days after Pearl Harbor. Those who wanted to enter World War II were called Interventionists, and those who did not were called Isolationists. Charles Lindbergh was the most famous isolationist.

The organization promoting Isolationism was called America First or the America First Committee. Lindbergh joined America First in 1940, but he maintained his independence and did not have his speeches approved by it.

President Roosevelt did not advocate entering the war but rather supplying allies with weapons. He also advocated for a military draft and a program called Lend-Lease, which allowed England to buy weapons it could not afford. Isolationists said supplying England with weapons would result in the U.S. entering the war and leave us unprepared to fight, because this had been the U.S. experience in World War I. They also advocated not shipping weapons to other countries so they could be used to defend ourselves.

This chapter is written in several sections. The first section is a table reviewing the two times Charles Lindbergh was adjudicated by the justice system. Both times no evidence was produced that he had any contact with a domestic nor international fascist organization.

The second section establishes criteria for the term "Nazi Sympathizer". It discusses American politics of the era to establish criteria to qualify as a Nazi Sympathizer and then applies them to Lindbergh.

The next sections define the principles of isolationism and how Lindbergh said he would conduct foreign policy had he been President.

The following section reviews the conflict between Lindbergh and Roosevelt and how Roosevelt tried to destroy Lindbergh's reputation and credibility.

The chapter closes with the author's personal thoughts which introduces the next chapter which reviews Roosevelt's record on foreign policy as it relates to the impending extermination of Europe's Jews.

1. The Historical Record: The Legal System's Adjudication of Lindbergh's Involvement with Fascist Organizations — Foreign and Domestic: There was no involvement.

Charles Lindbergh was investigated by the FBI and deposed under oath in a civilian court. In both cases, no evidence was produced demonstrating he had any interaction with any fascist organization. He did not pass information to a foreign government, nor, after his return to the U.S. in April 1939, have an interaction with any foreigner. He did not have any contact with any domestic fascist organization.

Table 1: Historical Judicial Record Regarding Lindbergh (L) and the *America First Committee* (AFC) regarding accusations of interactions with Nazi organizations

Accusation	Made by/ Accusation	Adjudication	Conclusion
L, AFC aided Nazi Germany	Individual, Chicago Tribune /L passed secrets to Nazis[1]	FBI investigation concluded February 1942: JE Hoover letter[2]	No contact with Nazis: L, AFC-no criminal activity, no treason[3,4]
L aided or had contact with American Nazi Movement	W. Pelley, Head of American Nazi "Silver Shirts"	L testified under oath after being subpoenaed, 8/4/42	L dismissed as a witness due to absence of evidence[4]

[1]*Chicago Tribune* published material considered militarily sensitive in 1942. Accusation – Lindbergh or AFC had provided the material to the *Chicago Tribune*. Separately, a military officer accused Lindbergh of

providing blueprints to the *Luftwaffe*. Both Lindbergh and AFC were cleared by the FBI.[3]

[2]JE Hoover letter: J. Edgar Hoover, Head of the FBI, letter to Edwin Watson, Secretary for President Roosevelt, February 13, 1942. Conclusion: no charges could be brought against Lindbergh due to absence of evidence of criminal activity.

[3]Wallace, 2003, pp. 306-8, [4]Berg, 1998, p. 445.

The FBI report contains only two exculpatory references to Lindbergh.[2] The FBI reported to the President that the isolationist movement was legally engaging in advocacy and no investigated member had a connection to fascism. Roosevelt responded by demanding a financial investigation of the AFC. He directed his press secretary to ask the FBI to investigate "who is paying for this?" (PSU, nd)

Lindbergh's innocence was public knowledge. When the *Chicago Daily News* demanded evidence Lindbergh was acting on behalf of a foreign government, Roosevelt's Secretary of the Interior, Harold Ickes, conceded, "Neither I nor any member of this administration ever charged that Mr. Lindbergh had any connection (nor communication) with any foreign government." (Cole, 1974, p.133)

2. What is a Nazi Sympathizer?

The table above demonstrates neither the FBI nor U.S. Justice System found evidence Lindbergh helped Nazi Germany nor had contact with any fascist organization. Innocence in our society is defined by an acquittal by the justice system. Lindbergh was acquitted twice. In his Pulitzer Prize-winning biography of Lindbergh, Berg wrote all the FBI uncovered was a report that while in Berlin in 1936, Lindbergh smiled and he had met people who might have contributed to "fringe" groups. (Berg, 1998, p. 409)

Since there is no evidence Lindbergh associated with nor helped any fascist organization, the question follows: why is he called a "Nazi sympathizer"? Terms used for anyone with whom the writer disagrees is name-calling. Terms must be defined. A review of who wasn't a Nazi-Sympathizer and contrasting them with those who were allows us to define the term and apply it to prominent figures of the era.

Who was not a Nazi Sympathizer?

1) Winston Churchill. He recognized in 1933 that, whatever "legitimate" grievances there were stemming from the Treaty of Versailles, Hitler's anti-Semitism was not only fundamental and inseparable from Nazism, but would also engulf Europe in war. He said in 1933, "There is a danger of the odious conditions now ruling in Germany, being extended by conquest to Poland and another persecution and pogrom of Jews being extended to this new area." (Gilbert, 1993) For that reason, Churchill said he would never consider negotiating with Hitler. Few American public figures made a connection between anti-Semitism and military aggression, most (including President Roosevelt) believed German anti-Semitism was an internal German matter.

2) Frances Perkins, U.S. Secretary of Labor 1933-1945. In her position as Secretary of Labor, she tried to facilitate the immigration of Jews from Germany. She reduced the fee for foreign students so more could come to the U.S. and arranged for 400 Jewish children to enter when the U.S. *Kindertransport* was killed by Roosevelt. She worked around State Department restrictions to allow roughly 200,000 Jewish "foreign visitors". (Downey, 2009)

The Hoover-era "public charge" restriction blocked immigrants without financial means to support themselves. This clause was used by the State Department to deny visas to Jews because Germany stripped them of assets prior to giving them an exit visa. Perkins created a "charge bond" system which allowed others to post a bond guaranteeing financial support. Challenged by the State Department, Perkins' plan was upheld by the Attorney General. (Americans and the Holocaust, n.d.)

Condemning anti-Semitism, refusing to negotiate with Hitler, and helping Jews leave Nazi Germany defines not being a Nazi-Sympathizer.

Who was a Nazi Sympathizer?

1) Joseph Kennedy, U.S. Ambassador to Great Britain (1938-1940). He told the Germans he agreed with excluding Jews because he had belonged to a golf club "...in which no Jews had been admitted in 50 years." (Perry, 2017) He said Jews could be mistreated but not with the "loud clamor" by which the Germans did it. He blamed the Jews for World War II and for controlling the media, "Jewish media...set a match to the fuse of the world." (Rosen, 2006, p. 81) He called Jews "kikes". (Perry, 2017)

In 1946, the U.S. Military found records of conversations Kennedy had before the war with two consecutive German Ambassadors to England, Joachim von Ribbentrop (later German Foreign Minister, hanged at Nuremberg) and Herbert von Dirksen in June 1938. Kennedy agreed with von Ribbentrop that Americans had a negative opinion of Germany because of "press agitation". Kennedy said he would do everything in his power to stem "press agitation". Then Kennedy identified the Jews as the "agitation" and said Americans were misinformed about Germany because everyone is afraid of the Jews. (Nasaw, 2012, pp.310-311) After Germany invaded Poland, Kennedy encouraged Roosevelt to negotiate a separate peace with Hitler. (Nasaw, 2012, p.498) (see pg. 283)

2)A famous aviator named Laura Ingalls (not the author of *Little House on the Prairie*). The *America First* movement failed to screen her and while speaking for them she was being paid by the Germans, which when discovered embarrassed isolationism. She was arrested by the FBI and served 20 months in prison. She gave Nazi salutes, actively distributed Nazi propaganda, met with German diplomats, and distributed seditious material. (Olson, 2013, p.332) (Laura Ingalls (aviator), n.d.)

3) James Conant, the President of Harvard from 1933-1953. Conant insisted Nazi academics were legitimate scholarship and encouraged academic collaboration with Nazi universities, despite Jews being barred from German institutions. Harvard instituted an admission system where applicants were rated J1 (definitely Jewish) through J3 (unlikely to be Jewish) to reduce Jewish admissions. The Jewish percentage of Harvard's enrollment in the 1930s fell to its lowest level since 1915. He tried to prevent a Jewish chemist whose lab produced 3 Nobel Prizes, Max Bergmann, from escaping Germany and taking a job with the DuPont Corporation. (Beir, 2006, pp.20-21)

4) John Foster Dulles, President Eisenhower's Secretary of State, 1952-1959: Like Lindbergh, Dulles was a wealthy powerful private citizen, who had connections to high-ranking Nazi government officials. Both made frequent trips to Germany prior to the war. But Dulles arranged loans to Nazi Germany and was pivotal in Nazi Germany's economic success in the 1930s. After *Kristallnacht* he publicly defended Germany and continued to travel there. (von Tunzelmann, 2016)

Based on Kennedy, Ingalls, Conant, and Dulles, a person can be considered a Nazi-sympathizer if they:

1. Advocated or acted to exclude Jews from society,
2. Denied the Jews were being persecuted or blamed the Jews for their own persecution,
3. Engaged in anti-Semitic activities, for example using slurs to refer to Jews,
4. Instituted Nazi-like procedures, such as labeling Jews, to deny them access to opportunities such as jobs or higher education,
5. Actively advanced Nazi interests. This includes blaming Jews for negative coverage of German actions,
6. Prevented Jewish emigration to the U.S.,

7. Did not publicly break with Germany after *Kristallnacht,* or
8. Advocated the U.S. negotiate a separate peace treaty directly with Hitler.

Does Lindbergh Meet Criteria to be Labeled a Nazi Sympathizer? No.

Lindbergh was neither Churchill nor Perkins, but he never used slurs, unlike Joseph Kennedy. Although investigated by the FBI, he was not found to have had any interaction with Nazi Germany in the U.S., unlike Ingalls. In direct contrast to Conant, Lindbergh obtained an exit visa for a Jewish scientist. Unlike Dulles, he stated he would not allow anyone to suspect he "seem(ed) to support" Germany after *Kristallnacht* and he made no material contribution to Germany's success. (Berg, 1998, p.380)

Lindbergh's foreign policy position was "I never wanted Germany to win this war." (Minneapolis speech, 5/10/1941) He was strongly opposed to separate U.S. negotiations with Germany.[5] (SF Speech, 7/1/41) He said the U.S. may have to negotiate with Hitler in the future depending on the outcome of the war, but he opposed all foreign entanglements including negotiations with Germany. (Olson, 2013) (Cole, 1974) (Chicago Speech, 8/5/1940) He shared intelligence with England to prepare them to fight Germany. He supported selling England defensive weapons. (Radio address, 5/19/1940)

Similarly, his statements regarding the mistreatment of Jews by Nazi Germany are the opposite of Kennedy's. He never justified the mistreatment of Jews. The public actions for which he was accused of supporting Germany were part of intelligence gathering. But even when being used by the Germans for public relations, he never publicly agreed with Germany. He gave a single speech in Germany in which he warned Germany it would be responsible for a European war. (Aeroclub Speech, July 1936) He did not blame the Jews for using their influence, starting World War II, nor being persecuted.

He was used by Germany for public relations, just as he was used by the U.S. to obtain intelligence, but he never arranged loans, nor made public trips to Germany after *Kristallnacht*, unlike Dulles.

Critics have searched through Lindbergh's private journals trying to find quotes like Kennedy's, but they aren't there. The journals are nearly devoid of anti-Semitism. He made observations about Germany which, today, are distasteful, but were made by many contemporary figures about Germany's ability to feed its people, demonstrate political stability, and prevent Soviet expansion. The U.S. foreign service, for whom he worked, felt similarly. (Nasaw, 2012) Even his critics acknowledge his personal journal demonstrates surprising compassion for the plight of German Jews. (Correll, 2014)

In January 1939, Lindbergh tried to help Jews flee Nazi Germany meeting the standard set by Perkins. (Lindbergh, 1970, p.142) He meets no criterion for being classified as a Nazi Sympathizer. Another important difference: neither Conant nor Harvard was ever held accountable their actions. Dulles has an airport named after him. Only Lindbergh is still held in contempt.

<u>Were other American Public Figures Nazi Sympathizers?</u> Sometimes

According to a Roper Poll in early 1940, only 2.5% of Americans supported entering the war, and even if, theoretically, Britain was on the verge of losing, the number increased to only 14.7%. The percentage of Americans who supported <u>selling</u> supplies to Britain was less than 40%. (Peters, 2005)

Due to political realities, few non-Jewish national figures consistently supported the Jews. German Americans were an important voting bloc and a factor in public opinion. (Peters, 2005) The German American Bund was a powerful force, which regularly held rallies in American cities in their Nazi uniforms, while observers engaged in the Nazi stiff-arm salute. (Taylor, 2017)

There were brave Americans who opposed Hitler, but they were frequently either Jews or Communists. The few politicians who supported Jewish interests were mostly from New York, where the majority of Jews lived. Fiorello La Guardia, the mayor of New York City from 1934-1945, vehemently opposed Hitler and his fellow Italian, Mussolini, from the beginning of his mayorship. But La Guardia's mother was born Jewish, so by Jewish law, he was Jewish, although he did not publicly identify as a Jew. (Vincent, 2018) Charlie Chaplin, the famous director and entertainer, mocked Hitler and uniquely publicized the plight of the Jews in his movie, *The Great Dictator*, for which he took enormous financial and professional risk and deserves credit. Chaplin too may have been Jewish, although there is no consensus on the subject. Albert Einstein told the *Jewish Telegraphic Agency* that Chaplin told him his grandfather had been Jewish. (JTA, 1931)

The Communists and supporters of Stalin were critical of Hitler when it suited them. But supporting one genocidal dictator (Stalin) while condemning another (Hitler) hardly makes them paragons of virtue. Arguably, they were more dangerous than Nazi sympathizers because Nazi sympathizers didn't infiltrate our government and compromise our security like Communists did.Between Stalin signing a non-aggression pact with Hitler in 1939 and Hitler's invasion of the Soviet Union in 1941, American Communists and Socialists supported America seeking an agreement with Hitler, which Lindbergh never did. (Peters, 2005)

An example of an American politician who was an anti-Nazi, Communist sympathizer is Henry Wallace, the U.S. Vice-President from 1941-1945. He was consistently an outspoken critic of Hitler and for this he deserves credit. Yet, he was intentionally blind to the terror and genocide in the Soviet Union and famously said, "there is no differences between the Soviet Union and the United States which can't be reconciled without sacrificing a single American principle." (Herman, 2000) As Vice President, he toured Gulags in Siberia and infamously called them "collective farms". (Black, 2013) He was compromised by Russian intelligence and when he ran for President in 1948, as a

Socialist, it is alleged his campaign was infiltrated by Soviet agents. Wallace got 2.3% of the vote in 1948. He left politics and denounced Communism in 1954. (Black, 2013)

There were a few non-Jewish American public figures between 1933-1941 who bravely sought to help the Jews and deserve credit. Senator Robert Wagner (D-NY) and Congresswoman Edith Rogers (D-Mass) tried to get 20,000 Jewish children admitted to the U.S.. But in general, non-Jewish national figures did not consistently oppose Germany nor support Europe's Jews. Refuge for Jewish adults was nearly universally opposed by non-Jewish politicians in the U.S.. (Dalleck, 2017)

Nearly any non-Jewish American public figure of the era, through the selective use of statements, could be portrayed as a Nazi Sympathizer. For example, quotes from Eleanor Roosevelt, President Roosevelt, and Harry Truman meet various criteria. (Medoff, 2017) (McCullough, 1992) (Cook, 2000)

Lindbergh's acquittal by the FBI isn't appreciated. The FBI rarely concluded an investigation without consequences. Laura Ingalls went to jail after an FBI investigation found she was getting paid by Germany. (Olson, 2013) Although no evidence was found Chaplin was a Communist, FBI director Hoover destroyed his reputation by releasing details of his private life. (Chaplin FBI File, 2015)

American politicians inconsistently supported Jewish interests:

Often politicians supported Jewish interests only when it was convenient. Sometimes these same politicians criticized Lindbergh. Lindbergh, not being a politician, was consistent in his beliefs and positions.

1940 Republican Presidential Nominee Wendell Willkie supported Jewish interests and was a critic of Lindbergh. But when it was politically convenient, he sounded like Lindbergh. Willkie was considered "anti-Nazi", and this was a factor in winning the nomination. As a corporate lawyer he criticized Hitler's treatment of the Jews, but not as the nominee. Needing German American votes in the Midwest, he said almost nothing critical about Hitler during the campaign. There is no record he mentioned the persecution of the Jews. (Peters, 2005)

To the extent he is remembered, Willkie is considered a hero for not opposing Roosevelt's decision to sell arms to Britain during the Battle of Britain. He did not criticize Roosevelt...until his poll numbers started dropping. On October 6, 1940, Willkie was trailing Roosevelt by 12 percentage points. From then until election day, he called Roosevelt a "warmonger" who had made a "secret deal to enter the war." His support for Roosevelt selling weapons to Britain suddenly became "...the most arbitrary and dictatorial action by the president in the history of the United States." (Peters, 2005)

Like Lindbergh, Willkie was never elected to any office. He made his anti-Nazi statements when few cared what he thought. (Peters, 2005) Willkie is a hero because he was "anti-Nazi" but when it mattered, he was silent. He is a hero because he didn't oppose the sale of weapons to Britain... that is until his campaign sank. Then he criticized Roosevelt for being a "dictator" and a "warmonger". Lindbergh charged Roosevelt with the same offenses, without the name calling, yet he is hardly considered a hero.

Selective statements to identify as opposition to an unpopular war — when it is convenient — is common in American politics. Barack Obama won the Democratic nomination because he claimed he had opposed the war in Iraq. He opposed the war in 2003 when he was a State Senator, and few people knew who he was nor cared what he said. When he had a national audience at the Democratic Convention in 2004 and an opportunity to oppose the Iraq War, he didn't. His only statement on the war was "There are patriots who support the war in Iraq and there are patriots who oppose it." (PBS, n.d.)

Donald Trump won the 2016 Republican nomination by claiming he, too, had been against the Iraq War. But when he could've been decisive, on *Fox Business* in 2003, he too gave a non-committal albeit much more rambling answer, "...we have to, you know, either do it or don't do it". He digressed to discussing Douglas MacArthur who he said "would go and attack. He wouldn't talk." (FactCheck.org, n.d.)

Just like both Obama and Trump used selective statements to later claim they opposed the Iraq War, focusing on certain statements and events and ignoring others can be manipulated to characterize many World War II era politicians' Nazi opposition credentials.

3. The Principles of Isolationism:

I) The Principles of Isolationism which Lindbergh promoted:

a. Both Germany and the West bore responsibility for the war, not just Germany.

Most isolationists, including Lindbergh, sided with England but felt England was also responsible for the war. The Versailles Treaty bankrupted Germany and enriched England and France. Post-World War I expansion of the British and French empires stole resources from others. The Treaty of Versailles added a million square miles and millions of subjects to a British Empire without anyone's consent. Lindbergh wrote in 1940, neither side had a "monopoly on right". (Cole, 1974, p.208)

b. Opposition to aid to England.

This opposition was based on World War I. The isolationist argument was that supplying England with weapons resulted in getting dragged into World War I, which wasted 116,000 American lives.

Lindbergh had a personal connection to this argument because his father had been a congressman from Minnesota who had opposed aid to England, and as a result lost his seat, his career, and was arrested pursuant to the Sedition Act. It was the German Navy's interception of U.S. merchant ships, either by boarding them or sinking them, that led to our involvement in World War I. As we expanded our aid to England between 1940 and 1941, and supply ships traveled the same route, isolationists predicted we would enter the European theater of World War II the same way. (Berg, 1998)

The passage of the Lend-Lease Act (March 1941) and a shift in public opinion led isolationists to relax this principle. Lindbergh supported an isolationist position that membership be provided to those who wanted to aid England as long as they opposed entering the war. (Press Release, Chicago, 4/17/41)

c. Aiding England was wasting our resources and our weapons: The garden hose analogy.

Roosevelt justified aid to England using the famous garden hose analogy: when your neighbor's house is on fire and he asks to borrow your hose, you don't quibble over payment. If the hose is damaged, compensation can be arranged later. (Peters, 2005) The isolationists refused to accept this argument. They pointed out that our neighbor wasn't "borrowing" our garden hose, it was handed to him without answering these questions: who started the fire, would it be returned, and what happened to "our hose" the last time he had a fire? Furthermore, "our hose" was really 100,000 American lives and when we had a fire, we'd have no hose.

Lindbergh opposed only "offensive weapons." He said he did not want to see American bombs killing European children even if the pilots were English. He supported the "unrestricted sale" of defensive weapons such as anti-aircraft weapons, to England. (Radio Address, May 19, 1940)

d. European Alliances were transient and unwise to predict, finance, and fight to defend.

Of all the loans we had made during World War I, the only nation who paid us back was Finland. Lindbergh pointed out that we aided Finland in 1938, but in 1941 Finland was allied with Germany. (SF Speech, 7/1/41) The remaining debt from World War I and the new debt we were incurring by aiding these countries again was the first argument Lindbergh made against giving arms to other countries. (Radio Address, September 15, 1939)

e. Roosevelt was exceeding his presidential powers.

He had run for a third term, and until November 1941, he gradually violated the Neutrality Acts with executive orders and not with Congressional consent, as required by the Constitution. The Neutrality Acts restricted the President to "selling" aid and mandated transport on unarmed non-U.S. ships. England couldn't pay. (Peters, 2005) Roosevelt invented future compensation and thus claimed he did not violate the Neutrality Act.[6] But the ships bringing aid were U.S. ships, and as the Battle of the Atlantic raged these ships were increasingly armed, and eventually escorted by battleships. In September 1941, Roosevelt allowed these "unarmed" ships to fire at enemy ships at will. (Berg, 1998, p.426) Isolationists considered Roosevelt a dictator for violating U.S. law with impunity to support England.

f. The Presidential Election of 1940 was not democratic and thus the American people had been denied the right to determine their future.

A major tenet of Lindbergh's advocacy was advocating a national war referendum. He sought Jewish support for this tenet of his advocacy because he believed it would protect Jews from being blamed for a U.S. war. (NYC, 5/23/1941) The reader might ask why the presidential election didn't suffice.

The presidential election of 1940 didn't pit an isolationist against an interventionist. Both candidates opposed entering the war and supported aiding England. Since there were no differences in the candidates' position toward a European war, Lindbergh said this about the 1940 election:

> "Both political parties had adopted platforms against intervention in this war. Both political candidates spoke constantly of peace. Many a sincere Democrat and Republican voted with full confidence that his man, if elected, would keep our country out of war. But it seems doubtful we even had two parties last November...the people of this nation were not given the chance to vote on the greatest issue of our generation – the issue of foreign war. And yet we are now told we must go to Europe to fight for the very principles of democracy which were denied to us in our own nation last November." (Minneapolis speech, May 10, 1941)

This was no one's fault but his own. He could have run for president, spoken at the convention, or supported a candidate. He chose not to.

g. Interventionism was the product of a small group of agitators who had control of the message Americans heard and spewed propaganda.

Lindbergh believed that a small group of Americans controlled the news, and absent this control, nearly all Americans would agree with him. This was one of his first arguments and in an early radio address he calmly advocated for his version of events, "If our people know the truth, if they are accurately informed, if they are not misled by propaganda, this country is not likely to enter the war now going on in Europe." (Radio Address, October 13, 1939) But as isolationists lost political battles and American public opinion shifted against them, this argument became shrill and nasty. "They (the media) attempted to stampede our people with fear and hysteria." (Philadelphia Speech, May 29, 1941)

In the fight over what news Americans received, Lindbergh saw a continuation of the battle his father fought opposing WW I. (Minneapolis, May 10, 1941) He claimed isolationists' free speech rights were similarly being suppressed. (Cleveland, August 9, 1941) In August 1942, he was subpoenaed in the criminal trial of William Pelley, leader of the American Fascists, also for sedition. He testified and was dismissed due to lack of evidence. (Berg, 1998, p.445) In his post-testimony press release he said the government had a right to prosecute true sedition, but "nothing could be more detrimental to our American system of government than the suppression of free speech and honest opinion." (Lindbergh, Press Release, 1942).

Lindbergh's criticism of "propaganda" bordered on hypocrisy. Everyone was entitled to free speech — even fascists — but those who disagreed with him peddled fear and hysteria.

h. <u>The American people overwhelmingly supported Isolationism</u>

Polling was primitive prior to World War II, but it was apparent few Americans wanted to enter another war when Lindbergh returned to the U.S. in 1939. However, Germany's invasion of Poland, its mistreatment of civilians, its bombing of London, and its defeat in the Battle of Britain changed American opinion. By 1940, polling showed more than half of Americans disagreed with the main principle of isolationism — opposition to aiding England. (Dalleck, 2017, p.421)

Isolationists exaggerated their popular support. Eunice Armstrong, *America First's* education director, claimed 88% of Americans opposed the Lend-Lease Act. (Armstrong, 1941) Lindbergh said 4/5ths (80%) of Americans both opposed aiding England (NYC, 5/23/1941) and the Selective Service Act. (Cleveland, 8/9/41) Americans didn't vote that way. Roosevelt easily won re-election in 1940 and used his election to promote these bills, which both passed in Congress with bipartisan support. (Dalleck, 2017, p.394)

II) The Principles of Isolationism which Lindbergh did not Promote: Some of Lindbergh's advocacy promoted principles also promoted by Presidents Roosevelt and Truman.

a. Lindbergh did not believe rearmament causes war.

Between 1934 and 1936, the U.S. Senate conducted hearings called the Nye Hearings regarding our efforts to arm our soldiers in World War I. These hearings contributed to a powerful national isolationist movement, but Lindbergh opposed the principles Senator Gerald Nye (R-ND) supported.

Our entry into World War I was too abrupt for our unprepared miniscule munitions industry. Munitions companies couldn't fill massive orders on short notice and American soldiers either went without or we ordered British munitions. Senator Nye held hearings which charged large American companies with profiteering in World War I. (Peters, 2005) Instead of the truth — that some companies made money providing inferior service — Nye promoted the narrative, and the American people believed that we went to war to enrich private companies. Future President Truman said Nye's commission seriously damaged U.S. preparation for World War II. It created a narrative European Wars were not a fight between good and evil, but rather munitions caused war. (Klein, 2013)

The fallacy that weapons cause war leads to the next logical step: disarmament produces peace. FDR was defeated in a legislative attempt to rearm America in 1937 because millions of Americans advocated disarming when we needed to rearm. (Moe, 2015) (Peters, 2005) Powerful Senators like William Borah (R-ID) refused to believe war was imminent. Borah was a fervent opponent of the Versailles Treaty, called World War II a "phony war", and believed Hitler was a reasonable man who could be negotiated with. He famously said when Hitler invaded Poland that had he been able to speak to Hitler "all of this (World War II) could have been avoided." (Dalleck, 2017, p.349)

Lindbergh's father, C.A. Lindbergh, also blamed business for dragging us into World War I, but Charles never minimized the threat of fascism nor blamed business for promoting American entry into World War II.

To the contrary, he told Americans that Germany was intent on war and their capabilities were formidable before Americans were willing to accept it. He promoted preparation, advocated the pre-war production of munitions, and helped Roosevelt rearm the country in 1939. His advocacy in the U.S. was the same as in England: prepare aggressively to defend yourself and do not squander your weapons trying to defend other countries. (Cole, 1974)

b. The U.S. could not enter World War II because it was not prepared.

This argument appears throughout Lindbergh's speeches: it is foolish to declare war if you could not fight a war. It seems few would disagree. For example, 1936 Republican Presidential Nominee Alf Landon said: "There is little disagreement as to the unity of effort necessary to speed vital production for national defense. We are facing a real emergency, and there must be no half-way efforts here." (Landon, 1941) Isolationists differed from interventionists in the wisdom of sending arms abroad, which they claimed prevented the U.S. from being prepared. (St. Louis speech, 5/3/41)

But there was disagreement. Young Americans opposed rearmament. Both FDR and Lindbergh argued with them. Lindbergh was invited to Yale University to address the leaders of young isolationists in October 1940. He proposed a compromise: the U.S. had to be prepared to fight a defensive war, but domestic society had to change as well. (Yale Daily News, 10/30/40)

Isolationism and Anti-Semitism: Isolationists were not anti-Semites.

The *America First Committee* (AFC) was tainted by anti-Semitism, either because some low-level officials made anti-Semitic comments or because its detractors publicized these comments to invalidate its political legitimacy. (Ross, 1964, p.314) But an FBI internal security report in December 1940 stated *America First* was not anti-Semitic, "(the) *Committee* is not anti-Semitic and...they are not drawing any line between themselves and the Jews." (PSU, p.4) Isolationism wasn't anti-Semitism because it neither advocated a German victory nor blamed the Jews for their persecution.[7]

Isolationists supported the right of English politicians to choose to negotiate with Germany, but did not advocate England losing the war. When Germany declared war on the U.S., it disbanded and pledged to fight. The isolationists made it policy to not allow fascists into their organization, and Lindbergh emphasized they weren't welcome. (SF speech, 7/1/41) With hundreds of local chapters, some fascists slipped in and attended rallies, but in a free country there was no way to prevent this. (Olson, 2013) *America First* tried to prevent fascist infiltration. In autumn 1941, they circulated instructions to local chapters, instructing them to make no arrangements with outside organizations in order to prevent infiltration by fascists. (AF doc, 1941)

Isolationism represented legitimate opposition to an elected American president. Lindbergh repeatedly emphasized he supported the Constitution and opposition must be peaceful. (Wallace, 2003, p.284) For example, FDR espoused 4 Freedoms (freedom from fear and want, of speech and worship) at his inaugural address in 1941. Lindbergh rebutted that FDR was denying the people freedoms. He emphasized we should have the "freedom to vote on vital issues" and "the freedom of information — the right of a free people to know where they are being led by their government." (Minneapolis speech, 5/10/41)

Lindbergh wrote a speech which was to be given in Boston on December 12, 1941. In the speech, he demanded that the inequality of Black Americans be addressed, but after the Japanese attack, the speech was canceled. Drafts of the speech emphasize that freedom for Black Americans must be guaranteed before we fought a war for democracy overseas. He wrote before we consider "...freedom and democracy abroad, let us decide how these terms are to be applied to the negro populations in our Southern states". (Cole, 1974) It's unfathomable a Nazi, fascist, or even an anti-Semite would emphasize the democratic rights of Black Americans in 1941.

Isolationists included important public figures for the next half century. The entire leadership of the opposition Republican party opposed Roosevelt's effort to aid Britain and resisted a peacetime draft. Famous isolationists include future President Gerald Ford, future Democratic Vice-Presidential candidate Sargent Shriver, and future Supreme Court Justice Potter Stewart. None of these men were anti-Semites nor Nazi Sympathizers. Some Jews joined the movement including their Publicity Director. (Berg, 1998, p.419)

Lindbergh's testimony before U.S. Congressional Committees, 1941

Lindbergh's testimony before Congress damaged his reputation. At a House Foreign Affairs Committee hearing in January 1941, he was asked by two Democratic congressmen to declare who he wanted to win the war in Europe. Lindbergh was on record wanting England to be victorious and had personally sacrificed to aid England. Yet, when asked the question by the House, and two weeks later by the Senate, he refused to answer. When asked "(are) you in sympathy with England's defense against Hitler?" He answered, "I am in sympathy with the people not with their (governments') aims." (Berg, 1998)

Lindbergh told the Senate it would be easy and beneficial for him personally to say he wanted England to win, but he didn't think anyone could 'win' the devastating war to come, nor was a prostrate Europe dominated by Russia in America's interest.

> "...an English victory, if it were possible, would necessitate years of war and an invasion of the continent of Europe (which) would create prostration, famine, and disease in Europe-and probably America-such as the world has never seen before." (Senate, 2/41)

Lindbergh's prediction came true. A human requires 2500 calories per day. In 1945, the average German consumed 1100 calories/day, and the average Austrian and Hungarian consumed 800 calories/day. (Steil, 2018, p.18)

He feared an English victory would also be a Russian victory — and his fears came true. (SF speech, 7/1/41)

> "I tell you that I would a hundred times rather see my country ally itself with England, or even with Germany with all her faults, than with the cruelty, godlessness, and the barbarism that exist in Soviet Russia. An alliance between the United States and Russia should be opposed by every American, every Christian, and every humanitarian in this country."

The next President, Senator Harry Truman, said the same thing a month earlier, "If we see...Russia is winning, we ought to help Germany." (Dalleck, 2013) Lindbergh's evasion has been legitimately criticized as supporting German aims, though he did not support Germany. He should have said then what he said later — he despised Germany's actions. (Cole, 1974) (SF Speech, 7/1/41)

Although the press and some Congressmen lauded his performance in front of the two committees, (Berg, 1998, pp.413-6) refusing to answer questions was a public relations mistake. 24-year-old John F. Kennedy recognized this. While advising his father for his testimony before the same committees, Jack advised, "Where I think Lindbergh has run afoul is in his declarations that we don't care what happens over there- that we can live at peace with a world controlled by dictators...I would think your (his father's) best angle would be that of course you do not believe this...it is important that you stress that how much you dislike the idea of dealing with dictatorships." (Nasaw, 2012, p.514)

Public relations errors are not the same as Nazi sympathizing. He had already answered the question of who he wanted to win the war. John Slessor, the Deputy Director of Planning for the Royal Air Force, was advised by Lindbergh before *Kristallnacht* and said of Lindbergh, "his attitude struck us as entirely sympathetic to the British." (Nasaw,

2012, p.339) He badly misjudged public opinion by refusing to answer questions directly; but this was his right.

4) Lindbergh Defines His Foreign Policy, Chicago, August 5, 1940

This speech, given in a brutally hot Soldier Field, is controversial. Historians write Lindbergh said the U.S. must accept a Europe ruled by Germany. (Klein, 2013) This is selective criticism of Lindbergh. If the U.S. wasn't entering the war, then no one was going to liberate Europe. Democratic Presidential Candidate Roosevelt said six times in one paragraph in a speech in Boston (10/30/40) that the U.S. would not enter World War II. Republican presidential candidate Wendell Willkie said it when he abruptly espoused isolationism on October 12, 1940. (Ambrose, 1983) Even the venerated Jewish hero Harry Truman was willing to accept Europe ruled by Germany rather than Russia. (Olson, 2013, p.346)

Truman, Roosevelt, and Willkie were accepting the status quo: Germany controlled continental Europe. There is no historical evidence Roosevelt ever intended to militarily confront Germany. On August 9, 1941, Roosevelt met Churchill in Newfoundland and told Churchill the U.S. had no intention of entering the war. (Olson, 2013, p.358)

The only American public figure held to a standard of determining the status of post-war Europe in 1940 was Lindbergh. What Lindbergh actually said:

1. It was not our decision who should rule Europe.
2. This was not a war for democracy because England and France were not democracies in the eyes of their colonial subjects.
3. It was not a war for the liberty of small, powerless nations because the U.S. had the ability to aid Manchuria, and England had the ability to aid Abyssinia when these nations were invaded by fascist powers and neither one did.
4. It was not a war for Western Civilization nor religious freedom because Russia destroyed thousands of churches.

5. England and France having been the "power centers" of Europe in the past, doesn't provide a right for them to be so in the future. The U.S. can't determine the power centers in Europe.
6. Europe's wars were not solvable by powers outside of Europe.
7. Since we can't choose the victor, we can't choose with whom we will eventually negotiate. (Lindbergh, Chicago, August 5, 1940)

In a national radio address 3 days later, he said he would make a proposal to the European powers,

> "Let us offer Europe a plan for the progress and protection of Western civilization, of which they and we each form a part. But whatever their reply might be, let us carry on the American destiny of which our forefathers dreamed…let us guard the independence that the soldiers of our revolution won against overwhelming odds." (Radio address, August 8, 1940)

His plan was vague, but his predictions came true. After World War II, England and France were not the "power centers" of Europe. The two power centers were Russia and a confederation of nations (NATO) including Germany and two of England's former colonies. He predicted and feared the post-war rise of Russia. His references to "western civilization" do not include Russia. Lindbergh usually considered Russia to be part of Asia, and often referred to Russians as Asians.

France would lose two wars (Algeria and Vietnam) and thousands of soldiers before it learned the lesson of Lindbergh's speech: Colonialism is immoral and unsustainable. Rather than heed Lindbergh's warning, France committed unspeakable atrocities. Between May 8-13, 1945, the French army killed an estimated 40,000 Algerians, roughly a thousand of whom were lynched. (von Tunzelmann, 2016) England too would commit atrocities and abandon Palestine and India because it too learned Lindbergh was correct. Neither country was held accountable.

Lindbergh never said the U.S. had to accept a Europe ruled by Germany and he certainly never said the U.S. should negotiate with Germany. He was opposed to a U.S. negotiated peace with Germany. (SF speech, 7/1/41) But this speech and a national radio address noted it could not be ruled out someday we would have to negotiate with Germany. (Radio address, August 8, 1940)

Lindbergh alone was held accountable for something both presidential candidates and the next President were also saying. The press chose how to cover it and because the president was conspiring to destroy him, Lindbergh had legitimate grievances as to how he was being portrayed by the press and who was responsible for it.

<u>What Lindbergh Wanted — A National War Referendum:</u> Lindbergh's policy was the U.S. should enter a war only via a national war referendum. He advocated for one because he thought the isolationists would win. He said in Cleveland (8/9/1941):

> "These interventionists who call themselves the defenders of freedom and democracy, dare not place the issue of war to a vote of our people. They dared not let us vote on the issue of war in our last election and they dare not let us vote on war today. They are afraid to put the issue to a referendum of the people or to a vote of Congress. They know the people of this country will not vote for war and they therefore plan on involving us through subterfuge."

This country had never had a war referendum. Roosevelt's political acts don't qualify as subterfuge because Congress approved the Selective Service Act and the Lend-Lease Act. Congress would soon rescind the Neutrality Acts and approve the declaration of war. Furthermore, Lindbergh never explained why the interventionists were to blame for the candidates chosen as the party nominees in the 1940 Presidential election. It would all be moot when we were attacked.

Lindbergh believed a national war referendum benefited the Jews and he appealed for their support in a speech he gave in New York City on May 23, 1941. It is discussed in a later chapter.

5)Lindbergh's Conflict with the Press and Roosevelt

Lindbergh and the press: Blaming Jews for press coverage you disagreed with was ubiquitous during this era. As an example of how common this was in pre-World War II America, in October 1939, U.S. Ambassador to England Joseph Kennedy, Sr., gave a much-criticized speech saying democracies and fascist dictatorships would have to learn to live with each other. President Roosevelt was furious, and although some Jewish journalists criticized him, most of the criticism came from non-Jewish journalists. Nevertheless, Kennedy's adult sons wrote letters to their father stating that but for the Jews, he would have received favorable coverage. Joe Jr. wrote that Jewish columnists were "knocking his head off" and 21-year-old Harvard undergraduate John said only the Jews were angry about what his father said, everyone else thought it was good. Rather than dwell on any mistakes he might have made, Joe Sr. spent the rest of his life blaming the Jews for criticism of his ambassadorship. (Nasaw, 2012, pp.353-7)

Unlike Kennedy's anti-Semitic victimhood narrative, Lindbergh was being targeted. The President and prominent journalists were conspiring to destroy Lindbergh's credibility. (Olson, 2013, pp.131-4) William White, publisher of the *Kansas Emporia Gazette,* recruited some of the most prominent journalists of the era, including Jewish journalists such as Walter Lippmann, to convince Americans of the need to enter the war. This group was informally called the "White Committee". The White Committee vilified isolationists and communicated with President Roosevelt regarding strategy. (Cole, 1974, p.139)

But Lindbergh emphasized his disagreement with the Jews was isolated to our national interest. He did not think a war was in the Jewish interest either. On August 23, 1939, in reference to the press and Jewish businesses boycotting isolationist programming he wrote, "I do not blame the Jews so much for their attitude, although I think it unwise." (Lindbergh, 1970, p.245)

Roosevelt and the Secretary of the Interior, Harold Ickes, Conspired to Destroy Lindbergh

Lindbergh is considered a Nazi sympathizer and an anti-Semite today, in large part because Roosevelt destroyed his reputation. Roosevelt couldn't defeat Lindbergh because he was financially independent and had no political office. Roosevelt had to disqualify him as a Nazi. Because Lindbergh would not speak to the press it was easy to vilify him. Secretary Ickes destroyed Lindbergh's reputation calling him a traitor and an appeaser. (Cole, 1974, p.130)

While Lindbergh was working for the U.S. in November 1938, Ickes said Lindbergh "forfeited his right to be an American". Ickes called Lindbergh a Nazi Sympathizer with increasing ferocity with each speech. For example, at Columbia University in December 1940 Ickes said, "(Lindbergh) is a peripatetic appeaser who would surrender his sword before it is demanded." In a speech at the *Jewish National Worker's Alliance*, April 1941, "(Lindbergh is) the Nazi's number 1 fellow traveler" and "the first American to raise aloft the standard of pro-Naziism". Ickes even went after Anne calling her book *Wave of the Future*, the "Bible of every American Nazi." (Berg, 1998, pp.423-4) (Cole, 1974, p.130)

On April 22, 1941, Roosevelt joined Lindbergh vilification at a press conference when he compared him to the infamous Civil War traitors, the Copperheads, and said Lindbergh was "an appeaser". (Cole, 1974, pp.130-1) Lindbergh responded by resigning from the Army Reserves. He wrote his "loyalty, character, and motives" were being impugned. He explained that he had served his country honorably and was only seeking to "exercise my rights as an American citizen to place my viewpoint before the people of my country in a time of peace", "I will continue to serve my country to the best of my ability as a private citizen." (NYT, 4/29/1941) He told his secretary, "If I take this insult from Roosevelt, more and worse will probably be forthcoming." (Berg, 1998, p.421) Previously, Lindbergh had not criticized Roosevelt by name, he only criticized "politicians". (Cole, 1974) But now, Lindbergh criticized Roosevelt's leadership by name, saying he deliberately misled and kept the nation misinformed. (St. Louis speech, 5/3/1941).

Ickes' abuse continued. The administration's strategy of "guilt by association", was a preview of McCarthyism; smearing Lindbergh by calling him a Nazi, though Ickes acknowledged Lindbergh had no connection with any Nazi. In 1941 Ickes began to call Lindbergh, "the knight of the German eagle" (the emblem on the medal) and said, "all of Lindbergh's passionate words are to encourage Hitler." Roosevelt wrote, "when I read Lindbergh's speech, I could not help feel that it was written by Goebbels." (Cole, 1974, pp.132-5) Unwilling to defend himself in the press, Lindbergh continued his letter-writing campaign to the White House, as if Roosevelt would see the error of his ways. Lindbergh's second letter written in June 1941, reminded Roosevelt of his service to his country, his rights as an American citizen, and said he expected an apology. He received no response except for a note from Roosevelt's Press Secretary, admonishing him for releasing his letter to the press. (Cole, 1974, p.133)

The June 1941 letter asked the President for a favor. He wanted Americans to be reminded of the circumstances which led to being awarded a German medal:

> "Mr. President, is it too much to ask that you inform your Secretary of the Interior that I was decorated by the German government while I was carrying out the request of your Ambassador to that Government… in the American Embassy, in the presence of your Ambassador?"

The only response he received was from the Secretary of the Interior describing his letter as "whining". (Ross, 1964, p.302) The circumstances of Lindbergh's medal debacle are still unknown, as is Roosevelt's dishonor. His administration asked Lindbergh to put himself in a precarious position and then unabashedly used the resulting events to destroy his reputation.

If the struggle consisted of dueling speeches between Lindbergh and the administration it might not have destroyed Lindbergh's reputation, but Roosevelt mobilized the press, the Attorney General, the FBI, and Congress against Lindbergh. Through the White Committee, Roosevelt used famous personalities to demonize Lindbergh. When Lindbergh spoke, airtime was immediately provided to a celebrity to attack Lindbergh's dedication to his country, orchestrated by the White House. (Cole, 1974, p.130-133) For example, Pulitzer Prize winning playwright Robert Sherwood told the American public Lindbergh was an "unwitting (purveyor) of Nazi Propaganda." (Berg, 1998, pp.409-10)

In May 1941, Roosevelt authorized the Attorney General and the FBI to use listening devices to monitor Lindbergh's communications and in November 1941, he impaneled a Grand Jury to investigate *America First's* financial support. (Cole, 1974, p.129) About Lindbergh, Roosevelt famously bragged he would "clip that young man's wings." (Berg, 1998) Lindbergh's phones were tapped as were hundreds of other isolationists. He moved his family to isolated Martha's Vineyard to escape harassment and he was then accused of using his new house to signal German U-boats. (Olson, 2013, p.326)

Quoted in a *Chicago Daily News* article, Ickes' responded to Lindbergh's letter to the White House in June 1941 by gloating about getting under Lindbergh's skin, and privately he pledged to be even more vicious. Lindbergh could end the spat, "He can cheer on England. He can unite with those who are prepared to defend American institutions." (Cole, 1974, p.133) The author considers Ickes' proposal a foreshadowing of

Communist self-criticism sessions. Ickes said all you need to do is think correctly, admit your faults, and we'll stop destroying you.

Defeating isolationism was not just a battle of ideas but an abuse of power to destroy those who disagreed. Roosevelt chose to "discredit and dismiss" his opponents. (Olson, 2013, p.310) Historian Wayne Cole wrote, "...any individual who spoke out on the noninterventionist side was suspect and had to be prepared to have his reputation besmirched and his wisdom and even his loyalty questioned." *NY Times* journalist Dorothy Thompson, who in 1936 called Black Americans "ignorant and illiterate", equated students who opposed entry into the war, like future President Gerald Ford and future Supreme Court Justice Potter Stewart, to the Hitler Youth. (Olson, 2013, pp.311-2)

6) Conclusion: Lindbergh was not a victim.

Lindbergh made choices knowing the power of the President he was criticizing. He could have spoken to the press and defended himself, and he certainly could have answered questions forthrightly in front of Congress. He could have offered more condemnation of Germany and more support for the Jews and Poles without violating his positions.

Roosevelt was the President. If Roosevelt thought Lindbergh was a Nazi, investigating him was his responsibility. Roosevelt's use of power during wartime pales in comparison to Lincoln, Wilson, or Nixon's enemies list. (Olson, 2013) Lincoln suspended the right of *habeus corpus* and banished a political opponent to the Confederacy. Wilson arrested his opponents for opposing U.S. involvement in World War I. Despite charges of tyranny against Roosevelt, major pre-World War II legislation was passed by Congress. (Berg, 1998)

Lindbergh was neither a Nazi nor a Nazi sympathizer. This has been confirmed by an FBI investigation and by testimony given under oath in the U.S. Justice system. Lindbergh stopped corresponding with friends in Europe in case they were in communication with a Nazi organization or foreign government. (Berg, 1998, p.420) He never publicly expressed sympathy with Germany, its aims, nor supported its activities, and all questionable statements in his private journal were unknown until Lindbergh released them in 1970. (Cole, 1974) (Correll, 2014) He made a public statement which today we know exaggerated Jewish influence in the pro-war movement and the press, but he never disrespected Jews nor engaged in the vicious anti-Semitism common in his era. (Berg, 1998)

Much of the criticism of Lindbergh is warranted, especially given his specious arguments (see pp.341-6), but he was not being criticized for the premise of his argument. The premise of Lindbergh's advocacy -- the cost of entering the war would be horrific, Germany's defeat would result in Russian domination of Europe, and the U.S. would never be able to extricate itself from European affairs – was true. (Radio address, 10/13/39) His opponents didn't deny it. A Lindbergh biographer wrote, "If Lindbergh overstated his case, at least he was stating it. Roosevelt, who saw the cost of entering the war clearly, had to pussyfoot...he could only fudge and hedge." (Ross, 1964, p.296)

We also know with 80 years' hindsight the isolationists did not delay our entry into World War II. Roosevelt won every legislative battle, and he never expressed any intention of declaring war on Germany, nor is there evidence he would have. (Olson, 2013) Roosevelt gets credit for sustaining England and its ability to oppose subjugation and occupation, establishing a draft, and getting money allocated for national defense but the latter is also a credit duly given to Lindbergh. (Nasaw, 2012, p.369) Perhaps Roosevelt is also due credit for "preparing the U.S. public to enter World War II" although events over which he had no control were a major factor in changing opinions and regardless, this is a hard accomplishment to define.

The U.S. made progress setting up an arms industry and producing some weapons in large numbers, but those weapons overwhelmingly were sent overseas. (Klein, 2013) Roosevelt made few preparations to fight a war; we had fewer men in uniform on December 7, 1941, than the British evacuated at Dunkirk a year earlier. (Ambrose, 1983) But Roosevelt's success arming and feeding England and Russia using American ships protected by American warships who could shoot at the enemy at their discretion is undeniable and was unimpeded by isolationists. (Beevor, 1998)

There would there be no national referendum. Isolationists failed to prevent Roosevelt from accomplishing his vision of our national interest. (Cole, 1974) Yet the U.S. was completely unprepared for the Japanese attack on Pearl Harbor, incarcerated Japanese Americans without due process, and suffered the worst military defeats in our history, e.g. Kasserine Pass and the surrender of the Philippines, after entering the war. Perhaps keeping our "hose" would have been better?

Despite his political victories, President Roosevelt did not prepare the U.S. for World War II. Only he should be blamed.

Personal Thoughts: On July 14, 1941, Ickes said about Lindbergh, "I have never heard this Knight of the German Eagle denounce Hitler or Naziism or Mussolini or fascism." This isn't completely true, for example, in San Francisco two weeks earlier, he called the Germans actions "horrors" and "gangster tactics". But it's mostly true. Lindbergh felt as a neutral nation criticizing combatants was a mistake. In a national radio address on June 5, 1940, he gave his reason for his reluctance to criticize Germany, "Nothing is to be gained by shouting names or pointing fingers across the ocean." But there was something to be gained — moral credibility.

Partly as a result, millions of Americans and specifically Jews hated him.

Lindbergh was hated and only Lindbergh should be blamed for it.

Despite the extent of German atrocities were not yet known, "independent" media collaboration with Roosevelt to destroy him, political conventions were different, and although he opposed German actions on occasion; Lindbergh failed to sufficiently condemn Germany's actions and didn't publicly support the victims. Having been to Nazi Germany he was the one person who should have seen their true nature. He never did.

It isn't fair to say he didn't like Jews because there's no evidence to support the charge, but clearly, once he returned to the U.S., he wasn't sympathetic to Jewish suffering. This was because he was an analytical person and Jewish concerns didn't affect his version of the national interest. Being overly analytical, he often failed to sympathize with others' suffering. He was insufferably demanding and was often not nice according to his children; but it was never based on others' ethnicity. (Olson, 2013, p.456)

But condemning Lindbergh for his insensitivity to the suffering of others, ignores that the "nice" people in positions of power who claimed to be sympathetic to Europe's Jews didn't help. Republican Presidential Candidate Willkie represented many politicians; when it was inconvenient to help Jews, they simply ignored them and seldom fought the legislative battles that needed to be fought. Legislative efforts to help European Jews, for example the Wagner-Rogers Bill or the Labor Department's efforts to provide visas to Jewish professionals with needed expertise, died due to neglect. (Morse, 1968, p.218) Most egregiously, Ickes' boss, President Roosevelt, acted as though he was sympathetic, but did not help the Jews even though he was aware his appointees in the State Department were interfering with those who wanted to help.

As sympathetic and interested as Roosevelt claimed to be in the plight of the Jews, he participated in thwarting the ability of Jews to flee Germany. While Lindbergh used whatever power he had to help Jews leave, Roosevelt was complicit in the murder of hundreds of thousands of Jews.

And that's a story worth telling. Keep reading.

[2]FBI report on *America First* and fascism -- references to Lindbergh: 1) he had no significant involvement with *America First.* The details of *AFC* meetings, e.g. lists of attendees and officers, do not include Lindbergh, 2) description of friendship with Robert McCormick, owner of the *Chicago Tribune* (see allegation in table 1, p.195). The FBI report the author located contained some redactions, but others have reviewed the entire report and found no additional evidence against Lindbergh. (see Berg, 1998, p. 409)

[5] Lindbergh opposed U.S. military alliances, notably the alliance between the U.S. and England. But he "opposed even more strongly a military alliance between the U.S. and Germany." (San Francisco, July 1, 1941) Therefore, quotes demonstrating Lindbergh supported negotiating with Germany <u>during the war</u> are distorted; they undoubtedly refer to U.S. policy <u>after the war</u>. Lindbergh's Chicago speech (August 5, 1940) is truncated to falsely portray Lindbergh supporting negotiating with Nazi Germany. (Friedman, 2007, p.186) The purpose of that speech was defining, "the relationship we will have with Europe <u>after the war</u>". His words, "In the future" are removed from the quote, "...an agreement between *us* could maintain civilization and peace" thus distorting his meaning. Also, "us" is defined as the U.S. and a hypothetical unnamed victor — it could refer to Russia, with whom we did negotiate.

[6] Some of the compensation Roosevelt arranged to receive from Britain, in order to comply with the Neutrality Acts, was only on paper. For example, the *Bases for Destroyers Agreement* in September 1940 gave the U.S. a "lease" to use British naval bases in exchange for 50 naval destroyers. U.S. ships had already been refueling at these bases without a lease.

[7] The *America First Committee* which disbanded in 1941 was unrelated to a racist anti-Semitic political party called the *America First Party* (1943-1952) founded by Gerald L. K. Smith. The former officers of the AFC disavowed this party as did its Vice-Presidential nominee in 1944. The words "America First" have been used periodically since by other unrelated political movements. (Feldman, 2011, p.324)

Works Cited

Some speeches available on CharlesLindbergh.com. Lindbergh's radio addresses are on line.

Ambrose, S. (1983). *Rise to Globalism.* USA: Pelican Works.

Americans and the Holocaust. (n.d.). Retrieved from USHMM: https://exhibitions.ushmm.org/americans-and-the-holocaust/personal-story/frances-perkins

Beevor, A. (1998). *Stalingrad.* New York: Penguin Publishers.

Beir, R. (2006). *Roosevelt and the Holocaust.* New York: Barricade.

Berg, A. S. (1998). *Lindbergh.* New York: Penguin Books.

Black, C. (2013). The Real Henry Wallace. *National Review.*

Chaplin FBI File. (2015). Retrieved from Internet Archive: https://archive.org/details/CharlieChaplin-FBI/page/n3/mode/2up

Cole, W. (1974). *Charles Lindbergh and the Battle Against Intervention in World War II.* New York: Jovanovich.

Cook, B. (2000). *Eleanor Roosevelt, The Defining Years.* New York: Penguin Publishing.

Correll, J. (2014, August). The Cloud Over Lindbergh. *Air Force Magazine,* pp. 76-82.

Dalleck, R. (2017). *Franklin Roosevelt.* New York.

Des Moines Speech. (1941, September 11). Retrieved from Charles Lindbergh an American Aviator: http://www.charleslindbergh.com/americanfirst/speech.asp

Dorthy Thompson. (n.d.). Retrieved from https://en....org/wiki/Dorothy_Thompson

Downey, K. (2009). *The Woman Behind the New Deal.* New York: Anchor Books.

FactCheck.org. (n.d.). Retrieved from https://www.factcheck.org/2016/02/donald-trump-and-the-iraq-war/

Feldman, N, *Scorpions*, Hachette Books, NY, 2010.

Friedman, D., *The Immortalists,* Harper Perennial, NY, 2007.

Herman, A. (2000). Joseph McCarthy. New York: The Free Press.

JTA. (1931). Retrieved from JTA Archive: https://www.jta.org/1931/03/12/archive/einstein-says-chaplin-is-half-jewish-his-grandfather-was-a-jew

Katz, R. (2003). *The Battle For Rome.* New York: Simon and Schuster.

Klein, M. (2013). *A Call To Arms.* New York: Bloomsbury Press.

Landon, A. (1941). *Vital Speeches of the Day*, 8.

Laura Ingalls (aviator). (n.d.). Retrieved from https://en....org/wiki/Laura_Ingalls_(aviator)

Lindbergh, C. A. (1970). The Wartime Journals of Charles Lindbergh. New York: Jovanovich.

McCullough, D. (1992). *Truman.* New York: Simon and Schuster.

Medoff, R. (2017). *The Jews Should Keep Quiet.* Philadelphia: University of Nebraska Press.

Moe, R. (2015). *Roosevelt's Second Act.* New York: Oxford Academic Press.

Morse, A. (1968). *While Six Million Died.* New York: Random House.

Nasaw, D. (2012). The Patriarch. London: Penguin Press.

Olson, L. (2013). *Those Angry Days.* New York: Random House.

PBS. (n.d.). Retrieved from Transcript of Barack Obama's Keynote Speech at the 2004 DNC: https://www.pbs.org/newshour/show/barack-obamas-keynote-address-at-the-2004-democratic-national-convention

Perry, K. (2017). Unveiling Joseph P. Kennedy. *All That's Interesting.*

Peters, C. (2005). Five Days in Philadelphia. New York: Publicaffairs.

Pressman, S. (2014). 50 Children. New York: Harper Collins.

PSU, Penn State University, America First FBI File, America First Committee - OneDrive (sharepoint.com)

Rosen, R. (2006). *Saving the Jews.* New York: Thunder Mouth Press.

Ross, W, *The Last Hero: Charles A. Lindbergh*, Harper and Row, NY, 1964.

Steil, B, *The Marshall Plan,* Simon and Shuster, 2018.

Taylor, A. (2017). American Nazis in the 1930s. *The Atlantic.*

Vincent, I. (2018, September 2). The Story Behind the Nazis Greatest Enemy. *NY Post.*

von Tunzelmann, A. (2016). *Blood and Sand.* New York: Harper Collins.

12: Larger Fish to Fry

FDR and the Jews, 1933-1945

Many books have been written about Roosevelt and the Jews. This chapter evaluates the relationship from the perspective of a series of math problems. This chapter examines the difference between the number of U.S. immigration visas available and those issued.

For every European country from which the Jews applied to emigrate, the difference was in the tens of thousands, even though there was a surplus of qualified Jewish applicants. As a result, between half a million and a million and a half Jews were murdered. According to the quotas established by U.S. immigration law they should have been safely in the U.S..

It has been known since 1943 that the denial of visas to Jews was the result of a deliberate policy of the U.S. State Department. The chapter addresses what motivated the State Department and to what extent Roosevelt bears responsibility.

In 1936, the Head of the Zionist Organization of America, Rabbi Stephen Wise, was lobbying President Roosevelt to support a boycott of German goods in support of the Jews in Germany. Future Supreme Court Justice Felix Frankfurter assured Wise that Roosevelt would support a boycott, "I feel sure he is watching this thing with sympathy and understanding."

Two weeks later Hjalmar Schacht, the Head of the German National Bank (Reichsbank), visited Washington, DC and Roosevelt gave him every courtesy and honor provided to visiting dignitaries. When U.S. diplomat James McDonald asked Roosevelt why he had ignored Wise's request and treated Schacht with full diplomatic privileges, Roosevelt said he had "...larger fish to fry" and he would make "no public statement" on behalf of the Jews. Instead, he gave a speech about the friendly relations enjoyed by the U.S. and Germany. Schacht reported back to Hitler that Roosevelt was "doubtlessly sympathetic to the...German chancellor". (Medoff, 2019, p.18-19) There was no economic boycott of Germany.

Between Hitler's rise to power in 1933 and our entry in World War II, 575,000 German Jews and 190,000 Austrian Jews were stripped of their rights, beaten in the streets, disappeared, murdered, or taken to concentration camps never to be seen again. Many of these Jews held American citizenship. These events were documented by the press and in reports to the Roosevelt administration as early as 1933. (Dalleck, 2017, p.160) No branch of the Roosevelt administration protested.

This chapter contains documentation from Roosevelt, his appointees, a memo provided to Roosevelt, his Vice President Harry Truman, First Lady Eleanor Roosevelt, and his own Treasury Department, documenting Roosevelt's motive: disregard for Jewish lives because there was no political benefit to be derived from acting otherwise.

Historical Context — Only Roosevelt Refused to Help the Jews:

In context of his predecessors' behavior (other presidents had political challenges too), Roosevelt was disinterested in the plight of the Jews, and the people he appointed to run the State Department were intent on not allowing Jews, and only Jews, into this country. Roosevelt was regularly briefed on these actions and approved of them. (Morse, 1968) For example, his predecessor Herbert Hoover was president for two months of Hitler's reign in Germany. Hoover faced many of the same challenges as Roosevelt, yet Hoover's ambassador to Germany protested the mistreatment of Jews. (Breitman, 2013, p.44) Roosevelt was president for nearly 9 years while Hitler was in power and didn't protest German actions. Roosevelt told his ambassador it was an internal German matter. (Downey, 2009, p.189) As a result of Roosevelt's policy, his Secretary of State Cordell Hull said, "the plight of German Jews was...a domestic German affair and hence above intervention." (Rolde, 2013, p.139)

Roosevelt maintained friendly relations with Jewish leaders at the same time his disdain for the Jews was unprecedented. In 1790, President George Washington assured the Jews of Newport, Rhode Island that Jews would enjoy the freedom provided to every citizen. Since then, every other American president formally protested and used U.S. power to protect Jews abroad. FDR refused because he decided the importance of maintaining friendly relations with an evil foreign government was more important. (Skwire, 2016)

Table 1: History of U.S. Presidential Intervention in Cases of the Mistreatment of the Jews

Year	President/ Secretary of State	Party	Country Mistreating Jews	Issue	Complaint Delivered/ Through	Result
1840	Van Buren	Dem	Syria/ Ottoman Empire	Pogrom	Yes, Egyptian Consulate	Refuge offered to Jews (1)
1855	Buchanan	Dem	Switzerland	Constitution gives rights only to Christians (2)	Yes	Rewritten in 1874 Jews given rights
1863	Lincoln / Seward	Rep	Morocco	Mistreatment/ Massacre in Marrakesh	Yes	Mistreatment stopped (3)
1867	Andrew Johnson /Blaine	Rep	Ottoman Empire	Jews expelled from Constantinople/ Massacre in Barfurush	Yes	Expulsions stopped (4)
1870	Grant	Rep	Romania/ Russia	Mistreatment of Jews/Expulsions	Spoke forcefully against actions	Appointed Jewish Consul to Romania (5)
1903 1906	Theodore Roosevelt	Rep	Russia	Kishniev Pogrom Bialystok Pogrom	Formal Rebuke	Protest to Czar (6)
1912	WH Taft	Rep	Russia	Mistreatment	Yes	Russo-U.S. treaty 1832 revoked (7)

1-4, ROAJTFGB20, n.d. 5. (Sarna, 2012) 6-7. (Singer, 2015)

No formal U.S. complaint about treatment of the Jews affected a domestic agenda, involved the consent of the opposition party, was not done because of concerns regarding the state of the economy, or required legislation. FDR's opposition often supported efforts to find refuge for Jews. (Medoff, 2019, p.201)

In the history of the United States, and in the history of 46 U.S. Presidents, Franklin Roosevelt, and he alone, refused to protest the mistreatment of Jews. Of course, German mistreatment of Jews was much worse during the Roosevelt administration than any foreign governments' during any administration.

<u>While Every Other President's Legacy is Critically Evaluated, Roosevelt's is often not Questioned:</u> Roosevelt's acknowledgement of *Kristallnacht* was weak, delayed, and conciliatory.

Richard Moe was Vice President Mondale's Chief of Staff. He wrote Roosevelt "was deeply affected by *Kristallnacht*". (Moe, 2013, p.28) Historian Robert Rosen wrote, "Roosevelt was shocked," but the documented Roosevelt is Eleanor, not Franklin. (Rosen, 2006, p.77) Did FDR care about *Kristallnacht*?

The only president to declare mistreatment of Jews an "internal matter" responded to reports detailing brutality of the Nazis towards German Jews with insensitivity and condescension. Once he counseled others to "...remind them (the Jews) they have been 'on the run' for about four thousand years" implying Nazi persecution was neither new nor worth complaining about. (Dalleck, 2017, p.324)

The traditional villains — Lindbergh, Chamberlain, and Kennedy — immediately criticized *Kristallnacht*, named the perpetrator, and the victims. (Nasaw, 2012, p.360) (Berg, 1998, p.380) Even Henry Ford criticized the Nazis by name. (Rosen, 2006, p.76) Roosevelt did not. He took 4 days to respond, never acknowledged the victims were Jews, and refused to name the perpetrators. When asked if he had anything to say he said, "No, I think not". Later, he read a statement which mentions neither victims nor perpetrators nor "condemns" or even "disapproves". People are "shocked", nothing more. The news came from Germany, but who did it isn't mentioned. Reporters described his mood as "jaunty".

> "The news of the past few days from Germany has deeply shocked public opinion in the United States. Such news from any part of the world would inevitably produce a similar profound reaction among American people in every part of the nation. I could scarcely believe that such things could occur in a twentieth century civilization." (Morse, 1968, p.231)

Asked if he had made a protest to Germany, Roosevelt said, "Nothing has gone that I know of". Asked if there would be any Jews admitted to the U.S. as a result Roosevelt said, "That is not in contemplation, we have the quota system." Jewish White House aide Ben Cohen wrote a draft for Secretary of the Interior Harold Ickes to read on CBS radio; the administration removed all references to 'Jews'. (Medoff, 2019, p.82) U.S. trade with Germany continued without restriction. Franklin Roosevelt made no other statement of concern nor criticized the Nazis for *Kristallnacht*, not even in private.

His Secretary of the Interior, Harold Ickes, used *Kristallnacht* to attack Lindbergh, who had expressed neither a political position nor political ambitions. At a Zionist conference Ickes berated Lindbergh for accepting a medal "at the hands of a brutal dictator who with that same hand is robbing and torturing his fellow human beings." (Cole, 1974, p.43) Ickes, too, couldn't say the victims were 'Jews'.

After *Kristallnacht*, Roosevelt recalled Ambassador Hugh Wilson from Germany. Historians claim the recall of the ambassador was a protest, (Rosen, 2006, p.77) but Roosevelt never stated this was his reason. (Breitman, 2013, p.114) Roosevelt never met with Wilson to discuss the situation. (Morse, 1968, p.231) When withdrawing an ambassador as a protest, presidents formally protest as President Theodore Roosevelt had done twice when Russia mistreated Jews in 1903 and 1906. (Dalleck, 2017, p.324)

For documentation, historians quote each other crediting Roosevelt for a bold action on behalf of Jews. But there is no quote from Roosevelt, even in private, giving this as his motivation. Then historians blame the leaders of other countries for not following Roosevelt's lead, (Rosen, 2006, p.77) but other leaders couldn't follow his "lead" without a reason.

Perhaps Roosevelt withdrew Wilson because he attended Nazi rallies and blamed the Jews for *Kristallnacht?* No one, including Wilson, noticed a change in policy. Rather than a reprimand, Wilson returned to a prime diplomatic job. (HW, nd) Roosevelt couldn't publicly reprimand Wilson for attending Nazi rallies because his Secretary of Commerce also attended a Nazi rally. (Medoff, 2019, p.34)

After *Kristallnacht*, Roosevelt received reports of hundreds of thousands of Jews being deported. His response was to joke at a press conference in October 1941 that Hitler was only trying to get the Jews to explain how they parted the Red Sea. (Breitman, 2013, p.189)

Roosevelt can be defended. For example, it can be pointed out Hoover was a lame-duck and FDR had other political considerations. Eleanor said, "Franklin frequently restrained from supporting causes in which he believed, because of political realities." (Morse, 1968, p.255) But historians have been disingenuous for 80 years by portraying his delayed, non-accusatory, weak response to *Kristallnacht* as a strong statement of condemnation. (Burns, 2022) He did not make such a statement.

He would neither condemn Germany nor support Europe's Jews for six and half more years — after we'd been at war with Germany for two and half years. In March 1944, he released a statement, "The wholesale extermination of the Jews goes on unabated every hour. That these people…should perish on the eve of triumph over barbarism which their persecution symbolizes, would be a major tragedy." Despite all the reports of atrocities it took years, but even then, he said too little. (Lelyveld, 2016, p.94)

Roosevelt's Actions and U.S. Immigration Law:

German and Austrian citizens were entitled to a certain number of U.S. visas according to the 1921 and 1924 Immigration Acts. (Breitman, 2013, pp.26-27) The Roosevelt administration obstructed issuing German and Austrian visas to Jewish Austrians and Germans but not to non-Jewish applicants. (Morse, 1968) (Rolde, 2013, p.11) Germany was granted 26,000 immigrants a year and Austria 3,000 a year, but only 26% of the visa spots were used and not due to lack of qualified applicants. German and Austrian Jews queued for hours to apply, for example the U.S. consulate in Stuttgart received 110,000 applications for 850 spots. (Morse, 1968, p.238) (Burns, 2022) Between 1933 and 1941 there were 261,000 visa openings allocated to German and Austrian citizens, but only 71,000 of them were used and 190,000 visa slots were wasted. (Morse, 1968)

Other American politicians behaved differently. Hoover limited immigration for all groups. (Breitman, 2013, p.29) Roosevelt's Republican opponents in the 1940s — Wendell Willkie, Robert Taft, and Thomas Dewey — all supported various initiatives and on occasion lobbied the Roosevelt administration to facilitate saving Jews. (Rolde, 2013) According to the Constitution, laws can't be ignored by the executive branch or applied only to some ethnicities. Congressman Emmanuel Cellar (D-NY) stated this in a public hearing, "When Congress passes immigration laws, the State Department has no right to reduce quotas 92%." (Morse, 1968, p.136)

The Roosevelt Administration Policy Was to Deliberately Deny Visas to Jews

Assistant Secretary of State Breckinridge Long established the State Department policy of preventing Jews from receiving visas in a State

Department memo, "We can delay and effectively stop for an indefinite length of time...immigration to the United States...by simply advising our consuls to put every obstacle in the way and to require additional evidence and to resort to various administration devices to postpone and postpone and postpone the granting of visas." (Dalleck, 2017, pp.395-6) (Pressman, 2014, pp.135-6)

These obstacles were specific to Jews: fear of spies only among Jews to delay granting visas, although no such "spy" would ever be found. (Medoff, 2017, p.92) (Morse, 1968) The administration deliberately refused to accept documents necessary for emigration only from Jews. (Rolde, 2013) Immigration quotas ensured spots from "other refugees", including those that were not subject to threats and were therefore not "refugees". (Rolde, 2013, p.11) (Dallek, 2017, p.352)

At the Evian Conference in 1938, the Dominican Republic offered to take 100,000 Jewish refugees. The Roosevelt administration feared these Jews would come to the U.S. and blocked the offer. The U.S. Virgin Islands offered to take Jews, but this was also blocked by Roosevelt. (Breitman, 2013, pp.130-2)

After *Kristallnacht*, the United Kingdom offered the use of its unused visa slots for Jewish refugees from wherever they might apply. In 1938, the UK did not use 62,356 entry visas to the U.S.. In the 4 years between the offer and U.S. entry into World War II, this amounts to more than 249,000 potential Jewish refugees. **The U.S. State Department denied the British offer as instructed specifically by the President because they were for Jews.** Sumner Welles, the Undersecretary of State, also decided "responsible" American Jews agreed with this decision.

> "I reminded the Ambassador that <u>the President</u> officially stated once more only two days ago that there was no intention on the part of this government to increase the quota already established for German nationals. I added that it was my very strong impression that the

> responsible leaders among American Jews would be the first to urge that no change in the quota of German Jews be made." (Morse, 1968, p.234)

The State Department did not make policy independent of Roosevelt. The individual who conducted policy, John Farr Simmons, Chief of the Visa Division of the U.S. State Department, said in 1938 it was Roosevelt's policy, "the drastic reduction in immigration was an obvious and predictable result of administrative practices." (Medoff, 2019, p.62) Breckinridge Long regularly briefed Roosevelt on these policies and said Roosevelt was "100% in accord with my ideas." (Medoff, 2019, p.284)

In September 1940, 80 Portuguese Jews arriving in Norfolk, Virginia were denied entry visas. The President sided with Long over his wife who protested. (Dalleck, 2017, p.396) In 1940, no immigration quota was filled and the quota for Portugal was ample for these Jews to enter the U.S.. (Morse, 1968, p.94) That same month, Eleanor Roosevelt was informed by the *Advisory Committee on Political Refugees* that the State Department was engaged in a deliberate "policy of obstruction... directed by the head of the State Department". Fiery arguments with the State Department and discussions with her husband were ineffective in changing the situation. (Kearns-Goodwin, 1994, pp.172-176)

<u>Let's Do the Math:</u> Table 2: Visas for German and Austrian Jews not used due to Roosevelt Administration policies, 1933-1941

Country of Destination	**Year(s)**	**Origin of Visa Allocation**	**Number of Unused Visas**	**Reason**
U.S.	Germany 1933-41 Austria 1938-41	1921 and 1924 Immigration Acts	190,000	Active Obstruction: FDR Administration
Dominican Republic	1938	Evian Conference Commitment	99,000	Blocked by FDR Administration

U.S.	1938-1941	Offered by United Kingdom, refused	249,000	Refused by State Department at FDR's directive

Total: 538,000

Reference: (Morse, 1968, p.94)

Let's put this number in context. There were 575,000 Jews in Germany prior to World War II. If the Roosevelt administration had simply filled existing quotas and not interfered with two foreign sovereign governments' offers, nearly every one of them could have left Germany.

The excuses historians make regarding legislative opposition to increasing quotas are straw-man arguments. For example, in the Ken Burns' documentary *The U.S. and the Holocaust*, Deborah Lipstadt said Roosevelt couldn't change immigration policy by executive action. No critic of Roosevelt ever said he should have, nor needed to do so. The existing quotas were not being filled. (Burns, 2022)

This is a conservative estimate: 1.3-1.5 million is a more accurate estimate.

Historian Arthur Morse calculated that the number of unused visas from all the European countries from which Jews applied to emigrate after Hitler seized power in 1933 exceeded **1.3 million**. (Morse, 1968, p.94) Consider the implication: had the Roosevelt administration complied with the law — the Immigration Acts of 1921 and 1924 — more than a fifth (22%) of the Jews murdered in the Holocaust would have found refuge in the U.S..

But even this number isn't comprehensive. It doesn't include other opportunities to save Jews, for example offers from the Virgin Islands, the Dominican Republic, and the 937 Jewish refugees on the ship the *MS St. Louis*. The *St. Louis* was bringing refugees from Germany and was sent back to Europe on June 6, 1939, after our government refused to let the Jewish passengers disembark. Roosevelt not only refused to intervene; he didn't respond. Roosevelt understood they were going to Germany. (Thomas, 1974)

There is documentation Roosevelt sought advice on "potential areas for settling displaced Jews." (Dalleck, 2017, p.325) But those areas were never in the U.S. and when other nations made offers, Roosevelt blocked them for fear the refugees would make it to the U.S.. (Breitman, 2013, pp.130-2)

<u>FDR was told the motivation was anti-Semitism:</u>

FDR was aware of the policies and the anti-Semitic motivation of the State Department. In addition to the above references, he was personally handed a memo which said, "(you are made) familiar…with the utter failure of certain officials in our State Department, who are charged with actually carrying out this policy, have failed (sic) to take any effective action to prevent the extermination of Jews in German-controlled Europe…responsible people and organizations have ceased to view our failure as the product of simple incompetence…they see plain **anti-Semitism** motivating the actions of these State Department officials." (Morse, 1968, pp.90-91) Eleanor told her husband the State Department's actions were motivated by fascism to which FDR responded, "you mustn't say that." (Medoff, 2019, p.91)

<u>Assistant Secretary of State Breckinridge Long Committed Perjury:</u>

Due to lobbying by Jews, on November 9, 1943, two congressmen introduced a resolution to aid refugees in Europe. (Breitman, 2013, p.228) Long testified before Congress against this initiative to save Jews. He complained such an effort would "duplicate functions already carried out by the (State) Department" and "would interrupt relationships already established". Under oath Long testified, "We have taken into this country since the beginning of the Hitler Regime and the persecution of the Jews, until today, approximately 580,000 refugees." (Rescue Resolution, n.d.)

Although this was a closed-door session, journalists exposed his lie: 580,000 was the number of German visa openings which existed since 1933, only half of them had been filled, and only half by Jews. The Secretary of the Treasury told Roosevelt that Long decided to "cover up his previous position" because he knew it was "indefensible". (Morse, 1968, p.91)

Long established U.S. policy of denying Jews visas and then testified under oath they had been issued. (Dalleck, 2017, p.395) That's the definition of perjury. If Long's statement had been true (i.e. the law was obeyed) nearly every German Jew would have escaped the Holocaust. He wasn't indicted for perjury.

<u>The Treasury Report of 1943 Documented Responsibility for the Murder of the Jews:</u> Inspired by Long's perjury, the Treasury Department investigated the State Department's actions.

It concluded the U.S. State Department deliberately obstructed opportunities to rescue Jewish refugees, blocked information regarding the treatment of Jews in Europe, and covered up their actions. (Rescue Resolution, n.d.) The General Counsel of the Treasury Department, Randolph Paul, submitted a report, *Report to the Secretary on the Acquiescence of This Government in the Murder of the Jews.* It concludes:

> (State Department Officials) have not only failed to use the Governmental machinery at their disposal to rescue Jews from Hitler, but have gone so far as to use its Governmental machinery to prevent the rescue of Jews.
>
> They have not only failed to cooperate with private organizations in the efforts to work out individual programs of their own, but have taken steps designed to prevent these programs from being put into effect.

> They not only have failed to facilitate the obtaining of information concerning Hitler's plans to exterminate the Jews of Europe but in their official capacity have gone so far as to surreptitiously attempt to stop the obtaining of information concerning the murder of the Jewish population of Europe.
>
> They have tried to cover up their guilt by a) concealment and misrepresentation, b) the giving of false and misleading explanations for their failures to act and their attempts to prevent action, and c) the issuance of false and misleading statements concerning the 'action' which they have taken to date. (Morse, 1968, p.89)

The report is conclusive: The administration's actions were inexcusable. Given his authority and documented knowledge of these actions, Roosevelt was complicit and ultimately responsible.

Roosevelt Repeated German Propaganda:

Prior to *Kristallnacht*, the U.S. foreign service believed Germany's behavior could be changed, or the U.S. and Germany could reach an agreement which would include refuge for the Jews. It thus discouraged boycotts or formal protests as counter-productive. (Nasaw, 2012) But after it, much of the foreign service stopped expecting Germany's behavior to change and some tried to help save Jews. But Roosevelt's solicitous behavior towards the Germans and his refusal to help Jews did not change.

Instead, Roosevelt showed understanding towards Germany's "specific and understandable complaints towards the Jews in Germany". In 1941, Roosevelt pointed out, "…while they (the Jews) represent only a small part of the population, over 50 percent of the doctors, lawyers, school teachers, college professors, etc. in Germany were Jews." (Medoff R., 2020) In addition, to being wild exaggerations (Jews made up less than 1% of teachers and they never constituted more than 16% of any profession), no other American President ever accepted and repeated enemy propaganda.

Jewish Pressure Against Germany Was Undermined by Roosevelt:

There were a few notable instances in which American Jews protested and surprisingly there was a modest effect, but each time our government refused to back the Jews. Prior to the war, each time the Jews planned a protest, the German government took notice and made "promises" the treatment of Jews would improve if protests were canceled. Of course, the promises were meaningless, but it demonstrated the Nazis were sensitive about their international image. Opportunity to help was missed. When our government was asked to approve of a protest, the response was the treatment of Jews in Germany was improving and the protest would make it worse. (Breitman, 2013, p.53)

Germany was sensitive to protests and Americans, other than the administration, supported actions against the Nazis. On July 26, 1935, a German ocean liner was met in New York harbor by protestors who tore down the Nazi flags on the ship and hurled them in the water. The charges against the six protestors were dismissed on the grounds that tearing down of the Nazi flag was justified. But in a repeating pattern the administration apologized to the German government. (Burns, 2022)

Roosevelt used dishonesty to reduce political pressure to help the Jews:

In 1938, the British High Commission on Palestine prepared to release a statement called the "White Paper" which would end Jewish immigration from Germany to Palestine. U.S. Jews protested. As a result of Roosevelt's policy, his Secretary of State Cordell Hull, instructed the U.S. Ambassador to Britain, Joseph Kennedy, to "unofficially inform (the British) that during the past few days the White House and (State) Department have received thousands of telegrams and letters from all over the United States protesting against the alleged intention of the British Government...to curtail or eliminate Jewish immigration." Kennedy did as he was told but knew it was posturing. His biographer wrote, "no matter what Roosevelt might say to Zionist leaders and sympathizers in Washington, the U.S. government was not going to involve itself". (Nasaw, 2012, p.388)

Joseph Kennedy knew in 1939 what is not acknowledged today — Roosevelt was disinterested in the plight of the Jews and wouldn't help. On May 1, 1939, Kennedy met with the Zionist representative in London (and future Prime Minister of Israel), Moshe Sharett. Kennedy kept the meeting short because he "had nothing to say that Sharett wanted to hear and saw no reason to prolong the discomfort." He knew the British would cut Jewish immigration to Palestine and Roosevelt would do nothing. (Nasaw, 2012)

Meanwhile, Roosevelt met with prominent Jews at the White House. The President assured them he had instructed Kennedy to "keep in touch with Prime Minister Chamberlain". The delegation believed this meant, and thus relayed to their organizations, that Roosevelt was "demand(ing) that he (Chamberlain) be especially attentive to the Zionist stance." However, the only instruction Roosevelt had given Kennedy was to ask if the British would delay the announcement. (Nasaw, 2012, pp.387-9)

Jewish Advocacy was effective but too late:

On November 8, 1942, the U.S. occupied French North Africa. Prior to the U.S. invasion, the Vichy French leaders imprisoned thousands of Jews in slave labor camps in North Africa. Churchill denounced the Vichy French government as collaborators who aided Germany's war against England. But Roosevelt considered it the legitimate representative of the French people. (Olson, 2017, pp.212-4) Thus, while Roosevelt denounced German atrocities against French non-Jews, he was silent when Vichy France deported Jews and these labor camps continued to function.

On December 17, 1942, the *New York Times* documented these slave labor camps still functioned and asked in an interview, "(whether) the abrogation of anti-Jewish laws (and) release of prisoners" would really happen? On January 1, 1943, at a Press Conference Roosevelt said "I think most of the prisoners have been released" but they had not. Once again, he wouldn't say "Jews".

Pressed further on the status of Jews in slave labor camps under U.S. custody, on January 17, 1943, Roosevelt said, "...the whole Jewish problem should be studied carefully, and that progress should definitely be planned." Finally, Jews refused to accept empty platitudes from Roosevelt. Jews protested and articles criticizing the situation appeared in the press. On February 14, 1943, the *American Jewish Congress* and the *World Jewish Congress* issued a joint public statement "the anti-Jewish legacy of the Nazis remains intact in North Africa." Jewish pressure worked. The camps began to close in March 1943 and the last inmates were freed in the summer, after roughly 8 months of internment under U.S. supervision. Jewish intervention and pressure freed them. (Medoff, 2019, p.135-7)

History could have been different. Jews overwhelmingly voted for Roosevelt many times. They could have demanded he act in their interests much sooner.

<u>Arguments made in Roosevelt's defense:</u> Similar to the straw-man arguments noted above, excuses made by historians are not reasonable and frequently lack historic documentation.

a) <u>Spies</u>: The first time Roosevelt expressed concern Jewish refugees included German spies was at a press conference on June 5, 1940. He said, "refugees out of Germany...especially Jewish refugees, they found a number of definitely proven spies," (Medoff, 2019, p.93) More than a hundred thousand ethnic Germans and Austrians emigrated to the U.S. prior to World War II. The FBI began arresting German-born spies in 1938, but Roosevelt never expressed concern (Patenaude, 2020); even after a German spy stole the design for an advanced bombsight in 1937. (Olson, 2014, p.335) He warned only about Jewish spies who lacked resources, connections, and motive. No Jewish spy was ever found.

Historians blame public hysteria for fear of spies obstructing Jewish immigration and point to a major anti-Nazi movie, *Confessions of a Nazi Spy* (1939) (Burns, 2022). But the movie was about German spies. Roosevelt encouraged refugees on a "broad religious basis." (Dalleck, 2017, p.352) Apparently, Roosevelt encouraged all religions to apply for visas, but when there was fear of spies it was specific for non-existent Jewish spies.

Meanwhile, German American disloyalty continued, sometimes in public. A German man was convicted of acquiring manufacturing information to pass to the Nazis. (O'Brien, 2022) Three German Americans were convicted of trying to give the German government details of American military installations on the East Coast in the Rumrich Spy Case. (Rumrich Spy Case, n.d.) The German Bund (Covenant) filled Madison Square Garden with 20,000 German Americans in February 1939, all of them publicly pledged support to Hitler. The head of the Bund, Fritz Kuhn, who called the Jews "enemies of the United States" was convicted of being a foreign agent, had his U.S. citizenship revoked, went to jail, and was deported to post-war Germany. (Fritz Kuhn, n.d.)

German American voters were a large undecided voting bloc in the 1940 election. (Peters, 2005) Did Roosevelt give a press conference which ignored established and publicly stated German American disloyalty and instead focused on non-existent Jewish spying because June 1940 was 5 months before a Presidential Election? Had Jewish voters been undecided, perhaps Roosevelt would have given a different warning?

b) Republican Opposition: Every Republican Presidential nominee between 1928 and 1948 and many of their Vice Presidential nominees publicly supported the Wagner-Rogers Bill to let 20,000 German-Jewish children into the U.S.. (Morse, 1968, p.253) (Breitman, 2013, p.150) If that wasn't enough Republican support, the widow of former Republican President Calvin Coolidge, Grace Coolidge, promised to personally arrange for the care of 25 Jewish children. The Bill passed both Congressional subcommittees with unanimous bipartisan votes. (Medoff, 2019, pp.84-86) (Grace Coolidge, n.d.)

Historians ignore unanimous bipartisan support and instead emphasize nativist opposition. (Burns, 2022) (Rosen, 2006) They could just as easily note celebrity actors and Eleanor Roosevelt supported it. (Breitman, 2013, p.148) Regardless, Roosevelt had significant accomplishments despite unified Republican opposition, e.g. supplying Britain, arming merchant ships, and reinstating a draft. The New Deal passed despite significant elected and judicial opposition. (Dalleck, 2017)

Roosevelt wrote "File. No action, FDR" on the Wagner-Rogers Bill. (Pressman, 2014) p.177) The bill failed, and children were murdered because Roosevelt personally chose to do so. He did so because he saw no political benefit in supporting the bill. (Rosen, 2006, p.85) (see initialed memo, figure 1)

c) <u>Unemployment</u>: While unemployment was a serious problem and affected many government policies, the State Department neither justified their actions based on unemployment nor were their actions consistent with reducing unemployment. President Hoover justified his immigration restrictions by giving the reason as reducing unemployment (Breitman, 2013, p.36) but the State Department said the justification was not giving the Jews special treatment (see quote below). The Jews were requesting equal application of laws which allocated visas to all those who applied to emigrate. Jews were qualified applicants and other than 1939 they were the only applicants. (Zucker, 2001) (Medoff R., 2020, p.87)

In order to reduce the number of Jews qualifying for these visas, the State Department not only obstructed Jewish applicants, but also made it a priority to give visas to other ethnicities (Rolde, 2013, p.11) based on Roosevelt's directive. (Dalleck, 2017, p.352) Qualified non-Jewish applicants were also entitled to visas, but since they needed jobs the motivation could not have been to reduce unemployment. The State Department sought to replace Jewish immigrants, many of whom would not have competed with Americans for jobs (e.g. doctors), with non-Jewish immigrants with no consideration of whether they would directly compete with Americans for jobs. (Morse, 1968, p.216)

Reducing domestic unemployment is the purview of the Department of Labor which supported the immigration of Jews because many had needed expertise. (Downey, 2009) The 'public charge' clause of the Immigration Acts denied visas to anyone who would require public financial support. This clause was particularly detrimental to Jews, because German and Austrian Jews had been stripped of their assets. When the Labor Department devised a 'Charge Bond' to allow others to post a bond and thus let Jews avoid this restriction, the State Department objected. Attorney General Robert Jackson decided Labor alone could interpret the law as it related to domestic unemployment. (Zucker, 2001)

The response of the Visa Division of the State Department to Jackson's decision proves the motivation was anti-Semitism — it never mentions unemployment — it blames Jews. The State Department's objection to the posting of a bond to allow an applicant to obtain a visa is it would give the public the impression Jews were getting special treatment because they "allege" to be victims of persecution:

> "Experience has taught that Jews are persistent in their efforts to obtain immigration visas, that Jews have a strong tendency, no matter where they are, to allege they are the subjects of either religious or political persecution, that Jews have constantly endeavored to find means of entering the United States despite the barriers of our immigration laws...unrestrained acceptance of bonds

> of Jewish aliens would soon develop the common understanding that for some reason the immigration laws of the United States operated to admit nothing but Jews." (Zucker, 2001)

Notice the statement meets the definition of anti-Semitism provided in the introduction. First, there's a problem, immigration. Second, the Jews are blamed. Third, a conspiracy theory is invoked: Jews invent persecution to violate the law. This statement goes further — it invents a motive. Apparently, the State Department's job isn't to comply with the law or enforce foreign policy, but rather to manage public opinion so Americans don't think immigration laws treat Jews differently.

If unemployment had been a reason, government policy would have improved as unemployment dropped. Instead its behavior became more anti-Semitic. In 1941, the U.S. was not at war and unemployment fell to less than 10%, but quotas were not filled despite receiving so many reports of German atrocities that intelligence stopped relaying them. (Burns, 2022) In 1942, the U.S. received reports of the construction of at least four concentration camps in Poland solely to murder Jews. Rather than allow more Jews to immigrate, State Department officials dismissed the reports as untrue. Unemployment was below 5%. (Dalleck, 2017, p.497) In 1943, Long committed perjury to prevent Jews from finding refuge. Unemployment was 1.9%. (Amadeo, 2022)

Unemployment was an important factor in politics, but it wasn't the reason Roosevelt obstructed Jewish immigration to the U.S..

d) <u>Exacerbation of Domestic Anti-Semitism:</u> Claims that Roosevelt's actions were inspired by wanting to avoid exacerbating anti-Semitism lack any documentation. (Dalleck, 2017, p.355) The Visa Division rejected Jews' documentation of marriage if they were married in a religious rather than a civil ceremony. Thus, for immigration purposes Jewish applicants weren't married, Jewish children were illegitimate, and the applicant was rejected for low moral character. The visa, allocated by U.S. law, went unused. (Rolde, 2013) There is no example of Christian documents being disallowed. If Roosevelt wanted to fight anti-Semitism, he could have done a lot. Contriving anti-Semitic means to deny Jews visas to leave Germany so they could be murdered wasn't one of them.

e) Roosevelt did not work behind the scenes to help Jews find refuge: The author has found no documentation of this commonly claimed exoneration. (Burns, 2022) This chapter contains documentation of Roosevelt working 'behind the scenes' three times to prevent Jews from finding refuge: 1. Dominican Republic's pledge to admit 100,000 Jews in 1939. (JTA, 1939) (Breitman, 2013, p.131-2) 2. The Virgin Islands' offer — Jews could have been admitted on visitors' visas. (Medoff R., 2020, p.87) 3. Congressional resolution to pressure England to let Jews into Palestine. (Dalleck, 2017, p.592).

Hagiography — Historians Assign Motives to FDR Without Documentation: Even when Roosevelt's motivation is documented historians invent alternative explanations.

In his documentary *The Roosevelts,* Ken Burns said Roosevelt notified the Germans they would be prosecuted for war crimes. This not only isn't true,[1] but Roosevelt told others why he would not. In autumn 1942, the Roosevelt administration received adequate intelligence the Germans planned to murder millions of Jews. Roosevelt decided notifying the Germans they would be prosecuted for atrocities would be a propaganda coup for the Germans and discourage sedition. Roosevelt told a group of Jewish leaders this on December 8, 1942. (Dalleck, 2017, p. 498)

Historians often ignore documented motives and instead ascribe benign motives to Roosevelt without documentation. Richard Breitman in *FDR and the Jews* repeatedly blames the Depression, politics, and wanting to solve problems "behind closed doors" but provides no references. (Breitman, 2013, pp.83,139,149) President Hoover's attempt to restrict immigration for all immigrants, not just Jews, has a reference that his motive was unemployment. (Breitman, 2013, p.69)

Breitman also makes two undocumented assertions to claim Roosevelt's inaction in the *St. Louis* incident has been "dramatized". He claims that because the Holocaust hadn't started in June 1939, FDR didn't know that the Jews would be mistreated upon their return to Germany, and gives FDR credit that none of the Jews would ultimately return to Germany. This is disingenuous. After *Kristallnacht*, Jewish persecution in Germany was well recognized and Roosevelt had been receiving intelligence since 1933 documenting the murder of Jews. (Dalleck, 2017, p.160) His decision to allow the Jews to return to Germany occurred four days before the other nations — each expecting an imminent German invasion — took them. Roosevelt made his decision knowing the Jews were going to Germany and then to concentration camps. 254 passengers were murdered in the Holocaust. (Breitman, 2013, p.139) (Thomas, 1974)

In 1945, Congress dealt with the anticipated need to resettle Jewish Holocaust refugees. FDR "worked behind the scenes" to <u>prevent</u> Congress from passing a resolution demanding England let survivors into Palestine. Robert Dalleck documented FDR's motive in his book *Franklin Roosevelt.* FDR told Senator Robert Wagner (D-NY) that Jewish immigration to Palestine exacerbated Arab anti-Semitism, "... there are approximately 70 million Mohammedans there who want to cut their (Jewish refugee) throats the day they land...I hope at this juncture no branch of government will act." (Dalleck, 2017, p.596). But before and anticipatorily after the war, Dalleck claims, without a reference, FDR's motive for blocking Jewish immigration to the U.S. was not exacerbating anti-Semitism. Instead of coming to the U.S., he claims Roosevelt's solution for displaced Jews anticipatorily after the war was Jewish immigration to Palestine, which he advocated on his return trip from Yalta. (Dalleck, 2017, pp.352,596-7)

Dalleck's ascribed motivations are contradictory. In 1945 the U.S. had not had a violent anti-Semitic event in recent memory, and the public was sympathetic towards Jews. (Welch, 2014) If the motive was preventing anti-Semitism, the best place for the survivors was the U.S. and the worst place would be Palestine — he told Senator Wagner this. Avoiding exacerbating anti-Semitism in the U.S. while inciting anti-Semitic violence in Palestine is contradictory and extraordinarily callous. A reasonable and consistent explanation for Roosevelt's actions is that preventing exacerbation of domestic anti-Semitism was neither Roosevelt's motivation in blocking Jewish immigration to the U.S. anticipatorily after the war nor encouraging it in Palestine. (Dalleck, 2017)p.596-7)

In Robert Rosen's book, *Saving the Jews*, reasons are given for Roosevelt's decision to kill the Wagner-Rogers Bill in June 1939. First, he was busy assembling a "secret coalition to obliterate Nazism" and the Jewish children would have interfered (no explanation is provided why domestic legislation would interfere with "secret" foreign policy). Second, supporting the bill would interfere with his effort to amend the Neutrality Acts because the Southern Democrats would have opposed it. The reference is a statement from another historian.[2] (Rosen, 2006, p.86)

These assertions are remarkable for the prescience it assigns to Roosevelt. In June 1939 the war hadn't started. Roosevelt didn't know who the combatants would be, for example he didn't know Hitler and Stalin would sign a non-aggression pact. The Neutrality Acts weren't amended until November 13, 1941. (Berg, 1998, p.431) So, the bill was defeated because Roosevelt was assembling a coalition to fight Nazism when no nation was fighting Nazism, and no one knew which nations would fight Nazism? Also, Roosevelt's motivation for denying visas to 20,000 Jewish children was winning a legislative battle more than two years in the future when he might no longer be President? Furthermore, if there was significant Congressional opposition, how did the bill pass committees in both houses of Congress unanimously?

In August 1941, England had defeated two fascist armies (Germany in the Battle of Britain and Italy in North Africa) and the Russians were locked in a brutal merciless war against the Germans. Wouldn't this have been the time to "obliterate Nazism"? Instead, Roosevelt told English Prime Minister Winston Churchill he had no intention of entering the war to fight Nazism. (Olson, 2014, p.358) If instead, Roosevelt was "secretly" arranging a coalition "obliterate Nazism" in June 1939 when there was no war, Russia was negotiating with Hitler, and the Prime Minister of England was Neville Chamberlain, historians are obligated to provide significant documentation.

Why solely in the case of Franklin Roosevelt's motives is hagiography considered historical scholarship?

<u>What was Roosevelt's documented motivation?</u>

In 1970, 86-year-old Harry Truman was asked to describe President Roosevelt's motivation. He said, "Inside he was the coldest man I ever met. He didn't care about you or me or anyone else in the world."(Fleming, 2001, p.560) Some historians acknowledge he was motivated solely by political considerations and Dalleck concluded his book calling his actions a "moral failure". (Fleming, 2001) (Moe, 2013) (Rosen, 2006, p.85) (Dalleck, 2017, p.626)

Eleanor said Franklin told her why he refused to support the Wagner-Rogers Bill, "I can't alienate certain votes I need for measures that are more important." (Morse, 1968, p.255) What issues were more than the lives of Jewish children and why didn't failing to save them "alienate votes"? Eleanor told her son James that her failure to stop the denial of visas to Jews was the greatest regret of her life, (Kearns-Goodwin, 1994, p.176) but Franklin never expressed regret.

It is an open historical question if Roosevelt had not been assured of Jewish votes whether he would have obstructed the immigration of Jewish refugees.

Roosevelt, the Jews, and Lindbergh after the war with Germany started on December 11, 1941:

U.S. involvement in the war in Europe started on December 11, 1941. The public conflict between Roosevelt and Lindbergh regarding U.S. foreign policy ended. Prior to the war Lindbergh opposed our entry; but once we were attacked, Lindbergh supported our decision to fight, unreservedly joined the war effort, and fought the Japanese. There are controversies regarding Roosevelt and Jews during the war but it's unrelated to Lindbergh. (Berg, 1998)

President Roosevelt won the war which ended the Holocaust. There are decisions regarding the Jews worth examining but those with military experience have explored them. The neglect of the Jews imprisoned in French North Africa is included because it demonstrates Jewish pressure did work; but there were military considerations involved in this controversy as well.

Roosevelt's Legacy:

Franklin Roosevelt was elected President twice as many times as any other American has or will be elected President. He is, by definition, the most successful politician in American history. Roosevelt may have been loved by more Americans than any other American President. The night of his death, April 12, 1945, thousands of Americans stood in silence all night beside the railroad tracks to salute the train bringing his body back to Washington, DC — a remarkable demonstration of gratitude and respect. The Atlantic Charter, written by Roosevelt and Churchill in August 1941, is as great an achievement in man's search for liberty as the Constitution or the Magna Carta.

Even his opposition recognized the greatness of his leadership. Senator Robert Taft of Ohio, who ran for the Republican nomination in 1940 to oppose Roosevelt, said "Men will thank God on their knees a hundred years from now, that Franklin Roosevelt was in the White

House." (Dalleck, 2017, p.620) As we approach 100 years since his first inauguration, such a statement from a current opposition politician is inconceivable.

The Jews were proud Americans, and they too loved him. And to be fair, Roosevelt did try to help Europe's surviving Jews enter Palestine and deemed his inability to do so his "one complete failure". (Dalleck, 2017, p.614) However, acknowledging Roosevelt's leadership does not change his legacy towards the Jews preceding World War II, nor does it change the deliberate obfuscation and excuses of this legacy made by Jews and historians — nearly uniformly lacking documentation.

A President's job is to pursue the national interest. <u>Were Roosevelt's policies in the national interest?</u>

1. The Treasury Department investigated the State Department and did not find their actions were in the national interest.
2. Despite the Treasury report and Long's perjury, no one was ever held responsible for malfeasance. Is impunity for government malfeasance in the national interest?
3. If Long was acting in the national interest, for example reducing unemployment, why would he commit perjury to hide it? Why commit perjury in 1943 when the U.S. needed workers? Is perjury in the national interest?
4. Losing Jewish doctors, dentists, and pharmacists didn't promote the national interest.
5. The impending war required scientific advances, for example, inventing synthetic rubber and addressing a shortage of tungsten which impeded the function of airplane engines. Jewish chemists and metallurgists were obstructed from getting visas to leave Germany. (Downey, 2009, p. 192) Was this in the national interest?
6. What was the motivation to dismiss only the intelligence reports of Jews being murdered? When is it in the national interest to dismiss reliable intelligence?

Consider the photo on page 260 of an 18-year-old mother and her baby, living in a squalid tent in a migrant camp in California in the late 1930s. Ask yourself, what was the quality of medical care these two Americans received in that camp? Multiply it by 2.5 million, the number of Americans displaced in the 1930s, and speculate on the loss of human potential caused by preventable death and morbidity due to lack of care. Tens of thousands of Jewish physicians, dentists, and pharmacists could not practice professionally and could not come to the U.S. because the State Department decided it had the power to deny them visas. The State Department based its decisions on a self-declared power to prevent Americans from feeling Jews were receiving "special treatment", when no such power exists. The visas for their immigration were unused. Roosevelt was made aware of the State Department's actions and did nothing about it.

How was this in America's national interest?

Was it anti-Semitism? Only Jews were subject to immigration obstruction, others were encouraged to apply. Only Jews had their documents invalidated. Only Jews had reports of their persecution considered lies. For no other group did the President say "spies" had been found when no such spy was ever found, even though spies were convicted from another ethnic group. For no other group did any president ever repeat enemy propaganda to justify persecution. No government official committed perjury, with impunity, other than to prevent Jews from achieving refuge. In every situation evaluated, Roosevelt's policies, statements, and appointees hurt Jews and only Jews.

Racism is a form of hatred that blinds its holders to their own interests and results in actions which compromise their interests. Roosevelt's actions compromised U.S. national interest and in some respect its security. There is no clearer example of presidential anti-Semitism in American history. This was all documented at the time.

For 80 years historians have promoted a narrative that Roosevelt wanted to help the Jews of Europe but couldn't. To support this narrative, historians have made assertions without documentation, contradicted themselves, misinterpreted Roosevelt's public statements, and give him credit for "bold action on behalf of the Jews" which were actually meaningless.[3,4] The State Department, whose officials Roosevelt chose and carried out his policy, was documented to have undeniably been motivated by anti-Semitism.

The author and some historians contend the historical record clearly demonstrates, at best, Roosevelt was disinterested in the plight of European Jews. He didn't care because American Jewish votes were neither contested nor important in the Electoral College (most Jews lived in Roosevelt's home state). As a result, Roosevelt enabled, and frequently contributed to, his State Department's anti-Semitic malfeasance. Some decisions catastrophic to Jews, for example the demise of the Wagner-Rogers Bill, were his alone.

<u>Conclusion:</u> Roosevelt enabled the murder of between half a million and 1.5 million people.

The number of humans who perished because German and Austrian visas were wasted, offers by sovereign nations to take Jews went unused due to U.S. interference, and the British offer to give its unused visa spots — refused specifically by President Roosevelt and solely because they were to be used by Jews — is roughly 540,000. The pre-war Jewish German population was 575,000. The total number of unused visas from every European country from which Jews sought to emigrate exceeded 1.3 million. Franklin Roosevelt enabled these deaths, forced the return of the *St. Louis*, refused to use tourist visas from the Virgin Islands, killed the Wagner-Rogers Bill plus other offers equals roughly 1.5 million humans.

Blame for 1.5 million deaths may still underestimate Roosevelt's culpability. Between 1938 and 1941, countries often based refusal to take refugees on the U.S.'s refusal. Although the Nazis massacred Jews prior to 1942, plans for the "Final Solution" were made in January 1942, only when it became apparent no country would take Jews. (Feingold, 1969, pp. 29-82) Had the U.S. acted in good faith, other countries may have done so as well. It is a legitimate question if there would have been a "Holocaust" as we know it.

Prominent works of fiction describe a U.S. Nazi regime. Philip Roth's *The Plot Against America* has a fictional American president named Charles Lindbergh and in Robert Harris' book *Fatherland* the role is played by Joseph Kennedy. These plots are unnecessarily complicated. In *Mein Kampf*, Hitler advocated two goals: conquer Europe and annihilate the Jews. The failed effort to prevent the inevitable war by which the Nazis would accomplish their first goal, led an administration elected by Americans, including Jewish Americans, to enable the Germans to achieve their second goal.

From 1933 until 1943, elected President Franklin Roosevelt deliberately interfered with the right of a minority, Jews and only Jews, to receive visas to which they were legally entitled although no such power is provided to the President. A congressman said it in a public hearing, his Treasury Department documented it, his appointee Breckinridge Long committed perjury in testimony before Congress to cover it up, and Roosevelt was handed a memo that said the motivation was anti-Semitism. His wife told him, and never forgave herself for letting it happen. No other American President, his predecessor, nor his Republican political opposition acted similarly. Indeed, four nations expecting an imminent German invasion took the Jews that Roosevelt refused to take.

Furthermore, Roosevelt himself repeated Nazi propaganda, resisted freeing Jews in labor camps, blocked a sovereign nation from taking Jewish refugees, sent representatives of the U.S. government to Nazi rallies, and refused to respond when 937 Jews were less than a mile from Miami and instead let them be returned to Germany. He publicly maintained he was doing all he could, but in nearly every instance, he refused to even say "Jew" nor name the perpetrators. But, when making callous and insensitive jokes the butt of the joke was the Jews.

The worst part is for 80 years American Jews believe Roosevelt's actions were unfortunately in the nation's interests. For these actions and only for these actions, by this president and only by this president, motivations are invented, and excuses made without evidence despite Eleanor and Harry Truman telling historians his motivation was pure political expediency. Because Roosevelt was assured of Jewish votes, he not only took them for granted; he decided the lives of Jews weren't important.

Roosevelt illegally obstructed Jews from finding refuge and always acted in the interest of good relations with Germany. He was personally complicit in the murder of 8% and perhaps enabled the murder of a fourth of the Jews murdered by the Nazis; every one a human being, every one just as much created in God's image as President Roosevelt.

Despite unanimous Republican support in Congressional committees and popular support, he not only condemned 20,000 Jewish children to death — he wrote his name on instructions to reject the bill. Then he allegedly told his wife he had more important matters to attend to.

Roth and Harris didn't need to invent villains.

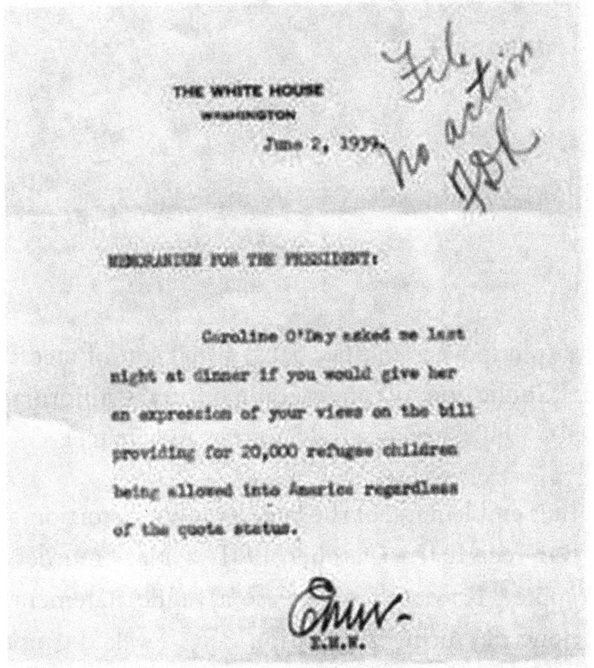

THE WHITE HOUSE
WASHINGTON

June 2, 1939.

File
no action
FDR

MEMORANDUM FOR THE PRESIDENT:

Caroline O'Day asked me last night at dinner if you would give her an expression of your views on the bill providing for 20,000 refugee children being allowed into America regardless of the quota status.

E.M.W.

The memo from Major General Edwin Watson (E.M.W), White House Appointment Secretary (today called Chief of Staff) to President Roosevelt. Roosevelt's instructions to kill the Wagner-Rogers Bill. (Courtesy of the FDR Presidential Library and Museum, (personal email, 10/14/2022))

Photo: 18 year old mother and her baby. What sort of medical care did they receive? (Public domain photograph of rural California, dust bowl refugees, 1930s-1940s, no copyright restrictions image)

[1] This untruth is emblematic of the hagiographic distortion of President Roosevelt's war record. In October 1941, a Nazi murder of French civilians prompted Roosevelt to release a vague statement, "seeds of hatred…will one day bring retribution". Roosevelt did not say there

would be an effort to hold anyone accountable for atrocities committed against any group, certainly not for crimes against Jews. Subsequent statements were neither intended for, nor received by, German officials. They were solely to placate national governments-in-exile. (see Kochavi, A, Diplomatic History, 19(4):1995, p.617 and www.presidency.ucsb.edu/node/210161)

[2] Rosen provided 4 secondary references regarding his statement Southern Democrats would have opposed the Wagner-Rogers Bill. The references state Southern Democrats generally opposed increasing immigration quotas. None of the references establish Roosevelt's motive.

[3] When Hitler annexed Austria in 1938, Roosevelt combined the visa quotas for Germany and Austria. Historians claim this helped Jews, but it didn't provide a single additional visa. If any German Jews were issued visas because of Roosevelt's action, they took them from qualified Austrian Jews. At the Evian Conference (July 1938), the U.S. representative publicized it as proof of a U.S. commitment to Jewish refugees, but other delegates said it was only a "sleight-of-hand". (Feingold, 1969, p. 31)

[4] An example of dishonesty is in *The U.S. and the Holocaust* (2022). It proclaimed the Roosevelt administration "admitted 225,000 refugees from Nazi terror, more than any other sovereign nation." "Refugees" is used instead of "Jews", because half of these "refugees" were not Jewish (it is debatable whether these non-Jews sought refuge). "Sovereign nation" deliberately excludes Palestine. How many Jews entered Palestine isn't known, but it may exceed the U.S. number. Regardless, it isn't true. More Jews sought refuge in the Soviet Union than all the "refugees" admitted to the U.S.. (U.S. Holocaust Museum (ushmm.org): German invasion of Poland, also *Jewish Journal*, 9/5/2023, WSJ, 9/21/2022)

Works Cited

Amadeo, K. (2022). *U.S. Unemployment Rate by Year.* Retrieved from The Balance: https://www.thebalancemoney.com/unemployment-rate-by-year-3305506

Berg, A. (1998). *Lindbergh.* New York: Berkley Biography.

Breitman, R. (2013). *FDR and the Jews.* London: Belknap Press.

Burns, K. (2022, September 17). The U.S. and the Holocaust. PBS.

Cole, W. (1974). *Charles A. Lindbergh, American Intervention in World War II.* New York: Jovanovich.

Confessions of a Nazi Spy. (n.d.). Retrieved from https://en....orga/wiki/Confessions_of_a_Nazi_Spy

Dalleck, R. (2017). *Franklin Roosevelt.* New York: Harcourt.

Downey, K. (2009). *The Woman Behind the New Deal.* New York: First Anchor Books.

Feingold, H, *The Politics of Rescue: The Roosevelt Administration and the Holocaust,* Rutgers University Press, 1969.

Fleming, T. (2001). *The New Dealers' War.* New York: Perseus Group.

Fritz Kuhn. (n.d.). Retrieved from FBI Records: https://vault.fbi.gov/fritz-julius-kuhn/fritz-julius-kuhn-part-03/view

Grace Coolidge. (n.d.). Retrieved from Wyman Institute: http://enc.wymaninstitute.org/?p=159

JTA. (1939, June 18). *JTA Archives.* Retrieved from http://pdfs.jta.org/1939/1939-06-19_164.pdf?_ga=2.247091460.149312393.1664189283-1320135280.1664189283

Kearns-Goodwin, D. (1994). *No Ordinary Time.* New York: Simon and Schuster.

Lelyveld, J. (2016). *His Final Battle.* New York: Knopf.

Medoff. (2019). The Jews Should Keep Quiet. Philadelphia: University of Nebraska Press.

Medoff, R. (2020). FDR, Nazis, and the Jews of Morocco. *JNS.*

Moe, R. (2013). *Roosevelt's Second Act.* London: Oxford Publishing.

Morse, A. (1968). While Six Million Died. New York: Random House.

Nasaw, D. (2012). The Patriarch. New York: Penguin Press.

O'Brien, R. (2022, November 8). Acquittal Raises Thorny Questions. *NYT,* A18.

Olson, L. (2014). *Those Angry Days.* New York: Random House.

Olson, L. (2017). *Last Hope Island.* NY: Random House.

Patenaude, B. (2020, October 8). The Nazi Spy Ring in America. *WSJ*, pp. https://www.wsj.com/articles/the-nazi-spy-ring-in-america-review-hoover-was-furious-11602198019.

Peters, C. (2005). *Five Days in Philadelphia.* NY: Public Affairs.

Pressman, S. (2014). *50 Children.* New York: Harper Collins.

Rescue Resolution. (n.d.). Retrieved from Wyman Institute for Holocaust Studies : http://enc.wymaninstitute.org/?p=474

Rolde, N. (2013). *Breckinridge Long.* Maine: PB and J Group.

Rosen, R. (2006). *Saving the Jews.* New York: Thunder Mouth Press.

ROAJTFGB20, en....org/wiki/Relationship of American Jews to the U.S. Federal Government before the 20th century

Rumrich Spy Case. (n.d.). Retrieved from FBI.com: https://www.fbi.gov/history/famous-cases/rumrich-nazi-spy-case

Sarna, J. (2012). *The Redemption of Ulysses Grant.* Retrieved from Reform Judaism.Org: https://reformjudaism.org/redemption-ulysses-s-grant

Singer, S. (2015, December 23). *Jewish Press.* Retrieved from President Taft and the Jews: https://www.jewishpress.com/indepth/front-page/president-taft-and-the-jews-a-remarkable-friendship/2015/12/23/

Skwire, S. (2016, September 20). George Washington's Letter to the Jews. Retrieved from Foundation for Economic Education: https://fee.org/articles/george-washingtons-letter-to-the-jews

Thomas, G. W. (1974). *Voyage of the Damned.* New York: Stein and Day.

Welch, S. (2014). American Opinion Towards Jews in the Nazi Era. *Social Sciences Quarterly*, 615-635.

Zucker, B. (2001). Frances Perkins and the German Jewish Refugees. *American Jewish History*, 3-6.

13. I just don't see it that way

A letter to Reeve Lindbergh

This is a brief introduction to the next chapter, an analysis of the speech Charles Lindbergh delivered in Des Moines, Iowa on September 11, 1941. Because it is personal thoughts it is written in the first person and contains no references. Complete references can be found in the next chapter's references, (Olson, pp. 389-391) and (Groom, p. 299).

Reeve Lindbergh was the youngest child of Anne and Charles Lindbergh. She was born in 1945. She is the only Lindbergh child who has written about their lives. She became aware of the Des Moines speech as a student at Radcliffe in the 1960s when her boyfriend's Jewish roommate refused to shake her hand. He told her it was because of what her father had said in Des Moines. She looked up the speech and was devastated.

She had grown up reading Anne Frank. She failed to understand how her father could have said something so insensitive. It isn't apparent from her writings whether she appreciated that in 1941 her father hadn't known the Holocaust would happen; the President didn't know until the fall of 1942. But she did recall she never heard her father say anti-Semitic nor racist things. As a young woman, her friends' parents said these things all the time.

I speak only for myself. But as a single Jewish voice, I would say to Reeve, "I just don't see it that way. I would shake your hand".

I was told Charles Lindbergh was an anti-Semite from the time I was a child. The pivotal event in his legacy was this speech he gave in Des Moines, Iowa three months before we entered World War II. This speech is considered not just a pivotal event in his legacy but a pivotal event in the history of domestic anti-Semitism. I have not just read the speech and watched video of it; I have read every draft of it, the reactions of dozens of people, both Jews and non-Jews, not just in the aftermath of the speech but to this day.

I understand why my grandparents' generation was so disturbed by this speech, but I don't live in 1941. I understand there were subjects that couldn't be addressed in 1941, but they should have been addressed. For no other group was there a convention which advocated public silence and private scorn. This convention served to deny us our Constitutional right to publicly address our grievances, a right which every American is granted.

Before I formed an opinion, I was obligated to listen to all your father's speeches, including those that celebrated religious diversity and those that proposed ways to protect Jews from anti-Semitic violence. I was obligated to read this speech and form an opinion based solely on what he said, not what others said he said. I was obligated to acknowledge some of what he said was supportive of Jewish interests and acknowledge that was neither perfunctory nor expected. The philo-Semitic passages were rarely stated in this era. No honest critic should mischaracterize what he said nor put words in his mouth.

Having done that, from the perspective of living in the twenty-first century, I can listen to your father's speech and ask, "is what he said true?". Like all political speeches, some of it was wrong, but some of it was true. Unfortunately, the truth was exaggerated.

Most importantly, I strongly believe the foundation of the conflict was American Jews' failure to give our definition of the national interest. That we did not, is not your father's fault. Had we done that prior to the speech, the speech would have been much different.

And whether I agree or disagree, I believe Charles Lindbergh, like every other American, had a First Amendment right to define his version of the national interest before we entered a war.

Some of the criticism is warranted, but blaming your dad is a distraction and accomplishes nothing. Your father said some anti-Semitic things, but that wasn't the problem, and it shouldn't be turned into the problem. In his era, many Americans said the same things, including two future Presidents: John F. Kennedy and Harry Truman. They received no criticism, they were much less diplomatic about it, and are lauded as Jewish heroes. His critics said worse. Often, they actively participated in anti-Semitism which your father did not. His critics certainly never advocated for Jewish interests.

The problem was no one was advocating for the Jews, not even most Jews. The people who criticized him didn't advocate for Jews, they told your father to shut up. They made the problem worse. We were on the verge of extermination. Someone had to say something. Maybe your father said the wrong thing but the criticism he received dissuaded others from speaking.

What exactly did your father's critics do for the Jews? Not a damn thing. And what did they do for this country? Some of your father's critics sacrificed for this country, but compared to your father, most didn't do a damn thing.

Those that said your father shouldn't have given the speech, bought into the great anti-Semitic conspiracy of the 1940s promoted by First Lady Eleanor Roosevelt — the Jews should solve their problems by blending into American society. It's circular reasoning: if Jews try to address anti-Semitism people will think they're not Americans, thus Jewish advocacy causes anti-Semitism. In other words, by trying to fix a problem, the Jews create the problem. Or even simpler, "blame the victim".

Jews desperately tried to be invisible and as a result failed to advocate for our interests. We were not only excluded from universities, hotels, and clubs but there were entire towns which did not allow Jews to buy or rent houses. Those that slipped through tried desperately not to draw attention to themselves. Those that could pick up the crumbs from the wealthy gentiles whose approval we so desperately craved were embarrassed by their co-religionists.

Your father didn't think the Jews were invisible. He was right. He didn't think we should try to be invisible. He was right again. Regardless, it wasn't his convention, so it wasn't his problem. If Jews felt threatened and if his reputation was destroyed it was all secondary to the future of our country.

So how did that "invisible thing" work out for us? Not real good. Eleanor Roosevelt's circular reasoning made no sense then and it makes no sense now. Anti-Semites don't care how we behave.

What Lindbergh's critics said, especially his Jewish critics, was "don't mention the Jews". That was the wrong approach. We desperately needed to be included in the conversation. When does not allowing people to speak help in any situation? Did anyone recommend this strategy for any other group?

I disagree with what he said, much of it was wrong, exaggerated, and condescending. But he had every right to say it— minus a few anti-Semitic stereotypes. If he had never said it, or apologized, or been silenced, how would history have turned out? Exactly the way it turned out. The speech made no difference. Neither this speech nor any of his advocacy hurt anyone.

While acknowledging political speeches are never completely true nor free of exaggeration, read the next chapter and ponder three questions: 1) Did Lindbergh address issues important to our nation? 2) Was there truth in Lindbergh's concerns? 3) Considering the hostility of political discourse in this era, was the speech respectful? If you answer "yes" to these questions, then much of the criticism of this speech advocated censorship.

Historian Winston Groom wrote, "The fact remains that what (Lindbergh) said was true, but", he then quotes Herbert Hoover, "(in politics you can't say things) just because they're true". Lindbergh didn't say it "just" because it was true, he said it because hundreds of thousands of young American men were about to be killed.

I close my thoughts by quoting one of my favorite writers. In 1941, Kurt Vonnegut was a student at Cornell. He dropped out in 1943 to join the army and was captured at the Battle of the Bulge. Anticipating he would soon be sent to fight, he responded to the criticism of Lindbergh's speech in the Cornell student newspaper,

> "The United States is a democracy, that's what they say we'll be fighting for. What a prize moment to that ideal-a cry to smother Lindy... 'Lindy you're a rat'. We read that somewhere, so it must be so. They say you should be deported. In that event, leave room on the boat for us."

Any time anyone is told they're not allowed to speak, any time there is a convention which says certain subjects may not be discussed, any time we listen to critics whose behavior is worse than those that are criticized, any time we take the side of the critic rather than the speaker, we run the risk, one day, we too, will not be allowed to speak. That's not the country I want to live in either.

One day we all may be on that boat. So... please save a spot on the boat for me too.

14: The Speech

Des Moines, Iowa 9/11/1941

This chapter reviews the most controversial and legacy forming speech in Lindbergh's life. Previous speeches, radio addresses, and his Congressional testimony dealt with foreign affairs, the status of our military, and criticized interventionists including President Roosevelt. Lindbergh had never directly mentioned Jews, but in two other speeches Lindbergh discussed religious tolerance, which was a reference to Jews. A link to the text of the Des Moines speech and the NYC speech of May 23, 1941, is provided in the references.

The Des Moines speech would mark him as an anti-Semite for the rest of his life.

This chapter is a modern analysis of one of the most controversial speeches ever made by an American public figure. Lindbergh did not say Jews were not Americans nor did he say "the Jews" were pushing the U.S. into World War II. He said three times <u>some Jewish leaders</u> were pushing the U.S. into war.

By 1934, Hitler had seized power in Germany and the extent of the oppression of the Jews was becoming apparent. The international Jewish organization, *B'nai B'rith*, summarized the Jewish response to oppression, "...a dignified silence, a silence with suffering, (which) may become more potent than emotion." Millions of Jews were silent about Jewish persecution in Europe.

Many prominent gentiles, including First Lady Eleanor Roosevelt, believed if Jews wanted to be Americans they must not complain. She said after *Kristallnacht* "I think it is important that the Jews remain unaggressive and remind everyone and stress the fact they are Americans first and above everything else...and, as far as possible, wipe out in their own consciousness any feeling of difference by joining all that is being done by Americans." (Cook, 1999) Prominent Jews feared being "too outspoken". Persecution of Jews could evoke sympathy, but Jews addressed FDR privately.

Charles Lindbergh refused to accept this convention. Lindbergh contended restricting free speech caused U.S. involvement in World War I, which led to the loss of 100,000 American lives and set conditions for World War II. He saw the U.S. about to repeat the same mistake. As he discussed his impending speech with his wife Anne, he told her it was inconceivable that there was a truth, relevant to a national struggle, and that truth simply could not be mentioned. (Berg, 1998, pp.425-6)

Lindbergh knew he'd be called an anti-Semite if he gave a speech about the role of Jews in America's debate over entering the war. He considered his reputation secondary. He thought perhaps admiring Jews, and showing compassion for German Jews, might prevent his message from being dismissed as blatant anti-Semitism. A draft of the speech demonstrated this:

> "I realize that in speaking this frankly I am rushing in where angels fear to tread. I realize that tomorrow morning's headlines will say 'Lindbergh attacks Jews'. The ugly cry of anti-Semitism will be joyfully pounced upon and eagerly waived about my name. It is so much simpler to brand someone with a bad label than to take the trouble to read what he says. I call you people before me tonight to witness that I am not anti-Semitic nor have I attacked the Jews." (Des Moines Speech, Handwritten Draft, circa September 1941)

He failed. His message was ignored, his legacy destroyed. He could not have succeeded. Those who wanted to enter the war wouldn't let an opportunity to label Lindbergh an anti-Semite pass. (Olson, 2013) Because Roosevelt considered Lindbergh his political opponent, he would seize any opportunity to vilify him. Using surrogates, President Roosevelt accused Lindbergh of anti-Semitism in 1938, a year before Lindbergh advocated any political position regarding any war. (Cole, 1974, p.43)

Was Lindbergh Motivated by Anti-Semitism? Arguable. Lindbergh's stated motivation was starting an "open and frank discussion." (Lindbergh, 1970, 9/15/1941)

Lindbergh opposed political positions Jews considered to be in their interests, was willing to be labeled an anti-Semite, and risked inciting anti-Semitic violence, but the evidence he was motivated by anti-Semitism is not convincing. It is documented he was motivated by opposition to a President usurping power from Congress. He was motivated by an unparalleled and personal knowledge of an enemy army he wasn't sure America could defeat and believed it would cost at least a million American lives.[3,4] He was motivated by 100,000 dead Americans in World War I, whose deaths were truly in vain. He blamed those deaths on muzzling opposition to entering the war, including the arrest of his father.

But why must he discuss the Jews' role in advocating entering the war but not mention others, for example the interests of Polish or German Americans? Is it rooted in anti-Semitism? He made statements supporting this anti-Semitic premise. Only in this speech, Lindbergh warned against the danger inherent in Jews having amassed power in the media and government influence which they had not. In a national radio address he criticized those behind the news, but did not mention Jews.[3]

However, he also stated his focus on Jews was because the Jews were uniquely vulnerable. He wanted Jews to support a national war referendum before the U.S. entered a war, otherwise he believed the U.S. might fracture along religious fault lines. (NYC, 5/23/1941) Jews alone were mentioned because he feared Jews alone would be blamed for the U.S. entering a war.

It must be emphasized, in this speech and at other times, he accepted Jews could use their influence to promote their interests. Anti-Semitism in his era was defined by blaming Jews for their persecution or exaggerating it using press coverage. Lindbergh did not. The major Jewish interest was increasing the emigration of European Jews, this Lindbergh may have supported. He advocated it when negotiating with the Germans in January 1939. (Lindbergh, 1970, p.140)

Furthermore, criticism of one Jewish influence statement ignores how common it was. For example, in response to *Kristallnacht* our ambassador to Germany, Hugh Wilson, said "the Jewish controlled (press)...sang a hymn of hate while people over here try to make a better future." (Larson, 2011) Congressman Rankin (D-MS) blamed Jews for pushing the U.S. into war in a speech at the U.S. Capitol (4/29/1941). There was nearly no criticism of either. After returning from Germany, Hugh Wilson received two honorary doctorates including one from Yale. (HW, n.d.) (JTA Archives, 1941)

Ultimately, Lindbergh's statement to his wife needs to be considered. If an issue is true and relevant to the national interest, then addressing it respectfully is not anti-Semitism and suppressing it is censorship. Lindbergh did not want to mention Jews but felt obligated to represent loyal Americans who wanted to address the Jewish Americans who influenced the national debate. (AML, 1980, p.195) Emphasizing Jewish interventionists was partly motivated by anti-Semitism, but censorship does not diminish anti-Semitism. Others noted this, Jewish Supreme Court Justice Felix Frankfurter wrote in a Supreme Court opinion "(keeping) all reference to anti-Semitism and anti-Catholicism hidden is the best kind of cover under which evil can operate." (Feldman, 2011, p.231)

<u>Historical Events the Week Prior to the Speech (September 4-10, 1941):</u>
The U.S. was neutral: 1) the *Greer* Incident, 2) The Senate Hearings on Motion Picture War Propaganda — the Jews were blamed for a possible U.S. entry into World War II.

On September 4, 1941, German submarines shot torpedoes at the U.S. battleship, *Greer*, off the coast of Iceland. President Roosevelt responded by giving U.S. Naval vessels the right to fire on German vessels at will. As had been done in the *Luisitania* incident in World War I, events were distorted to create a *causus belli* (i.e. justification to declare war). The *Greer* was fired on with legitimate cause, it was tracking a German submarine for British aircraft. (Dalleck, 2017, p.434) Also, as Lindbergh emphasized, Congress had not approved the deployment of American warships to a war zone as required by the Constitution. (NYC, 10/30/41)

President Roosevelt's mother, Sara, died on September 7, 1941, delaying FDR's change in U.S. policy due to the *Greer* incident. Some advisors were advocating declaring war. FDR's response was to allow arming merchant shipping, another violation of the Neutrality Acts of 1937 and 1939.[1] (NA, n.d.) This announcement occurred immediately before Lindbergh's speech. (Dalleck, 2017) Lindbergh's frustration is documented; perhaps partially due to waiting for FDR to announce further steps drawing the U.S. closer to war. (Berg, 1998, p.426)

On September 9, 1941, the Senate held hearings investigating Hollywood's role in influencing U.S. opinion to enter World War II. In his opening statement, Senator Gerald Nye (R-ND) said, "Our Jewish Citizenry"... wanted "(our) sons taken into this foreign war", furthermore he said because Jews advocated war, Jews were contributing to anti-Semitism. Nye was criticized, but mostly for attacking free speech by criticizing movies he admittedly hadn't seen. Although some criticism of Nye was for anti-Semitism (Streich, 1990) (JTA Archives, 1941) it was mild compared to the criticism Lindbergh would receive, despite Lindbergh never blaming the Jews for inciting anti-Semitism. (Olson, 2013, p.372)

<u>The Speech:</u> "Who are the war agitators?" Des Moines, Iowa given on September 11, 1941, about an hour after Roosevelt gave his fireside chat regarding the *Greer* Incident. (<u>Underline</u> added by author)(link below)

The speech starts off by noting a slide towards war which Lindbergh claims most Americans oppose. He said the anti-war movement had always been honest, as opposed to the British and Roosevelt administration which have not been willing to have their allegations analyzed or reviewed. He made another appeal for a national war referendum before the U.S. enters the war.

Lindbergh then mentioned the debt incurred by World War I and then stated the reason America is being pulled towards war is subterfuge and propaganda. He named minor groups pulling America towards war: capitalists, Anglophiles, and intellectuals. He also named the Communists.

He named three major groups influencing American thought: the British, the Jewish, and the Roosevelt administration. Lindbergh did not err; he did not say nor intend to say, "the Jews". The unspoken noun following the adjective "Jewish" is "agitators". It is in the title. He follows this accusation with "I have named the major war agitators" and then 'agitators' are "a small minority of **our people**", i.e. **Americans**.

He then spoke of the British spending large sums of money to get us involved in the war and the debt we will incur should we enter it. He claimed Britain would have made peace with Germany but for the arms we are supplying, and we will again incur a non-paid debt as we incurred in World War I.

Then he discussed the Jews: first reference-

> "It is not difficult to understand why Jewish people desire the overthrow of Nazi Germany. No person with a sense of dignity of mankind can condone the persecution of the Jewish race in Germany. But no person of honesty and vision can look on their pro-war policy here today without seeing the dangers in such a policy both for us and for them."

He then made a statement about tolerance, mentioned Jews who were active in the isolationist movement, and then said Jewish influence and ownership of the media is dangerous (reference 2):

> "Their greatest danger to this country lies in their large ownership and influence in our motion pictures, our press, our radio and our government."

There is a later paragraph which said the media glorified the war by portraying atrocities committed by the Germans and Japanese and smeared opponents of war as traitors. Lindbergh's critics add this paragraph to Jewish influence accusations but given its history of smearing him personally, this probably referred to Roosevelt administration influence.

The third reference:

> "Instead of agitating for war, the <u>Jewish groups</u> in this country should be opposing it in every way for they will be the first to feel its consequences."

Fourth reference:

> "I am not attacking the British or the Jewish peoples. Both races I admire. But I am saying the <u>leaders</u> of both groups for reasons that are as understandable from their point of view as they are inadvisable from ours, for reasons which are not American, wish to involve us in war.
>
> We cannot blame them for looking out for what they believe to be in their own interests, but we must also look out for ours. We cannot allow the natural passions and prejudices of <u>other peoples</u> to lead our country to destruction."

Final (fifth) Reference: doesn't specifically mention Jews and is not in the typewritten text. It's written in the margin in his handwriting. He defined "agitator". His accusations did not apply to all Jews:

> **"I am speaking here only of war agitators, not of the sincere but misguided men and women who, confused by misinformation and frightened by propaganda, follow the lead of the war agitators."**

He then discussed the Roosevelt administration's use of emergency power to amass the greatest debt the country had ever known. He said that because the Roosevelt administration could not get America to enter the war in 1939, it instead used its emergency power to steadily erode limitations on its power, including its unprecedented third term. He accused it of using the media to convince Americans to go to war, by creating a series of propaganda incidents to force us to enter the war, and by suppressing free speech by preventing isolationists from using public venues to speak. He was denied use of a venue in Oklahoma City on August 29, 1941, but despite it and death threats, the speech proceeded.

He concluded, "we are on the verge of a war for which we are still unprepared, and for which no one has offered a feasible plan for victory — a war which cannot be won without sending our soldiers across an ocean to force a landing on a hostile coast against armies stronger than ours." A premonition of D-Day? Finally, "…we can still make our will known. And if we, the American people, do that, independence and freedom will continue to live among us. And there will be no foreign war."

<u>What did he say about the Jews that was good?</u>

Two phrases Lindbergh used: "For reasons which are understandable" and "we cannot blame them for what they believe to be in their own interests" are, in the author's opinion, the most important. They comport with his journal, in which he says it is the Jews' right to act in their interests. (Lindbergh, 1970) (8/23/39) Legitimately earned democratic power to pursue Jewish interests violates a basic principle of anti-Semitism: the Jews amass power to control events and destroy the non-Jewish world. (Rosenberg, 2022) To qualify as anti-Semitism, Jews must be definitionally nefarious in the use of power. Lindbergh is saying the opposite, he is saying Jews are justified in their intentions, but he disagrees with their goal.

As important is his admiration for the Jews. In 1941, people didn't say they admired Jews, speakers emphasized they didn't like them. When British Prime Minister Neville Chamberlain accepted 10,000 Jewish children in the *Kindertransport* he defended himself, "The Jews aren't lovable people. I don't care about them myself. But that isn't sufficient to explain the pogrom." (7/30/39, HC) Lindbergh made a remarkable statement. As a contrast consider Joseph Kennedy, Sr. who said about the Jews, "as a race they stink". (JPK, n.d.)

The prominent acknowledgement of the mistreatment of the Jews was unusual and laudatory. Mainstream national publications ignored it or buried it on back pages. (Wallace, 2018, p.124-129) Anti-Semites claimed the persecution of Jews was manufactured or blamed it on the Jews as Senator Nye had done. After *Kristallnacht*, anti-Semite Father Charles Coughlin used his radio address to blame the Jews, "Jewish persecution only followed after Christian persecution first." (CC, n.d.)

<u>What did he say about the Jews that was bad?</u> Lindbergh didn't say Jews were not Americans and he didn't say "the Jews" were pushing the U.S. into World War II.

Nothing Charles Lindbergh did in a life lived in the public spotlight would generate more criticism than his reference to the British and the Jews as "other peoples". The allegation is he said the Jews weren't Americans. These two words were seized upon as so blatantly anti-Semitic that in the public memory, they undid nearly everything Lindbergh accomplished in his life. Half a century later Philip Roth would use these words as inspiration for writing *The Plot Against America*. (Bailey,

2021) On April 10, 2022, in an article about religion in politics, the *Wall Street Journal* wrote, "By defining Jews as 'not American' Lindbergh effaced more than a century of religious toleration." (Contenetti, 2022) He never said it; he said they were part of our people.

Lindbergh kept extensive records of his thoughts and never hesitated to express controversial opinions. He left volumes of writings, hundreds of speeches and letters, and dozens of articles and interviews. Although it was common in his era to question "American-ness" (e.g. Eleanor Roosevelt), Lindberg never said nor wrote any group wasn't American. He never used anti-Semitic stereotypes nor made derogatory comments about Jews. The accusation ignores 16 speeches and five national radio addresses[3-8] Lindbergh had just given. In this speech, he had just said he admired the Jews.

If Lindbergh believed Jews were not Americans, he not only would not have admired them or included them in 'our people', but he would have noted it clearly somewhere else. Few non-Jews and no anti-Semite of his era ever said they admired Jews. One never has to analyze speeches or get a dictionary to find anti-Semitism in 1941 America.

Analysis of his previous speeches: Lindbergh divided Americans into "peoples" based on political viewpoint not ethnicity.

Lindbergh used 'people' in the collective, the way President Obama used the word 'folks', as a demographic relevant to a political discussion (e.g. gun owners). (Templeton, 2014) Today 'a people' is a nationality or ethnicity (e.g. 'the Irish people' are of Irish descent) and Lindbergh's use is archaic. For example, one would not call intellectuals "a people who read books", but Lindbergh used 'a people' that way. (Minneapolis, 5/10/41) Lindbergh gave 20 national speeches and five national radio addresses and 'a people' always referred to a political demographic[4-6] and never to a nationality.

Lindbergh emphasized Americans had been artificially divided into two "peoples", interventionists and isolationists, by "agitators"[5] and the two American "peoples" were quarreling. The "people", i.e. demographic, who agreed with him he called "our people" (Philadelphia, 5/29/41)[4-6] and those who disagreed were either a "people of another kind" or had ideas "of another kind". (NYC 10/30/41, Minneapolis, 5/10/41) But they were all Americans. For example, in a radio address he said, "We need not fear a foreign invasion unless American peoples bring it on through their own quarreling."[5] In a different radio address, he said groups like those identified in the Des Moines speech, i.e. those pushing the U.S. towards war, represent a small minority "of the American people".[7]

Lindbergh used the term "not American" as an adjective modifying the word "reasons", i.e. entering the war was not in America's interest. Those who did not act in America's interests were a different 'people'. For example, he called the presidents of American universities a "people" "of another kind". (Cole, 1974) He blamed them for pushing the U.S. into World War II, for our involvement in World War I, and for the Versailles Treaty, but he didn't say they weren't Americans. (Minneapolis, 5/10/41)

This Speech: 'Jewish War Agitators' referred to a few Jewish leaders, *the Jews* were not pushing the U.S. into the war.

In his special on the U.S. entry into World War II, documentarian Ken Burns accused Lindbergh of blaming the Jews for pushing the U.S. into war, but Lindbergh never mentioned the Jews. (Burns, 2022) He refers to Jews in the collective ("the Jewish race" and "the Jewish people") only in positive statements: acknowledging Jewish persecution in Germany and admiring Jews.[8] In negative statements he specifically refers to Jewish leaders or Jewish groups as defined by the word "agitators". He clearly said they are distinct from the rest of the Jews in the fifth reference above (in **bold**).

When Lindbergh blamed Jewish war agitators, he was referring to those who were collaborating with Roosevelt to vilify him. (Cole, 1974, pp.132-6) They called him a Nazi (Cole, 1974, p.150), said he had a "poisoned mind" (Berg, 1998, p.409), and labeled him "the Lone Ostrich". (WW, n.d.) Lindbergh's designation of agitators as either Jewish groups or Jewish leaders, but never *the* Jews, is also underlined above in references 3 and 4. He had legitimate grievances with the accusations of disloyalty leveled at him, but Lindbergh never said those who criticized him weren't Americans.

To qualify as an "agitator", one's advocacy had to oppose his version of the national interest. He was sympathetic with Jewish efforts to protect fellow Jews. They were "sincere" but "misguided", "confused", and "frightened." He is speaking to his fellow Americans whose support he desired. Regardless, "other people" had a right to advocacy, and he never said they weren't Americans.

<u>Another claim made by historians:</u> "other" meant the Jews were outsiders in America

To their credit, some historians did not accuse Lindbergh of saying the Jews weren't Americans. (e.g. Groom, Olson, Berg) Instead, they accuse Lindbergh of a lesser but similar and common transgression of this era: saying Jews were not 'real Americans' or outsiders. (Berg, 1998, p. 427) For example, the novelist Raymond Chandler said, "the Jews are to some extent still foreigners". (Olson, 2013, p.364) Fictional Senator Geary said it about Italians in *Godfather II.* But Lindbergh <u>never</u> said anything like it about Jews nor anyone else.

Ironically, it was his adversaries, the Roosevelts, who said the Jews were not real Americans. Franklin said "...this is a Protestant country. The Jews and Catholics are here under sufferance." (Olson, 2013, p.383) Eleanor said:

> "The difficulty is that the country is still full of immigrant Jews, very much unlike ourselves. I don't blame them for being as they are. I know what they've been through in other lands, and I'm glad they have freedom at last, and I hope they'll have the chance, among us, to develop all there is in them. But it takes a little time for Americans to be made...One day I hope, we'll be Americans together." (Cook, 1999, pp.315-7)

New York City, May 23, 1941: Lindbergh advocated the antithesis of what he is accused of advocating.

Lindbergh was introduced in a sold-out raucous Madison Square Garden rally to thunderous applause and shouts of "our next President". Approximately, 23,000 people were in the auditorium and 10,000 who could not get in, stood outside dangerously mingling with protestors and listening to the speech on speakers. (Cole, 1974, p.147) The police had to break up brawls and enter the crowd to restore order. (Olson, 2013, p.325) Anne expressed fear for her husband's safety. (Berg, 1998, p.420) Lindbergh had an opportunity to whip the crowd into an anti-Semitic frenzy.

Instead, he calmly emphasized our diversity and said the threat of religious violence evolved from entering a war without a chance for the people to vote on it:

> "The United States is a nation of mixed races, religions and beliefs. We came from every part of Europe and from every portion of the earth. Here, in this country, we have learned to live peacefully together. Here we have developed a racial tolerance such as the world has never known before. Here we have developed a civilization in many ways never previously approached. Why must all this be jeopardized by injecting the wars and the hatreds of Europe into our midst?" (NYC, 5/23/1941)

Anne wrote the crowd didn't like her husband's "calm and unemotional" speech but left peacefully. (AML, 1980, p.169) Months later he repeated this message, emphasizing every religion was an integral part of this nation. (NYC, 10/30/1941)

The text of the New York speech (May 1941) is available on the web, but a search is more likely to show doctored photographs of Lindbergh giving a Nazi salute, something he never did.[9] The absurdity of celebrating minority inclusion in American society and suggesting ways to protect Jews while giving a Nazi salute is never noted. Apparently, his critics haven't read the speech, considered the potential violence he diffused, nor considered the damage caused by the Roosevelts choosing 'real' Americans. Instead, they emphasize fascist attendees, as if Lindbergh selected the audience.

<u>Conclusion — Reference to "Other People":</u>

Lindbergh said every religion was part of our nation in two national speeches and in this speech said, "the Jewish" were "our people". Jews were his fellow American citizens whose support he desired. "Other people" were defined as those who used their power to influence U.S. foreign policy contrary to his version of the national interest, whether Jewish or not. Despite "others'" vilification of him, he never said they did not have a democratic right to advocate as they saw fit and certainly never said they weren't Americans.

Stating the average Jew is sincere but misguided is condescending, but it violates a principle of anti-Semitism: Jews must act with nefarious intent as part of a conspiracy. (Rosenberg, 2022) A "misguided" person needs to hear the truth. Lindbergh wanted to convince all Americans to adopt his version of the national interest, and the last thing he wanted to do was insult those he was trying to convince. He thought Jews, in particular, would be receptive to the idea of a national war referendum because he believed they would see it was in their interest.

<u>What about the other references to Jews?</u> These references were anti-Semitism.

The reference to Jewish influence is anti-Semitism. Identifying powerful people collaborating with a President to vilify you is legitimate; attributing it to their faith is anti-Semitism. But his motive is clear. When he said "they will be the first to feel its consequences" he is warning Jews — if we declared war on Germany and lost, Jews may have been blamed.

Nevertheless, it was an anti-Semitic statement because Lindbergh needed to have said in Des Moines that any decision to enter a war is a national decision and no group should ever be judged solely responsible.

Notice the difference between Joseph Kennedy's statement to the German Ambassador in June 1938 and Lindbergh's. Kennedy said Jewish 'control' of the media falsely portrayed Germany as mistreating Jews so Americans would oppose Germany. Lindbergh said some Jews used their earned 'influence' to emphasize real persecution, which was justified. However, he warned this was dangerous for Jews because Americans might blame them if the U.S. entered the war. Kennedy's statement is anti-Semitism. Lindbergh's may also be because he named the agitators' religion — but it was the attack on Pearl Harbor three months later, which no one anticipated, which made Lindbergh's concerns unwarranted.

<u>What did Americans hear in 1941?</u> In politics it may not matter what a speaker meant if the audience heard something else.

Lindbergh's speech terrified Jews, this was inexcusable. (Wallace, 2003) But most other Americans already had an opinion of him, and this accusation didn't change the discussion because he had been vilified in the press so often. This accusation was mild. The president called him a Copperhead (i.e., a traitor) and famous *NY Times* columnist Dorothy Thompson wrote "Lindbergh is pro-Nazi". Another column said about Lindbergh, "In our first fight for freedom we got rid of Benedict Arnold. In this fight for freedom, let's get rid of all the Benedict Arnolds." (Cole, 1974, pp.131,140)

Both sides were name calling in a very tense political climate. Lindbergh's allies called Roosevelt a tyrant (Olson, 2013). Lindbergh didn't use the word "tyrant", but he said Roosevelt was denying Americans basic democratic rights. (St. Louis, May 3, 1941) Although there were some Americans who believed the accusation of tyranny, most Americans understood real tyranny. Although FDR clearly violated the Neutrality Acts it hardly qualified.[1] (Dalleck, 2017, p.436) (NA, n.d.)

Likewise, Americans knew real anti-Semitism because they saw it every day. The movie *Gentleman's Agreement* won the Oscar for Best Picture in 1947 by portraying it. (GA, n.d.) Lindbergh's two words, no matter the interpretation, didn't qualify as the anti-Semitism Americans knew then but not today. Lindbergh's critics hadn't objected when apartments, universities, and hotels were "restricted" to gentiles, (Groom, 2003) so how could they honestly be offended by Lindbergh's speech? Americans in 1941 understood Lindbergh's critics seized an opportunity to label him an anti-Semite to win a critical debate. Today people are unfamiliar with the climate of hostility and anti-Semitism in 1941, nor do they appreciate the stakes of the debate. Only one of many political accusations is remembered.

How accurate was the speech?

Much of the speech was wrong, but accusations Roosevelt used the press to influence American public opinion to support entering the war and violated the Neutrality Acts to supply England with weapons were true. (Fleming, 2001) (Olson, 2013) Accusations some Jews were advocating entering the war were true. Their influence was exaggerated.

The war and American public opinion were changing, and the isolationists were losing. If Lindbergh admitted Germany was evil and Britain would not lose, then U.S. aid not only worked but was morally imperative. Lindbergh's position was increasingly undefendable. He acknowledged isolationism was losing on his way to Des Moines. (Berg, 1998, p.426)

Americans increasingly understood the real situation in Europe and were beginning to believe if Britain could defeat Germany, then America certainly could. A poll in October 1940 revealed half of Americans wanted the U.S. to arm England because they believed Hitler would invade the U.S. next, slightly more wanted to give England more aid. (Dalleck, 2017, pp. 391-3) Instead of acknowledging the truth, isolationists increasingly blamed "propaganda" and exaggerated public support for their positions.[4,6]

Lindbergh's contention U.S. foreign military aid was futile and but for our aid Britain would reach a peace agreement with Germany was no longer correct (also said in SF Speech, 7/1/41). Perhaps after the fall of France in June 1940, U.S. refusal to help would have induced England to sign a peace agreement with Germany; but by September 1941 England had defeated Germany in the Battle of Britain and humiliated the Italian army in North Africa.

The "agitators" were accused of spreading "propaganda", but this ignored the same First Amendment he is championing and as previously noted bordered on hypocrisy. Major media outlets, particularly *Life* and *March of Time* movie news reels, had the same First Amendment right as Lindbergh. They chose to report on the brutality of the Germans and the suffering of the people they occupied. (Olson, 2013, pp.364-5) "Agitators" didn't fill the news with stories of atrocities, the Germans did that on their own. The coverage wasn't "propaganda", it was true whether Lindbergh believed it or not, but regardless it was constitutionally protected free speech.

Overwhelmingly, Jews wanted to enter the war to help Europe's Jews, but saying Jews had "...large...influence in our motion pictures, our press, our radio" is an exaggeration. (Berg, 1998, p. 429) There were Jews in major media companies, but few controlled content. Many Jewish movie studio owners wouldn't produce anti-Nazi movies, but a notable few did. Belying allegations Hollywood supported the war, 20th Century Fox had sent its employees to hear Lindbergh speak at the Hollywood Bowl three months earlier. (Cole, 1974, p.150) A study done at Notre Dame in 1941 concluded Jews controlled 3% of media content, exactly the Jewish percentage of the U.S. population. (Berg, 1998, p.429)

Jewish influence in the government seems minimal by today's standards: one cabinet member and five representatives. However, for its era, the 12 prominent Jews in the administration and numbers of Jews appointed to federal positions was unprecedented. (Feingold, 1969, p.

9) Furthermore, Lindbergh's insinuation that Jews secretly influenced policy was based on some truth. Justice Frankfurter was publicly silent about his fellow European Jews, but privately advocated intervention in World War II. (Fullilove, 2013, p.116) (Wyman Institute, n.d.) His connections freed prominent Austrian Jews from concentration camps, including his 82-year-old uncle. (Feldman, 2011, pp.154-7)

If the speech is understood as Lindbergh said it, his much-criticized statement was true — a few Jewish leaders were advocating the U.S. enter the war. The most powerful and influential columnists of the era, Walter Winchell and Walter Lippman, were both Jewish, supported entering the war, and vilified Lindbergh through their collaboration with Roosevelt. (Cole, 1974, p.140) Other prominent Jewish interventionists included Eugene Meyer, publisher of the *Washington Post,* the actor Edward G. Robinson (who starred in the pro-interventionist movie *Confessions of a Nazi Spy* (1939)), and those active in interventionist advocacy organizations *Century Group* and *Fight for Freedom.* (Olson, 2013, p.385) (Nasaw, 2012, p.508) *Century Group* recruited the most effective interventionist speaker, General John Pershing, and Lippman wrote his speeches. (Peters, 2005, p.163)

Jack Warner was perhaps the most influential "Jewish war agitator". The co-founder of Warner Brothers was born in Canada, the fifth son of an immigrant Jewish tailor. In 1939, he made *Confessions,* which because it enraged Hitler led to U.S. staff leaving Berlin in November 1939. President Roosevelt pressured him to stop making "propaganda pictures", but Warner Brothers made more anti-Nazi movies including Casablanca. (JW, n.d.) Lindbergh had criticized the Jewish owner of *Movietone News,* William Fox, in 1940. The most watched newsreel's coverage of the war, especially the London Blitz, had unparalleled influence in U.S. public opinion because newsreels were Americans only exposure to audiovisual news. (Berg, 1998, p.412)

If Lindbergh had to name more "Jewish war agitators", certain movie producers would have been proud to be named. Walter Wanger was an avid interventionist. (Olson, 2013, p.361) His pro-war movie *Foreign Correspondent* (1940) was nominated for 6 Academy Awards including Best Picture but did not win any. (Olson, 2013, p.366) (FC, n.d.)

Movie producer Fritz Lang also qualified. He was baptized as a child by his Jewish mother. Because his religious lineage was unknown, he was offered a position as head of a German film studio by Joseph Goebbels. He fled Germany penniless, but quickly received a U.S. immigration visa. Despite movie studio executives denying him access to the editing room when they discovered his intentions, he produced four anti-Nazi movies. His most acclaimed was *Man Hunt* (1941) which drew on his experiences living in Nazi Germany and exposed viewers to details of German persecution like making victims wear labels. (FL, n.d.)

<u>Conclusion — Lindbergh's comments to Jews:</u> Three speeches relating to religious tolerance (Des Moines/two NYC speeches) need to be evaluated in their entirety, rather than two words taken out of context.

Lindbergh criticized critics who were calling him a traitor. (Berg, 1998, p.409) Just as Lindbergh was forced to move his family to Europe in 1935, he was forced to move his family to Martha's Vineyard in 1941 to protect them from press hysteria. The "agitators" would be proven right about our national interest, but whether they had a First Amendment right to destroy Lindbergh's reputation and endanger his family is a legitimate question.

Lindbergh didn't blame "our Jewish citizenry", as Senator Nye had done. He addressed specific Jews designated as "agitators" and for the remainder of American Jews he expressed admiration. Undoubtedly, these Jewish activists advocated entering the war because of their Jewish identity. After respectfully acknowledging that these Jews had the right to advocate for Jewish interests, he could then address their motivation. This was because a critical national decision, in the interest of all Americans, was being influenced by prominent Jews, motivated mainly because they were Jewish. His point was valid: Those of other faiths may not have shared the same definition of the national interest as Jewish activists.

Jews considered the speech inflammatory and potentially dangerous. Anne agreed. But everyone has the right to defend themselves. The term "agitator" is not nice, but it pales in comparison to his Jewish critics' personal attacks.

The author acknowledges Lindbergh made anti-Semitic statements, but American society was so imbued with anti-Semitism in 1941 each statement can't be reviewed separately. Doing so removes the speech from its era, and applying this standard uniformly renders nearly every non-Jewish public figure in 1941 an anti-Semite, including both Roosevelts and Truman. An evaluation of the message, based on all his speeches, indicates Lindbergh's message was there can be only one foreign policy and it must be in the interest of all Americans — which included Jews. Lindbergh's goal was to convince everyone, especially Jews, to support a national war referendum. His message was not anti-Semitic.

<u>Analysis of the Criticism of the Speech by non-Jews:</u> Much of it was espoused by anti-Semites.

There are three problems with the non-Jewish criticism of Lindbergh. First, quite a few of Lindbergh's critics were virulent anti-Semites. Second, they were inconsistent. Others who expressed the same sentiment in public, with much less empathy and tact, escaped criticism. Third and most important, Lindbergh's critics didn't advocate for Jewish interests. Some media commented on the hypocrisy of the criticism of Lindbergh, noting the criticism was not because the critics supported Jewish interests, but rather because Lindbergh said it and he was Roosevelt's chief political opponent. (Cole, 1974, p.178)

The group the Committee to Defend America (CDA) was created by FDR to oppose isolationism and prepare Americans for U.S. entry into World War II. The CDA chapters viciously criticized Lindbergh as an anti-Semite. An isolationist in Greenwich, Connecticut, Professor Gregory Mason, challenged the head of the CDA to a debate on anti-Semitism in America. He was turned down because the CDA chairman was also the chairman of the Greenwich Real Estate Board which refused to rent or sell houses to Jews. In response Professor Mason said, "A great deal of hypocrisy has been evidenced by smug citizens in our midst who sounded off to condemn Lindbergh on the hasty reading of two or three sentences lifted from his Des Moines address. Many such citizens practice anti-Semitism every day of their lives." (Cole, 1974, pp.181-2)

This hypocrisy was noted at the time. The magazine *Christian Century* wrote, "...hotel clubs and foyers rang with denouncement of Lindbergh...(all of them) barring their doors to Jews." (Breitman, 2013, p.188) The head of the Socialist Party, Norman Thomas, said "(Lindbergh is) not as anti-Semitic as some who take the opportunity to criticize him." (Ross, 1964, p.314)

The two Republican Presidential nominees of the era condemned the speech because it was ammunition to attack Republicans, but their objections were vague. The 1940 nominee Wendell Willkie said it was "the most un-American talk made in my time". The 1944 and 1948 nominee Thomas Dewey, said, "(it was) an inexcusable abuse of the right of freedom of speech." (Cole, 1974, p.175)

Republican presidential nominees should have more upset about worse sentiments emanating from a Republican Senator two days earlier, but Dewey said little about it. Besides, if they were so upset, perhaps they should have supported Jewish interests? Willkie only criticized Hitler when he wasn't running for President. During the 1940 campaign he didn't criticize Hitler and adopted virulent isolationism when it improved his polling. (Peters, 2005, pp.174-9) The major Jewish political interest was increased immigration of Jews from Europe. Both Willkie and Dewey advocated restricting immigration.[2] (Republican Platform, 1940) (Yang, 2020, p.117-8) Willkie, to his credit, criticized Senator Nye for spreading anti-Semitism. (JTA, 9/17/41)

Lindbergh wasn't criticized for harming Jewish interests, but rather for violating the convention presented in the introduction: Jewish interests must not be mentioned in public. John Flynn, an isolationist journalist, said, "no one could mention (the Jews without)...incurring the guilt of the religious and racial intolerance." (Cole, 1974, p.181) In her diary Anne asked why nobody minded his naming the British or the Administration as pro-war, but "to name 'Jew' is un-American-even if it is done without hate or bitterness or even criticism?" (Berg, 1998, p.427)

The *New York Herald Tribune* had backed Lindbergh when defamed by the administration, but after the Des Moines Speech, it would no longer support him. It wrote that the speech, "(marked) the climax of a series of innuendos and covert illusions by Isolationist leaders opening new and ugly vistas." (Mosely, 1976, p.302) This was valid criticism: He might have worsened anti-Semitism (i.e. "ugly vistas"). It was repeated by three other newspapers that had previously supported him.[10] When *America First's* local chapters made "anti-Semitic innuendos" they were reprimanded but not expelled by the national organization. (Ross, 1964, p.314) However, Lindbergh wasn't responsible for the statements of others, especially because he never engaged in "innuendos" regarding any issue. He always said what he thought.

A modern critic of Lindbergh, historian Richard Breitman, defined the anti-Semitism in Lindbergh's speech as "crossing the line between private mutterings and public prejudice...(by saying) Jews led the push for war". (Breitman, 2013, pp.187-8) This criticism doesn't address Lindbergh's motivation. These "lines" put the country in danger and in World War I they wasted 100,000 American lives. Nor does it ask whether a "line" forbidding the discussion of Jewish political interests reduced anti-Semitism. The logical follow-up question also isn't asked: If public silence was beneficial in minimizing anti-Semitism why wasn't it recommended to manage all forms of racism, e.g. address Jim Crow by not talking about it? Obviously, it made anti-Semitism worse. This strategy was a complete failure, recommended only for Jews, and despite that it is still defended today. Furthermore, those who still advocate for the appropriateness of its use in 1941 continue to criticize Lindbergh for not abiding by it.

Breitman echoes the *Herald Tribune's* criticism of Lindbergh for opening "new vistas". In 1941, this was stated exclusively by non-Jews. For example, *Liberty Magazine* wrote, "leaders of anti-Semitism were shoddy little crooks...(but Lindbergh) has stood up in public and given brazen tongue to what obscure malcontents have only whispered." (Berg, 1998, p.428) In 1941 America, Jews faced public discrimination in housing, employment, and education. In *Gentleman's Agreement* denying Jews hotel rooms was portrayed. (GA, n.d.) Only those who didn't face daily discrimination considered anti-Semitism "new vistas", "private mutterings", or "only whispered". A Senator and Congressman had accused Jews of pushing the U.S. into war in official government proceedings in the previous 6 months. Our Ambassador to Germany said it in the aftermath of *Kristallnacht.*

Statements blaming Jews for U.S. pre-war policy were said often in public, by elected Americans in taxpayer funded government proceedings, with much less tact before Lindbergh did so. The criticism of government officials was comparatively mild and in the case of our Ambassador to Germany, Hugh Wilson, there was none.

<u>What did the Jews say about the speech?</u> A paralyzing fear of anti-Semitism caused the Jews to miss an opportunity to advocate for themselves.

While nearly every religious organization and individual Rabbis criticized Lindbergh's speech, there was no effective Jewish response. (Leaders of All Religions, 1941) The Anti-Defamation League (ADL) said no national Jewish organization advocated entering the war, and despite his accusations of Jewish influence in the media, Lindbergh had no trouble getting radio time to espouse his views. (JTA Archives, 1941)

American Jews were rightfully upset by Lindbergh's speech. There was a real fear of anti-Semitic violence. In Europe, Jews were daily victims of violence, and the U.S. had a substantial Nazi presence. Anne warned her husband the anti-Semitic violence risked by his speech was unacceptable, and she preferred to enter the war than see this violence in her country. However, there was no anti-Semitic violence, only an increase in anti-Semitic letters which today are preserved in archives because Lindbergh insisted on the preservation of "the bad as well as the good". (Berg, 1998, p.429)

By September 1941 American politics and society had changed. Unemployment had fallen to less than 10% and anti-Semite Father Coughlin had been taken off the radio. Americans were receptive to Jewish complaints about German persecution. It is one reason Lindbergh's speech was uniformly criticized. A poll in November 1938 demonstrated 94% disapproved of Nazi persecution of the Jews, 83% wanted Germany to lose any future war, and 61% supported boycotting German goods. (Dallek, 2017, p.325) A poll in the aftermath of Lindbergh's speech found only 8% of Americans blamed the Jews for pushing the U.S. towards a war. (Breitman, 2013, p.188)

The 1938 poll showed 83% opposed increasing immigration quotas, (Dalleck, 2017, pp.325-6) but the immigration conflict (e.g. Labor's conflict with the State Department) regarded complying with existing laws, not increasing quotas. (USHMM, n.d.) The Secretary of Labor advocated immigration of needed Jewish professionals: doctors, pharmacists, economists, and scientists. But no one else did. As a result, efforts to give visas to certain Jewish professionals died quietly. (Downey, 2009, p.192)

Lindbergh's speech was an opportunity for the Jews to aggressively advocate for the emigration of Europe's Jews. Because Jews weren't publicly advocating, Lindbergh did not know Jews with access to Roosevelt were mostly using it to advocate for Jewish emigration. He might have agreed. He helped a Jewish colleague get out of Germany and facilitated meetings between the head of the Reichsbank, Hjalmar Schacht, and his father-in-law's friend, the head of the *Intergovernmental*

Refugee Committee to facilitate Jewish emigration in January 1939. (Berg, 1998, p.381), (Lindbergh, 1970, p.139)

1941 America was ripe for the conversation Lindbergh might have started. Non-Jewish Americans used Jewish stereotypes, but they understood what was happening in Germany, opposed it, and disagreed with Lindbergh. Had Jews emphasized existing quotas were not filled and needed professionals were available to fill them, many would have supported retroactively filling quotas with specific professionals. Lindbergh avidly promoted recruiting scientists and a Jewish cardiologist out of Germany. (Hessen, 1984, p.152) Perhaps he would have supported the selective immigration of Jewish physicians and scientists?

<u>The Speech's Legacy:</u> Judged in the context of its time, the transgressions made while mentioning Jews does not justify dismissing this speech as anti-Semitic.

Historians consider the speech a disaster that ended the *America First* movement. (Herman, 2000) This is hindsight. A poll showed support for isolationism plummeted in the immediate aftermath of the speech, (Breitman, 2013, p.188) but public opinion is fluid. Lindbergh's speeches that followed were sold out. He had other speeches scheduled — Boston on December 12, 1941, and Seattle in January 1942 — but they were canceled, and isolationism ended because we were attacked on December 7, 1941.

The isolationist organization, *America First*, considered censoring Lindbergh, but they didn't. Lindbergh issued no retraction although he offered to make a statement that he expressed his own opinions and not those of *America First*. His offer was declined. (Lindbergh, 1970) (Berg, 1998, p.429)

The speech's legacy should be a debate whether it was legitimate free speech and therefore protected by the First Amendment. Lindbergh's message, there must be a single national interest, is as valid today as it was in 1941. Lindbergh never regretted giving the speech. He wrote, "I prefer to go down fighting for what we believe, if we must go down at all." (9/17/1941, Lindbergh, 1970)

Conclusion: In Exodus 3:1-4:17, God appears to Moses in the form of a burning bush and tells him, despite his fears and speech impediment, he must speak to Pharoah to demand an end to the oppression of the Jews. Thus, Jews are commanded to represent Jewish interests, and non-Jews can't do it for them. In this case, they did it very badly.

Based on the advocacy of prominent Jews and the ADL comments, the author would propose the Jewish response to Lindbergh: *Primarily, the U.S. must act in good faith to facilitate the emigration of as many Jews as possible from Europe. Entering the war is a secondary interest which can be de-emphasized if doing so helps to get the Jews out of every European country from which they seek to emigrate.* First, it's a request to comply with the law. Second, if Jews were leaving Europe freely, entering the war would hurt the ability to extricate them. Had this been stated publicly, Lindbergh might have agreed.

Jews could have asked why the Dominican Republic's commitment to take 100,000 Jews or Labor's initiative to issue visas to Jewish professionals hadn't been fulfilled. Neither in his speeches nor any public statement did Lindbergh ever advocate restricting Jewish immigration.

While Lindbergh was speaking, millions of Americans were agreeing with accusations Roosevelt was a tyrant for violating the Neutrality Acts with impunity. Yet, at the FDR Presidential Museum in Hyde Park, NY the only mentions of the Neutrality Acts are dates. This political accusation has been forgotten. Yet a different accusation, Lindbergh was the anti-Semite because he said two nebulous words in a country where Jews couldn't rent apartments and faced quotas in higher education, is accepted as truth solely because it is convenient to do so.

Neither widespread American anti-Semitism, Jewish silence, selective press reporting, Roosevelt's actions, the hypocrisy of his critics,

Lindbergh's advocacy for German Jews in January 1939, nor the anti-Semitism of government officials like Nye, Wilson, and Rankin excuse Lindbergh's anti-Semitism. But an honest assessment of what Lindbergh said which constituted hate speech and thus possibly unprotected by the First Amendment, would have left no one to criticize him. The non-Jewish American public figures who criticized him didn't advocate for the Jews, engaged in anti-Semitism in their everyday lives, and were silent about the threat facing Europe's Jews when it was politically expedient.

Some people who defined Lindbergh's legacy had legitimate motives. They wanted to enter the war because it was in the national interest. Their chief political opponent gave them the opportunity to destroy him, and they took it. That was politics then and now. But 80 years later it needs to be understood — the vilification of Lindbergh was a political diversion to win a debate that ended in 1941. Jews must recognize the anti-Semitic phrases were not Lindbergh's message and were commonly said by elected public figures, some of whom are now considered heroes by contemporary Jews.

With 80 years hindsight it's easy to decide what lessons Lindbergh *should* have learned from his visits to Nazi Germany. But the lesson Lindbergh did learn was nations easily splinter along religious lines. He believed because a handful of people were "injecting...the hatreds of Europe into our midst" (NYC, 5/23/1941) it would happen here. Although he never questioned their constitutional right to advocate, he felt it was his obligation to warn his fellow Jewish American citizens of the societal danger of advocating entering the war, regardless of what it did to his reputation or legacy. Lindbergh learned the wrong lesson, but lack of ability to predict the future does not make one an anti-Semite.

Lindbergh was not a politician. He said what he thought needed to be said. He never retracted his words nor accepted any restrictions on speaking. Nor should he have. His intent was not to malign Jews. It was to promote his definition of the national interest. As a future combat pilot, but also simply as an American, he had a First Amendment right to define our national interest. Those who disagreed were obligated to answer before we entered a war. The author hears Lindbergh pleading, "tell me why it's in my interest and the interest of 130 million non-Jewish Americans to fight this war". He was entitled to ask the question and he was entitled to an answer.

The reader may hear something else, but even so, the reader should acknowledge an in-depth discussion of the meaning of "other peoples" and whether it connotes anti-Semitism at a time when every aspect of American society was imbued with real anti-Semitism is pointless. Furthermore, the labeling of Lindbergh as an anti-Semite by those who wouldn't rent to Jews and a President who enabled the murder of Jews is hypocrisy.

The villain was a convention that said Jewish interests could not be discussed. This convention is unacceptable and dangerous in every era for every form of racism. No one benefits, especially Jews, from not being part of the national conversation. Of course, it would have been better if Lindbergh had changed some of the wording, but Lindbergh spoke the way people spoke in his era. There was no way he could address the Jews and not be called an anti-Semite because he was Charles Lindbergh. He tried. He said even "Jewish war agitators" were part of "our people". He acknowledged the reality of Jewish persecution and the legitimacy of Jewish advocacy. He wrote on the speech in his own handwriting that he was criticizing only those Jews who vilified him, not "the Jews". He said 3 times in the Des Moines speech he wasn't referring to all Jews and twice in other speeches that every religion is an integral part of this nation. This has been ignored for 80 years. Given an opportunity to destroy his reputation his enemies took it then and they still take it now.

Lindbergh's speech made no difference to the Jews. Those who criticized him did nothing for the Jews. If only a handful of brave Americans were willing to advocate for the Jews in Europe, what difference did it make that Lindbergh mentioned Jews in Des Moines, Iowa? The attention it received, and still receives, is not solely based on a misinterpretation; it is intentional. The reader should acknowledge Lindbergh clearly said his accusations weren't referring to all Jews, and those accusations he made about Jewish leaders were exaggerated but true. Critics are willfully ignoring what he said. The speech is still used as a diversion from what was about to happen, and who was truly to blame.

The villain was neither Lindbergh nor the Jews. As weak and powerless as the Jews felt they were, many Americans, Lindbergh included, wanted them to openly advocate for their interests. Those who criticize Lindbergh's speech, even today, offer no alternative or course of action which should have been employed to fight anti-Semitism in 1941. They never recommend other ethnic or racial groups accept private scorn and public silence as a strategy to fight racism.

Lindbergh emphasized adherents of every religion were Americans and never excluded any group, especially not Jews, from "American-ness". Lindbergh's poor judgment and condescension is not the reason he is still criticized. It is convenient to blame him. He is criticized for the opposite of what he said. Those who criticized him, the President and First Lady, said Jews weren't Americans.

Regardless, Lindbergh wasn't the one who was silent or who had the power to do something and didn't. Indeed, in 1939 he was one of the very few who tried to help. The blame should be directed at a convention which enabled millions of Jews to be murdered without people advocating for them and those who so emotionally defended this convention.

Those two words hardly mattered. President Franklin Roosevelt's State Department refusal to comply with the law resulted in hundreds of thousands of Jews being murdered. There is your villain.

[1]The Neutrality Acts of 1937 and 1939 both forbade the use of American ships to transport munitions to belligerent nations. Roosevelt had been violating these provisions since Hitler's invasion of western Europe. He allowed the ships to be escorted by battleships and then allowed them to be armed. On September 11, 1941, he allowed them to fire at

German vessels at will. All these were violations of the Neutrality Acts and sending sailors into a war zone without Congressional approval was a violation of the Constitution. The Munitions Control Board was to approve the sale of munitions but the author found no instance it ever denied or even modified a sale that Roosevelt announced. (NA, n.d.)

[2]In 1941, Thomas Dewey was a rising figure in Republican national politics and didn't oppose immigration of Jews. However, as a presidential candidate Dewey opposed the Displaced Persons Act which President Truman signed and gave U.S. visas to 200,000 overwhelmingly Jewish refugees. (Yang, 2020) Two of those displaced persons were the author's father-in-law and the author's wife's grandfather who had survived Dachau.

Text of the Des Moines Speech and New York Speech (May 23, 1941) can be found at the listing for the America First Committee at charleslindbergh.com.

[3-7] Five national public radio addresses given by Charles Lindbergh from 1939-1940 in chronologic order. Available at Our Drift Toward War : Charles A. Lindbergh : Internet Archive. The titles and dates of his 5 national radio addresses are in the Index, under Lindbergh's entry.

[8]He also made a reference to the "Jewish position" in one of the drafts, "I oppose such persecution (of Jews) and feel we must keep it from our own nation. I stand opposed to such persecution and I am in sympathy and understanding with the Jewish position". Unfortunately, he never said it.

[9]Photos of Lindbergh making Nazi salutes are fraudulent; there's no evidence he ever gave one. During the May 1941 NYC speech, the *New York Times* reported Lindbergh repeatedly waved to the crowd, but not that he gave a Nazi salute. (Mosley, 1976, p.290) In a movie of the speech, available on the *Smithsonian Magazine* website, cheering is audible after he said, "England is losing the war". Lindbergh held his hand up to quiet the audience — his hand motion resembled a Nazi salute, but clearly wasn't. Photographs of Lindbergh with his arm outstretched were a Bellamy Salute, a patriotic

salute originating in the 19th century (palm is upright, as opposed to a Nazi salute in which the palm is down), during the Pledge of Allegiance. In these photographs, interventionists either cropped out his hand or the American flag. (Feldman, 2011, p.180)

[10]The three other newspapers which had consistently defended Lindbergh but criticized him after the Des Moines speech were the *Des Moines Register*, the *Kansas City Star*, and the *San Francisco Chronicle.* The criticism was notable because these newspapers neither endorsed Roosevelt's policies nor were influenced by interventionist organizations. (Mosley, 1976, p.301)

Works Cited

AML, Lindbergh, Anne M., *War Without and War Within: Diaries and Letters of Anne Morrow Lindbergh, 1939-1944,* Harcourt, Brace, and Jovanovich, 1980.

Armstrong, E. (1941, February). *Letter Against Lend-Lease Act.* Educational Director, America First.

Bailey, B. (2021). *Philip Roth.* New York: WW Norton and Company.

Berg, A. S. (1998). Lindbergh. The Free Press.

Breitman, R. (2013). *FDR and the Jews.* London: Belknap Press, p. 188.

Burns, K. (2022, September 17). U.S. and the Holocaust. PBS.

CC. (n.d.). *Charles Coughlin.* Retrieved from https://en....org/wiki/Charles_Coughlin

Cole, W. (1974). *Charles Lindbergh and the Battle Against American Intervention in World War II.* New York: Jovanovich.

Contenetti, M. (2022). The Return of the Old American Right. *Wall Street Journal*, C1-C2.

Cook, B. (1999). *Eleanor Roosevelt.* New York: Viking Publishers.

Dallek, R. (2017). *Franklin D. Roosevelt.* New York: Penguin Publishing.

Downey, K. (2009). *The Woman Behind the New Deal.* New York: Anchor Books.

FC. (n.d.). *Foreign Correspondent.* Retrieved from https://en....org/wiki/Foreign_Correspondent_(film)

FL. (n.d.). *Fritz Lang.* Retrieved from https://en....org/wiki/Fritz_Lang

Feingold, H, *The Politics of Rescue: The Roosevelt Administration and the Holocaust,* Rutgers University Press, 1969.

Feldman, N, *Scorpions*, Hachette Books, NY, 2011.

Fleming, T. (2001). *The New Dealers War.* USA: Perseus Books.

Fullilove, M. (2013). *Rendezvous With Destiny.* NYC: Penguin Press.

GA. (n.d.). *Gentleman's Agreement.* Retrieved from https://en....org/wiki/Gentleman%27s_Agreement

Groom, W. (2003). *The Aviators.* Washington, DC 2013: National Geographic Society Publishers, p. 264-300.

Herman, A. (2000). McCarthy, A re-examination of the legacy of America's most hated senator. The Free Press.

Hessen, R. (1984). *Berlin Alert: The Memoirs and Reports of Truman Smith.* Stanford, CA: Hover Institute Press.

HC: Retrieved from The Holocaust Chronicle: http://www.holocaustchronicle.org/ staticpages/165.html

HW. (n.d.). *Hugh Wilson.* Retrieved from https://en....org/wiki/Hugh_R._Wilson

JPK. (n.d.). Retrieved from https://en....org/wiki/Joseph_P._Kennedy_Sr.

JTA. (1941, September 17). Retrieved from Isolationists Challenged to Denounce: https://www.jta.org/archive/isolationists-challenged-to-denounce-lindberghs-and-nyes-anti-semitic-statements

JTA Archives. (1941, September 17). Retrieved from http://pdfs.jta.org/1941/1941-09-18_234.pdf (coverage of Nye's hearings into Hollywood)

JW. (n.d.). Retrieved from https://en....org/wiki/Jack_L._Warner

Larson, E. (2011). *In the Garden of Beasts.* New York: Broadway Paperbacks.

Leaders of All Religions. (1941, September 16). Retrieved from Jewish Telegraphic Agency: https://www.jta.org/1941/09/16/archive/leaders-of-all-religions-sharply-condemn-lindberghs-anti-jewish-address

Lindbergh, C. (1970). *The Wartime Journals of Charles Lindbergh.* Jovanovich: New York.

Medoff, R. (2017). *The Jews Should Keep Quiet.* University of Nebraska Press: Lincoln.

Morse, A. (1968). *While Six Million Died.* New York: Random House.

Mosley, L, *Lindbergh: A Biography*, Doubleday, 1976.

NA. (n.d.). *Neutrality Acts.* Retrieved from https://en....org/wiki/Neutrality_Acts_of_the_1930s

Nasaw, D. (2012). *The Patriarch.* New York: The Penguin Press.

Olson, L. (2013). *Those Angry Days.* New York: Random House.

Peters, C. (2005). *Five Days in Philadelphia.* New York: PublicAffairs.

Republican Platform. (1940, June 24). Retrieved from The American Presidency Project: https://www.presidency.ucsb.edu/documents/republican-party-platform-1940

Rosenberg, Y. (2022, January 19). Why So Many People. *Atlantic Magazine.*

Ross, W, *The Last Hero: Charles A. Lindbergh*, Harper and Row, NY, 1964.

Streich, B. (1990). The Roosevelt Administration and Hollywood. *Humboldt Journal of Social Relations*, 48-50.

Templeton, J., Buzzfeed, October 30, 2014, Confirmed: Obama Says The Word "Folks" A Lot (buzzfeednews.com)

Wallace, M. (2003). *The American Axis.* New York: St. Martins Press.

Wallace, M. (2018). *In the Name of Humanity,* New York: Penguin.

WW. (n.d.). *Walter Winchell.* Retrieved from https://en....org/wiki/Walter_Winchell

Wyman Institute. (n.d.). Retrieved from Felix Frankfurter: http://enc.wymaninstitute.org/?p=197

Yang. (2020). *One Mighty and Irresistable Tide.* New York: W.W. Norton.

15: High Altitude Aviation

One of Lindbergh's Most Enduring Scientific Accomplishments

Some authors consider the research Lindbergh performed on high altitude aviation to be of secondary importance, the author disagrees. The author was the first to document the details of this research for medical posterity. (Reich, 2022) The research is remarkable for its bravery, patriotism, and legacy.

Once Hitler declared war on the U.S. on December 11, 1941, Lindbergh advocated an end to isolationism and all the isolationist organizations were disbanded. Lindbergh wrote, "If I had been in Congress, I certainly would have voted for a declaration of war." (Lindbergh, 1970, p.561) Lindbergh desperately wanted to join the war effort, he wrote in his journal, "I simply cannot remain idle while my country is at war. I must take some part in it." But while he was willing to ignore past grievances towards Roosevelt, he would not ask Roosevelt to reinstate his commission, "I do not know a single man who has known Roosevelt, friend or enemy, who trusts what he says from one week to the next. And the President has a reputation, even among his friends, for being a vindictive man." (Lindbergh, 1970, p.567)

Roosevelt was indeed vindictive. Roosevelt would never have allowed Lindbergh to return to active duty, but his animosity extended to preventing Lindbergh from having any role in the war effort. Lindbergh's antagonist and Roosevelt's Cabinet Secretary, Harold Ickes wrote the following memo to President Roosevelt, "...he (Lindbergh) is a ruthless and conscious fascist, motivated by a hatred for you personally and democracy in general...I ardently hope that this convinced fascist will not be given the opportunity to wear the uniform of the United States. He should be buried in merciful oblivion." Roosevelt responded to his memo, "I agree wholeheartedly." (Berg, 1998, p.436)

Bowing to administration pressure, Pan American Airlines and Curtiss-Wright Aviation, on whose boards of directors Lindbergh sat, refused to let him resume any role. But there was one man who was not intimidated by Roosevelt, Henry Ford. Ford owned many of the factories that would produce the weapons to fight the war and was constructing the largest ever in Willow Run near Detroit, Michigan at a cost of over $200 million. There Lindbergh could consult in the construction of airplanes and test fly new military aircraft. Lindbergh visited the plant and test-flew the newest model of bomber, the B-24C. He made suggestions for improvement. Ford hired him and paid him a salary of $666/month, exactly the pay he would have received if he had kept his commission in the Army Air Corps. (Berg, 1998, p.440) The War Department was made aware of this arrangement. (Wallace, 2003)

He moved his family, and pregnant wife, to Detroit. For 8 months Lindbergh worked full-time (and over a year and half part-time) to get the Willow Run factory functioning. Primarily he worked as a test pilot, flying the new combat aircraft as they came off the assembly line, making recommendations and then improving the planes Americans would fly in combat. His 16-hour day included reviewing procurement and assembly line designs. He made assessments of the efficiency and morale of new employees; many were women and Black Americans who moved to Michigan for work.

In August 1942, Anne gave birth to their fifth child (a son named Scott) and on September 18, 1942, President Roosevelt came to visit the Willow Run factory. Lindbergh wasn't there that day. Eventually the plant functioned 24/7 and would produce a combat airplane (mostly B24 bombers) every hour, and made jeeps. (Berg, 1998, pp.443-6) (Wallace, 2003)

On September 22, 1942, Lindbergh and several Ford executives flew to Rochester, Minnesota, where he was introduced to Dr. Walter Boothby, who was the head of a new field in medicine, aviation medicine. (Lindbergh, 1970, pp.718-9) In 1938, Dr. Boothby and two other doctors had applied for a patent for the first oxygen mask for high elevation flights named the BLB mask. (Cooper, 2017)

Dr. Boothby was the director of the recently established Mayo Clinic Aeromedical Unit for Research in Aviation Medicine and constructed a high-altitude simulator, basically a steel tank with an air lock. It allowed the air pressure and oxygen level to be adjusted to simulate the different physiologic conditions at different altitudes. (Lindbergh, 1970, p.719) This would allow the doctors to study a new field in warfare, high altitude combat, arbitrarily defined as combat at elevations exceeding 40,000 feet (13,000 meters). (Hawkins, 1995)

Note to the reader: the chapter will now become technical and delves into high altitude physiology. It is written at a level below that of a physician, and thus the interested reader may want to understand the medical challenges of engaging in airborne combat above 40,000 feet in altitude. By understanding these challenges, the reader can appreciate Lindbergh's role in advancing the field. Those who have no interest in medicine or technology may skip to the conclusion after reviewing the bullet points below. This field is the author's major contribution to original Lindberghian research, the material comes directly from Lindbergh's notes and has not previously been documented by others.

The reader should also note in 1942 Lindbergh was too old to be required to serve (he was 40 and the upper age of the draft was 36 years). (Olson, 2013) Many men of this age had non-combat volunteer jobs. For example, the author's grandfather was 38 years old, he volunteered as an air raid warden. Lindbergh had 4 small children including a newborn son. His actions demonstrated remarkable bravery and patriotism. Giving the U.S. the slightest advantage in a war he had vigorously opposed, inspired him to perform very dangerous experiments. In the spring of 1943, he nearly died when due to instrumentation failure he lost consciousness at 43,000 feet elevation. Sensing he was losing consciousness, he put the plane into a dive and the plane descended 20,000 feet unpiloted. At an altitude of approximately 20,000 feet the higher atmospheric oxygen level enabled him to regain consciousness and he was able to regain control of the airplane. (Berg, 1998, p.447)

Key points:

1) Similar to the race to develop an atomic weapon, the ability to engage in combat above 40,000 feet in elevation was a new frontier in warfare. The European combatants were competing to accomplish it first because of the military advantage it would provide.
2) High altitude aviation has both medical and technological aspects to it. Some aerospace issues of flying at high altitudes had been solved in peacetime in the 1930s, but many oxygen supply issues had not. Without supplemental oxygen above 40,000 feet elevation a human loses consciousness in roughly 10-20 seconds. (Kehrt, 2006) Oxygen tanks in the 1940s were heavy, flammable, and as dramatized in the movie *Midway* prone to chemical contamination which caused irreversible lung damage.
3) Absence of oxygen causes hypoxia which causes confusion, euphoria, impaired decision making, and eventually loss of consciousness. Even with sufficient supplemental oxygen there are physiologic issues which needed to be overcome including nitrogen metabolism and memory loss.
4) Maneuvers specific to combat made overcoming physiologic challenges of high-altitude aviation more dangerous than achieving it in peacetime. Maneuvers which needed to be considered and incorporated into the experiments included pilot ejection and rapid ascents and descents. These maneuvers had significant hazards associated with them.
    A) Pilot ejection was a particularly difficult problem to solve. A pilot's oxygen supply couldn't remain in the cockpit, or the pilot would die from the low oxygen at high elevations once they ejected.

B) Lindbergh experimented with apparatus designed to provide a pilot who ejected with an adequate oxygen supply and different masks called "jump-masks".

5) Unlike the cardiac bypass pump there is not a single accomplishment for which a picture can be shown. The advances Lindbergh made are more subtle and technical and thus require more physiologic explanation, but these accomplishments were significant and unlike the bypass pump they were adopted by aviation and medical sciences.

These advances included:

A) Testing and combat-simulation use of a portable oxygen supply including improvements in pilot masks and jump-masks. Lindbergh improved the simulation of descent and established the optimal flow rate for oxygen.

B) Improvements of the efficiency of the design of the cockpit, oxygen equipment, and masks to allow more efficient use of supplemental oxygen.

C) Experimentation that demonstrated "denitrogenization" could be performed safely and would prevent complications of rapid ascent.

D) The development of an official pilot training protocol to prepare pilots for high altitude combat.

6) Unlike the cardiac bypass pump, the author has seen no criticism of this work by Lindbergh's critics. (Reich, 2022)

Above 13,000 feet elevation (4,000 m) pilots and airmen require supplemental oxygen. During World War II, the average bomber mission took place at between 16,000 and 23,000 feet (5-7,000 m) elevation. Routine reconnaissance flights approached 40,000 feet (13,000 m) elevation. (Kehrt, 2006)

During the 1930s, pressurized pilot suits and pressurized cabins were developed by all the combatants to prepare for a war to be fought at these elevations. The Germans however had also developed high altitude chambers, similar to the Mayo Clinic, to train their pilots in the proper use of oxygen masks and developed masks that automatically delivered higher percentages of oxygen at higher elevations in the late 1930s. (Kehrt, 2006)

The physiologic issues of high-altitude aviation are complicated and not completely solved by providing supplemental oxygen. Because air pressure is low, breathing pure oxygen at 40,000 feet, a pilot's arterial oxygen saturation drops from 99% to 84% and at 50,000 feet it drops to 15%. (Hall, 2006) The metabolism of nitrogen is a problem distinct from oxygen metabolism and known to scuba divers as "the bends". There are also chronic health issues from repetitive exposure to high altitude. Indeed, a recent study showed that pilots repetitively exposed to high altitude demonstrate adverse cognition side effects such as impaired memory and reduced reflex times. There is more we need to learn about this challenging field. (Nation, 2017)

I) Oxygen Metabolism at High Altitudes:

A. Acute Changes

As a human ascends to higher altitudes the partial pressure of oxygen (pO2) in the atmosphere decreases but the partial pressure of carbon dioxide (pCO2) remains relatively constant. As a result, the ratio of pO2/pCO2 decreases. The chemoreceptors in the body sense this as elevated carbon dioxide (hypercarbia) rather than low oxygen (hypoxia). The compensatory mechanism induced, hyperventilation, reduces the amount of carbon dioxide in the blood. Because carbon dioxide acts as an acid in the blood, a reduction in the PaCO2 (the partial pressure of carbon dioxide in the arterial blood) causes a respiratory alkalosis (the pH of the blood > 7.45).

The body compensates for a respiratory alkalosis by inducing a metabolic acidosis. This is achieved at the level of the kidney. The kidney compensates for the elevated pH (caused by the low pCO2) by secreting bicarbonate into the urine (instead of a base returning to the blood, it is excreted in the urine). The lack of bicarbonate in the blood lowers the blood's pH, i.e. it induces a metabolic acidosis. Eventually the pH of the blood approaches the normal upper level of 7.45. Unfortunately, this takes 2-3 days. In the meantime, the effects of alkalosis are sleep disturbances, impaired mental performance, weight loss, and decreased exercise capacity.

This constellation of symptoms is referred to as *acute mountain sickness* and today it can be prevented by using the diuretic acetazolamide prior to ascending to high altitudes. Acetazolamide replicates the body's compensation for respiratory alkalosis. It prevents the kidney from reabsorbing bicarbonate. As the person ascends in altitude the induced acidosis buffers the alkalosis the lower levels of oxygen causes. Acetazolamide has side effects, most notably it lowers serum potassium, which in turn can cause arrhythmias if adequate potassium supplementation is not provided.

The body's blood vessels respond to hypoxia either by either dilation or constriction depending on the relative importance of the organ being supplied with oxygen. The most important organ, the brain, experiences significant vasodilation so it can preferentially be supplied with oxygen. Often this results in a potentially lethal complication, fluid leaking into the brain or a condition called High-Altitude Cerebral Edema (HACE). Another similar and often lethal complication of acute mountain sickness is High-Altitude Pulmonary Edema (HAPE). HAPE is the result of uneven constriction of pulmonary vasculature forcing more blood through fewer open vessels. This causes localized areas of high pressure resulting in fluid leaking into the lungs.

B. Chronic Changes

There are also chronic compensatory effects of low oxygen, called *chronic mountain sickness*. First, the molecule hemoglobin binds oxygen in the blood and then releases it in the tissues. As a human becomes more alkalotic, hemoglobin binds tighter to oxygen making it more difficult to deliver adequate oxygen to the tissues (the hemoglobin-oxygen dissociation curve shifts to the left). This causes cellular hypoxia (low level of oxygen in the cells).

A hormone called erythropoietin is released by the kidneys to compensate for cellular hypoxia. In response to erythropoietin, the bone marrow makes more red blood cells which increases the viscosity of blood. Because the pulmonary blood vessels are very thin to allow for air exchange, thicker blood has trouble traversing the capillaries in the lungs. This increases pressure in the lungs and leads to chronic changes in the pulmonary vasculature, which results in a potentially lethal and difficult to treat complication called pulmonary hypertension. The increase in red blood cell mass and pulmonary pressure also leads to thickening of the heart muscle, called ventricular hypertrophy.

Much of this was known, although not completely understood, in 1942. For example, pulmonary hypertension (originally called pulmonary vascular sclerosis) and high-altitude pulmonary edema were both described in the 19th century and erythropoietin had been discovered in 1906. (Hackett, 1990) The first textbook of Aviation Medicine had been published in 1939 and contained many of these principles. (Lindbergh C. A., 1970)

The challenge for Lindbergh and the Mayo Clinic was preventing complications due to sudden exposure to extremely high altitudes. Due to the exigency of war, chronic complications were not evaluated in Lindbergh's experiments but are a foundation of aviation medicine.

C. The effect of acute fluctuations in external pressure on the metabolism of nitrogen

The air we breathe is 79% nitrogen. At sea level, nitrogen passes inconsequentially into the various tissues and out of the body. Nitrogen has no physiologic effect and acts as an inert bystander throughout nearly our entire lives. More than half of our body's nitrogen resides in our fat cells, this is because nitrogen is more soluble in fat than in liquid.

Because nitrogen dissolves at different rates in different tissues, the effect of nitrogen metabolism when exposed to changes in outside pressures depends on the length of time someone is exposed to the change in pressure. For example, scuba divers can descend to deep depths for short periods of time without experiencing adverse effects of rapid ascent. This is because in short periods very little nitrogen dissolves.

Decompression sickness has many names, some of them are: the Bends, compressed air sickness, Caisson Disease, Diver's Paralysis, and Dysbarism. In historical literature, it is sometimes referred to as the Staggers. A sudden change from high to low pressure produces nitrogen bubbles. This happens if suddenly exposed to low pressure at high elevations or a return to sea level after experiencing high pressures while submerged. The bubbles lodge in various tissues. If they lodge in the bones; they cause bone pain, i.e. the patient is bent over in pain thus — *the bends,* or if it lodges in the brain; it affects cognition, i.e. the patient stumbles around thus — *the staggers.* (Hall, 2006)

The physiology of nitrogen metabolism when exposed to abrupt changes in external pressure, was well known in 1942. Doctors had studied and reported on workers on the Golden Gate Bridge in 1933 who descended to very high external pressures to work on the foundation deep in San Francisco Bay. If they returned to the surface quickly, they got sick. It was also understood that peacetime ascent to high altitudes in the 1930s was brief and did not allow for nitrogen to form bubbles, so these pilots were not at high risk of decompression sickness. (Hawkins, 1995)

However, warfare required extended periods of time at high altitude as well as sudden ascent and descent, so significant research needed to be done to prevent decompression sickness in pilots.

Experiments and Advances In High Altitude Aviation Made by Charles A. Lindbergh, September 1942-April 1944

Between the dates listed above, Lindbergh performed simulated flights and parachute jumps as well as actual flights exceeding 40,000 feet elevation for extended times in various aircraft but mostly the P-47 fighter plane. (Lindbergh C., 1942) He would test oxygen supply in the cockpit and make recommendations for improving efficiency. He would develop equipment for oxygen supply both in the cockpit and for pilot ejection. Lindbergh would demonstrate effective denitrogenization (ridding the pilot's body of nitrogen prior to ascending) could be accomplished. He would also organize and propose the first formal protocol for prospective pilot training for high-altitude aviation. (Lindbergh, circa 1943)

A. Experiments dealing with supplemental oxygen

Historians have credited Lindbergh with making improvements to oxygen apparatus as well as the efficiency of the cockpit design in maintaining adequate levels of oxygen. (Berg, 1998, p.447) Lindbergh's tests on a negative pressure demand oxygen mask with a constant flow feature in simulated flights at 40,000 feet resulted in recommendations for masks with higher pressure sealing. Lindbergh demonstrated 43,000 feet was the limit for the standard BLB mask but using specialized pressure masks Lindbergh reached a peak altitude of 48,000 feet in the simulator without demonstrating ill effects indicating the pilot oxygen supply was adequate for combat pilots to reach this altitude with the right equipment. (Feb. 11, 1944, experiment notes, (Lindbergh C. A., 1970))

He also demonstrated pilots could recognize hypoxia and take corrective action as he had in the spring of 1943 when he lost consciousness at 43,000 feet. In the simulator he had the oxygen supply either discontinued or disabled without his knowledge. Recognizing disorientation, he would switch to an alternative oxygen supply. (Berg, 1998, pp.446-7) (experiment notes, 1942)

Many of the records which resulted in improvements in oxygen supply involve supplemental pilot oxygen supply in simulated parachute jumps. Initial simulations demonstrated standard U.S. military pilot oxygen equipment was inadequate and in initial simulated parachute descents Lindbergh demonstrated ill effects of hypoxia, including altered consciousness and impaired decision making, forcing him to reconnect to the simulator's non-portable oxygen supply. (Experimental notes, 9/26/42)

Pilot ejection simulations consisted of Lindbergh sitting in the altitude simulator and when the air pressure and oxygen levels simulated 40,000 feet, Lindbergh would remove his BLB mask, replace the mask with a jump-mask, then perform exercises equivalent to a pilot preparing to eject (some experiments involved simulating the hatch jamming). Once "out of the plane", the simulator would approximate atmospheric changes consistent with a parachute jump, i.e. the oxygen level and air pressure would gradually increase per minute simulating a pilot returning to sea level (over time the protocol more accurately represented atmospheric changes). (experimental notes, 1942-43)

The jump-mask consisted of a mouthpiece attached to a parachute oxygen bottle. Lindbergh chose the optimal oxygen flow rate and made equipment recommendations, particularly for the jump-mask mouthpiece. At least three times Lindbergh passed out in the simulation chamber from hypoxia. On one actual flight the cockpit filled up with smoke. (10/24/1942) (Lindbergh C. A., 1970)

B. Denitrogenization

Charles Lindbergh worked on protocols to rid the pilot's body of nitrogen before ascending to high altitudes. He would undergo "denitrogenization", then rapidly ascend to altitudes of 40,000 feet for at least an hour. In the simulator, he performed rapid ascents to 35,000 feet in less than 3 minutes and to 40,000 feet in seven minutes. Later (February 1944) he performed similar maneuvers exceeding 40,000 feet in flight. Demonstrating no ill effects of "the bends", Lindbergh demonstrated "denitrogenization" could prevent the adverse medical effects of nitrogen metabolism in combat pilots. (10/2/1942, experimental notes) (Lindbergh C. A., 1970)

The initial protocol consisted of vigorous exercise for at least half an hour while breathing different mixtures of inhaled air which contained no nitrogen. Once this was proven an effective means of ridding the pilot's body of nitrogen, Lindbergh worked on perfecting a technique more appropriate for the exigencies of combat. He worked on reducing the length of time of exercising and various breathing techniques which could shorten the time a pilot needed to rid his body of nitrogen in preparation for combat at elevations exceeding 40,000 feet. (Lindbergh C. A., 1970).

C. Pilot Training Protocol

German pilots had been undergoing high altitude training for years prior to Lindbergh's recommendations and Lindbergh had visited pilot training programs at his first visit to Nazi Germany in July 1936. (Kehrt, 2006) (Berg, 1998)

The Mayo Clinic records include an undated 5-page manual written by Lindbergh detailing the first known training program for U.S. pilots attempting to engage in combat at altitude exceeding 40,000 feet elevation. This document (circa 1943) details 3 months of lectures and training procedures to ensure safety at high altitudes. (Lindbergh C., circa 1943)

D. The A-14 Aviation Mask

This mask replaced the BLB mask as the standard mask for combat aviation. Compared to the BLB mask it had less oxygen loss and provided more efficient removal of water vapor. It was significantly more comfortable than other iterations of combat masks and became standard issue among American pilots. (Dill, 1954) Lindbergh performed experiments with this mask and credited it with saving his life in the incident in 1943 when he lost consciousness. (Lindbergh, 1948, p.7) Lindbergh, Boothby, and the Aeromedicine Unit at the Mayo Clinic were given significant credit for the development of this mask. (Keys, 1974) (Dill, 1954)

Other pilots tested the A-14 aviation mask before it was used in combat, but Lindbergh deserves credit for important testing done in dangerous conditions. He ascended to altitudes exceeding 43,000 feet in test flights repeatedly to ensure the mask worked effectively even though no U.S. airplane would ascend to this altitude in combat in World War II. (Lindbergh, 1970, p. 754)

Conclusion: On April 24, 1944, Charles Lindbergh would get his wish and leave the U.S. for combat against the Japanese in New Guinea and Palau in the South Pacific. There he would fulfill his dream of fighting in combat for his country. This would end any further experimentation in the new field of high-altitude combat.

High-altitude combat would not occur with any frequency during World War II, but would in the Korean and Vietnamese Conflicts. It was also an important part of espionage for two decades. Lindbergh's contributions to the field are recognized for their importance but also for the bravery required to conduct these experiments. Because standard issue military oxygen equipment prior to 1942 was so ineffective and resulted in pilots losing consciousness should they need to eject, Lindbergh and Boothby deserve credit for saving the lives of American pilots through the Vietnam War. (Berg, 1998)

But before we go off to war...

The Legacy of These Experiments

High altitude aviation had a brief window in espionage and combat before the advent of satellites and radar avoidance technology. Lindbergh and Boothby's improvements in masks, oxygen supplies, and denitrogenization enabled pilots to ascend to altitudes exceeding 40,000 feet for roughly two decades.

High altitude aviation is often considered only the U2 incident of May 1, 1960. U.S. Pilot Francis Powers was shot down over the Soviet Union and imprisoned for several years. He was later released in a spy swap and died in the 1970s in a helicopter accident. (Reel, 2018) Often high-altitude aviation is considered a mistake because the U2 incident was a disaster for U.S. public relations. The Eisenhower administration badly handled the incident, but like many public relations disasters, mishandling was based on several assumptions which were incorrect.

When Powers' plane failed to land in Norway, the CIA knew the plane had either crashed or been shot down. But for nine days they released information that was obviously untrue, for example the government issued statements a weather plane had crashed, or the plane had not entered Soviet airspace. Why? Because the CIA assumed the plane had been destroyed by a self-destruction mechanism and no human could survive ejecting from 68,000 feet. It took 9 days, May 10, 1960, for President Eisenhower to speak the truth: the U.S. was spying on the Soviet Union, but he would not apologize. He said all nations spy on each other. (Hitchcock, 2018)

Both CIA assumptions were incorrect. The self-destruction mechanism failed because, while falling from a disintegrating airplane, Powers couldn't activate it, and he did survive the descent from an altitude with no oxygen, -50 degrees C, and an air pressure one-fourteenth of sea level (Anderson, 1989) — an air pressure so low skin would peel off your body. For this Lindbergh deserves much credit. The Russians captured Powers alive and knew he was a CIA pilot because he had his identification on him. (Hitchcock, 2018)

Eisenhower wouldn't apologize nor claim he didn't know. He could have said it was payback for Julius Rosenburg or any of the 400 spies the Soviet Union placed in the Roosevelt and Truman administrations, but there was a superpower summit imminent, and he chose to be less abrasive. If he had told the truth on May 2, 1960, the event may not currently be considered a disaster.

The legacy of the flights should be the intelligence gathered by the U2 planes. The intelligence provided the Eisenhower administration with a reliable estimate of Soviet nuclear capabilities. Knowing this enabled the administration to withstand pressure to donate more resources to missiles and weapons, which at best would have been a waste and at worst contributed to an environment of worsening hostility. With an election year approaching, the candidates competing for the 1960 Democratic Presidential nomination, including Senator John Kennedy of Massachusetts, tried to do outdo each other as tough on the Soviet Union. They warned of a non-existent "missile gap". Although the administration knew the charges weren't true, they couldn't release the source of the intelligence. This made their competitors more strident and hysterical in their accusations. (Hitchcock, 2018)

Powers' U2 flight resulted in a halt in U2 flights over Russia, but U2 flights over Cuba produced the evidence which resulted in the Cuban missile crisis (October 16-November 20, 1962). High altitude surveillance flights reduced the chance of nuclear confrontation. When the U.S. Ambassador to the United Nations, Adlai Stevenson, confronted the Soviet Union about these missile bases at a United Nations Security Council session on October 25, 1962, the Soviet missiles in Cuba were not fully operational. The intelligence gathered by these flights both prevented a wasteful arms race and reduced the pressure for a nuclear confrontation in the Cuban missile crisis. (Reel, 2018, pp. 175-296)

Lindbergh's legacy includes making these flights possible and these flights helped reduce the possibility of a nuclear war. Of all his accomplishments, this legacy may have made Lindbergh the proudest.

Works Cited

Anderson, J. (1989). *Introduction to Flight.* New York: McGraw Hill.

Berg, A. S. (1998). *Lindbergh.* New York: Berkeley Biography.

Cooper, M. S. (2017). High Altitude Hypoxia, A Mask. *Anesth Intensiv Care,* pp. 45-48.

Dill, D. (1954). Walter Boothby: Pioneer in Aviation. *Science,* 688.

Hackett, P. R. (1990). High Altitude Pulmonary Edema. *Journal of Wilderness Medicine,* pp. 1, 3-26.

Hall, G. A. (2006). *Medical Physiology.* Philadelphia: Elsevier and Saunders.

Hawkins, M. (1995, December). Some Problems of High Altitude Aviation in the 1930s. *Aviation, Space, and Enviornmental Medicine,* pp. 66:1214-1214.

Hitchcock, I. (2018). *The Age of Eisenhower.* New York: Simon and Schuster.

Kehrt, C. (2006, November). Higher Always Higher. *Endeavor,* pp. 30(6):138-143.

Keys, T. (1974). Walter Boothby, Historical Vingette. *Anesth Analg,* 219-220.

Lindbergh, C. (1942, December 19). Letter to Boothby. Bloomfield Hills, MI.

Lindbergh, C. (1943?). Outline for 3 Month Indoctrination Program. Rochester, MN.

Lindbergh, C. (1948). *Of Flight and Life.* New York: Scribner and Sons.

Lindbergh, C. A. (1970). *The Wartime Journals of Charles Lindbergh.* New York: Harcourt, Brace, and Jovanovich.

Nation, D. e. (2017, Jan). Mechanism of Memory Dysfunction During High Altitude Hypoxia Training in Military Aircraft . *J Int Neuropsych Soc*, pp. 23(1):1-10.

Olson, L. (2013). *Those Angry Days* . New York: Random House.

Reel, M. (2018). *Brotherhood of Spies.* New York: Doubleday Publishers.

Reich, J. (2022, Summer). Charles Lindbergh's Contribution to High Altitude Aviation. *Pharos.*

Wallace, M. (2003). *The American Axis.* New York: St. Martin's Press.

16: War

1944-1955

Although Charles Lindbergh had held the rank of colonel in the U.S. Army Air Corps Reserve prior to U.S. entry in World War II and would receive an honorary appointment to Brigadier General in 1954, he was only on active duty for a few months between 1939 and 1940. He went to New Guinea as an "observer" or a "technician", without formally being part of the U.S. armed service. He paid for his own uniforms and had he been captured by the Japanese he would not have qualified for P.O.W. status and theoretically the protections granted by the Geneva Conventions. Of course, the Japanese didn't respect the Geneva Convention and treated POWs with horrific barbarity. (Dalleck, 2017)

Lindbergh arrived in New Guinea on April 26, 1944, and was assigned to the 475th Fighter Group of the Fifth Air Force. He was immediately given a P-38 and the next day went on a bombing run deep into enemy territory and strafed an enemy barge.

According to those who served with him, he was an outstanding fighter pilot. His commanding officer, Colonel Charles MacDonald, said of him:

> "Lindbergh was indefatigable. He flew more missions than was normally expected of a regular combat pilot. He dive-bombed enemy positions, sank barges, and patrolled our landing forces on Noemfoor Island. He was shot at by almost every anti-aircraft gun the [Japanese] had in Western New Guinea." (Berg, 1998, p.451)

After a few weeks in the Pacific, Lindbergh made another remarkable contribution to the American war effort. He recommended modified throttle settings for airplanes using the Allison V-1710 engines. The mechanics noticed that Lindbergh's plane returned with more fuel than the other planes. When asked, Lindbergh explained that by setting the throttle to a higher manifold pressure, the engine could achieve the same speed using less fuel. (Berg, 1998) The pilots were concerned it would cause the engines to fail, but Lindbergh knew the engine's capabilities and convinced them otherwise:

> "The problem is that the newer pilots, and many of the old ones, cruise their engines at too high an r.p.m. and often leave their mixture controls in auto rich during an entire flight. They have never tried low r.p.m. cruising and cannot believe that it will not injure their engines-or make such a difference in fuel consumption." (7/3/1944, (Lindbergh, 1970))

So astonishing was Lindbergh's recommendations that he was asked to present them directly to General MacArthur. (Berg, 1998, pp.456-7) The adjustments to throttle settings gave U.S. planes more range. Some Japanese targets thought they were beyond airplane range, but they weren't.

After New Guinea was secure, the U.S. Navy and Marines began the invasion of a chain of islands called Palau (the island in the chain where the fighting took place is Peleliu) starting in September 1944. There was an internal military debate regarding the range of the fighter planes required to provide cover for bombers whose job it was to bomb Japanese fortifications prior to the invasion because the island chain of Palau is 1000 miles north of New Guinea. (Berg, 1998, p.454) (History.com, 2009)

General George Kenney, was the commander of the Fifth Air Force and the commander of the Palau air campaign. He said, "When Lindbergh joined us the P-38s were considered to have a range of 400 miles. Under his training the P-38s were able to escort bombers...for a 950-mile mission." This allowed the U.S. to begin the attack on Palau and eventually liberate the Philippines sooner. General Kenney continued, "Lindbergh's contribution shortened the war by several months and saved thousands of American lives." (Ross, 1964, p.332)

General Kenney's comments need context. The German Me-109 was faster and more agile than the British Spitfire, but it had the range of a P-38, prior to Lindbergh's improvement. During the Battle of Britain, the Me-109 had to return to occupied France to refuel after 15 minutes of combat; this left their bombers undefended. Had a German pilot similarly increased the Me-109's combat time, it would have changed the war. (BattleOfBritain1940.com)

Lindbergh had an intrinsic ability to understand engines which led to these advances. When he was a boy, private ownership of automobiles was in its infancy. There were no organized system of gas stations and mechanics. Automobile owners needed to repair their own engines. Teenage Lindbergh was the town mechanic and repaired many of Little Falls' cars. (Berg, 1998)

His knowledge of engines extended to the maximum payload these planes could carry and still engage in combat. In September 1944, Lindbergh carried a payload of 4,000 pounds during the bombing of several small Japanese controlled atolls north of New Guinea. This was the highest payload ever carried by the Corsair F4U. (Berg, 1998, p.455) Although he piloted test flights after returning from the Pacific, this may have been the final contribution Lindbergh made to the war effort. It is hard to think of another American who made as many.

For a man whose philosophy was to never show emotion, Lindbergh's reaction to combat was surprisingly emotional. He struggled dealing with the lives he had taken and the damage he had done. An example of his internal anguish from his journal, May 29, 1944:

> "You press a button and death flies down. One second the bomb is hanging harmlessly in your racks, completely under your control. The next it is hurtling down through the air and nothing in your power can revoke what you have done. The cards are dealt. If there is life where that bomb will hit, you have taken it... The world is the same. The sky is the same. Only that column of smoke, settling now, dissipating. How can there be death down there? How can there be writhing, mangled bodies?" (Lindbergh, 1970)

Lindbergh said for the rest of his life he prayed for the souls of the Japanese soldiers or anyone else he'd killed. (Berg, 1998) Odd behavior for a man often accused of being a racist.

Lindbergh's sensitivity extended to taking umbrage at disparaging comments regarding the Japanese made by U.S. soldiers. He was critical of his fellow soldiers if they disregarded the humanity of the enemy. He frequently criticized what he called atrocities committed by U.S. soldiers against Japanese soldiers. The problem is, the combat logs and Lindbergh's own journal entries indicate he didn't witness the atrocities. His journal consists of stories he heard (e.g. 6/21/1944 and 6/28/1944). He saw mutilated Japanese corpses and attributed the mutilation to U.S. soldiers, but he never witnessed ground combat. (Lindbergh, 1970) (Berg, 1998) He does mention the excessive brutality of the Japanese, but felt as "upholders of all that is good" our obligations were greater. What Lindbergh never mentioned was that Japanese atrocities were frequently against civilians (Dalleck, 2017) and Lindbergh relates no stories of similar U.S. atrocities. An example of Lindbergh's criticism:

> "What is courage for us is fanaticism for him. We hold his examples of atrocity screamingly to the heavens while we cover up our own and condone them as just retribution for his acts." (7/21/1944, (Lindbergh, 1970))

Throughout Lindbergh's combat experience there were conflicts with his superior officers regarding engaging in combat without being a member of the armed forces. For example, on July 12, 1944, Lindbergh related a conversation he had with General Kenney. General Kenney told him flying as a civilian was against all regulations and the Japanese would chop his head off immediately if he was captured. (Lindbergh, 1970) Yet, Lindbergh continued to fly combat missions until September 1944. How was this possible?

In the history of the U.S. military there have been civilians who have grabbed weapons in the heat of combat and engaged the enemy — usually orderlies or cooks. But in the annals of the U.S. military, the author is unaware of another civilian being handed a million-dollar piece of equipment and being allowed to engage the enemy repeatedly despite the objections of commanding officers, indeed over the expressed wishes of the commander-in-chief.

This continued because Lindbergh was an outstanding pilot, and the other pilots wanted him in the fight. Their objections convinced the commanding officers to look the other way. At the briefings, Lindbergh's opinion was always requested and considered. The other men looked to him for leadership. Lindbergh's record of his conversation with General Kenney ends as described above, but afterwards Colonel MacDonald claimed he interceded and convinced General Kenney to let Lindbergh continue to fly. Kenney was reported saying "nobody in the U.S. needs to know". (Berg, 1998)

After he had flown his 50th combat mission, Lindbergh was sent home. He arrived in San Diego on September 16, 1944, notified his wife and his mother that he was back in the U.S., and waited for transportation home. By this time, Anne had moved the family back to Connecticut. (Berg, 1998) Unusual for him, he spoke to the press briefly in San Diego correcting errors of where he had fought. He established the highest altitude he flew in combat was 30,000 feet. After correcting these errors, he refused to speak to the press further. Despite his combat service, Roosevelt refused to restore his commission. (Lindbergh, 1970)

For 8 months Lindbergh resumed his old job as a test pilot for two military contractors. During this period, President Roosevelt died, and the Germans surrendered. In May 1945, the U.S. military asked Lindbergh, again, to go to Germany and collect intelligence, this time on the status of the German rocket program and their development of jet engines.

The Europe he found was in ruins and without food. It was very different from the Europe he left 6 years earlier. He described two cities he remembered, Paris and Munich, as "hellish death…death without dignity, creation without God." Once again, he repeated stories he heard about looting and wanton murder committed by Allied soldiers, and he commented often on the starvation and deprivation of German women and children. (Berg, 1998)

On June 10-11, 1945, Lindbergh traveled to the Mittlebau-Dora Complex, the location for the manufacture and storage of the V-2 and V-1 weapons. The complex contained a sub-camp of the Buchenwald Concentration Camp. On their own, Lindbergh and a Navy Lieutenant who spoke German, went to see the sub-camp, the crematoria, and the evidence of the horrific events that took place. (Berg, 1998, pp.467-9) The inmates had been forcibly evacuated, but there was an emaciated 17-year-old former inmate to guide them and provide details. Corpses of murdered Jews and pits of human ashes remained. (Mittelbau-Dora Concentration Camp, n.d.) (Lindbergh, 1970, pp.990-8)

His thoughts at the time are complicated and often intersected with his own memories of war, but he was clearly affected by the horror of what he witnessed. He wrote in his journal, "Of course, I knew these things were going on, but it is one thing to have intellectual knowledge, even to look at photographs someone else had taken, and quite another to stand on the scene yourself, seeing, hearing feeling with your own senses." Upon seeing the crematoria, he wrote, "Here was a place where men and life and death reached the lowest form of degradation. When the value of life and the dignity of death are removed what is left for man?" (Lindbergh, 1970)

Did seeing what Nazi Germany did make Lindbergh re-examine his pre-war stance? During the brief period between his visit to Buchenwald and the defeat of Japan he condemned the atrocities the Germans committed, but he never came to terms with his advocacy. The longer the U.S. failed to confront Hitler and the less aid the U.S. gave England and Russia, logically the worse Germany's atrocities would be. Had the U.S. done what he advocated, more Jews and in particular English Jews would have suffered the same fate. This he never came to terms with. His response would be a war solely in the east was obtainable. This was not just a denial of reality, but the atrocities in the east were as bad or worse.

He acknowledged he was wrong about Hitler's intentions and accepted he misunderstood the Nazis were motivated by evil. Lindbergh was an advocate of trying Nazis for war crimes, including his former acquaintance Hermann Goering. (Berg, 1998, p.465) (Lindbergh, 1970) But he continued with moral equivalency. First, he separated the Nazis from the German civilians and then separated defeating Germany from destroying it. To Lindbergh, America too was evil for destroying German cities, killing civilians, and mistreating the civilians after the war. (Lindbergh, 1970)

Opposition to U.S. bombing policy was not unique; the famous aviator James Doolittle also felt the wanton destruction of Germany was unnecessary. (Hansen, 2008) Nor was Lindbergh's advocacy for displaced German civilians unwarranted. Watching a family with small children leave their house with meager belongings so the U.S. military could use the house, he wrote, "I know Hitler and the Nazis were the cause. But we in America are supposed to stand for different things." (Lindbergh, 1970)

Lindbergh was responding to a U.S. policy which was formulated while he was fighting in Asia. While Lindbergh was engaged in combat over Palau in September 1944, President Roosevelt met Churchill in Quebec City. There Roosevelt explained post-war policy would not simply punish the Nazis; rather the entire German population was to be held responsible for World War II. "We have to be tough with Germany, and I mean the German people not just the Nazis…you have got to treat them in such manner so they can't go on reproducing people who want to continue the way they have in the past." (FDR, September 14, 1944, (Dalleck, 2017))

One should not underestimate the vindictive inclinations of people who had fought two wars with Germany and were repulsed by their atrocities, but Roosevelt's motives were not purely vindictive. The Nazis had risen to power by the popular appeal of an anti-Semitic conspiracy German myth called *dolchstosslegende*, or the legend of having been stabbed in the back. The legend derives from a Richard Wagner opera, in which the hero, Siegfried, dies by being stabbed in the back. Every German knew the opera and the legend. The Nazi argument was the Germans didn't lose World War I; the politicians, the Jews, and the Communists stabbed the army in the back. (Stephens, 2020) This time Roosevelt would make sure the Germans knew they'd lost World War II, if only to prevent another war.

Germany had, of course, lost World War I. The people were starving, the army had been defeated, and its soldiers were engaged in mutiny. The Kaiser had abdicated, and the surrender had been arranged by politicians who reflected the will of the people and had the support of the generals. But because the German army was still on French soil and its cities weren't shelled, it was easy for the people to accept the Nazi version of events. (Stephens, 2020) This time Roosevelt would not let this happen. He rejected proposals to bring Germany quickly into the family of nations, "every person in Germany (was) to realize that this time Germany is a defeated nation…collectively and individually. (This is) to be so impressed on them that they will hesitate to start a new war. (It will be driven home) that the whole nation has been engaged in a lawless conspiracy against the decencies of modern civilization." (Dalleck, 2017)

Lindbergh and Moral Equivalency

Lindbergh's arguments had some merit. The bombing of cities like Cologne and Dresden were not done for an obvious military purpose, nor is there evidence they shortened the war. Hundreds of thousands of civilians died gruesome deaths and the motivation was in some respects political. Allied air forces were under pressure to show results and bombing true military targets, like the ball bearing factory in Schweinfurt, were just too costly in men and material. (see p. 361) The Allies argued these were legitimate military targets because Axis workers required housing and "dehousing" them was strategic.

This is a contemporary discussion. At the time few were interested. Many contemporaries of Lindbergh argued no fascist nation respected any separation between military and civilian targets. Its infrastructure was therefore a legitimate target no matter the military relevance. (Hansen, 2008)

Lindbergh also may not have known it was a strategic presidential policy to treat German civilians this way. Perhaps Lindbergh knew and disagreed implicitly with Roosevelt's policy? In the author's opinion, it doesn't matter. It was in Lindbergh's interest to conclude the U.S. was being cruel because if he acknowledged the culpability of the German people, he'd have to acknowledge he'd been wrong. Lindbergh knew the German people deserved blame. He saw their orgasmic fealty to Hitler at the 1936 Olympics. Weren't the people he felt sorry for the sisters, wives, parents, and children of the non-civilian Germans who had humiliated, robbed, dehumanized, and murdered millions?

Lindbergh's reaction was always to see both sides as wrong no matter how contrived his reasoning. He had seen both England and Germany as wrong in his testimony to Congress and to some extent he was willing to see both sides as wrong while he was fighting in Asia. Until his death when asked, he never accepted any personal blame for any of his actions, only blaming all of humanity for its descent into deprivation. (Berg, 1998) When asked about Nazi Germany's crimes, he would often devolve into a false moral equivalence comparing German war crimes with what he claimed he had seen in New Guinea and post-war Germany. However, what he had to say was hearsay, dealt with military conflict, and involved the deprivation of food and housing which are often associated with post-war occupations. His counter-accusations didn't list atrocities against civilians.

How Accurate Were Lindbergh's Pre-War Predictions?

When confronted with the realities of what the Nazis did and asked to evaluate his advocacy for isolationism, Lindbergh defended himself by emphasizing his pre-war predictions. He claimed much of what he had predicted had come true:

The Accuracy of Lindbergh's Pre-War Predictions: (source: Cole, 1974) (Radio Address, 10/13/1939)

Prediction	Outcome	Comment
U.S.-Germany war would last 15 years and cost a million U.S. lives	The European war lasted 4 years and cost 230,000 U.S. lives	Lindbergh's prediction was excessive and pessimistic
War would result in the destruction of Europe	Europe experienced widespread destruction, hunger, and deprivation	Lindbergh was correct
Russia would dominate post-War Europe	Russia controlled Eastern Europe for 45 years	Millions were imprisoned or denied opportunity to achieve their potential. Lindbergh was correct.
U.S. would accrue massive debt. England would not re-pay its debt to the U.S.	In 1945, U.S. debt = 113% of GDP, highest % ever.[1] UK finished repaying debt to U.S. in 2006, total debt in 2011.[2]	At his death (1974) Lindbergh was correct

[1] (Phillips, 2012) [2] (Thornton, 2006)

In Lindbergh's own words, "...the disturbing fact remains that while our soldiers have been victorious in arms, we have not so far accomplished the objectives for which we went to war. We have not established peace or liberty in Europe. There is less security there now than perhaps ever before, and less democracy...The ideals of justice and tolerance have practically vanished from the continent. Freedom of speech and action is suppressed over a large portion of the world, especially in so-called 'liberated nations', many of which have simply exchanged the Nazi form of dictatorship for the Communist form." (Berg, 1998, p.470)

Although much what he predicted came true, this statement is a continuation of his pre-war selective blindness. It was nonsense before the war and after the war it was worse.

There was more security and democracy after World War II than when Germany was conquering Europe. The "liberated nations" were not those Russia took from the Nazis. Not every nation would be liberated in Lindbergh's lifetime, but unquestionably 7 conquered European countries were liberated by the Allies (France, Netherlands, Belgium, Luxembourg, Denmark, Norway, and Greece). There were other nations with complex histories (e.g. Sweden, Italy) whose citizens were also provided with liberty because of the Allied victory. World War II provided liberty and freedom to millions in Europe and Asia and Lindbergh's statement ignores this quite impressive accomplishment. Europe during the Cold War had problems, but the "ideals of justice and tolerance" hardly vanished.

Furthermore, Lindbergh refused to answer the question: What about the Jews? If England had entered into a peace agreement with Germany, as Lindbergh proposed in his congressional testimony, what would have happened to the Jews in England (would they have been subject to a Vichy-like arrangement)? Lindbergh never answered the question. He would digress into a discussion of various irrelevant historical events, for example England entered the war by coming to Poland's defense which he advised it not to do. Sometimes he would resort to retelling his father's grievances regarding England's behavior preceding our entry into World War I. His refusal to answer the question honestly, and his fairy-tale version of what would have happened had England and France listened to him, deserves disdain.

He should have admitted when he had been wrong and point out when he had been right? Anne admitted they had been wrong and expressed remorse, "we were both very blind, especially in the beginning, to the worst evils of the Nazi system." (Berg, 1998, p.469) After his death, she good-naturedly said his Swedish cultural background did not permit admitting errors. "He was a stubborn Swede, and he himself never felt the need to explain his feelings." (Mitgang, 1980) For what it's worth, another famous American of Swedish descent, Chief Justice Earl Warren, was a champion of civil rights on the Supreme Court but when he was the attorney general of California, he was the person most responsible for sending 112,000 Japanese Americans to internment camps and depriving them of all their rights. Like Lindbergh he never accepted responsibility nor acknowledged it was a mistake, and like Lindbergh his reasoning was convoluted. (Newton, 2006)

Whether it was his Swedish heritage or some other reason, as an old man Lindbergh was remarkably stubborn when asked to consider decisions he had made as a young man. Most famous was his decision to refuse to consider that accepting and then refusing to return the medal Goering gave him in 1938 was a mistake. As described in an earlier chapter, Harold Ickes, Roosevelt's Secretary of the Interior, asked, and appropriately so, how Lindbergh could have resigned his Army Reserve commission so quickly but held on to a Nazi medal? (Cole, 1974, p.132-3) Millions of Americans agreed and hated Lindbergh because he accepted and then refused to return it. Twenty years after he accepted the medal Lindbergh said, "(it) never caused me worry, and I doubt it caused me any difficulty." (Berg, 1998)

Lindbergh's Post-War Reputation:

Most Americans had either stopped listening to Lindbergh or were not interested during their victory parade. Reporting on Lindbergh reminded Americans of distorted versions of what they believed Lindbergh said. For some his war service improved his status, but for millions it did not. *Harper's Magazine* wrote,

> "(To Lindbergh) the Jews didn't seem to matter nor the Poles nor the Czechs nor the Greeks. The destruction of France didn't seem to matter, nor the invasion of Russia, nor Holland, Belgium, Norway, Denmark. Massacre, the bombing of Coventry or Warsaw or Rotterdam didn't seem to matter, the enslavement of millions, the starvation of millions, the slaughter of millions. What the hell?" (Berg, 1998, p.470)

This is also nonsense.

For all his errors in policy recommendations between 1939 and 1941, Lindbergh could not have known the Germans intended to "massacre" or "slaughter" the Jews because although the Roosevelt administration had been receiving reports of Jews being persecuted, they didn't receive reports of what would be called the "Holocaust" until the fall of 1942. (Dalleck, 2017, pp.497-8) Furthermore, perhaps Lindbergh didn't anticipate these atrocities, because Roosevelt's own Treasury Department documented Roosevelt's State Department withheld the news from the American people. (Morse, 1968, p.89) Since Roosevelt's State Department refused to believe it, expecting private citizen Lindbergh to anticipate it and condemn it is unreasonable. (Dalleck, 2017, p.497)

Furthermore, U.S. policy supplied England with weapons and Lindbergh didn't prevent this. Achieving interventionist objectives, i.e. supplying England with weapons, didn't stop any atrocities. Apparently, Lindbergh is being condemned for opposing a policy that didn't affect the atrocities he is accused of ignoring. Lindbergh's legitimate arguments that the aid violated the Neutrality Acts and was unconstitutional because Congress hadn't approved sending Americans into a war zone, weren't addressed by his critics either.

What Lindbergh did know about German mistreatment of the Jews, he acknowledged, criticized, and said the Jews had every right to advocate the U.S. going to war to stop, which was a position few of his contemporaries or his political opponents were willing to advocate. Where were Lindbergh's critics, in this case *Harper's Magazine*, when the Jews were in trouble? It neither advocated Jewish immigration nor gave prominent coverage to German persecution of Jews. Which major American publications supported helping Jews flee Germany, mentioned Roosevelt's obstructionism, condemned Breckinridge Long's perjury, advocated for the disembarkation of the passengers on the *St. Louis*, or even supported Jews advocating for their cause as Lindbergh did?

How many of Lindbergh's critics used their public appearances to acknowledge Nazi Germany was mistreating the Jews in 1941, like Lindbergh did? How many warned Germany in 1936 that it would be responsible for war like Lindbergh did? Only a handful of people did, and the author is unaware they were the ones who mocked Lindbergh after the war. Silence was the worst strategy. If *Harper's Magazine* was silent, it hardly gave it the moral authority to mock Lindbergh.

Despite 80 years of vilification and disdain by Jews, Lindbergh never ignored nor condoned the persecution of the Jews. He wrote "I oppose such persecution (of Jews) and feel we must keep it from our own nation. I stand opposed to such persecution and I am in sympathy and understanding with the Jewish position". (Des Moines draft, 1941) He certainly should have said more, and he gets no credit for something he didn't say, but this was his position. Contrast this sentiment with President Roosevelt excusing Jewish persecution a month earlier, "(the

Germans had) specific and understandable complaints towards the Jews in Germany". (Medoff, 2016)

Lindbergh didn't say enough, but for no ethnic group's suffering or occupation did Lindbergh say, "what the hell" and he certainly did not say this regarding the extermination of the Jews. Quite the opposite, he felt everyone's suffering; including the civilians of the countries we defeated.

In every speech Lindbergh made regarding World War II, he exercised his First Amendment right to express his opinion that U.S. entry into another European war would not help solve the problems of the persecution and mistreatment of all civilians. It did not help in World War I, and his view was it wouldn't help and didn't help in World War II either. Lindbergh was wrong regarding Allied victory in World War II, because it ended not just the Holocaust but all Nazi persecution of civilians, including for example, Nazi atrocities committed against Italian civilians during Germany's brief but brutal occupation of Rome. (Katz, 2003) Like Anne, he should have admitted when he was wrong. But it is unlikely it would have changed anyone's opinion.

Lindbergh's Post-War Advocacy:

Lindbergh's experience led many to seek his opinion. He advised Republican congressmen and circumnavigated the globe doing work on commissions and fact-finding missions for the Air Force. In addition to choosing the location of the new U.S. Air Force Academy; he helped re-organize the Strategic Air Command, test flew new jets, and recommended missile strategy. He also worked for Pan American airlines consulting on supersonic commercial transportation. (Berg, 1998, pp.476-7) In 1954, Eisenhower promoted him from Colonel to honorary Brigadier General. (Berg, 1998, p.488)

Lindbergh wrote two best-selling books. *Of Flight and Life* was published in 1948 and *The Spirit of St. Louis,* an autobiography of his famous flight, was published in 1954 and made into a motion picture. Both were best-sellers and the latter won the Pulitzer Prize. He was honored to receive the Daniel Guggenheim Medal for advances in aviation in 1954, because it gave him an opportunity to resolve any tensions in his relationship with Harry Guggenheim remaining from World War II.

He was offered professorships and honorary degrees but in 1955 he started turning them down. He wrote appreciative notes saying for privacy he no longer accepted honors. But privacy did not mean spending time with family; he traveled on various enterprises of dubious value and did so extensively through the 1960s. He built homes in Europe and Hawaii but spent little time in either. (Berg, 1998)

In the 1960s he made three notable public appearances. In 1962, he and Anne accepted an invitation from President Kennedy to attend a state dinner at the White House. Lindbergh wanted the opportunity to meet Joseph Kennedy's son. Few people recognized the older balding Lindbergh. He enjoyed meeting President Kennedy and Anne started a friendship with Lady Bird Johnson that lasted into their mutual widowhoods. In 1968, he accepted an invitation from President Johnson to honor the Apollo astronauts and participated in a photo opportunity. Later that year he stunned the Alaska State Legislature by speaking about a bill regarding whale conservation. (Berg, 1998, p.532)

On August 30, 1970, the *New York Times* published an interview with Lindbergh on the front page. It was titled "Lindbergh says the U.S. lost World War II". Rather than a current photo, the Times used a three-decade old photograph of Lindbergh with Nazi Hermann Goering. (Whitman, 1970) The photo and headline distort Lindbergh's message. While Lindbergh didn't admit errors, he had emphasized for two decades that the conflict with interventionism was over, "We fought the war together and we will face the future together as Americans." (Berg, 1998, p.473)

Lindbergh's contention was the U.S. lost the peace after World War II, because "Western Civilization is less respected". (Cole, 1974, p.237) During the era of Vietnam and CIA backed coups, this was valid criticism. Senator Frank Church (D-ID), who many consider a hero, would repeat Lindbergh's arguments in a speech in the U.S. Senate a year later. (10/29/71, Risen, 2023, p.146)

In 1972, he published an op-ed in the *New York Times* against the use of commercial supersonic transport for environmental reasons. It may be the final time he would be proven right. Despite many believing commercial air travel would be supersonic, supersonic commercial flight ended in 2003 partly due to environmental reasons. His last public act was to help establish a nature preserve on the Minnesota-Canada border. (Berg, 1998, p.538)

<u>Illness and Death:</u>

Charles Lindbergh was diagnosed with lymphoma in 1974. He arranged with Hawaii to buy a plot of land in an abandoned church graveyard over-looking the Pacific Ocean. Although old and dying, and wealthy enough to hire someone, he cleared the brush himself so he could be buried. On August 26, 1974, in the company of his wife and some of his children, Charles Augustus Lindbergh passed away.

As one final reminder of their lives, Anne couldn't spend time with him alone. She needed to escape the press. Anne had his body moved quickly to the funeral site. He had, per his request, a traditional Hawaiian funeral. His remains lay there now, alone, facing the Pacific Ocean. (Berg, 1998)

The reader may be surprised that a man whose earliest memory was of the Mississippi River and whose fame was achieved crossing the Atlantic Ocean wanted to be buried facing the Pacific Ocean, but it's oddly appropriate. The crossing of the Atlantic Ocean in 1927 was an accomplishment of technology, but also a triumph over internal adversaries: fear, inexperience, hunger, thirst, and sleep deprivation. But crossing the Pacific Ocean in 1944, was a reward for persevering against external adversaries: the President, the media, and public opinion. His legacy was formed as much by what he accomplished overcoming his own limitations as the battles he fought with others.

Lindbergh was a complicated man and his actions and motivations were often inconsistent. He crossed the Pacific because he desperately wanted to fight in a war which he prepared the U.S. to fight. But he vehemently did not want the U.S. to enter it. He so opposed entering the war, he became the chief enemy of the President and millions of Americans hated him for his stance which became his legacy. The President did everything he could to prevent him from fighting in that war. But while fighting it, he was an outstanding pilot who saved the lives of countless pilots and soldiers whose statements he often criticized and sometimes accused of war crimes he hadn't witnessed.

Such are the contradictions in Lindbergh's life.

Works Cited

Battle of Peleliu. (2009). Retrieved from History.com: https://www.history.com/topics/world-war-ii/battle-of-peleliu

Berg, R. (1998). *Lindbergh.* New York: Penguin.

Cole, W. (1974). *Charles Lindbergh and the Battle for U.S. isolationism.* New York.

Dalleck, R. (2017). *Franklin Roosevelt.* New York: Harcourt.

Hansen, R. (2008). *Fire and Fury.* New York: Caliber, p. xi.

History.com. (2009). Retrieved from Battle of Peleliu: https://www.history.com/topics/world-war-ii/battle-of-peleliu

Katz, R. (2003). *The Battle for Rome.* Simon and Shuster: New York.

Lindbergh, C. A. (1970). *The Wartime Journal of Charles A. Lindbergh.* New York: Harcourt, Brace, Jovanovich.

Medoff, R. (2016). *The Jews Should Keep Quiet.* Lincoln, NE: University of Nebraska Press.

Mitgang, H. (1980, April). *Lindbergh said to regret misperceptions.* Retrieved from Chalres Lindbergh.com: http://www.charleslindbergh.com/ny/105.asp

Mittelbau-Dora Concentration Camp. (n.d.). Retrieved from https://en....org/wiki/Mittelbau-Dora_concentration_camp

Morse, A. (1968). *While 6 Million Died.* New York: Random House.

Newton, J. (2006). *Justice For All.* New York: Penguin.

Phillips, M. (2012). The Long Story of U.S. Debt. *Atlantic Monthly.*

Risen, J, *The Last Honest Man*, Hatchette Books, NY, 2023.

Ross, W, The Last Hero, Harper and Row, NY, 1964

Stephens, B. (2020, November 3). Trump Contrives His Myth. *NY Times.*

Thornton, P. (2006). Britain Pays Off Final Installment of U.S. Debt. *The Independent.*

Whitman, A. (1970, August 30). Lindbergh says U.S. lost World War II. *New York Times*, p. A1.

17: Legacy

"Nothing fails like success." Attributed to the historian Arthur Toynbee

(Engineering concepts are simplified to make them understandable to a lay public.)

The expression means once a person has been successful at something they believe their abilities extend to the next endeavor. They will stubbornly persist doing what they previously did, even if it leads to failure and public mockery.

Linus Pauling founded quantum chemistry and was a pioneer in molecular biology. He won two Nobel Prizes, but later in life advocated dietary supplements and claimed megadoses of Vitamin C could treat 75% of cancers. Medicine refused to adopt his theories. Pauling, who did not have a medical degree, performed two sham clinical trials to support his position which were published because of his name. Three well-researched papers in the late 1970s found no evidence large doses of vitamin C could treat or prevent cancer. Later his own researcher found Vitamin C made tumors grow faster. Instead of admitting he was wrong, Pauling sued him. (Gorski, 2008)

Pauling's and Lindbergh's legacies have some parallels. Both became remarkably successful in the field of their education but then declared themselves to be experts in a field in which they had no credentials. They advocated for theories which were demonstrated to be wrong and in the process were potentially responsible for great harm. They were both mocked. They were also the same age.

Pauling's legacy is divided into his remarkably important work and quackery, but Lindbergh's legacy can't be divided because of significant differences. First, Pauling's work in chemistry and molecular biology were only peripherally related to medicine, while Lindbergh's expertise in aeronautics was directly related to his foreign policy recommendations. Second, Pauling's theories of megavitamins could be proven with clinical experiments *before* he made the claims. His studies were amateur, widely derided, and performed *after* he made the claims. Lindbergh advocated for foreign policies which could be proven wrong only with hindsight.

Third, once Pauling embarked on his second career, he stopped making contributions to chemistry and molecular biology. Lindbergh's contributions to aeronautics continued through the 1950s. He made the U.S. safer, and it could be argued he directly reduced the possibility of a Cold War superpower conflict.

So why not accept that Lindbergh's legacy regarding U.S. foreign policy prior to World War II is that all public figures can be wrong? Lindbergh had a First Amendment right to his opinion, so why not accept he couldn't predict the future? Because Roosevelt isn't held to the same standard. If Roosevelt's actions aren't excusable, despite his motivation or his invented motivation, then neither are Lindbergh's. Lindbergh has to be held to the same standard.

Lindbergh made not only truly dangerous and offensive statements, but he was guilty of false moral equivalency. This, not anti-Semitism, should be the dark half of his legacy.

The Dark Side — Lindbergh's advocacy for isolationism and False Moral Equivalency: Review what Lindbergh said in San Francisco on July 1, 1941:

"Have you ever stopped to realize that Russia and Germany would have been at each others' throats two years ago had it not been for the interventionist interference of England and France? This conflict, between Germany and Russia, which the interventionists all applaud now would have taken place then if only they had shown a little more insight. The Germany armies were prepared to march eastward; but what happened?...They beguiled Poland into a futile war and when Germany turned east, they attacked her in the west. Instead of pushing on to Russia, they drew the German onslaught to their own countries."

This is wishful thinking buttressed by German propaganda. Lindbergh knew war was inevitable but believed this war could be isolated to eastern Europe. (Lindbergh, 1970, p.160) By July 1941, it was obvious Hitler was determined to conquer all of Europe and beyond.

England and France didn't beguile Poland into a war. Poland was attacked on September 1, 1939, for refusing to surrender territory. It did not refuse to negotiate with Hitler because England and France told it to. It refused because it would not surrender its sovereign territory, especially after Czechoslovakia made concessions and was then conquered. Czech citizens were horribly mistreated, including a massacre at Lidice, which was presented at Nuremberg as evidence supporting a new charge: Crimes Against Humanity. (Taylor, 1992, p.302) England and France declared war on Germany after offering to negotiate for two days.

Despite their promises, in 1939 the Allies provided nearly no support to Poland. England sent a ceremonial force to France whose troops advanced 5 miles into Germany and then withdrew. Allied declarations of war were the result of a promise to defend Poland. Perhaps it was a mistake, but Hitler turned his army away from Russia because of the non-aggression pact he signed with the Soviet Union. It was that treaty, not an English or French declaration of war, which prevented a German-Russian war in 1939. Lindbergh was deliberately dishonest by ignoring this pact.

But more egregiously, the paragraph advances a theory that nations enter treaties with no expectation they should be kept, and then should either break them or make new treaties with no regard to an existing obligation. No country would ever sign a treaty under such circumstances. No reasonable person believed after Hitler broke the Munich Agreement and the non-aggression pact with Stalin, there was any value in negotiating with him, yet Lindbergh was advocating England do so. In that paragraph he ignores or advocates the abrogation of multiple treaties but then advocates negotiating new ones which will somehow be complied with?

Even Lindbergh suspected this was nonsense. In a national radio address on August 8, 1940, he respectfully gave the opposition point of view its due:

> "The opposite view, of course, has not believed that the Chamberlain policy of appeasement was successful. They wonder if all modern precedent does not indicate that appeasing an aggressor is the fastest and most certain way of arming an opponent and placing yourself more firmly than ever on the road to war against a country allegedly appeased."

Why did Lindbergh cling to a position even he suspected made no sense? Because nothing fails like success. He had been right for so long, and those who now opposed him had been so wrong throughout the late 1930s, that he simply couldn't accept he was wrong now:

"It would be interesting to trace the personal records of the interventionists through the years preceding this war. I would like to know, for instance, what they were doing while Germany was rearming, and while the Siegfried line was being built. I would like to know where they were when I was advocating a stronger air force for America and England. In those days, when there was still time to have prevented this war, the people who shout so loudly now were hard to find. I could find very few people interested in military aviation when the German air force was beginning to be built. But now there are thousands of experts on trans-Atlantic bombing. I suspect that some of our interventionists did not believe in war five years ago. I understand some of them even opposed an increase in our military forces." (Philadelphia speech, May 31, 1941)

Thinking you're right is natural, but contriving ridiculous examples to justify a policy of allowing evil to flourish makes the reader question the speaker's motives. Consider another statement made in Philadelphia on May 31, 1941:

"Our own President says that the safety of America lies in controlling the Cape Verde Islands off the coast of Africa. Even Hitler never made a statement like that. Suppose the Germans said that the safety of Europe lay in controlling the Fernando Noronha Islands of the coast of South America. Obviously, this country would go to war. If we take the attitude that we must control the islands of the eastern hemisphere, Europe has just as much reason to demand control of the islands of the western hemisphere. If we say our frontier lies on the Rhine, they can say theirs lies on the Mississippi...Mr. Roosevelt claims that Hitler desires to dominate the world. But it is Mr. Roosevelt himself who advocates world domination when he says it is our business to control the wars of Europe and Asia, and that we in American must dominate islands lying off the African coast."

The author doubts many readers had any idea the Cape Verde Islands played a role in World War II. With the Suez Canal shut down due to combat, the Cape Verde Islands were a major refueling depot for ships bringing supplies to Europe. Portugal controlled these islands, and although neutral, it supported the Allies; for example some Verdeans fought for the allies. In mid-1941, a plan that was never used by the military, called Operation Alacrity, came to public attention. In it, the army proposed a military operation to ensure the continued operation of the naval refueling facility on Cape Verde Islands. However, because the Cape Verde Islands were never threatened by Germany (it had a weak surface navy), the plan was never needed. (Cape Verde Islands WWII, n.d.)

Did Lindbergh really believe a plan to safeguard a militarily necessary possession of a friendly government that was never used is the equivalent of Hitler's crimes? Did he really believe this meaningless military operational plan to secure a refueling depot is the equivalent of conquering countries, subjugating their populations, stealing their resources, and murdering Jews? Is he really charging Roosevelt with crimes like Hitler's because of this obscure unused military plan? It is hard to believe his experience visiting Germany, and discussing affairs with foreign dignitaries, led him to this conclusion. But he said it again in Cleveland that August. (Cleveland, August 9, 1941)

Inventing grievances or exaggerating events to draw a conclusion that both sides are evil, and therefore no one is evil, is called <u>false moral equivalency</u>. Lindbergh may have been the worst practitioner of this calumny, and he would be for the rest of his life. Of all his public statements, this statement appearing in the *Atlantic Magazine* in March 1940 may be the worst:

> "The English and French claim they are right in fighting to maintain their possessions and their ethics, and the status quo of their last victory. The Germans, on the other hand, claim the right of an able and virile nation to expand — to conquer territory and influence by force of arms as other nations have done at one time or another throughout history.
>
> This war in Europe is not so much a conflict between right and wrong as it is a conflict between differing concepts of right — a conflict in which the 'defenders' are represented by the static, legal 'right' of man, and the 'aggressors' by the dynamic, forceful 'right' of nature. No nation has been consistent in its concept of either."

There is no "right" to conquer other humans' sovereign territory. That other nations did so does not make it a "right". Besides can you compare the U.S. acquisition of Hawaii, which became a state and produced an American President, to what the Germans did to the civilians of the countries they occupied, even their ally Italy?

The Germans did not claim the right to conquer their neighbors because they were an "able and virile nation". They justified their actions on theories of racial superiority. Their neighbors, not just the Jews, were *Untermenschen,* less than men. Of all people, Lindbergh should have known this. This equivalency is reprehensible and false moral equivalency deserves to be a significant part of his legacy.

Even after he saw what the Germans did with his own eyes, he continued blaming everyone: "What the German has done to the Jew in Europe, we are doing to the [Japanese] in the Pacific...What is barbaric on one side of the earth is barbaric on the other...It is not the Germans alone, or the [Japanese], but the men of all nations to whom this war has brought shame and degradation." (Lindbergh, 1970, 6/11/45)

No, Charles, the men and women who fought fascism, resisted oppression, and especially those Germans who refused to be complicit with the atrocities committed in their names earned legacies of honor and glory. Although Lindbergh too fought fascism, his legacy is quite different. Perhaps deservedly so? This article should be his legacy, not the speech he gave in Des Moines.

Lindbergh's Legacy the Bright Side:

1) Lindbergh helped organize the Strategic Air Command (SAC):

On August 29, 1941, Lindbergh delivered a speech in Oklahoma City. Historians have ignored its message because they don't appreciate its significance. Instead, historians focused on the controversy generated by the Municipal Auditorium breaking its contract, and the speech instead taking place at a minor league baseball stadium amid threats of violence. Lindbergh needed a police escort and thugs threatened to burn down the wooden spectator stands. While "only" 8,000 people were brave enough to attend, the speech was broadcast nationwide by the Mutual Broadcasting Network. (Cole, 1974, p.88)

This wouldn't be the first time Lindbergh was denied the ability to speak. He was being denied a fundamental right and highlighted the hypocrisy of a movement that sought to fight a war to defend freedom abroad while denying freedom to those at home:

> Where is freedom when it becomes disunity for citizens to meet and discuss their beliefs on the fundamental issues of their nation? Where has freedom gone when we in America are not even informed of the underlying intentions of our government; when the agents of a foreign power are encouraged to speak and to travel throughout our land, while the same lecture halls that are open to them are closed to those of us who place the welfare and independence of our own country above the interests of any foreign power?" (Cleveland, August 9, 1941)

Historians have done a disservice by ignoring a remarkable speech. It contains the usual isolationist points, but more importantly it established the foundation of an American air defense strategy that was different than what was being pursued by most militaries. His strategy was introduced in testimony to the House Appropriations Committee in 1939. Lindbergh proposed the U.S. limit the size of the air force to 10,000 airplanes at a time when the others were recommending building as many airplanes as possible. (Testimony, U.S. House of Representatives/House Appropriations Committee, May 17, 1939)

He explained the strategy in his third national radio address, "The Air Defense of America", given on the Mutual Broadcasting Network on May 19, 1940:

> "Air defense depends more on the establishment of intelligent and consistent policies than the construction of huge numbers of airplanes...until we have decided on a definite policy of defense, the mere construction of large number of aircraft won't be adequate for our national defense. In fact, without a strong policy of defense we won't even know what kinds of planes to build."

He discussed different potential air strategies and then recommended the key to national security is small air bases be built in other countries, as our strategic needs demand, and then the bases moved as the national security situation changes. (Radio speech, 5/19/40)

In Oklahoma City and in San Francisco (SF Speech, 7/1/1941), he recommended small bases be maintained around the world and criticized Roosevelt because the Portuguese Cape Verde Islands were too far from Europe to be a strategic choice. Instead, he listed locations of bases which were worth the resources strategically and others that were not. For example, he predicted our base in the Philippines was too large and therefore undefendable, and if not, then unsustainable financially. It proved to be both. He even recommended which types of airplanes to build. (Cole, 1974) He repeated the recommendation for fewer more modern planes stationed at smaller bases in the Oklahoma City speech.

Why was Lindbergh recommending a smaller air force? Because, unlike other 'experts', he had seen the advances coming in aviation and concluded a large air force would be expensive to maintain and make strategy inflexible. Limiting airplane production would allow for greater flexibility in incorporating new advances and adjusting strategy accordingly.

The contribution he made after the war as a consultant to the Secretary of the Air Force is an adaptation of the Oklahoma City speech. He wrote in his first report to the Air Force generals, "the standards of performance, experience, and skill which were satisfactory for the 'mass' air forces of World War II are inadequate for the specialized atomic forces of today." (1947, in Berg, 1998, pg. 476)

On this basis, he helped reorganize the Strategic Air Command, making it a priority to recruit the most promising Air Force officers and used his name and access to politicians to acquire sufficient funding. He flew across the country and assessed the war capabilities and preparations of every Air Force base, developed standards for jet pilot training, and flew simulated missions with the 509th Atomic Bomb Group. He was an avid supporter of the anti-Communist Truman Doctrine and advised the SAC on nuclear strategies in the event of Communist invasion of Europe. (Berg, 1998, pp.476-7)

Much of what Lindbergh advocated before World War II was wrong, but a consultant is judged on the ability to adapt a vision of the future to present strategy. His advice on the future of air power strategy was unique for his time. It was a remarkable incorporation of a future vision into a current strategy.

2) Lindbergh's Contributions to the U.S.'s Ability to Produce Jets at the start of the Korean War

It was recognized in the 1930s that conventional piston engines were limited in thrust and altitude. These limits would be reached in the 1940s. Conventional diesel piston engines could not power an airplane to speeds more than 420 miles per hour. Fuel injection gave German airplanes a slight advantage in speed, with some German planes reaching speeds of 450 miles per hour. This advantage allowed some German pilots to escape and fight another day. (Jet Engines, n.d.)

No Allied jet airplane saw action in World War II, but when the Korean War started in 1950, piston engine airplanes were obsolete. This meant the U.S. had only 5 years to develop jet airplanes.

Jet engines compress air entering the engine to very high density, combine fuel, and the subsequent combustion turns turbine blades, which provides thrust and in return powers the compressor. The component of the jet engine which determines power is the compressor, and the premier compressor of the World War II era was the axial compressor. The German engine company *Jumo* developed it while Lindbergh was given extensive tours of its factories. How much exposure he had to it is unknown.

The key parameter which determines the thrust produced by a jet engine is the engine pressure ratio (EPR) which is the turbine discharge pressure divided by the compressor inlet pressure. The higher the EPR the more thrust the engine produces.

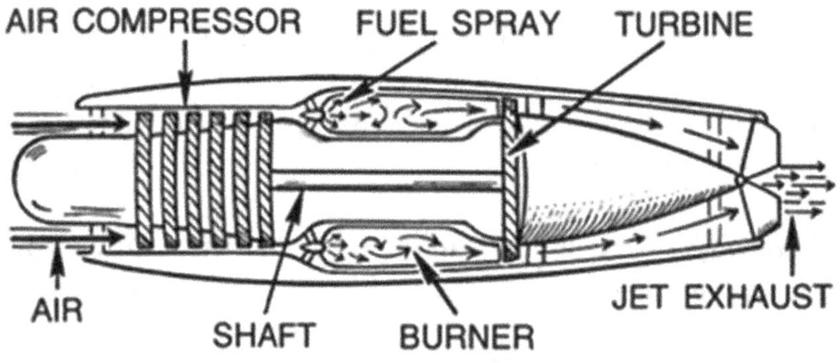

Jet engine design had been proposed prior to 1920, and in 1928, an English engineer patented it. But it was the German engineer Hans von Ohain, with the help of German industrialist Ernst Heinkel, who first developed a functioning jet engine in 1935. The first jet airplane, the He (Heinkel) 178 flew on August 27, 1939. (Jet Engines, n.d.) At this time the U.S. jet engine program was in its infancy.

Whether Lindbergh was given specific access to the axial compressor is not known. Lindbergh was given tours of the most secret German airplane research facilities as well as the Jumo engine factories. Major Smith said there was no significant U.S. exposure to jet technology, but

Smith was not allowed to attend this visit. (Smith, 1938) In Lindbergh's testimony to Congress in 1939, he told Congress of Germany's research facilities, their excellence, and the need for the U.S. to produce similar facilities.

> "...they (the Germans) have four or five such establishments, and I know that their research facilities are much larger than ours. In fact, Germany has greater research facilities than any country in Europe. Certainly, they have several times as much in the way of basic research facilities as we have today." (testimony before the House Appropriations Committee, May 17, 1939)

In April 1939, Lindbergh met with NACA (precursor of NASA) and American engine manufacturers, at his own expense. Jet technology was likely discussed, and the meeting with NACA on April 20, 1939, resulted in an additional critical allocation of money for aviation research. (Ross, 1964, p.290)

While in Germany in October 1938, Lindbergh befriended the legendary jet engineer, Willy Messerschmitt. (Lindbergh, 1970, p.104) Messerschmitt developed the first two jet fighter planes to see combat. The Me 163 Komet was introduced in 1942 with a top speed of 624 mph and an unmatched climb rate however its armaments had too short a range. The Me 262 was introduced in 1944 with a top speed of 540 mph, and in the few instances in which it engaged in combat with the premier U.S. fighter plane, the P51 Mustang (top speed 415 mph), it shot down four times as many planes than were lost. Although the kill ratio was lopsided, by 1944 the Allies had such an overwhelming advantage in airplanes it didn't affect the war. The Germans produced 1,300 Me 262 jets but fewer than 300 saw action. The Allies had destroyed so many airfields these airplanes often had to take off from highways and many crashed. (Klimek, 2022) Had the war had lasted longer, these engines would certainly have affected the outcome.

When he returned to Germany in May 1945, Lindbergh located Messerschmitt hiding from the Allies in a barn. Through a translator, Messerschmitt described the details of German advances and his vision of the future of jet technology. (Berg, 1998, p.465) Lindbergh's detailed notes also describe the remnants of German jet infrastructure, examinations of intact Me-242s, and the EPR of German jet engines. Lindbergh recruited at least three prominent German jet engineers, but Messerschmitt declined. He served two years in an Allied prison, and then chose to remain in Germany. (Lindbergh, 1970, pp.955-9)

Aerodynamic considerations: *Drag* is the force that opposes the forward motion of an airplane. *Lift* is the force that enables an airplane to ascend in altitude.

This is a simplified explanation of German engineering advances in the development of jet airplanes which American engineers had not achieved at the end of the war. Some terms are used here interchangeably which in engineering are not interchangeable.[1]

At all speeds, the air surrounding the wing is compressible, but at conventional engine speeds the compressibility is minor and of no aerodynamic consequence. However, as an airplane's speed approaches 500 mph (transonic) the air surrounding the wing density changes significantly. This is termed the "compressibility effect", in which the density of the air is designated by the Greek letter rho (p).

The ratio:

p_1/p_2, (where p_1 is the baseline density of air) = the compressibility factor.

p at sea level = 1.2 kg/m^3 (Anderson, 1989, p.87)

The Mach number (M) defines the speed of aerodynamic flow divided by the speed of sound (343 m/s or 767 mph). Thus, a Mach number > 1.0=supersonic air flow. (Anderson, 1989, p.108)

A wing is characterized by its critical Mach number (M_c). M_c has a definition provided in the footnote, but for a non-engineer it describes the ability of the wing to absorb the effect of air compression at high speeds.[1] When the speed of the plane exceeds the critical Mach number, drag increases exponentially and lift decreases parabolically. The higher the critical Mach number the better the wing can tolerate higher and eventually supersonic speeds. (Anderson, 1989, pp. 86-87)

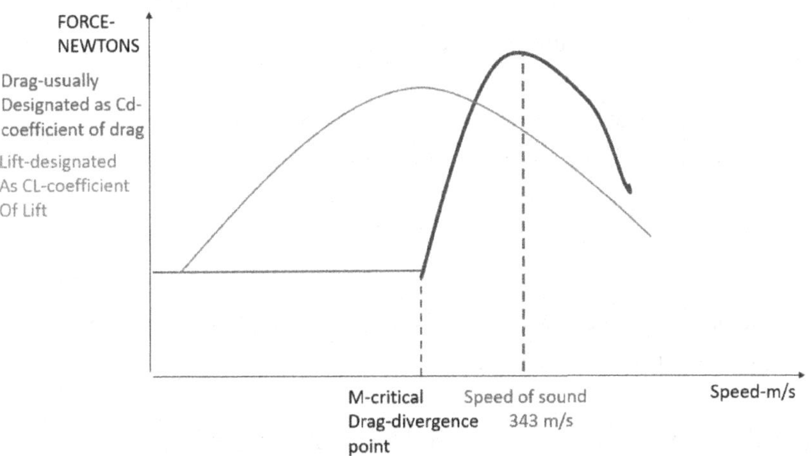

Graph 1: An overly simplified representation of how lift and drag could vary for an arbitrary wing size (S_{CL}) at an arbitrary air density (p). Notice at speeds generated by a conventional diesel engine, the drag (Cd-coefficient of drag) is constant and relatively low. Once the speed of the air flowing across the wing reaches M_c, (for this example 60% of the speed of sound, i.e. 200 m/s), drag increases and lift (CL) falls. (for an engineering example see Anderson, 1989, pp. 207-215)

A wing with a low M_c experiences a shock wave at a lower speed. There is a sudden loss of lift and an increase in drag. Airplane speed exceeding the wing's critical Mach number can stall and dive, i.e. a "Mach tuck". (CMN, n.d.) "Inexperienced pilots" can lose control of the airplane and since no pilot had flown that fast, all pilots were inexperienced. (Mach Number, n.d.)

<u>Adaptation of German Engineering to American Combat Airplanes (1945-1950):</u>

Among other advances, German engineers developed the "swept" wing. This development helped keep pilots from losing control at higher speeds. German engineers understood that angling a wing allowed an effective increase in the critical Mach number equal to:

> M_∞/cosine of the angle of the sweep, (M_∞ is called the "freestream Mach number")
>
> Or for a straight wing with a M_{cr}=0.7 (515 mi/hr), a swept wing at a 30 ° angle would demonstrate the $M_c = M_\infty/\cos 30 = 515/0.8 = 590$ mi/hr

So, for the same wing size, shape, and materials an airplane could fly an additional 75 miles/hr before reaching M_c or M drag-divergence by angling it at 30 degrees. (Anderson, 1989, p.226)

The U.S. program was so far behind technologically that the first U.S. jet plane (the P-80) not only had conventional wings, but they were thick, inflexible, and unsuited for faster speeds. (CMN, n.d.) Under pressure to provide jet airplanes for combat, crashes killed three U.S. jet test pilots and seriously injured another one. (Lockheed P-80, n.d.) At the end of the war, the Air Force reported, "…the Me 262 was superior to the P-80 in acceleration (and) speed…The Me 262 apparently has a higher <u>critical Mach number</u> (the Me 262A's <u>being at M 0.86</u>), from a drag standpoint, than any current Army Air Force fighter." (Ethell, 1994) This meant the Me262 could fly 660 mi/hour before losing lift and experiencing a dramatic increase in drag due to the compression effect.

Although not an engineer, Lindbergh understood the importance of the swept wing in aviation. His journal specifically mentioned the advantages of this wing design, his effort to examine airplanes with this type of wing, and the subsequent discussions with German engineers about this feature. (Lindbergh, 1970, pp.984-5) It is possible the engineers he recruited were chosen specifically for their expertise in designing and adapting innovations like the swept wing.

The Air Force had to adapt German jet technology quickly. Five years is a very short time to develop combat ready aircraft. Despite being a top priority, it took Germany four years to progress from demonstrating a working jet engine to test flights, another three years for a jet airplane to see combat, and two more for the Me 262 to demonstrate combat effectiveness. (Jet Engines, n.d.) The German engineers, including those Lindbergh recruited, helped American engineers create a new version of the P-80, the P-80C, by borrowing German wing design, wing slots, and armament design from the Me262. (Marco, n.d.) The axial compressor was adapted; U.S. airplanes used a very similar compressor. Lindbergh flew the P-80 as a test pilot during this process. (Berg, 1998, p.476) When the Korean War started in 1950, the P-80C was combat ready.

The Kilner Board (1939) is an exception because it allows for definitive documentation of a Lindberghian contribution to engine technology. For the development of jet airplanes there's nothing comparable. The historical record demonstrates: First, Lindbergh was exposed to embryonic German jet technology at the Lilienthal Conference in 1937 and then visited the most confidential German testing facilities. Second, because Lindbergh saw some German research, he either knew or could identify the most important engineers whom he subsequently recruited. (Lindbergh, 1970, p.959) Third, he provided this intelligence to the U.S. military, military manufacturers, and performed dangerous test flights. (Berg, 1998, pp.465-6,476) Lindbergh deserves significant credit combat ready jet airplanes were available to fight in the Korean War.

Lindbergh similarly recruited rocket scientists for the U.S. rocket program and his contribution to high altitude aviation, as previously documented, was unparalleled. U.S. preparedness for conventional air combat, an effective rocket program, a prepared Strategic Air Command,

and the ability to engage in high altitude aviation, all prepared us for future nuclear standoffs with the Soviet Union and in so doing helped reduce the likelihood of a future nuclear war.

Conclusion: Nothing Lindbergh did in his life is without controversy nor easily summarized. He made tremendous advances in U.S. security, while at the same time he engaged in immoral false moral equivalency. Perhaps like Pauling he should have only commented on subjects he was qualified to speak about? Unfortunately, he won't be the last celebrity to take up a controversial cause for which they lack qualifications and as a result do great harm.

These two legacies can't be reconciled. A person's legacy is comparable to the scales of justice. The good weighs on one side and the bad on the other. Lindbergh has significant weights on both sides. Which way the scale tilts, depends on the readers' interests and view of history. The author tried to present both sides of the scale accurately and neither ignore accomplishments nor disgraceful comments.

Lindbergh was not an anti-Semite, but he was perhaps the worst unapologetic practitioner of false moral equivalency. But his world view was consistent, and he never hesitated to help his country even at the risk of his own life. For example, unique for his time he vilified the U.S. for the use of the atomic bomb, while at the same his actions reduced the likelihood of another nuclear war.

Unlike historians' assessments of Franklin Roosevelt, the author refuses to rationalize the disgraceful comments Lindbergh made, nor the harm he did. The author will not assign benign motives to Lindbergh for actions nor statements without documentation. False moral equivalency did great harm in the Great Debate and continues to do great harm when espoused by contemporary figures.

Although lionized by some, Lindbergh no longer had prominence in public debate after World War II. As a result, his later false moral equivalence was hardly noticed, and his statements did little harm. This doesn't excuse them nor make them unworthy of note. However, neither do they discount the contributions he made. Reconciling this conflict can't be easily done.

Perhaps Lindbergh ought to be given the last word on his legacy? The conclusion of his speech in Ft. Wayne, Indiana, given on October 3, 1941:

> "In making these addresses, I have no motive in mind other than the welfare of my country and my civilization. This is not a life that I enjoy. Speaking is not my vocation, and political life is not my ambition. For the past several years, I have given up my normal life and interests; first, to study the conditions in Europe which brought on this war, and second, to oppose American intervention. I have done this because I believe my country is in mortal danger, and because I could not stand by and see her going to destruction without pitting everything I had against that trend. I am moved by no personal interest or animosity. I do not speak out of hate for any individuals or any people. But neither have I tried to avoid facts in order to have my speeches politically popular. I have tried, and I continue to try, as long as it is possible, to give you the truth without prejudice and without passion." (Cole, 1974, p.202)

The author has also tried to present the truth to the best of his ability. The final judgment is up to the reader.

[1] The critical Mach number (Mc) is the speed at which the faster air on the superior part of the airfoil reaches the speed of sound. In this chapter, the critical Mach number is used interchangeably with the Drag-Divergence Mach number because the Air Force intelligence reports used them that way. The two measurements are related, but Drag-Divergence Mach number is the correct term for the speed at

which the plane experiences the increase in drag described above, and the terms are not interchangeable.

At speeds generated by a conventional diesel engine, the relationship between lift and velocity is provided by a simple equation: for a constant air density (p), area of the wing, and angle of the airplane, lift increases relative to the velocity squared. But for transonic velocities, the relationship includes many other variables. Graph 1 is overly simplified. At Mc there is a sudden loss of lift which along with the sudden increase in drag, contributes to a Mach tuck.

Works Cited

Anderson, J. (1989). *Flight.* New York: McGraw-Hill.

Berg, A. (1998). *Lindbergh.* New York : Berkley Biography.

Cape Verde Islands WWII. (n.d.). Retrieved from https://en....org/wiki/Cape_Verde_in_World_War_II

CMN. (n.d.). Retrieved from https://en....org/wiki/Critical_Mach_number

Cole, W. (1974). *Charles A. Lindbergh and the Battle Against American Intervention.* NY: Jovanovich.

Downey, K. (2009). *The Woman Behind the New Deal.* New York: Anchor Books.

Ethell, J. (1994). *Wings of War.* Washington, DC: Military Books.

Gorski, D. (2008, August 8). *High Dose Vitmain C and Cancer.* Retrieved from Evidence Based Medicine: https://sciencebasedmedicine.org/high-dose-vitamin-c-and-cancer-has-linus-pauling-been-vindicated/

Hitchcock, I. (2018). *The Age of Eisenhower.* New York: Simon and Schuster.

Jet Engines. (n.d.). Retrieved from https://en....org/wiki/History_of_the_jet_engine

Klimek, C. (2022). First Jet into the Fight. *Air and Space Smithsonian*, 72-73.

Lindbergh, C. (1970). *The Wartime Journals of Charles Lindbergh*. NY: Harcourt.

Lockheed P-80. (n.d.). Retrieved from https://en....org/wiki/Lockheed_P-80_Shooting_Star

Mach Number. (n.d.). Retrieved from NASA: https://www.grc.nasa.gov/WWW/k-12/airplane/mach.html

Marco, S. (n.d.). *6 Innovative German Aircraft Designs of World War II*. Retrieved from Aerocorner: https://aerocorner.com/blog/german-jet-aircraft-ww2/

Ross, W, *The Last Hero: Charles A. Lindbergh,* Harper and Row, NY, 1964.

Taylor, T. (1992). *The Anatomy of the Nuremberg Trials*. New York: Knopf.

18: Epilogue

Lindbergh and his critics

> "The trouble is that many people...never think about any of the practical problems involved in waging a successful war. They just say "fight" and there all their ideas end. A few years ago, many of the same people were shouting for peace and disarmament. And their ideas ended with their shouts then, too."
>
> Charles Lindbergh, March 19, 1939

War evokes emotions of horror and courage, but wars are not won solely by emotion. They are also won by obtaining intelligence and then using it to develop superior weapons. But neither matters unless one can solve practical problems of tactics, weapons, and logistics. Soldiers need superior weapons in large quantities. Lindbergh's critics didn't consider these practical problems in the 1930s and they aren't considering them now.

Two vignettes from World War II demonstrate the critical contribution Lindbergh made to providing intelligence and superior weapons and how it won the war:

1) The Big Week, February 20-25, 1944

"The Big Week" was the code name for U.S. Air Force operations against the *Luftwaffe* and its essential infrastructure in February 1944. The Allied air forces destroyed a decisive percentage of German airplanes, airfields, airplane factories, and fuel depots. Without the Big Week, D-day and the subsequent liberation of the concentration camps would not have been possible. (The Big Week, n.d.)

A brief chronology of pivotal U.S. Air Force missions in World War II, including the two worst defeats in Air Force history followed by a complete reversal of fortune:

a. Operation Tidal Wave — August 1, 1943: an Allied Air Force offensive against oil fields in Ploesti, Romania lost 53 airplanes, 310 Airmen killed, and over 100 captured. 88 airplanes returned to base of which 55 were seriously damaged and the damage done to the oil fields was quickly repaired. (Operation Tidal Wave, n.d.)
b. Black Thursday — October 14, 1943: the Air Force bombed a ball bearing factory in Schweinfurt and lost a quarter of its planes and over 600 men (22% of the Airmen). The raid halted the production of ball bearings for only six weeks. (Second Schweinfurt Raid, n.d.)

Then a victory which led to the end of the war:

c. The Big Week — Four months later, the Air Force devastated the *Luftwaffe's* infrastructure and earned air superiority for the rest of the war. In dozens of sorties the air forces suffered losses of less than 5% of airplanes and airmen.

Strategy changed, but the outcome of the Big Week was different than the other raids primarily because two new superior fighter planes, the P-51 Mustang and the P-38, became available in large numbers. (The Big Week, n.d.) Both airplanes used liquid-cooled engines. The P-38 used the Allison V-1710 engine. The P-51 Mustang initially used the Allison V-1710 engine but later the engine was replaced by a more powerful liquid-cooled engine.

No two missions are the same and tactics are different, but between October 1943 and February 1944 the pilots and air defenses were the same. The availability of superior airplanes required intelligence and a national commitment years prior to the event. Lindbergh's intelligence reports led to the first allocations of resources to upgrading our air force since the start of the Depression. Lindbergh began advocating for this commitment immediately upon his return to the U.S. in April 1939, and prior to this the U.S. effort to build a competitive air force probably would have been insufficient. Lindbergh not only advocated for the mass production of the specific engines that powered these two planes when the military had limited interest, he made it the official policy of the U.S. military.

Lindbergh visited both U.S. companies that made liquid-cooled engines and discussed the equivalent German technology with their engineers who then requested German engines from the military. Lindbergh's committee recommendation was years before the military demonstrated the necessary interest in these engines and a year before these engines would prove themselves in the Battle of Britain.

Without Lindbergh's advocacy when would these airplanes have arrived? In Italy's case, they arrived too late. Perhaps without Lindbergh's advocacy the same would have been true of the U.S.?

2) The Fall of the Philippines, December 8, 1941-May 6, 1942

Based on casualties and prisoners of war, the Japanese conquest of the Philippines was the worst military defeat in U.S. history. The fall of the U.S. garrison in the Philippines demonstrates how lack of the type of intelligence Lindbergh provided compromised national security and led to a military disaster.

Intelligence on Japan's air force was limited and ignored, i.e. there was no "Japanese Lindbergh" to provide intelligence and warn Americans of a real threat. A lack of "Lindbergh-like" intelligence led the U.S. military to underestimate Japanese ambitions, prowess, pilots, and planes. For months prior to the Pearl Harbor attack, the military told Roosevelt the Japanese wouldn't attack, and if they did, we would "knock Japan out of the water." (Feldman, 2010, p.212) U.S. intelligence incorrectly believed Japanese torpedo bombs wouldn't function in shallow harbors like Pearl Harbor. Those bombs sunk 6 battleships, 3 cruisers, and 2 destroyers at Pearl Harbor. (Fleming, 2001, p.129)

When Japan attacked the Philippines in December 1941, America's largest foreign air force garrison (277 combat airplanes) was quickly destroyed. Most of the airplanes were destroyed on the ground, 9 hours after warnings of an imminent attack were received. (Feldman, 2010, p.212) Lindbergh was briefed that the airplanes weren't just on the ground, they were parked in a straight line. (Lindbergh, 1970, pp. 651-2)

General Douglas MacArthur had only disrespect for Japanese air power. When attacked, he wired his superiors 'German pilots must be flying Japanese airplanes', implying Japanese pilots would be incompetent. (Fleming, 2001, p.129) The premier historian of the campaign, Walter Edmunds, wrote "in the Philippines the personnel of our armed forces almost without exception failed to assess accurately the weight, speed, and efficiency of the Japanese Air Force." (Phillippines Campaign 1941-42, n.d.)

The U.S. had an accurate assessment of the German air force due to Lindbergh. Lindbergh provided the specifications of nearly every German airplane. In 1939, primarily due to Lindbergh's visits, the Embassy in Berlin provided the military with the location, size, and production capacity of nearly every German airplane factory and airfield. (Hessen, 1984, p.164)

Instead of recognizing these contributions, Lindbergh's critics "shout" terms like "anti-Semite" and "Nazi sympathizer" ignoring evidence and historical context. It is expected that Lindbergh would use common expressions and Jewish stereotypes of the era, as did Harry Truman. But if Truman was an anti-Semite, the word has no meaning. Why? Because Truman recognized the State of Israel in 1948. As important as this recognition was, why does it supersede the defeat of the *Luftwaffe* and thereby the defeat of Germany and thus the end of the Holocaust?

If an American spy had managed to obtain the details of one of the enemy's finest and yet unknown combat airplanes, he'd be considered one of our greatest spies. Lindbergh not only performed this feat for a dozen airplanes but reported on how they were manufactured, their novel technologic components, spoke to the designer, sat in their cockpits, saw them train their pilots, and in many cases piloted these airplanes. He did this when there was a paucity of other intelligence, consider our knowledge of Japan's air force. He sat down with the President, the Secretary of War, the Army Air Corps, and nearly every U.S. military manufacturer and explained in depth everything he had learned. This was a remarkable feat, which truly ought to be better appreciated even by his detractors.

When we entered World War II in 1941, nearly everything we knew about the *Luftwaffe* was because of Lindbergh. Because of Lindbergh we knew the strengths and weaknesses of every German combat airplane, pilot training, strategy, production and performance goals, future airplane designs, and research the Germans were prioritizing. Just as Lindbergh was responsible for the allocation of millions of dollars to build American combat aircraft, he was responsible for dozens of technical factors which made airplanes capable of engaging in combat and improved pilot safety. He designed the oxygen equipment on the most used American aircraft.

These accomplishments have been well-documented; for example, the official history of the U.S. Air Force acknowledges all these advances were enabled by the Kilner Board, on which Lindbergh sat, and whose recommendations were made public. (Craven, 1958) He also saw German research facilities and was an expert on the development of jet airplanes. Without his efforts to develop comparable U.S. jet technology we might have lost the Korean War.

Just as his critics state as fact that Lindbergh was an "anti-Semite", they state as fact he "exaggerated" German airpower. (Nasaw, 2012) They refuse to acknowledge Lindbergh was right, and the popular wisdom of the day was wrong. (Nasaw, PC, 2020) While Lindbergh was advising the British and the French that in the upcoming war with Germany they were incapable of defending themselves and needed time to build an air force, John F. Kennedy, was visiting Europe. The future President told his father he had been told France was too well prepared for Germany by the *New York Times* correspondent in Rome. (Dalleck, 2003)

Perhaps Lindbergh's critics should ask the Poles, the Dutch, or the French if Lindbergh "exaggerated" the power of the German air force that laid waste to their countries and forced their armies to surrender quicker than anyone else anticipated or considered conceivable?

Lindbergh's critics either refuse to acknowledge or don't understand the yawning chasm between German and Allied aeronautical engineering and our fundamental lack of intelligence in 1938. This gap was as large as the disparity in commitment to military preparedness. These disparities were responsible for the utter annihilation of the armies defending continental Europe in June 1940. Lindbergh was the pivotal figure publicizing these disparities and trying to remedy them. No matter what evil labels you want to apply to Lindbergh, the author implores the reader to ask, how would have the war have proceeded without Lindbergh's advocacy and intelligence?

Lindbergh opposed aiding England because he remembered World War I. The English were deceitful prior to World War I. Their debt was not repaid, 116,000 Americans were killed, 200,000 seriously wounded, and the result of all this sacrifice was the Versailles Treaty. The Versailles Treaty not only led to the rise of Nazi Germany but the addition of millions of colonial subjects to Britain and France's rule without consent. He did not oppose aid to England because he was an anti-Semite or wanted Germany to win the war. He wanted to avoid repeating our errors and abhorred colonialism.

Prior to World War II England was again dishonest and spying on U.S. citizens; nor was it blameless in Germany's rise. He opposed aiding

England because we didn't have enough weapons to defend ourselves, and he was right. He opposed aiding England because he saw a European war leading to Russian domination of Europe, and this happened. But in Congressional hearings he refused to blame Germany; and he was wrong. But it must be remembered that his opponents did not want to fight Germany either, and England by itself was not going to liberate Europe. So, it is unfair to accuse Lindbergh of being complacent when faced with the possibility of a Europe ruled by fascists. U.S. politicians, including President Roosevelt, were resigned to this fate prior to the attack on Pearl Harbor.

Roosevelt was right and Lindbergh was wrong in the Great Debate which consumed the U.S. between Germany's invasion of Poland on September 1, 1939, and Hitler's declaration of war on the U.S. on December 11, 1941: Isolationism was immoral, and oceans did not protect us.

But the debate was about supplying England and Russia with weapons. Roosevelt and Lindbergh both advocated not entering the war. Roosevelt made perfectly clear in September 1939 the U.S. was not going to enter the war unless we were attacked, and there is no evidence he ever would have declared war on Germany. In October 1940, at a speech in Boston, he said 6 times in one paragraph we would not enter the war, and in August 1941, in Newfoundland, he told Churchill we would not. (Moe, 2013) (Olson L., 2013) It was also not about the U.S. rearming because in this respect Lindbergh and Roosevelt also agreed. The disagreement was solely whether arms should be sent to others, including the Soviet Union. Our military unpreparedness at the start of the war and Russia's war crimes, to this day, prove Lindbergh's arguments had merit.

While Lindbergh is not blameless, the conflict with the Jews was unnecessary and this blame lies elsewhere. Lindbergh saw the U.S. heading toward war and Jews were understandably supporting this effort. He never criticized the Jews for wanting to enter the war but felt (and this is anti-Semitism) he couldn't oppose U.S. policy without addressing the role of the Jews. Jews wanted to enter the war because their families couldn't get out of Europe. Had Assistant Secretary of State Breckinridge Long's sworn testimony to Congress been true, nearly every Jew would have left Germany. If Jews were leaving Europe according to U.S. immigration quotas, the Jews wouldn't want to enter the war because it would interfere. The conflict was mostly due to administration dishonesty and a code of silence (Jewish political interests could not be mentioned) for which Lindbergh was not responsible.

Calling Lindbergh's conflict with the Jews "anti-Semitism" ignores his motivation. Lindbergh advocated removing emotion from decisions. Indeed, he refused, and tried to make Anne refuse, to be emotional about the kidnapping and murder of their son. He endorsed a foreign policy conducted "as impersonal as a surgeon with a knife". (Radio address, 10/13/39) But even a surgeon must consider the emotional state of the patient. A patient may be demented in five years, but to say that to the patient in those words is cruel. Lindbergh never acknowledged emotional realities and refused to discuss them. The English, for all their faults, were heroically standing up to evil and the remedy required fighting the Germans. His testimony before Congress refused to acknowledge or address this. He was wrong and it's inexcusable.

The author has read dozens of Lindbergh's speeches and articles, his journal, and books he wrote. Not once did he say anyone, especially not the Jews, were not Americans. Lindbergh showed remarkable respect for the Jews. In his era, both behaviors were unusual. Racists view individuals through the lens of ethnicity or race and then apply stereotypes to their behavior. But Lindbergh rarely applied stereotypes to people, and he never used anti-Semitic slurs. Throughout his life, the good (his friend Harry Guggenheim) and the bad (Charles Levine) experiences with Jews passed without any stereotype or even an acknowledgment of the religion of the person.

To the contrary Lindbergh credited the Jews with something very few of the opponents of Jewish interests ever do — the same Constitutional right to petition the government to address grievances as every other American. He acknowledged Jews were justified in using their influence to promote their interests and never questioned, criticized, nor assigned nefarious motives to it. In his opinion, what the Jews advocated wasn't in the national interest, and saying so was his democratic right.

There is no evidence Lindbergh was motivated by anti-Semitism nor did he engage in malicious anti-Semitism which was so common. To dismiss his message as anti-Semitism is sad. The author sees Lindbergh offering Jews a courtesy he rarely offered anyone. Lindbergh was willing to consider the Jews' position and situation and stated it was reasonable. For Lindbergh this demonstrated profound respect. Lindbergh's children often said their father believed there were two ways to solve any problem: his way and the wrong way. (Berg, 1998)

When Lindbergh advised the English and French, he had no personal stake in their decision. He knew his family would return to the U.S.. But in the fight over U.S. intervention in World War II every American had a life and death stake in the result. Every American had every right to their position and to demand all Americans, including Jews, defend their position.

Events would demonstrate defeating Nazism was in the national interest, but it is not Lindbergh's fault Jews refused to answer him. Jews were not powerless, the fight to release Jewish prisoners in North Africa in 1942 proved it. It isn't forbidden to mention Jewish political interests and Lindbergh was not obligated to pretend it was. It is never in the Jewish interest to be excluded from the national debate.

No other group subjected to racism has ever advocated nor willingly adhered to a strategy of being quiet and thought it was effective. Only for the Jews, and only for the worst impending genocide, was such a strategy advocated. It's inconceivable that those who did not adhere to it are criticized 80 years later.

Britain defeated the *Luftwaffe* in 1940 and this often cited to prove Lindbergh exaggerated the capacity of the *Luftwaffe*. Lindbergh's intelligence regarding the strength of the *Luftwaffe* was not wrong, let alone an exaggeration. Lindbergh provided his intelligence before the first successful use of radar, which enabled England to defeat the *Luftwaffe*. The advice Lindbergh gave England prior to the Munich Agreement was right. England could not defend eastern Europe. In trying to defend western Europe, England lost nearly half its airplanes and pilots as well as nearly all its tanks, machine guns, and armored personnel carriers *in six weeks*. (Klein, 2013) England would have been better served by conserving its resources to defend itself — which is exactly what Lindbergh said and what he wanted the U.S. to do.

That Lindbergh's intelligence and advocacy was a critical factor in defeating the Germans isn't the author's opinion; it is the opinion of the dean of U.S. journalists, U.S. intelligence, the Chief of the Army Air Corps, and the official history of the U.S. Air Force. This should be his legacy.

Lindbergh's emotionless approach works for spies and pilots, but not for husbands or fathers. It also makes poor foreign policy. But often western democracies did not consider morality in foreign policy in the 1930s. The example of Britain allowing the Italian army to pass unmolested through the Suez Canal to attack Ethiopia (Abyssinia) and commit horrible atrocities must be re-emphasized. Both England and Abyssinia were members of the League of Nations and England had committed to defend any members of the League that was attacked. Yet England not only refused to defend Abyssinia, they refused to stop shipments of oil and poison gas to the Italian army through the Suez Canal. (Bouverie, 2019) In the 1930s, no democracy did anything about Japanese atrocities in China nor Fascist atrocities in the Spanish Civil War. Lindbergh's approach to foreign policy represented the policies of his era.

Today moral judgments are integral to foreign policy. By ignoring morality and by engaging in false moral equivalency Lindbergh made two terrible mistakes. In general, Germany's propaganda efforts in the U.S. were amateurish. Conversely, the British had an extensive espionage and propaganda effort in the U.S., of which Lindbergh and other isolationists were targeted. (Olson, 2013, p.336) Because the Germans failed to establish an effective propaganda network in the U.S., isolationists unintentionally became their spokesmen and Germany's *de facto* foreign policy advocates.

Neither the *America First* movement nor Lindbergh supported Nazi Germany, minimized the seriousness of the persecution of Jews, nor advocated the defeat of England. In his speech in San Francisco (July 1, 1941), Lindbergh specifically said those who do are not welcome in the isolationist movement. The isolationist movement tried to exclude Nazi supporters. (Olson, 2013) But becoming Germany's spokesmen could have been avoided by speaking often and forcefully about Germany's crimes. That Lindbergh, and other isolationists did not do this often or forcefully enough can't be excused.

Second, his stubborn belief system, that the truth is to be spoke regardless of consequences, led him to ignore the climate American Jews were living in. The speech in Des Moines elevated the Jews to a position they did not hold; they were not the third major force compelling the U.S. to enter World War II along with President Roosevelt and the British. While the author agrees the truth must be spoken and the foundation of the conflict was opaqueness, he put the Jews in danger.

On the other hand, had Jews advocated for themselves and been transparent in their objectives in lobbying Roosevelt, Lindbergh might have agreed. Certainly, the speech he would have delivered in Des Moines would have been very different.

As a private citizen it was not Lindbergh's job to address Jewish political concerns and certainly not through exaggeration. As Anne told him the next day, it was too dangerous. He risked accidentally starting a "pogrom" like the Tulsa Race Riots of 1921. American Jews felt threatened by his speech. While there was no violence, he took a risk that he could have been responsible for violence. Noting it is legitimate criticism. However, it is also legitimate to note he may have prevented just such a riot in New York City on May 23, 1941.

Prior to World War II, few American politicians, including Lindbergh's critics, supported Jewish interests. Nearly all of Lindbergh's critics made the problems of Jewish Americans worse. So why is Lindbergh's speech the iconic example of pre-war American anti-Semitism? Wouldn't Breckinridge Long's perjury while testifying before a Congressional committee be a better example? It motivated the Treasury Department to reveal the State Department's complicity in the murder of a million Jews. No one was ever held responsible.

There are other definitions of anti-Semitism besides the one in the introduction. America's 7.4 million Jews never do anything together nor all agree. The popular perception is Lindbergh referred to American Jews as a unified block, but he did not. Furthermore, some authors have defined any reference to Jewish influence or any term which portrays Jews pursuing a single interest as anti-Semitism. (Wallace, 2003) If Lindbergh said some Jews were pursuing a national agenda rather than individuals, why can't it be said he was an anti-Semite?

Because he wasn't. Lindbergh clearly referred to individual Jews with whom he disagreed, not Jews as a unified mass. Nearly all non-Jewish American public figures, including those we consider heroes, discussed Jewish influence as part of the national discourse. In his era, this was not considered anti-Semitism, indeed if no blame is attached to the discussion it's not clear it's anti-Semitism today.

Neither Anne nor any of their children could recall him saying anything anti-Semitic in their presence — not one joke, not one private comment. (Mitgang, 1980) Two people who knew Lindbergh better than anyone who wasn't family also said he was not an anti-Semite. Major Truman Smith said Lindbergh so "abhorred" anti-Semitism he canceled a much-encouraged visit to Germany's newest airplane factories after *Kristallnacht*. Lindbergh's best friend was Jewish. Harry Guggenheim vouched for Lindbergh's lack of anti-Semitism at times when he was uniformly despised by American Jews.

Having Jewish friends is not a defense against anti-Semitism. Joseph Kennedy, Sr. had Jewish friends too. For example, Carol Rosenbloom, the owner of the Baltimore Colts, was his friend. But in letters Kennedy routinely uses anti-Semitic stereotypes. (Nasaw, 2012) In Lindbergh's 43-year friendship with Harry Guggenheim, there is rarely a mention of religion in their communications. Neither the Jewish lawyer who prosecuted his son's murderer, the Jewish movie producer who produced his life story, nor the Jewish publisher who published Anne's most famous book said Lindbergh said anything anti-Semitic. (Berg, 1998) David Wilentz, the Jewish attorney who prosecuted Hauptmann, left retirement to defend the Lindbergh verdict a decade after Lindbergh died. Would he have done that for an anti-Semite?

Lindbergh blamed everyone and found fault in every side of every conflict, but never the Jews. He blamed the English for being bombed by Germany. He criticized his fellow soldiers for speaking disrespectfully about the most amoral army the modern world has known, the Japanese. He criticized the U.S. Air Force, which he helped develop, for destroying German cities. He criticized U.S. soldiers for their treatment of German civilians in the aftermath of World War II. He may be the only American who fought the Japanese and condemned the atomic bomb as a war crime. But he never blamed the Jews for their predicament, their political stances, nor even for using what influence they had in their own interests. Both Franklin and Eleanor Roosevelt did find fault with the Jews, for either not being "American enough" or for dominating Germany's professions, which was a lie. As blaming the Jews for their predicament was the definition of anti-Semitism in the

1930s and 1940s, and Lindbergh did not, it as close to proof as can be made that he was not an anti-Semite.

One could argue that it doesn't matter if Lindbergh wasn't an anti-Semite in his personal affairs because in public, he opposed Jewish interests, and Jews felt threatened by one of his speeches. If we acknowledge, first, the speech in Des Moines was a mistake, second, perhaps unintentionally, he represented Germany's interests, and third, he engaged in false moral equivalency his entire life, even after he had seen the Buchenwald concentration camp, can it be argued this is all that matters?

It matters, and it's worthy of criticism, but it's not all that matters. Lindbergh's legacy was invented by Roosevelt in order to win a political battle, and Roosevelt personally acknowledged the plight of the Jews wasn't important. Additionally, he said the plight of Jewish children was unimportant. Lindbergh must be credited for believing it was important. He tried to facilitate Jewish emigration from Europe in 1939 and made Jewish refuge part of peace negotiations. He must be remembered for the remarkable risks and expense he undertook and the successes he was responsible for, and that it was done purely out of love for his country. Those successes helped end the war and there was nothing more beneficial for Jews.

More than nearly any other American, he prepared this country for World War II. He sacrificed more and took greater risks than nearly any other American. He had absolutely no obligation to fight in World War II, he was too old, and the President did everything he could to prevent it. Yet having lost a son and with a wife and four young children, he risked his life for his country out of personal patriotism.

The discounting of the intelligence he provided by people who have little background in aviation and the discounting of his medical advances by people who may have no medical training is the definition of disingenuity.

The accusation of anti-Semitism and Nazi sympathizing is also disingenuous because it ignores successful espionage requires giving your target the opportunity to use you for propaganda. It ignores the evolution of Lindbergh's actions towards the Jews mimics the position of the government on whose behalf he was acting — at his own expense. In other words, the accusation ignores Lindbergh's actions followed the U.S. foreign policy position: a settlement between Germany and the U.S. was the solution to Jewish persecution. After *Kristallnacht*, Lindbergh recognized such an agreement was impossible and stopped any public visit or action which could be interpreted as support for Germany. (Cole, 1974)

Lindbergh stated his reason for stopping public visits to Germany was Germany's treatment of the Jews. Unfortunately, our President did not change the U.S. policy toward Nazi Germany after *Kristallnacht*. FDR refused to comment. When Franklin Roosevelt did comment he refused to mention the victims had been Jews or the perpetrators had been Germans, let alone Nazis.

The accusation is disingenuous because it ignores Lindbergh's uncharacteristic sympathy for the Jews of Germany, the recognition of their persecution, the acknowledgment of the virtue of a Jewish pro-war stance though it contradicted his own, the visit to the concentration camp, and his enthusiastic support for exacting justice on the perpetrators of atrocities. Each of these actions individually are inconsistent with the behavior of anti-Semites in his era, and taken together make the label fraudulent. A half dozen men, including U.S. Assistant Secretary of State Sumner Welles, negotiated with Germany for a peaceful settlement. The historical record demonstrates only Lindbergh included the Jews in his negotiations. He used his position to help Jewish refugees by giving those in a position to help Jews access to the German government.

The accusation is disingenuous because Jews were obligated to present our version of the national interest. Jews failed to do so. Jews believed a President was their friend who did not believe their interests were important. Disagreeing with a Jewish version of the national interest does not make someone an anti-Semite. All Americans have a right to express their opinion without being investigated, vilified by our President, or used as a scapegoat. Americans have a right to petition their government to address grievances, but if Jews believed in the 1940s that to do so was unamerican that wasn't Lindbergh's fault. If today, Jews are afraid of being accused of dual loyalty it is no one else's fault.

Characterizing Lindbergh as an anti-Semite is a distraction. It is a charge which inaccurately simplifies events. Its simplicity makes it untrue. The charge ignores Jewish inaction and the duplicity of his critics.

It is a distraction because Lindbergh, for all his faults, was not responsible for the failure of our government to abide by the law. The President that Jews overwhelmingly voted for four times, and who labeled Lindbergh a traitor, was <u>personally responsible</u> for the murder of half a million Jews, or 8% of the Holocaust victims. This is because he either instructed, or was made aware of and still permitted, his State Department to prevent German and Austrian Jews from filling visa openings to which they were legally entitled. It is reasonable to project that had someone else been President, not only might a million Jews have escaped the Holocaust, but our government undoubtedly would have made it policy to formally protest Germany's actions. Every other man elected President of the U.S., his political opponents, the previous president, and the Prime Minister of England, Neville Chamberlain, protested when Jews were mistreated.

Where are the speeches or memos which justify Roosevelt's actions being necessitated by domestic concerns, fear of anti-Semitism, the economy, or having been motivated by anything other than callousness, cruelty, and perhaps anti-Semitism? There are documents which provide a motive for Roosevelt's actions, and they state the motive was either callousness or anti-Semitism.

If Roosevelt had a legitimate domestic political or geopolitical reason for deliberately refusing to fill German and Austrian visa openings with Jewish Germans and Austrians, then why would Assistant U.S. Secretary of State Breckinridge Long have committed to perjury to obscure it? The Secretary of the Treasury told Roosevelt why Long committed perjury: the administration's actions were indefensible. Why wasn't he indicted?

Where is the evidence the State Department obstructed the immigration of non-Jews to the U.S. during the Depression because it would worsen unemployment? Perhaps the reason Long committed perjury is because he couldn't answer why Jewish immigrants would worsen the Depression, but non-Jewish immigrants wouldn't? Not only did non-Jewish immigrants from Germany and Austria fill half the visas, but Roosevelt made policy specifically to encourage non-Jews to fill visa spots. (Rolde, 2013, p.11) (Dalleck, 2017, p.352) It is a hard question to answer if you consider that a large percentage of the potential Jewish immigrants had jobs that were in desperate need, such as doctors, pharmacists, and scientists.

The same anti-Semitic themes are active today. After *Kristallnacht* in 1938, Sumner Welles turned down Britain's offer of 68,000 unused visa slots per year to be used by German Jews to emigrate to the U.S.. Welles said not only that President Roosevelt did not want Jews using these visas, but took it upon himself to declare that "responsible Jews" did not want other Jews to use them. (Morse, 1968) In 2022, Amnesty International declared not only that Israel should not exist as a Jewish state but that American Jews agreed with them. Apparently, anti-Semites are not only entitled to their own opinions but to Jewish opinions as well — in 1938 and in 2022. (Kampeas, 2022)

Every president who preceded FDR lodged formal complaints with governments which mistreated Jews, while President Roosevelt wouldn't even say the word "Jew" when discussing the crimes committed by Germany. Efforts to remove Jews from the history of the Holocaust started with President Roosevelt and continue to this day. In 2017 Canada inaugurated its Holocaust Memorial but didn't mention the victims were Jews, neither on the monument in Ottawa nor in Prime Minister Trudeau's remarks. (BBC, 2017) That year, President Trump also released a statement which didn't mention Jews were the victims of the Holocaust. (CNN, 1/28/2017) While Canada apologized for the "oversight" and made a new plaque for the monument, removing the Jews from the Holocaust is a form of Holocaust denial and is therefore anti-Semitism.

In the rush to demonize Lindbergh, the passengers on the *St. Louis* have been forgotten. It has been forgotten that many important Republican politicians supported the Wagner-Rogers Bill to give 20,000 Jewish children refuge in the U.S. and Congress demonstrated bipartisan support. A former Republican First Lady's pledge to personally take care of 25 Jewish children didn't stop FDR from killing the bill with a handwritten note. He told his wife he couldn't sacrifice "more important" political objectives.

Jews have refused to teach the Treasury Report that specifically blamed Roosevelt's State Department for refusing visas to hundreds of thousands of Jews who were legally entitled to them and were murdered because of these illegal actions. The report says the motive was anti-Semitism. Ignoring history doesn't make what happened Lindbergh's fault.

Lindbergh makes a convenient villain. He never held political office. He had no legislative achievements. His success in espionage is hard to quantify and understand. He is criticized for the Munich Agreement, but he was asked to give his opinion and his predictions of the future war were correct. He isn't to be blamed that England and France experienced a decade of political turmoil and could not defend themselves, let alone Czechoslovakia. He took it upon himself, knowingly sacrificing his reputation, to address what he believed was critical to the national interest. He said Jews wanted to enter the war and were advocating for it. Both were true. He demanded Jews defend their interpretation of our national interest, and the Jews desperately needed to have done so.

Lindbergh associated with Republicans who had opposed Jewish interests for decades: they had opposed workers' rights when Jews worked in sweat shops, closed the U.S. to immigration in the 1920s-1930s, supported isolationism, accused munition makers of profiteering, and opposed the international organizations like the U.N. that created Israel.

Most importantly, Lindbergh never defended himself and none of his children ever took up his case. He was who he was, and he did what he did; neither he nor his family ever defended his legacy nor felt the need to do so. He almost never spoke to the press, what they said about him went unchallenged.

But there is danger in choosing your villains because they're convenient and other than one controversial speech, there is nothing he did nor said that was anti-Semitic. There were convicted Nazi Sympathizers, but an FBI investigation and a civilian court both found no evidence Lindbergh had any contact with any fascist organization; neither foreign nor domestic. Harvard labeled Jews to deny them opportunities in higher education (exactly as the Nazis did) and no one has been held accountable. Harvard has never apologized. These are the standards by which Americans should be judged.

Jews only prosper by learning from history. The villains are the President, the people he appointed, and Jewish perception of weakness. Jews mostly refused to speak publicly for fellow Jews when times demanded it. Jews have never held those accountable who truly victimized Jews such as Harvard University. The true villain was, and is still, fear. The fear of exacerbating anti-Semitism caused paralysis.

Lindbergh's legacy:

1) He did more to prepare the U.S. to fight and win World War II than nearly anyone, which isn't acknowledged because the people telling the story aren't qualified,
2) One speech was ill-advised and dangerous, but was not motivated by anti-Semitism:
    a. it resulted from Jews not advocating for themselves. The primary Jewish objective was legal emigration from Germany. Had this been stated clearly, he might have agreed,
    b. he repeated what was said by others with more power at tax-payer expense. They said it with less tact and sympathy and yet were essentially not criticized,
    c. it was of no importance in future events. Those who criticized him did nothing for Jews. They only condemned Hitler when it was convenient.
3) He did not delay U.S. entry into World War II nor did he hurt anyone other than the Japanese he killed in defense of his country. This tormented him the rest of his life.

He was a complicated flawed man with a complicated legacy, and he deserves better than facile judgment pronounced by people like Philip Roth and Arthur Schlesinger, Jr..

There are few people more responsible for Lindbergh's reputation than Philip Roth. Roth's book *The Plot Against America,* presented a new generation of Americans with a portrayal of Lindbergh as an anti-Semite. Decades earlier Roth wrote *The Conversion of the Jews* (1958) a title taken from an anti-Semitic Catholic prayer. It is perhaps the most anti-Semitic story ever written by a Jew. Jews are portrayed as mumbling, weak, foolish, and without principles. The moral is, Jews pray but don't believe in God, and mass conversion to Christianity is amusing. (COTJ, n.d.) He refused any religious rituals at his funeral deeming them fairy tales. (Dolstein, 2018) He has no credibility to accuse anyone of anti-Semitism.

Arthur Schlesinger, Jr. coined the term "Lindberghian future" — a scenario in which the U.S. allies itself with tyrannies out of amoral expediency. He was a great speech writer, but he never served in combat, so he never fought tyranny. Lindbergh did and according to those who served with him, he was an outstanding brave pilot who saved many American lives. His engineering innovations, tested at great personal risk, gave U.S. planes more range and larger payloads. Schlesinger failed his military entrance exam. Who was he to call Lindbergh disloyal? (AS, n.d.)

Lindbergh never apologized…ever…to anyone. He regretted his legacy included being called an anti-Semite, but he felt his achievements stood on their own and people could think what they wanted. He had no reason to apologize after two adjudications of no evidence. Lindbergh risked his life for his country, committed his time and resources to this country, but because he exercised free speech he was demonized. No one mentioned he'd been cleared. Who would apologize in those circumstances?

Truth is, he didn't care what anyone thought of him.

And those who demonized him — Philip Roth, Arthur Schlesinger, Jr., *Harper's Magazine*, and Reeve Lindbergh's college boyfriend's roommate, did what for Jews? Did they risk their lives to win World War II? Doing nothing and staying silent are much worse. It's certainly worse than two possibly anti-Semitic words in a lifetime of accomplishments which dwarf his critics' accomplishments.

<u>The Lesson for the Jews:</u> The Jews of Lindbergh's era never honestly addressed their own failures to help the Jews of Europe. Because those lessons were never taught, they were never learned. Jews are still hesitant to defend our interests and quick to apologize for exercising the same

rights given every American by the Constitution — to petition our government to address grievances.

Jews never acknowledged who was to blame for the catastrophic U.S. domestic political failure prior to World War II. Jews are still ignoring internal problems by finding more convenient villains.

The villains of the era are obvious, but rather than honestly address the lessons, Jews made a scapegoat. Choosing a scapegoat allowed the guilty to escape opprobrium. We allowed it to continue by not teaching our children what happened to their great-grandparents. Blame can be found outside of the Nazis and their accomplices. It lies with our elected representatives and ourselves, not with Lindbergh.

And in the end, our elected representatives are ourselves. It is our fault. Let's teach that to our children.

<u>The Lesson for America:</u> Every nation that fought in World War II invented a national myth. Other nations have been forced to re-evaluate theirs, but the U.S. has not.

The French convinced themselves they had resisted the Nazis and freed themselves. Years of litigation forced French companies to acknowledge they profited from Jewish slave labor. The French government collaboration with the Nazis freed thousands of German soldiers and significant resources to be reallocated to fight our Allies. While the French establishment escaped accountability, powerless French women accused of consorting with Germans received brutal misogynist 'justice', without an opportunity to defend themselves. In 1995, French President Jacques Chirac admitted that the French version of its history "...is convenient. But it is false." (Boissoneault, 2017)

The Japanese taught their children their army liberated Asia from colonial powers. They ignore their sadistic abuse of their fellow Asians, especially the Chinese, Filipinos, and Koreans. Japanese war crimes committed against Asians were much worse than any colonial power.

The English stood up to Germany alone. But their heroic narrative does not include deception prior to World War I, spying on U.S. citizens prior to World War II, facilitating Italian war crimes, consenting to the conceding of Czech territory to Germany without consulting Czechoslovakia, nor the immoral legacy of their colonialism which included war crimes of their own.

Canada pictures itself as a bastion of liberty and justice, but for decades they've ignored their Prime Minister admired Hitler. Recently, Canada was forced to acknowledge it harbored hundreds of Nazi War Criminals. None was ever convicted. (CBC, 9/28/2023)

The U.S. liberated much of Europe and Asia and lost half a million men. But we refused to do anything about the extermination of Europe's Jews until Germany declared war on us. So, we too, invented a myth: A few villains, particularly Lindbergh, prevented us from helping earlier.

The truth: Our government documented in 1943 that it had enabled Nazi crimes. Our government refused to close slave labor camps when the imprisoned were Jews. News of Nazi atrocities were suppressed, few people cared, and even fewer did anything. When they did, our government apologized to the Nazis. The most elected and perhaps most loved President in American history, stated Jewish lives were not worth saving because there was no political benefit.

Perhaps it's time for America to re-evaluate its national myth?

Works Cited

AS. (n.d.). Retrieved from https://en....org/wiki/Arthur_M._Schlesinger_Jr.

BBC. (2017, October 4). *Canada Forgets to Mention Jewish People at Holocaust Memorial.* Retrieved from BBC News: https://www.bbc.com/news/world-us-canada-41506700

Berg, A. (1998). *Lindbergh.* New York: Berkeley Biography.

Boissoneault, L, *Smithsonian Magazine*, 11/9/2017

Bouverie, T. (2019). *Appeasement.* New York: Random House.

CNN, 1/28/2017, https://www.cnn.com/2017/01/28/politics/white-house-holocaust-memorial-day/index.html

Cole, W. (1974). *Charles A. Lindbergh and the fight against U.S. Intervention in World War II.* New York: Harourt, Brace, and Jovanovich.

COTJ, (n.d.), n.wikipedia.org/wiki/Conversion_of_the_Jews

Craven, W. a. (1958). The Army Air Forces in World War II. In *Final Rpt. of Air Corps Board on Revision to the 5-Year Experimental Program, 28 June 1939* (p. Volume II). University of Chicago Press.

Dalleck, R. (2003). *John F. Kennedy, An Unfinished Life.* New York: Little, Brown, and Company, pg. 51.

Dalleck, R. (2017). *Franklin Roosevelt. New York: Viking.*

Dolstein, J. (2018, May 26). Phillip Roth won't be having a Jewish funeral. *Times of Israel*, https://www.timesofisrael.com/philip-roth-wont-be-having-a-jewish-funeral/.

Feldman, N, *Scorpions*, Hachette Books, NY, 2010

Fleming, V. (2001). *The New Dealers War.* New York: Perseus Books.

Hessen, R. (1984). *Berlin Alert: The memoirs and reports of Truman Smith.* Stanford, CA: Hoover Institute.

Kampeas, R. (2022, March 12). *Jerusalem Post.* Retrieved from JTA: https://www.jpost.com/diaspora/antisemitism/article-701054

Klein, M. (2013). In *A Call To Arms.* New York: Bloomsbury.

Lindbergh, C. (1970). *The Wartime Journals of Charles A. Lindbergh.* New York: Harcourt.

Mitgang, H, 1980, see charleslindbergh.com

Moe, R. (2013). *Roosevelt's Second Act.* London: Oxford Publishing.

Morse, A. (1968). *While Six Million Died.* New York: Random House.

Nasaw, D. (2012). *The Patriarch.* New York: Penguin Press.

Olson, L. (2013). *Those Angry Years.* New York: Random House.

Operation Tidal Wave. (n.d.). Retrieved from https://en....org/wiki/Operation_Tidal_Wave

Phillippines Campaign 1941-42. (n.d.). Retrieved from https://en....org/wiki/Philippines_campaign_(1941%E2%80%931942)

Reich, J. (2022). Charles Lindbergh's Contribution to High Altitude Aviation. *Pharos.*

Rolde, N. (2013). *Breckinridge Long.* Solon, ME: PB and C.

Second Schweinfurt Raid. (n.d.). Retrieved from https://en....org/wiki/Second_Schweinfurt_raid

The Big Week. (n.d.). Retrieved from https://en....org/wiki/Big_Week

Wallace, M. (2003). *The American Axis.* New York: St. Martin's Press.

19: The Apocrypha

Lindbergh in the Afterlife

Charles Lindbergh felt there was no need to defend his legacy. He was who he was, he did what he did, and he was proud of the life he had led. People would think what they chose to think.

Undoubtably, he knew his motivations, actions, and legacy were being distorted. When he agreed to have his journal published in 1970, this was widely noted. The journal's publisher, Harcourt, Brace, and Jovanovich was criticized for even publishing the journal – 3 decades after we entered World War II.[1] But he could not have anticipated that misuse of his journal and demonization of his legacy would become much worse half a century after his death.

The most prominent critic of the Harcourt, Brace, and Jovanovich company in 1970 was Frank Mankiewicz (1924-2014). He was the Press Secretary for Robert F. Kennedy's Presidential Campaign and the Campaign Director for George McGovern's Presidential Campaign. Mankiewicz' stated reason for opposing its publication was Lindbergh was a racist and an apologist for the Nazis. Also, he stated 1970 was a fraught time for Israel and this journal would inflame public opinion against Israel.[1]

The author is unaware there has ever been another attempt to suppress the publication of a diary of a major political figure. In April 1983, the British newspaper *The Sunday Times* and the German newspaper *Bild,* announced they had obtained copies of Hitler's diary. While forensic experts quickly concluded the diary was a fake, there is no record anyone opposed the publication of the diaries because Hitler was a racist or Israel's political situation was too fragile. (HD, nd)

No one opposed the publication of Joseph Goebbel's diary in 1993. James Kilpatrick (1920-2010) was the editor of *The Richmond News* and a major segregationist public figure. Mr. Kilpatrick kept a detailed journal, parts of which have been published. No one ever criticized the publisher nor tried to suppress its publication.[2]

The author wonders why critics such as Mankiewicz were so adamant that Lindbergh's journal not be published. The argument that publishing a diary three decades after it was written, which was a time when Israel did not exist, would inflame opinion about Israel, is a truly specious argument. Nor, even if true, would be a reason not to publish something of immense historical value. An effort to suppress an historic record of nearly unparalleled importance, detailing events in a critical and controversial era of American history, is unprecedented and can't help but make the author speculate why Lindbergh alone is treated this way.

Perhaps it was because the reviewers who judged Lindbergh's legacy also came to a different conclusion than the commonly accepted narrative. These reviewers stated he was an anti-Semite, but they also believed it neither defined who he was nor meant his thoughts and legacy were not worth considering.

These reviews describe Lindbergh as a complicated man, not motivated by anti-Semitism, and do not call him a racist. They emphasize the importance of his work and describe his thought process as unique and in the words of *The New York Times*, "a genuine humanist in the modern American condition."[3] They also point out Lindbergh is rarely quoted correctly and his mistreatment by the press, during the period from 1939-1941, was being repeated in 1970.[1] His mistreatment is much worse today.[9]

Here are excerpts from a book review published in *The New Republic* in October 1970. Notice the similarities between it and the author's premise[1] (underline added by the author):

"What Mankiewicz and Braden (an advocate of not publishing Lindbergh's journal) did…is so characteristic of journalistic criticism of Lindbergh in general, during the years of his glory and infamy, that all of Lindbergh's hatred of journalists, and the reasons for it, are immediately brought to mind. In the first place they didn't read the book apparently, but only promotional material *about* the book; and in the second place they were thoroughly intemperate in their description of him.

At worst Lindbergh has been perhaps a snob, a sucker for old-world manners.

But at best Lindbergh is a genuinely civilized man who, from the time of his Paris flight, has been surrounded by Yahoos and literally driven into anti-democratic isolation. There is no more depressing testimony to the brutishness of American journalism than that which Lindbergh has seen for nearly half a century — and Mankiewicz and Braden have added to the record.

It is one of Lindbergh's continuing complaints that journalists have only rarely quoted him accurately and represented his position fairly. The chances of their now representing the *Journals* fairly seem equally slim. After all, he was an isolationist and a culture vulture; he hated Roosevelt and was…anti-Semitic. He had enormous capitalist connections, knew the conservative Western military mind like an open book, and believed that cleanliness is next to godliness. Does this not damn him?

Yet the liberal who does not recognize in Lindbergh, beyond these qualities, an extraordinarily strong and characteristic American intelligence, and fails to see the complications of such a character behind the anti-liberal

> views that he displays, will never, I am afraid, understand America very well.
>
> This is an important book. Lindbergh is an important man, with a spacious mental life that is not well represented if one takes into account only his America First connections. Much of that life is committed to the art, science and romance of flying (and) much more to preserving and making habitable the private life that Yahoo journalists always were anxious to turn to nightmare.
>
> And even in the parts of the *Journals* that journalists might call obscene we see less evidence of racism and the like than of the reasoning of a military specialist.

It is perhaps more remarkable that this reviewer came to this conclusion without the evidence of Lindbergh's contribution to American security that the author has documented, without reviewing an accurate text of the speech Lindbergh gave in Des Moines, nor noting that Charles Lindbergh did not mention "Jewish war agitators" in public prior to September 11, 1941.

Since then, his critics have consistently combed through his journal to vilify him but ignore good entries. Even removed entries are known, and his critics have been eager to use them as well. (Berg, 1998, p.393) (Sparrow, 2024, p. 11)

Hovering above all the misuse and deceit, facts remain unassailable:

1) Despite calling him a traitor, the administration did not accuse him of being an anti-Semite prior to September 1941.[4] Had there been any public anti-Semitic action undoubtably his critics would have noted it.

2) The percentage of days between the start of Lindbergh's advocacy and his mention of the Jews in public defines 90% of his advocacy as being devoid of any mention of Jews. This undermines the accusation that Lindbergh was motivated by anti-Semitism.[4]
3) People have known for half a century that Lindbergh is being misquoted.
4) Despite his works on "race" being widely published and read, and his legacy being widely evaluated, it is unusual to find references to him being labeled a "racist" prior to his death. In his era, it is unclear anyone accused him of being a racist.

Major American political figures have opposed every war. Yet, Senator Eugene McCarthy's opposition to the Vietnam War, or Senator Robert La Follette's opposition to World War I is attributed to the motivation they presented. Lindbergh too clearly stated his motivation to have been legitimate geopolitical interests and sparing the lives of young Americans (national radio address, 10/15/39).[5] Why is Lindbergh alone accused of an ulterior motive: anti-Semitism? (Sparrow, 2024, p. XIV) How could someone "motivated by anti-Semitism" have spent 90% of his political lifespan without even mentioning the Jews?[4] Why would he mention them only once and accompany the mention with three remarkably philo-Semitic statements?

This accusation lives on for 80 years because Lindbergh's critics overcome the lack of evidence by misquotes, quoting unverifiable private conversations,[6a-b] and because of a series of stories about Lindbergh which are reported as fact despite the lack of a reliable primary source. Absent a verifiable source for these private statements and alleged actions these stories are apocryphal. It is not the author's responsibility to search for the source of legends. It is historians' responsibility to document their work. Until they do so, this *Aprocrypha* should be ignored.

Five apocryphal accusations about Charles Lindbergh which are used to define his legacy:

1. Charles Lindbergh refused to be photographed by Jewish photographers. (Lecture by Paul Sparrow, former director of the Franklin Roosevelt Presidential Library, 6/16/2024)

Lindbergh's hatred of the press is well-documented. He began writing about it in 1927, soon after he landed in Paris. Many historians have written that his hatred was justified. *Christian Century* wrote in 1940, the "attack against Lindbergh has gone far beyond the ordinary canons of debate. It is pulsed with venom." (Berg, 1998, p. 409) But Lindbergh never specified his hatred of the press was specific for Jewish photographers.

The author believes this allegation is based on an event in October 1940. Lindbergh refused to have one his speeches filmed because he feared the Jewish owner of *Movietone News,* William Fox (born Fuchs), would edit in a manner that treated him unfairly. However, on October 22, 1940, he watched a *Movietone News* reel covering him and stated that he was encouraged by the coverage and the audience's reaction. (Berg, 1998, p. 406) Lindbergh's speeches were filmed.

This allegation ignores that Lindbergh regularly contracted with Jewish media companies.

a. The Culture of Organs (1937): This medical textbook was co-written by Lindbergh and Dr. Alexis Carrel. It was published by P.B. Hoeber, Inc.; a publishing house in New York City. Paul Hoeber, the founder and president of the company, was Jewish. Hoeber published other scientific texts in which Lindbergh was a co-author.
b. Pantheon Publishers: The Jewish couple, Kurt and Helen Wolff, started Pantheon Publishers in 1942. They published at least 4 of Anne's books. (Berg, 1998, p. 497)

c. *The Spirit of St. Louis* screenplay: In 1956, Lindbergh sold the rights to his Pulitzer-prize winning life story to Jewish movie producer Billy Wilder (1906-2002). Wilder fled Europe in 1933. Lindbergh was impressed by Wilder's previous work, most notably a movie about Allied POWs, *Stalag 17* (1953). To prepare for the movie, Wilder and Lindbergh formed an unusual friendship as they traveled together to see the locations of Lindbergh's life. The movie received positive critical acclaim but was a commercial failure. Lindbergh never criticized Wilder. (Berg, 1998, p. 500-2) Wilder would direct two major Hollywood hits, *Some Like it Hot* (1959) and *The Apartment* (1960).

Since Lindbergh chose Jewish publishers and a movie producer, it seems likely the concern regarded a single news outlet which happened to be owned by a Jew. Given the hostility of the era, he may have had legitimate concerns as to how he was being portrayed.

2. Lindbergh criticized the Jews prior to 1941, however he did it using code words.

In modern political terminology, this is called a "dog-whistle". The accusation is that when Lindbergh criticized those promoting U.S. entry into World War II, he used terminology which was widely understood by his listeners to refer to the Jews. For example, in his book *1941,* Marc Wortman wrote that when Lindbergh criticized "the elements of personal profit" in a radio address in 1939, "nearly all his listeners knew he was referring to the Jews." (ref: The Air Defense of America, broadcast December 12, 1939, as cited in Wortman, 2016, p. 138) Wortman does not provide a reference.

There were public figures of this era who used code words to refer to the Jews. For example, the anti-Semitic radio personality, Charles Coughlin, used the term "money changers" as a slur referring to the Jews. (Warren, 1996) President Roosevelt also referred to "money changers" in his first inaugural address in 1933 but wasn't referring to the Jews. In this speech Roosevelt was providing Americans with confidence in our financial system. This example underlies the need to provide the context for all public figures' statements, including Lindbergh's. (see section 3)

Wortman's accusation is specious because the author was unable to find criticism of Lindbergh prior to 1941 for being an anti-Semite (see details of the author's search in next chapter). While the author can't search every newspaper article, it is a fact the administration did not accuse Lindbergh of anti-Semitism. Because the topic of the radio address was "The Air Defense of America", and the content was opposing exporting weapons to the Allies, it seems logical listeners heard Lindbergh's reference to "the elements of personal profit" as a reference to the manufacturers of weapons. In Lindbergh's journal, he finds fault with the Jews for media coverage promoting entry into the war, but never for a profit motive. This blame is assigned separately to non-Jewish manufacturers of war materiel. (Lindbergh, 1970, 5/1/1941)

It is possible Lindbergh was, in part, referring to the Jews. It is also possible that some listeners knew it and that there are articles criticizing Lindbergh for being an anti-Semite prior to 1941. It's more likely the charge is hindsight. Famous journalists and the administration were furiously criticizing Lindbergh in 1940 for worse transgressions, i.e. treason. It seems unlikely even hidden anti-Semitism would have been mostly ignored if "nearly everyone" knew Lindbergh was engaging in it. Certainly, the Roosevelt administration would not have let it pass, they never missed a chance to call Lindbergh an anti-Semite.

To demonstrate how unlikely it is that a major political figure could engage in code word addresses or dog-whistles to make a racist appeal to a critical demographic, especially months before a presidential election, and his political enemies could have missed it, consider Ronald Reagan's presidential campaign in 1980.

At a 1980 election rally in Neshoba County, Mississippi (where three civil rights workers were murdered in 1964), Ronald Reagan said "I believe in states' rights". The reaction was swift and furious. Many civil rights notables, such as former U.N. Ambassador Andrew Young, immediately criticized Reagan for using code words for white supremacy. The Secretary of Health and Human Services, Patricia Harris, became an "Ickes-like" figure. She furiously hammered Reagan for anything possibly racist. For example, she criticized him for endorsements by the Ku Klux Klan, despite Reagan having nothing to do with them. (Perlstein, 2020, pp. 832-3)

It is extremely unlikely that if "nearly everyone knew" Lindbergh was engaging in dog-whistles that the administration and the press would have let it pass. Dogs don't wait a year to hear the whistle.

3. References to Lindbergh wanting to discuss "The Jewish Problem and how it could be handled in <u>this</u> country" (i.e. the U.S.)

It would be particularly malicious to falsely put Nazi terminology in Lindbergh's mouth. The accuser must document the date and setting that Lindbergh used these words, and document he used them to refer to American Jews in a Nazi-like context. Once again, the author can't find the source.

Wortman alleged Lindbergh said it at a dinner party in 1940. He provides no reference. (Wortman, 1996, p. 126) Another author, Craig Nelson, repeats Wortman's description of this party conversation nearly verbatim, but changes this line to the passive form, i.e., someone at the dinner party said it, but not Lindbergh. His reference is nearly unverifiable. (Nelson, 2020, pp. 141-2) (see the discussion of this dinner party in section 4) This conversation appears to be "hear-say".

Like Roosevelt's use of "money changers", context is critical. Lindbergh addressed "the Jewish question" during his many of his pre-war visits to Germany. (Berg, 1998, p. 383) However, the context is the opposite of the context Wortman and Nelson assigned to Lindbergh's apocryphal dinner conversation in 1940. Berg wrote Lindbergh used this term because he "consistently" sought a solution to anti-Semitism in Germany. Lindbergh's solution, as noted in Chapter 10, was helping the Jews leave Germany. He expressed frustration that he was unsuccessful in changing the mind of the Germans he encountered. (Berg, 1998, p. 381)

One wonders if Lindbergh said anything like what he is accused of saying. His accusers certainly provide no evidence he did.

4. Lindbergh said he wanted American Blacks disenfranchised

Lindbergh's journal displayed dismay for the plight of Black Americans and as the Boston speech text demonstrates (December 11, 1941), he saw Black Americans as potential allies in the fight against U.S. involvement in World War II. Therefore, this accusation is not only extraordinarily improbable but requires meticulous documentation. The existing documentation strains credibility.

Wortman wrote Lindbergh said Black Americans should be disenfranchised at the same dinner party on November 5, 1940, that he mentioned the "Jewish problem". This was the night of the presidential election of 1940, in which Republican Wendell Willkie was defeated, thus allowing President Franklin Roosevelt to serve an unprecedented third term. Wortman writes as the "state by state election tallies" came in, Lindbergh became depressed and lashed out making anti-Semitic and racist statements. There is no reference. (Wortman, 2016, pp. 142-3)

As noted above, Nelson repeats these accusations verbatim and then references a box of documents in the Yale archives that span roughly a year. The reference lists three dates. (also December 3, 1940 and May 1, 1941, Nelson, 2020, pp. 141,387) In a personal communication, Mr.

Nelson admitted this alleged conversation is actually three conversations condensed into a single conversation.

This is extraordinarily odd. First, neither Berg, Anne's journal, nor Charles' journal report a conversation of note, nor any other event, on these other two dates. On May 1, 1941, Charles' journal contains a short entry which mentions Jewish influence in the media, but none of those alleged quotes. These two other dates appear to be of no historic significance.[7] Second, is it acceptable historical scholarship to combine three conversations into one, thereby dropping the context of two of them? Third, why is distortion of historical events only allowed when impugning Lindbergh? Fourth, shouldn't historians document which alleged anti-Semitic or racist Lindbergh statement occurred at which event and what was the context of each statement? Fifth, how is it possible that Berg spent weeks going through these boxes and either didn't find these documents or chose not to mention them? The author has also spent time reviewing boxes and didn't find this either.

Mr. Nelson refused to provide the author with these documents.

Most importantly, the story is chronologically implausible and conflicts with Lindbergh's journal. In 1940, election results took hours to be tallied and released to the public. Attendees at a dinner party on election day in 1940 could not have heard "state by state" tallies on the radio because these results would not have been available until much later. In Lindbergh's journal entry for November 5, 1940, he wrote he went to a dinner party where they discussed politics. Contrary to Wortman's description of his mood, Lindbergh wrote he was optimistic that Willkie had "an even chance". As he drove home from the party, around midnight, initial election results were reported and he heard them for the first time.

Because ballots were counted by hand, only small precincts could complete counting and report results within a few hours of the polls closing at 7 PM. (TPL, 1940) Thus, any election results available earlier than when Lindbergh heard them, would have been from small towns, not indicative of the general election results, and favored the Republicans – certainly not "state by state" results. In 1944, President Roosevelt didn't start reviewing election returns until after 9 PM, and in 1948 (albeit a closer election, but television could disseminate results) Truman wasn't presented with election results until after 2 AM the next morning. (Roll, 2024)

The next day when Roosevelt was declared the winner, Lindbergh wrote, "I guess Roosevelt will be president for the next 4 years." He was neither depressed nor angry, he was realistic. (Lindbergh, 1970, pp. 413-4) Anne's journal contains no entry for November 5, 1940, but she wrote in 1941 that her husband was never "bitter" when he discussed current events and when he privately discussed the role of Jews, collectively or individually, promoting U.S. entry into World War II he did so "truthfully, moderately, and without bitterness or rancor".[8] (AML, 1980, p.195)

The only credible documentation undermines this accusation. These accusations are most likely gossip, hear-say, or entirely fabricated.

5. Lindbergh said, "The more feeling there is against the Jews, the more they band together, and the more the feeling against them rises."

If Lindbergh said this, in public, it would be critically important. In the chapter on the Des Moines speech, the author emphasized Lindbergh *never* blamed the Jews for causing anti-Semitism. However, if he said the quote above, in the context of justifying anti-Semitism in the U.S., then Lindbergh could be accused of having partly blamed the Jews for anti-Semitism. The alleged quote blames the Jewish reaction to anti-Semitism, it does not blame the Jews for causing it.

Regardless, the author can't verify that he said it. He certainly never acknowledged he said it. Neither Berg nor Anne note he ever blamed the Jews for anti-Semitism.

The source, once again, is the apocryphal chronologically impossible dinner party conversation of November 5, 1940, that was apparently three heretofore unknown conversations of unknown context with unknown participants over the span of months. (Wortman and Nelson, *ibid*).

Yet, despite the credibility issues already noted, the author is unwilling to dismiss the charge as hear-say. This is because a verifiable quote of this nature would be too consequential. So, the author performed an extensive search to find the source of this legend.

Different artificial intelligence search engines consistently attribute this statement to Lindbergh's journal, as an entry written on September 18, 1938. The author's copy of Lindbergh's journal does not include this statement, and the author was unable to find an alternative version of the journal, or a reference to an expunged entry, confirming this is true. However, if this entry exists for this date, the context is critically important.

On September 18, 1938, Lindbergh was in Paris. The Munich negotiations were underway, and Chamberlain had agreed in principle with Hitler, but Lindbergh was not yet directly involved. On that date, Hitler gave a major speech about the Munich negotiations. Lindbergh retained two German translators to translate the speech into English. Notice Lindbergh's mistrust of the press. Although a private citizen and uninvolved in the Munich negotiations on this date (Ambassador Joseph Kennedy summoned him to London the next day), Lindbergh spent his money so he could form his own opinion of Hitler's speech and not rely on the newspapers' interpretation.

If Lindbergh had written this statement on that date, it would seem the context may be the opposite of what has been alleged. Not being in the U.S., Lindbergh likely would have been referring to German Jews. Perhaps he was explaining little could be done for the German Jews, because whatever the Jews did, it only made German anti-Semitism worse?

The author is speculating. But it isn't the author's job to explain an alleged Lindbergh statement which has questionable documentation. The historians alleging Lindbergh said it are obligated to document when, where, and in what context it was said.

<u>Misquotations:</u> Lindbergh's inaccurate legacy is not only being perpetuated by dishonest apocryphal historical scholarship, but some authors simply change what he said to support their allegations. The author provides three examples -- certainly he could provide more.

First, authors start Lindbergh's quotes in the middle of the sentence.

Samuel Freedman wrote one of the most important books about contemporary American Jewish life, *Jew vs. Jew* (2000). It was nominated for the Pulitzer Prize. In 2023, Freedman wrote a book misquoting Lindbergh. Freedman took the quote from the Des Moines speech referring to Jewish influence in the press, "Their greatest threat", and removed the word "Their". He replaced it with the word "the". He changed the meaning of the sentence. Lindbergh said *certain influential Jews' use of <u>their</u> earned influence is "<u>their</u> greatest danger to this country".* Freedman changed it to *"<u>the</u> greatest danger" to this country is Jewish influence.* He accused Lindbergh of saying, "the greatest danger to this country was not Hitler's fascism but Jewish ownership and influence in the press and motion picture industry." (Freedman, 2023, p. 183)

Lindbergh never said "Jewish influence" was the greatest danger to this country. He said the Soviet Union was the greatest danger to this country. (Testimony, U.S. Senate, February 6, 1941)

By putting the word "the" outside the quotation marks, Freedman demonstrates he knew what Lindbergh said and changed it. In a convoluted obeyance of scholarship rules, Freedman felt the need to not put words Lindbergh didn't say in quotes while changing the meaning of what he said. Why would an author who was nominated for a Pulitzer Prize change a quote, so it means what he wants it to mean? Why would he stringently honor the rules of scholarship while significantly distorting what a man said?

Second, authors use ellipses to remove philo-Semitic statements.

Lindbergh referred to Jews in the collective only in compliments; criticism is reserved for Jewish leaders. This detail is not an impediment to writers who want to vilify him. In her book, Candace Fleming simply puts ellipses over Lindbergh's specific designation of his criticism for certain Jewish leaders, his condemnation of German mistreatment of the Jews, and the discussion of the national interest. She combined two passages into one statement. This way she can allege Lindbergh said the Jews were not Americans:

> She combined: *"No person with a sense of the dignity of mankind can condone the persecution of the Jewish race in Germany" and "the* ***leaders*** *of the Jewish races, for reasons which are understandable from their viewpoint as they are inadvisable from ours, for reasons which are not American..."*

into "the Jewish races...are not American". (Fleming, 2020, p. 273) Lindbergh did not say the Jews were not Americans.

Third, authors attribute statements to Lindbergh which he wrote others said.

During Lindbergh's sojourn in Germany, he wrote about anti-Semitism he experienced. His critics write, "Lindbergh wrote...". As if it was

Lindbergh who said it. The author doesn't explain that Lindbergh wrote about these experiences because he found what the Germans said to be offensive. (Friedman, 2007, p. 146)

If Lindbergh were truly evil, why would it be necessary to misquote him?

Conclusion: Since everyone knows "Lindbergh was evil", historians demonstrate no compunction in misquoting him or inventing stories about him.

It doesn't matter to historians if Lindbergh didn't really say the Jews are the biggest threat to this country, or blacks should be disenfranchised, or Jews cause anti-Semitism, or that Jews are not Americans, because Lindbergh was so evil he must have believed it regardless. The patina of evil covers anything Lindbergh did in his life after he landed his plane in 1927.

The author knows this personally. In 2022, he published an anodyne scientific article in a medical journal about Lindbergh's work on high-altitude physiology. The response accusing him of being an anti-Semite demonstrates nothing good can ever be written about Lindbergh. (Pharos, 2022) Hysterical and specious criticism of Lindbergh must devalue everything he did – the cardiac perfusion pump, military intelligence, efforts to get Jews out of Germany, the philo-Semitism in the Des Moines speech, advances in high-altitude aviation, life-threatening testing of the A14 aviation mask, bravery in combat, and advances in U.S. security after World War II. None of it can be mentioned. Those who reviewed his journal in 1970 also realized it is "unacceptable" to judge Lindbergh fairly.[1,3]

The academic malfeasance in this chapter was mostly published in the last 8 years. The demonization of Lindbergh is getting worse. Misquotations, an apocrypha, and even fantasy are replacing honest historical scholarship.[9] While Lindbergh said controversial, distasteful, and poorly expressed ideas, he was not evil. If he were quoted correctly, it would demonstrate he was mostly speaking a truth that wasn't permitted to be spoken publicly. The fallacy would end.

Honest historic scholarship, e.g. Berg's book and Lindbergh's journal reviewers in 1970, explain that Lindbergh represented the opinions of a loyal segment of American society that did not want to enter World War II. He felt obligated to address the influence of certain Jewish Americans because it was an important issue in America's debate over its national interest. He did not dislike the Jews, did not want to attack the Jews, and took no joy in addressing this issue. He felt he had no choice.

Granted, anti-Semitism influenced many Americans who believed Jews were influencing our foreign policy. Furthermore, it is undeniable that anti-Semitism exaggerated the importance of Jewish influence. Nevertheless, because it was a valid issue it was valid for Lindbergh to address it. Suppressing a national discussion never suppresses anti-Semitism, or any form of hate speech.

Anne expressed this better than anyone else ever could. Her journal entry on September 11, 1941, as she alone knows what her husband is about to say (C. stands for Charles):

> "I dread the reaction on him. No one else mentions this subject (the Jews' influence) out loud though many seethe bitterly and intolerantly underneath (but C. does not). C., as usual, must bear the brunt of being frank and open...the other soft-spoken cautious people who say terrible things in private would never dare be as frank in public as he. They do not want to pay the price." (AML, 1980, p.195)

Lindbergh indeed paid the price and continues to do so half a century after his death. Perhaps those who lived through this era were too traumatized to be objective, although some were objective. But his legacy's distortion by supposedly objective historians after this generation passed, is a disgrace. To prove a narrative that is not based on events; lies and apocrypha have taken the place of a debate over Lindbergh's public position and his contribution to American security and medical science. Anyone who argues otherwise must be an anti-Semite – even the author.

In his defense, the author emphasizes a fundamental principle of Judaism, expressed by the great teacher Hillel. "If I am not for myself who will be for me, but if I am only for myself who am I?" We must be for ourselves. We owe allegiance to our grandparents' generation. We are obligated to understand how vulnerable they were, and it is perfectly legitimate for them, or even for us, to hate Lindbergh because this generation feared the reaction to what he said. It is not disqualifying that the feared reaction never materialized.

Nevertheless, everyone owes a higher allegiance to the truth. If we seek to deny the truth, or refuse to even seek the truth, then we can't learn from history. Nothing is more important for both Jews and Americans than learning from the mistakes of the past.

If we do not commit ourselves to the truth, then we are only "for ourselves". And if so, who are we?

[1] Whittemore, R, "The Flyer and Yahoos", *National Review,* October 30, 1970, https://newrepublic.com/article/91517/charles-lindbergh-war-germany-nazis

[2] James Kilpatrick's journal was not published in its entirety, however segments of it were published in "The Southern Case for School Segregation", Crowell-Collier Press, 1962. He was given a national microphone, including often appearing on the CBS news show *60 Minutes*, to express his views.

[3] Goldman, E, "The Wartime Journals of Charles A. Lindbergh", *NY Times,* September 20, 1970. https://archive.nytimes.com/www.nytimes.com/books/98/09/27/specials/lindbergh-journals.html

[4] During the period between Lindbergh's first national radio address on September 15, 1939, and the Des Moines speech on September 11, 1941, Lindbergh did not mention Jews and the administration did not criticize Lindbergh for anti-Semitism. The fight over American involvement in World War II ended less than 3 months after the Des Moines speech, therefore the period in which Lindbergh's advocacy which was devoid of any public mention of Jewish influence constitutes 89.2% of the days of Lindbergh's advocacy (i.e. 727 days (9/15/39 – 9/11/41) / 815 days (9/15/39 – 12/7/41)).Ickes did criticize Lindbergh in 1938 for accepting the medal from Goering, which because it was said in front of a Jewish audience, can legitimately be considered criticism of Lindbergh for anti-Semitism.

[5] Lindbergh stated his motivation for his opposition to U.S. involvement in World War II in a national radio address in October 1939: hatred of Russia, abhorrence of colonialism, not desiring another unpaid English debt, and aversion to involvement in European affairs. He also stated another motivation for his opposition in U.S. Senate testimony: he estimated the U.S. would suffer a million casualties should we enter World War II. (2/6/1941)

[6] On August 23, 1939, Lindbergh had a political strategy session with two prominent isolationists: columnist Fulton Lewis and former U.S. Ambassador William Castle. They discussed the imminent war, and they identified that Jews with influence in the media would be part of their political opposition. Contrary to others, the author contends it was a legitimate political strategy discussion and does not believe simply discussing Jewish influence is anti-Semitic. (see Sparrow, 2024, p. 13)

[6a] Lindbergh's journal's report of this conversation described legitimate political discourse. For example, there was discussion of an anti-Semitic movement forming in the U.S. and how this would be dangerous for the Jews. No one said they wanted to incite it nor that this would be good, but rather that it might happen and be dangerous. Furthermore, a careful reading of Lindbergh's journal entry demonstrates he is reporting

what *was* said, not what *he* said. (Lindbergh, 1970, p. 245 also see Berg, 1997, p. 393) Distinguishing what Lindbergh said is critical for those honestly evaluating his legacy, but for those whose already decided it is of no importance.

[6b] Private political strategy meetings have been held by every major political figure in recent history. These sessions are notorious for the frank and brutal discussions of how to defeat their opponents, which invariably includes exploitation of demographics and minority groups' voting priorities. No other political figure is judged on what was said by others at one of these meetings. Other political figures are judged only by the public strategy that emerged from these meetings.

[7] No date during World War II is of "no historic significance", there were U.S. domestic legislative conflicts every day and a war. Yet, these particular dates do not contain significant journal entries, nor is there a notable historic event on these dates which might have engendered an emotional reaction from those opposed to entering World War II.

[8] Anne's journal entries describing Charles' lack of an emotional reaction either to U.S. political events or Jewish advocacy for entering World War II were written before he gave the speech in Des Moines. She did not know the extent of the outcry it would engender. Therefore, it seems unlikely she wrote it to defend him.

[9] In 1993 a book was published accusing Lindbergh of killing his son. The authors admitted they had no evidence. (www.mhsnj.org/page-18154). In 2020, this allegation was resuscitated. The 2020 book review by the Medical History Society of New Jersey states the premise is nothing more than a recycled conspiracy theory. The very fact that someone can get nonsense published, even after its originator admitted in 1993 it is unsupported by evidence, is indicative of how widespread the vilification of Lindbergh has become.

References:

AML, Lindbergh, Anne M., 1980, *War Within and Without: Diaries and Letters of Anne Morrow Lindbergh, 1939-1944*, Harcourt, Brace, and Jovanovich.

Berg, AS, 1998, *Lindbergh,* The Free Press

Fleming, C, 2020, *The Rise and Fall of Charles Lindbergh,* Schwartz and Wade.

Freedman, S, 2023, *Into the Bright Sunshine,* Oxford Press.

Friedman, D, 2007, *The Immortalists,* Harper Perennial.

Lindbergh, C, 1970, *The Wartime Journals of Charles Lindbergh.* Jovanovich: New York.

Nelson, C, 2023, *V is for Victory,* Scribner.

Perlstein, R, 2020, *Reaganland: America's right turn: 1976-1980,* Simon and Schuster.

Pharos, Autumn 2022, letters to the editor, pp. 35-7.

Roll, D, *Ascent to Power,* Penguin Random House, 2024

Sparrow, P, *Awakening the Spirit of America,* Pegasus Books, 2024.

TPL, Ballot Counting, 1940 | Tacoma Public Library (tacomalibrary.org)

Warren, D, *Radio Priest: Charles Coughlin, The Father of Hate Radio,* Free Press, 1996.

Wortman, M, *1941,* Atlantic Monthly Press, 2016

Glossary

HEADQUARTERS
FIFTEENTH AIR FORCE
APO 520

GENERAL ORDERS)
NUMBER 1647)

18 July 1944

Award of the Silver Star I
Awards of the Distinguished Flying Cross II

* * * * * * *

SECTION II - AWARDS OF THE DISTINGUISHED FLYING CROSS

Under the provisions of AR 600-45, as amended, and pursuant to authority contained in Circular No. 26, Headquarters NATOUSA, 6 March 1944, the Distinguished Flying Cross is awarded the following named personnel, Air Corps, United States Army, residence and citation as indicated:

JOSEPH S. KAPPEL, O-806991, First Lieutenant, 345th Bomb. Sq, 98th Bomb Gp. For extraordinary achievement in aerial flight as pilot of a B-24 type aircraft. On 24 April 1944, Lt. Kappel participated in a bombing mission against vital enemy installations in Rumania. Over the target, following a successful bombing run enemy anti-aircraft fire knocked out one (1) engine, causing the aircraft to fall behind the protective formation. Immediately twelve (12) enemy fighters attacked the crippled aircraft, knocking out two (2) turrets. Lt. Kappel, exercising great skill, maneuvered his aircraft to evade the enemy and bring his guns to bear on the attackers and finally drove them off. Later, the formation fell back to cover the crippled bomber. Returning to base, Lt. Kappel successfully negotiated a landing although his hydraulic system had been shot away. By his outstanding professional skill, courage and devotion to duty, his combat record of fifty (50) successful missions against the enemy, Lt. Kappel has reflected great credit upon himself and upon the Armed Forces of the United States of America. Residence at appointment: Brooklyn, New York.

* * * * * * * * * * * * * *

By command of Major General TWINING:

R. K. TAYLOR,
Colonel, G.S.C.,
Chief of Staff.

OFFICIAL:

/s/ J. M. Ivins,
J. M. IVINS,
Lieutenant Colonel, AGD,
Adjutant General.

A True Extract Copy:

G. G. CHAMBERS,

RESTRICTED

The order, signed by General Taylor of the U.S. Air Force, bestowing the decoration of the Silver Star and the Distinguished Flying Cross to Lieutenant Joseph Kappel (the author's great-uncle) on July 18, 1944, for bravery in combat.

Additional Historical Notes

The accusation that Lindbergh supported a separate peace treaty with Hitler (discussed on p. 200) is supported by a reference which is misquoted. The historians who make this accusation claim Lindbergh said it in the speech he made in Chicago in August 1940. The author's footnote on page 226 documents that Lindbergh is misquoted, perhaps deliberately. The author is confident that an honest critic of Lindbergh who reads the Chicago speech and the San Francisco speech (7/1/1941) in their entirety, will conclude that Lindbergh didn't support a separate U.S. peace treaty with Hitler. Lindbergh said if our interests one day aligned, it could not be ruled out Nazi Germany and the U.S. would need to negotiate.

Two other accusations made by historians, and noted in this book, do not include references. Based on his research, the author believes he knows where these myths originated and chooses to address these charges. Because the accuser does not provide a reference, the author is under no obligation to speculate on the source of the accusation and provide a rebuttal. However, in the interest of an honest historical debate about Lindbergh's legacy, and to anticipate and refute future criticism of this work, the author has chosen to do so.

<u>Lindbergh spread anti-Semitism on American Radio</u>

On page 3-4, the accusation that Lindbergh was on American radio in the 1930s spreading anti-Semitism is addressed. In private Lindbergh addressed Jewish political interests, but in no public appearance did Lindbergh mention the Jews prior to 1941, so this accusation is based on the accuser interpreting what Lindbergh said and concluding it referred to Jews. It would appear this specific accusation is taken from a radio address he gave on September 15, 1939, in which Lindbergh said Americans need to "look behind every article we read and every speech we hear" (discussed on p. 272). The premise that news is affected by the source is expressed often, to this day, because it is a prudent way to analyze how news is presented. It did not automatically refer to the Jews then and does not do so now.

The author reviewed the *New York Times* articles which mentioned Lindbergh between 1939 and 1941 and found no reference to any radio address, specifically those in 1939, which criticized passages for referring to the Jews. The famous *NY Times* journalist Dorothy Thompson wrote scathing criticism of Lindbergh through 1940, but the author did not find an example of her calling him an anti-Semite in the aftermath of his radio addresses. (Berg also reviewed Thompson's criticism prior to 1941 and does not cite a charge of anti-Semitism, p.397) The accusation this radio address was anti-Semitic appears to be hindsight. After the speech in Des Moines on September 11, 1941, critics searched for other public examples of Lindbergh's anti-Semitism to support legitimate criticism of the Des Moines speech. All they found was non-specific statements in radio addresses, for which they used hindsight to decide they referred to Jews.

Furthermore, it must be pointed out that in the next sentence Lindbergh said we need to investigate "the nationality" of those behind the news. No one in 1939, not even the most ardent Zionist, referred to the Jews as a nationality. If Lindbergh had been referring to the Jews, it would have constituted a remarkable philo-Semitic statement. It appears this admonition almost certainly referred to the English. It has been extensively documented English agents, including Lindbergh's brother-in-law, were influencing the news Americans heard.

It is possible Lindbergh's statements about the press referred, in part, to Jews, but it appears at the time, no one suspected it. Thus, he could not have been "spreading anti-Semitism".

<u>Lindbergh and the intelligence he collected.</u>

On page 34-5, the accusation that Lindbergh's intelligence was "already known" is presented. The author believes the critics who allege this are misquoting Major Truman Smith's memoirs (p. 143). In May 1939, Charles Lindbergh, fresh off the boat from Europe, took a trip to the U.S. Military Academy in West Point, New York, to meet with General "Hap" Arnold, the Chief of the U.S. Army Air Corps. General Arnold had scheduled a two-hour lunch meeting, but the conversation lasted much longer. After lunch, Arnold and Lindbergh were kicked out of West Point's cafeteria and they found their way to the baseball stadium, where they ostensibly watched an Army – Columbia baseball game. But they were discussing the *Luftwaffe* for several more hours. It was after this meeting that Arnold provided the quote on page 94, which stated that Lindbergh provided him with the best briefing on the *Luftwaffe* he ever received. (Berg, p. 387)

Understandably, Smith takes offense at Arnold's statement because it implies that the information Lindbergh provided to Arnold at this meeting was newly presented to him. It had been Smith's job for 17 years to provide this information to the U.S. military. Smith's memoirs do not state that Lindbergh's intelligence was "already known", but rather that Lindbergh's intelligence had already been presented to Arnold. He states the intelligence Lindbergh provided to Arnold was already present in the military intelligence reports sitting in Arnold's files. Smith's pique is expected, but Arnold wouldn't be the first military official to not read all his reports. Regardless, an honest critic who reads Smith's memoirs will acknowledge the intelligence originally came from Lindbergh, regardless of how Arnold received it. Indeed, many of the reports that Smith emphasized were in Arnold's file cabinet were written by Lindbergh.

Another source of assertion that Lindbergh's intelligence was already known may be from a letter Lindbergh wrote to Smith in 1937. In the letter Lindbergh explains that he did not attempt to obtain intelligence that "wasn't offered freely". (Wallace, p. 158) This sentence is true, Lindbergh did not betray the trust of his hosts. But the information the Germans offered willingly was critically important, unknown to Western Intelligence, and on two occasions the Germans themselves realized that he shouldn't have been shown it. (pp. 100, 105)

It is also possible the author is over-thinking the lack of respect for Lindbergh's espionage work. The accusation could be nothing more than the "sloppiness" which has infected historical scholarship regarding Lindbergh and is documented in the Preface. For example, one author's discussion of Lindbergh's intelligence contribution contains a statement that, "In later years, Lindbergh's defenders would claim his missions to Germany were clandestine missions to obtain secret military data on behalf of the U.S. government." (Wallace, p. 158) The purpose of Lindbergh's mission was not invented later by Lindbergh's defenders. The letter from Truman Smith to Charles Lindbergh on the letterhead of the American Embassy on May 25, 1936, clearly stated this was his mission. The letter is available in Lindbergh's papers at the Yale archives, and anyone can access it. The author has a copy of it and provides specific details of what information Smith requested Lindbergh obtain. The author does not currently have permission to reprint it. (see pp. 97-8)

Lindbergh: Eugenics and Race

Eugenics was dangerous, and the author does not intend to minimize the damage it did. It was an enormously popular scientific discipline in the era covered by this book, and Dr. Alexis Carrel was an advocate of it. The author mentions Carrel's advocacy briefly on page 73. The author does not claim to be an expert on Carrel and is making no effort to defend him -- his intention is only to provide differing opinions provided by others who have written about Carrel's legacy. Other critics contend Carrel did tremendous harm to society with his theories and writings. (Wallace, p. 99) Because Carrel was a Nobel Laureate, he had unparalleled influence in the debate, and he can be criticized for not anticipating his writings would be misused. The author refers these arguments to the fourth ground rule presented in the introduction. Lindbergh is only responsible for his own actions.

Eugenics' heyday corresponded with Lindbergh's era of diplomacy and advocacy prior to World War II. But he hardly mentioned eugenics. His

1,000-page wartime journal contains only a single reference to eugenics. One of Lindbergh's guests brought it up during a dinner conversation and Lindbergh wrote he found the conversation interesting. However, Lindbergh wrote prolifically about race and race-related issues and the author made a deliberate decision not to address these writings; except for a cryptic reference on page 216, which explains that Lindbergh referred to Russians as Asians. He defined 'Asians' as Russians in a much-criticized *Reader's Digest* article in November 1939 which discussed the future of aviation.[1] In this era, Slavic peoples were sometimes labeled "Asiatic".[2]

There are three reasons the author decided not to discuss Lindbergh's writing about race. First, the word "ethnicity" did not appear in the English language until the end of Lindbergh's life. Often, Lindbergh's references to "race", e.g. the French race, are references to ethnicities. Second, Lindbergh wrote so prolifically about this subject, writers can find anything they want. If writers choose to make Lindbergh appear to be a racist, it can certainly be done, but if they want to say that he only promoted the achievements of certain ethnicities that were solely the result of hard work, that can be done as well. The author has no interest in trying to decipher statements about "race" when the conflict is between English-speaking countries and Russia. He chose not to do so because Lindbergh is writing about a conflict between ethnicities not races.

Third, the writer suspects Lindbergh's societal musings may have meant something at the time they were written, but whatever impact they had, today they are meaningless. The author has read hundreds of pages of his thoughts about spirituality and race; they are mind-numbingly boring and often cringy. The author does not believe they are worthy of historical investigation. The author feels that actions are more important than writings.

Lindbergh's actions relating to other racial groups:

1) He is the only public figure, the author is aware of, who demanded a public discussion of the role of Black Americans in American society in 1941. The speech was cancelled because the Japanese attacked Pearl Harbor. Lindbergh would have given the speech otherwise.
2) He is the only public figure, the author is aware of, who publicly advocated for the humanity of the Japanese in 1945.
3) In the winter of 1935-6, Lindbergh nearly lost his life supplying food to Chinese peasants who had become isolated because of a flood. This was one of many humanitarian missions Lindbergh participated in as part of his commitment to serve humanity.

These actions are not meaningless, his writings about race are.

The accusation Lindbergh was a racist is mostly posthumous. During the Great Debate (1939-1941), Lindbergh was called a traitor but not a racist, despite his writings on race and society having been published and widely read. Readers understood his writings to be "humanism", a spiritual disciple devoid of a deity. In humanism, the purpose of life is for the human spirit to excel, and aviation was a spiritual endeavor to Lindbergh. In these articles, he is explaining how the qualities of different ethnicities either propel or impede spiritual development.[3] Biographies written during Lindbergh's life, e.g. Ross' biography (final edition, 1968), don't mention racism. The charges are hindsight.

Munich:

The author argues in Chapter 9 that Lindbergh's involvement in the Munich Agreement was minor and took place after the decision to acquiesce to the demands of Hitler had already been made. The author is aware that in 1939 Joseph Kennedy gave an interview to Walter Winchell in which he said he presented Lindbergh's letter to English Prime Minister, Neville Chamberlain. The author believes Kennedy was either mistaken or bragging. Kennedy met with Chamberlain six days before he met with Lindbergh, and Chamberlain met with Hitler twice before Lindbergh even wrote the letter. If Chamberlain saw Lindbergh's cable, it couldn't have affected the events that took place.

Finally:

On page 467, Berg wrote Lindbergh visited the Bergen-Belsen Concentration Camp on June 11, 1945. Lindbergh did not mention the name of the camp he visited. The author believes Berg is mistaken. Bergen-Belsen is over 100 miles from the Nazi rocket facility at Camp Dora that Lindbergh was in Germany to evaluate. There is no record of Lindbergh having made a 200-mile round-trip journey through post-war Germany, nor was there a reason for him to have done so. Camp Dora contained a sub-camp of the Buchenwald Concentration Camp. It is reasonable to assume that this is the camp Lindbergh visited.

[1] Lindbergh, C., "Aviation, Geography, and Race", *Readers Digest,* 1939, vol. 35. This is the most cited reference in which Lindbergh specifically referred to a "race" as "white" rather than "European" or "Christian". Berg's discussion of this article does not mention anyone criticized it for "racism". (p.395) The criticism for "racism" mostly began with the publication of his journal (1970).[3]

[2] Refer to the controversial statements made by political figures regarding immigration, radicalism, labor strife, and Communism at the end of World War I. Specifically, see Hochschild, A, *American Midnight,* Mariner Books, 2022, p.240.

[3] Goldman, E, "The Wartime Journals of Charles A. Lindbergh", *NY Times,* September 20, 1970. https://archive.nytimes.com/www.nytimes.com/books/98/09/27/specials/lindbergh-journals.html

Index

Printed in the United States
by Baker & Taylor Publisher Services